Kardiac Kids

KAR

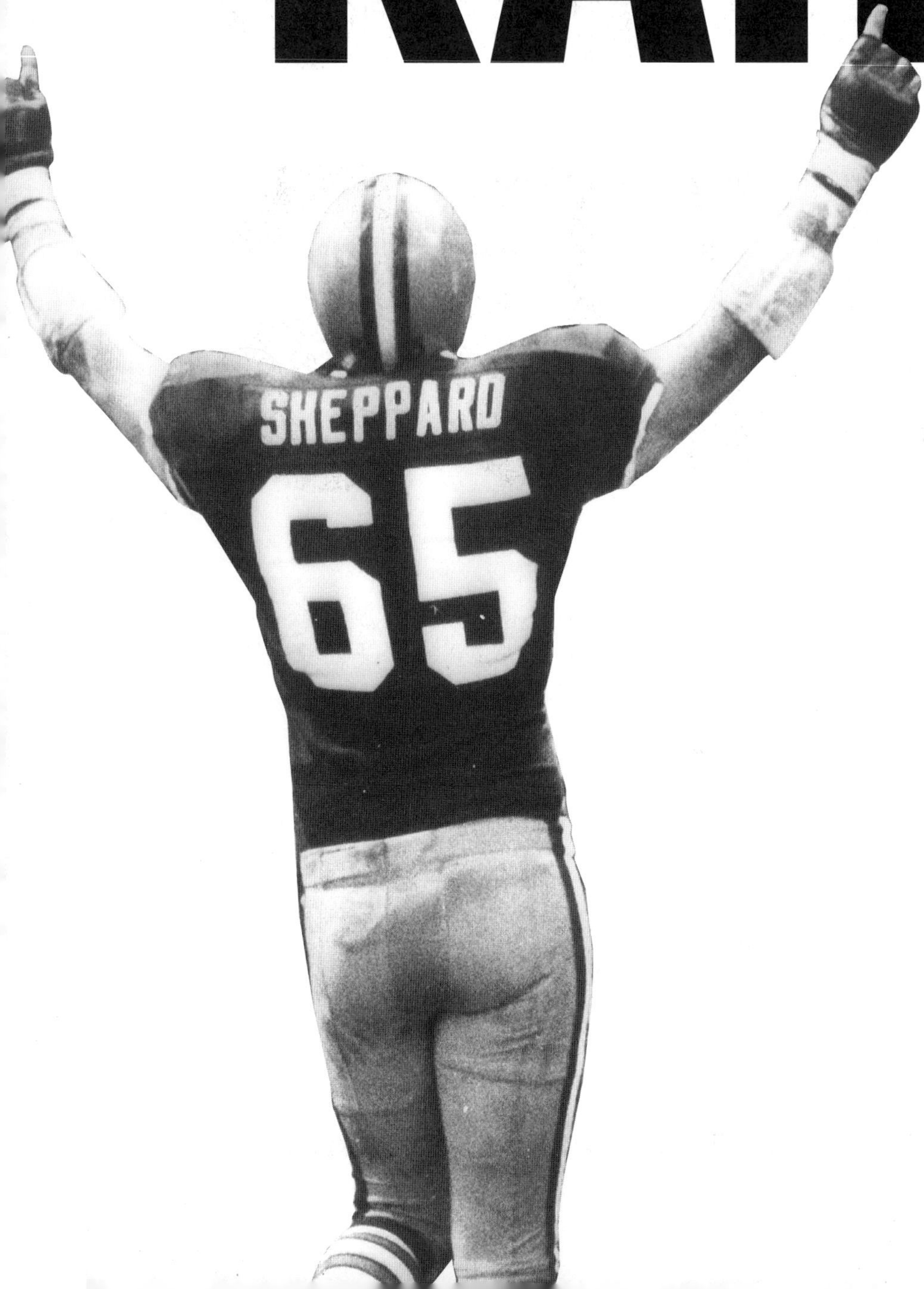

KARDIAC KIDS

THE STORY OF THE 1980 CLEVELAND BROWNS

JONATHAN KNIGHT

THE KENT STATE UNIVERSITY PRESS • KENT AND LONDON

© 2003 by The Kent State University Press, Kent, Ohio 44242

All rights reserved

Library of Congress Catalog Card Number 2002006659

ISBN 0-87338-761-9

Manufactured in the United States of America

07 06 05 04 03   5 4 3 2 1

Library of Congress Cataloging-in-Publication Data

Knight, Jonathan, 1976–

Kardiac kids : the story of the 1980 Cleveland Browns / Jonathan Knight.

p.   cm.

Includes bibliographical essay and index.

ISBN 0-87338-761-9 (pbk. : alk. paper) ∞

1. Cleveland Browns (Football team : 1946–1995)—History. I. Title.

GV956.C6 K65 2003

796.332'64'0977132—dc21

2002006659

British Library Cataloging-in-Publication data are available.

For my parents, who taught me how to be a good person,

And my wife, for making sure I stay that way.

The citizens may find many things to complain about in the way the town is governed, going up or down economically, gaining or losing population, but they all identify with a winning team.
—PHILIP WILEY PORTER
    Author, *Cleveland: Confused City on a Seesaw*

Hearts are stronger than swords.
—WENDELL PHILLIPS

Contents

Foreword by Sam Rutigliano

Why do so many people remember the Kardiac Kids so fondly?

First, it was like a good movie. People will still watch classic movies and classic television shows. It was like the good guys against the bad guys, and there would always be that late charge after we were counted out. It just happened time after time. We saw it first in 1979, and it certainly peaked in 1980.

Second, it was the dramatics we provided in the way we won. It was incredibly exciting and entertaining. I'll be at the grocery store today, and people will come up to me and say "thanks." Whenever I'm at an airport or a mall, people are always, always reminding me of how wonderful it was. It was so much fun. It was a great run, and it means a great deal to me.

People tell me that the 1980 season provided the best times in Browns' history. How ridiculous can that be after having Paul Brown and Blanton Collier as former coaches? People put us up there with those guys. People really enjoyed how we played, week after week. It was magic, and people would just sit and wait for it to happen.

Another reason why I think so many people identified with that team was that the nation itself was in need of a comeback. The unemployment percentage in the United States was in double digits at the time. In Youngstown, unemployment was at 20 or 25 percent. With so much going wrong in so many people's lives in Northeast Ohio, they rallied around that team. It provided a great sense of community pride. Winning Coach of the Year in 1979 and 1980 was a great honor, but the most important thing to me was sharing the success with the city. It taught me a great lesson about coaching. I probably enjoyed myself more in those years than a lot of coaches who did a lot better than me ever enjoyed themselves.

I think Brian Sipe was the epitome of that team. He was a thirteenth-round draft choice and came in when the Browns were going with Mike Phipps. The necessity for Phipps to perform well was even more dramatic than it has been with Tim Couch in recent years, because not only was Phipps the No. 1 pick in the draft in 1970, but the Browns had given up Paul Warfield, a Hall-of-Fame receiver, to get him. So automatically, Brian Sipe became the underdog. He became the guy that rose out of the ashes, then did exactly that so many times when we were the Kardiac Kids.

The way it all ended, "Red Right 88" and Brian's last-minute interception in the playoffs, reflected our personality. We had always put everything on Brian's shoulders. From that day to the present, I have never second-guessed that call. My answer at the press conference that day was, "My mother told me the girl you take to the dance is the one that you take home." Brian Sipe got us there, and we put the ball in his hands.

We all would have preferred to go on to San Diego the next week and then to New Orleans and win the Super Bowl. But I think we're remembered more for the way it ended.

The Browns accomplished more and went further in the playoffs in later seasons than we did in 1980. But consider what the AFC Central was like when Marty Schottenheimer coached, when Bud Carson coached, and when Bill Belichick coached. Now think of what that division was like in 1980. It's amazing how much we overcame. All three teams in that division had better talent than us, yet we overcame it to become champions.

Because of that David-vs.-Goliath mentality, that team captured the hearts of a lot of young people who are now in their thirties and forties. I often hear guys tell me about how their fathers would buy tickets, and they'd sit together on the forty-yard line, and that's how they were introduced to the Brownies. That relationship between fans and the team demonstrates how Cleveland is a unique city, especially when you look at it in terms of how it responded to the Browns leaving. Most other cities that lost teams in football and in other sports—Los Angeles, Oakland, St. Louis—just said "good riddance." Cleveland didn't do that, and to me it's no surprise.

We weren't about the people in the loges, the fat cats who, when it got cold, closed the doors and windows. We were about the people in the bleachers who borrowed money on Saturday to buy tickets for the game on Sunday. We identified with the lunch-pail community. I think that's why the legacy of that team has held on. We were popular where the roots of Cleveland are, at the heart and soul of a great ethnic city.

Recently, an older gentleman told me that after we beat Cincinnati in the 1980 season finale and were preparing for the playoffs around Christmastime, there was a big sign hanging in Mayfield that said, "God Bless Sam Rutigliano." I never saw that stuff at the time, and when people tell me about it now, I think it had to have been a movie. Somebody must have just made this up, it didn't really happen.

But it did.

Preface and Acknowledgments

In the fall of 1980 when the Kardiac Kids were in the middle of their legendary division-championship season, I had no idea it was happening. There were other things on my mind at the time, like learning to read and playing with action figures and getting my mom to take me to see *The Empire Strikes Back*. That October, I turned four.

Though I had been bombarded with Browns pajamas and sweatshirts seemingly since birth—which is only natural for the son of a lifelong Browns' fan—I didn't start following the team myself until later and missed out on the adventures of the Kardiac Kids. Still, their legacy was passed down to me long before I ever watched a football game. Before I ever knew why, I knew there was something special about 1980. My dad had a Kardiac Kids t-shirt, and he hung a picture of the 1980 team (back when Sohio used to give them away after a fill-up) on my bedroom wall.

As I grew older I began to piece together the story of that season from different tales my father would tell. Before I'd ever watched him play, Greg Pruitt was my favorite player; I knew Brian Sipe was really, *really* good at what he did—whatever that was—and there was a sadness surrounding something called "Red Right 88."

I became a Browns' fan in 1985—a reconciliatory stroke of remarkable good timing—and have followed them religiously ever since. There have been ups and downs, as with anything worth loving, and I always link a good portion of my growing up with the Browns. Each stage of my young life was connected with theirs. Fourth grade was The Drive; fifth grade was The Fumble; eighth grade was 3-13; eleventh grade is when they cut Bernie Kosar. But I missed out on the carnival that was the Kardiac Kids, and I was always kind of bitter about that.

As each new season began I secretly hoped it would mark the second coming of the Kardiac Kids so that I could get a chance to live through what my dad and all those other Browns' fans experienced. Granted, I have some wonderful memories of the late 1980s, but all too soon came the lost years of Bud Carson, Bill Belichick, Vinny Testaverde, and eventually Art Modell's bailout—which put a serious dent in my freshman year of college. The Kardiac Kids never returned.

And to my surprise no one ever truly captured on paper the full magnitude of that season. Sure the Kardiac Kids always warranted a chapter in any of the handful of well-written tomes on team history that I read over the years, but I never felt these abbreviated passages captured the operatic drama and the sheer importance of that team.

I watched the highlight films, I read the Browns' history books, I scoured through the media guides. I had a general idea of what happened, but most accounts I'd come across simply focused on the way it ended—the frosty playoff loss to Oakland. They didn't go into detail about the equally thrilling victories that were that team's hallmark. I knew it was a memorable season. I knew there were a lot of close games, and I knew how some of them finished, but I wanted to know more. I knew Dave Logan caught a touchdown pass to beat the Green Bay Packers, but why was it so amazing? I knew the Browns came from behind to beat the hated Steelers, but from how far behind? I knew that before he worked for NBC, Ahmad Rashad had caught a desperation touchdown pass to give the Browns a taste of their own medicine in Minnesota, but why was it such a big deal? And, ultimately, was Red Right 88 a horrible decision or sound thinking spoiled by poor execution? We'll explore all of these issues over the next few hundred pages.

As I slowly realized how unique it was, how I'd probably never get to experience a season that exciting, and how a year like that could only happen once in a lifetime—maybe not even that often—I wished for a time machine. I longed to go back in time to 1980 and experience that season for myself.

So I did the next-best thing.

What you're about to read was ultimately created for a selfish purpose. This project initiated simply because I wanted to live through the 1980 season since I missed it the first time. So for nearly two years that's what I did. I scoured through back issues of the *Plain Dealer* and the *Cleveland Press,* day by day. I got my hands on old videotapes of those 1980 games and eventually visited with several key members of that team—most of whom were a combination of a Roman warrior, a movie star, and a crazy uncle who'd make milk come out of your nose at the dinner table.

Along the way I discovered that the 1980 Browns were even more impressive than I'd originally thought. Yes, they had a great deal of talent but interestingly not enough talent to warrant what they accomplished. There was something inexplicable about that team, something magical. It was made up of a bunch of guys who simply loved playing in the clutch and by and large were as colorful as their uniforms (and I'm sure I'm not the only one who has the occasional pang of longing for the brown-jerseys-and-orange-pants combination that went by the wayside in 1983).

But more than just what transpired on the field, I found out how much the city of Cleveland needed this team, maybe more than any city ever needed a team in the history of professional sports. The 1980 Browns didn't win the Super Bowl—didn't even make it to the Super Bowl—but just the fact that they believed they could seemed to light up a city that, like the Browns, had been downtrodden for far too long. Cleveland's civic renaissance in the late 1980s and 1990s was complicated and made up of a hundred different variables, but I doubt I'm the only one who believes the comeback began, appropriately, with the Kardiac Kids.

Every Browns' fan remembers Brian Sipe's ill-fated final pass of the 1980 season. Like the heartbreaking AFC Championship losses to Denver that would follow in the coming years, it was another in a long line of instances of Cleveland sports fans getting the short end of the stick. I suppose the theme of all this is that heartbreak in sports is contingent upon previous success whether you're talking about a single game, an entire season, or a lifetime. And it's important that said heartbreak does not rinse away the memory of what got you to that point. Much as we hate to admit it, it *is* better to have loved and lost than never to have loved at all—or as in the case of the Browns, to have driven down the field in the final minutes and then turned the ball over than never to have made the playoffs. The end of the 1980 season was excruciating, no doubt. But in a strange way, it makes the preceding successful moments—of which there were many—even sweeter.

I'd always come to this part in a book and wonder, "C'mon, just how many people does it take for one person to write a book?"

Now I know. Any book, like success itself, has a hundred fathers. First and foremost I'd like to thank my wife Sara for her never-ending support and encouragement during this process. You are without a doubt the greatest thing that's ever happened to me, and I'm really looking forward to the rest of our lives together.

Several others laid a bedrock of support and encouragement long before this book became reality:

My parents, whom I'll never completely appreciate for all they've done for me, even though I'll spend the rest of my life trying. I love you both.

Jack Suter, the first true Browns' fan I ever met outside my family and, incidentally, a clever and determined fan who finagled his way into the Cleveland locker room at Riverfront Stadium following the Browns' division-clinching wins there in 1980 *and* 1986. He saw something in a geeky little kid in gym class at West Main Elementary in Beavercreek, Ohio, in the mid-1980s and a homespun newsletter called *Only Dogs Allowed* and inspired that kid to become a writer without ever handing him paper or a pencil. Jack, thanks for everything.

Phil Neal, who's three times the writer I'll ever be and my literary inspiration since high school. I expect to see your stuff on the shelves very soon, Splinky.

Last but not least, the handful of wonderful educators who touched my life in so many ways, from kindergarten through college, but those in particular who molded me into a writer. My seventh-grade English teacher, Carolyn Bailey (who incredibly was a Bengals fan), comes to mind since she was the one who laid down my foundation in grammar and writing that made everything afterward that much easier. Another early influence was Timothy Fleck, who in fifth grade first showed me how to link history and writing. For every book you'll ever read, thank a teacher.

Once I got into the nitty-gritty of the research and writing process, I quickly realized this project would have been impossible without the Ohio Historical Society archives and library—a virtual Walt Disney World for historians—and the friendly and cooperative staff there. Also helpful were the staff of the Pro Football Hall of Fame library, another oasis for a gridiron history buff, and the staff of the Columbus Metropolitan Library ("Oh, the microfilm is loaded backwards?"). For every nonfiction book you read, vote "yes" for library funding.

On the same note, since the foundation of the research for this book is based on the newspaper coverage of the 1980 Cleveland Browns, I must thank those who covered and commented on that team so wonderfully and eloquently the first time around, particularly Russell Schneider, Dan Coughlin, Bob Dolgan, Chuck Heaton, and even a young Tony Grossi of the *Plain Dealer,* anchored by venerable sports editor Hal Lebovitz; and Jim Braham, Doug Clarke, Bill Scholl, Bob Schlesinger, and sports editor Bob Sudyk of the *Press.*

And though he was stuck as the Indians' beat writer for the *Plain Dealer* in 1980, I'd like to thank Terry Pluto for becoming a professional role model for me, both in column and book writing. Ever since the age of thirteen when I read my first Terry Pluto book *48 Minutes,* I was enamored with the idea of writing one of my own. Thank you, Mr. Pluto, and keep up the great work.

Also a huge thanks to the members of the 1980 Cleveland Browns who donated generous amounts of time to reminisce with me: Dick Ambrose, Ron Bolton, Joe DeLamielleure, Tom DeLeone, Doug Dieken, Thom Darden, Mike Pruitt, and Cody Risien. And, of course, a hearty thank-you to head coach Sam Rutigliano for his help—there have been some great coaches in the rich history of the Cleveland Browns, but in my opinion they've never had a finer all-around human being directing the team than Sam Rutigliano.

Also thanks to Dino Lucarelli, the Browns' manager of alumni relations, for getting me in touch with those men, and operations director Carla Hostettler for getting me in touch with Mr. Lucarelli.

Special thanks to the staff of the Cleveland State University Library in charge of special collections, especially Joanne Cornelius, for helping me sift through old photographs from the *Cleveland Press* and finding some really good ones. They made the process far easier than I ever thought it would be. Also a big hats-off to the *Press* photographers who braved the heat, rain, and cold to illustrate the team so well in 1980. All photographs are from the *Cleveland Press* collection at the Cleveland State University Library.

I'd also like to acknowledge the creators of the legendary "The Twelve Days of a Cleveland Browns Christmas" song, which I refer to. My publisher and I tried to locate you to request specific permission to use the lyrics to your wonderful tune, but we were unsuccessful. Regardless, thank you for your creativity and ingenuity.

And of course all this is possible because the folks at The Kent State University Press, led by assistant director and acquisitions editor Joanna Hildebrand Craig, shared my vision and took a chance on a subject a little bit off their beaten path. Also a big thanks to Joanna and managing editor Kathy Method for their encouraging words during the long, *long* editing and pre-publishing process. And my gratitude to copy editor extraordinaire Mike Busam, who boosted my confidence when he enthusiastically plowed into this thing.

But I suppose the ultimate "thank-you"s must go to all the Browns' fans who, whether directly or indirectly, made me understand the importance of that 1980 team over the years. Without this understanding and appreciation I would never have been inspired to do all this.

And lastly I'd like to thank that angel of serendipity who whispered in my ear one beautiful spring morning in 1998 in Athens, Ohio, as I was walking home from class at Ohio University. Because of her (or him or it) I was able to do something I never thought possible and enjoy each and every second of the journey.

Much like the 1980 Cleveland Browns.

So to quote the great Nev Chandler, to those of you with heart pacemakers, get the batteries recharged right now. I believe that the Kardiac Kids are facing a pretty big play in Cincinnati . . .

Prologue: The End of the Beginning

The Cleveland Browns broke the huddle and marched up to the line of scrimmage. After more than five months of blood, sweat, and tears, the entire season hinged on the outcome of this one play on the slick Astroturf of Cincinnati's Riverfront Stadium on a solemn, gray December afternoon.

Rarely in professional sports does a team's season come down to one single play. The final outcome of most campaigns is determined slowly, over a period of weeks. Playoff teams usually clinch their bids prior to the last game, and even if their postseason hopes are still up in the air at that point, it's unusual for that final contest to go down to the wire.

For this Browns team, going down to the wire was nothing new. It had begun nearly four months earlier with a last-minute drive in regulation that forced overtime against the Jets in New York on opening day. A last-minute Browns field goal in sudden death set the stage for what would be a thrilling season—arguably the most thrilling in team history.

The heroics continued the following week in Kansas City with another last-minute score, this one for the win, and a seventy-four-yard pass play in the final minutes set up a game-winning field goal in Week Three against Baltimore. The beat went on all year, win or lose. During one midseason home game sportswriters noticed a banner hanging from a concourse at Cleveland Stadium calling the heart-stopping Browns the "Kardiac Kids." The name stuck.

They started the season 4-0, then dropped three straight, then won four of their next five and stood at 8-4 with four games to play. The Browns had a great shot at ending their seven-year playoff drought but lost two of their next three to take themselves out of the postseason driver's seat. Fittingly, though, this nerve-racking season during which eleven of the first fifteen games had been decided by seven points or less would come down to one final snap.

Regardless of the outcome this game would become the twelfth contest decided by a touchdown or less for the 1979 Browns. The question was: would it result in their tenth victory of the year or their seventh defeat?

Quarterback Brian Sipe marched up behind center Tom DeLeone and surveyed the Cincinnati Bengals' defense. Whether or not he delivered now Sipe had enjoyed a career year. He'd thrown for a team-record 3,793 yards and twenty-eight touchdowns as he engineered one of the most prolific offenses in the National Football League.

But for the 1979 season to be a truly successful one for the Browns and their fans, Sipe would need to add five more yards and one more touchdown to his season totals.

Five seconds remained. The 9-6 Browns trailed the 3-12 Bengals, 16-12, in a game Cleveland should have wrapped up long before had it not been for a smorgasbord of costly mistakes. Kicker Don Cockroft had missed a short thirty-nine-yard field goal as well as an extra point costing the Browns the four points they now needed. Wide receiver Ricky Feacher, playing for injured starter Reggie Rucker, had dropped a potential touchdown pass late in the first half that would have given Cleveland the lead. Another potential score, a twelve-yard Sipe-to-Dave Logan pitch in the third quarter, was wiped out on a holding penalty.

But the most critical mistakes were four turnovers, including a pair of fumbles by punt returner Dino Hall. The second came at the Cleveland thirty-one with 2:17 remaining and the Browns down one. The Cleveland defense held, but a forty-three-yard field goal by Chris Bahr with 1:51 to play made it 16-12 and ensured the Browns would need a touchdown, not a field goal, to win.

As they had all year Brian Sipe and the Cleveland offense responded in the clutch. For the sixth time in 1979 the Browns drove down the field in the final two minutes while trailing. This time the drive started at the Cleveland thirty-one. It appeared that all was lost moments later when a fourth-down Sipe pass fell incomplete, but Cincinnati defensive tackle Wilson Whitley was penalized for roughing the passer, giving the Browns an automatic first down and keeping their hopes alive. After a nine-play march the Browns were at the Cincinnati five following a twenty-three-yard Sipe-to-Feacher pass and a toss out of bounds to stop the clock with five precious ticks left. Rucker, the veteran receiver who had injured his right hamstring in the first half, had started to come in for the final play to replace Feacher, but Sipe waved him back to the sideline. Feacher was healthy and already involved in the drive. Besides, the play was designed to go to second-year tight end Ozzie Newsome.

A touchdown would keep the Browns' playoff hopes alive. To snag the second Wild Card spot and a trip to Houston to face the Oilers the following weekend the Browns needed three things to happen: First and foremost, they had to win in Cincinnati. Second, the 9-6 Oakland Raiders (who had defeated Cleveland the previous week) had to lose at home to the Seattle Seahawks later that afternoon. And third, the 10-5 Denver Broncos would have to lose (and lose big) to the San Diego Chargers on Monday night.

If those three conditions came to fruition the Browns and Broncos would have the same overall and conference records (10-6 and 7-3) and the next tiebreaker was net-point differential. Entering Week Sixteen the Browns were plus-11, while Denver was plus-37. As they lined up for the final play in Cincinnati the best the Browns could do was improve their differential to plus-14, which meant Denver would have to lose to the Chargers by twenty-four points for the Browns to sneak into the playoffs. It was a long shot, but the 1979 Browns had already succeeded in the face of longer odds than this.

The Oakland contest was just under way, but if the Browns couldn't score here it didn't matter what happened in California or in primetime the following night. In five seconds the Browns would either take a big step toward making the play-offs for the first time in seven years or be on their way back to Cleveland for a brief layover before embarking into the long, dark months of the off-season.

Sipe barked the signals, took the snap, and dropped back to pass.

Things were spoiled from the get-go. Newsome couldn't get open and Sipe couldn't find anyone else to throw to. He scrambled in the backfield, stalling, hoping someone would break free as the clock reached zero. He was running out of time before the Bengals' pass rush would reach him.

Then Sipe saw Feacher streaking across the back of the end zone. Feacher wasn't exactly wide open—he had two defenders near him—but he was Sipe's only hope. Sipe cocked his celebrated right arm and fired his final pass of the 1979 regular season.

As the football blitzed through the leaden air many Browns' followers experienced a prescient mental flash. It would be the perfect end to the most thrilling single season in Browns' history. They would clinch a playoff spot on the strength of the final play of the final game of the regular season then in the playoffs face a team they'd just defeated two weeks earlier. After that, anything was possible, even a rematch with archrival Pittsburgh for the AFC championship less than two months after the Browns had all but clinched an important victory over the Steelers in Pittsburgh only to lose by a field goal in overtime.

All those hopes rode on that pass as it catapulted through the air and into the end zone. All Feacher had to do was catch it.

But in the final moment before it reached him, the ball was tipped. Bengals' safety Dick Jauron, who didn't even know where Feacher was, got a finger on the ball and altered its course ever so slightly. Feacher tried to adjust to the change in direction, but he slipped on the slick turf, and with cornerback Ray Griffin flanking him as well, his vision was partially blocked. He reached out anyway in a final desperate attempt to send the Browns toward the playoffs.

The football glanced off Feacher's hand, then his shoulder, and fell incomplete. The game, and consequently the season, was over.

Feacher crumbled to the ground and sat in the end zone as the Bengals celebrated off the field. A long and miserable cacophony of a season for Cincinnati had ended on a sweet note. The Bengals had defeated the team their owner, Paul Brown, had founded and coached for seventeen years before being unceremoniously terminated after the 1962 season by Art Modell, then a young and unproven owner, who on this December day was still the Browns' monarch. It also marked the second straight year the Bengals had defeated the Browns in Cincinnati in the season finale, but this time the home team had prevented the visitors from reaching the playoffs. It was as sweet a triumph as the Bengals had enjoyed in a long time, especially since victory had shown its face only eight times in the previous two years.

The Browns, who had now lost seven consecutive season finales, marched off the field slowly, heads down, to the locker room. They passed Feacher along the way as he remained planted in the end zone, dejected. Once the team passed him Feacher got up slowly and turned to follow. As he did, a bag of rain-soaked peanuts thrown by a fan sliced out of the stands and struck the ground at his feet, exploding all over the Astroturf. For the Browns, anyway, it symbolized the moment perfectly. "Without question," Browns' head coach Sam Rutigliano said in the locker room, "the ball bounced a thousand different ways, and we had some great opportunities. But at the end of the game, it didn't bounce our way."

Three hours later the Browns learned that the Seahawks had indeed upset the Raiders. And the following night Denver did lose to San Diego but not by enough at 17-7. Even if Feacher had caught Sipe's pass the Browns still would have missed the playoffs. But had the Browns not made so many mistakes against the Bengals and won by at least seventeen points, which they probably should have, they would have reached the postseason. Instead the Browns, who finished their season at 9-7, trudged quietly into the off-season, dreaming of how things would be different next year. "A year from now if the final game is here it won't mean a thing," Browns' running back Mike Pruitt said, "because we'll already have the playoffs locked up."

"It kills me that we have to walk away as we are, without going any further," Sipe said, "but I am planning to do it next year because I know we can."

"It would have been good to wind up this exciting 1979 campaign with a victory," wrote Chuck Heaton in that Monday's *Plain Dealer*, "but the future seems bright even in defeat. The Browns have a young and improving team, a pleasant good mix of youth and experience. Difficult as this would seem 1980 just might be even more exciting."

It just might.

1 · Between Heartbeats

After closing the books on a decade marred by Vietnam and Watergate, among other national crises, the United States of America was in transition in July 1980.

Republican Ronald Reagan and Democrat Jimmy Carter were closing in on securing their parties' nominations to run for president that November. Though Carter was the incumbent, the poor economy and global problems of the previous four years weighed on his chances for re-election, and Governor Reagan of California already held a steady lead.

The Cold War was still going strong. In June a computer malfunction reporting a Soviet missile attack nearly catapulted the United States into nuclear war. Following the Soviet Union's invasion of Afghanistan the year before the United States took political action, halting grain sales to the USSR and disallowing Soviet fishing in American waters. More noticeable was Carter's decision for the United States, followed by fifty other nations, to boycott the summer Olympic Games set to begin in August in Moscow.

It had been eight months since a mob of students had seized the U.S. embassy in Teheran, Iran, and taken ninety Americans hostage. Fifty-two hostages remained in Iran that summer. The United States had endured even more embarrassment in April when an ill-advised rescue mission ended with an American military helicopter colliding with a transport plane in the Iranian desert, killing eight U.S. soldiers.

Domestically things were not good either. The nation was in the midst of an energy crisis. Unemployment and interest rates were up, the economy was down, and inflation was rising. Personal bankruptcies in the United States were at their highest level in five years. Typifying this stagflation, Ford Motor Company, one of the mightiest corporations in the world, would lose a U.S.-record $595 million in its third quarter.

In May eighteen people were killed in Miami as the result of the worst race rioting since the late 1960s, following an all-white jury's acquittal of four white policemen of the murder of a black businessman in Tampa. Also that month in Washington State, Mount St. Helens erupted, destroying hundreds of square miles of wilderness, buried under tons of ash.

Cleveland, Ohio, was also suffering. After flourishing as one of the largest and most attractive cities in the Union in the first half of the twentieth century, the late 1960s and 1970s had crushed Cleveland financially and psychologically. It's hard to say exactly when the city's slump began, but by 1970 the entire nation had heard the "mistake-by-the-lake" jokes, and most thought of Cleveland as dirty and dangerous—not a place you'd like to visit and certainly not somewhere you'd choose to live.

A looming factor in the city's social decline was one of the elements that had once upon a time made it one of the most unique burgs in America: its smorgasbord of ethnic backgrounds. Cleveland was a microcosm of America in the early twentieth century. It was a settling ground for Czechoslovakians, Hungarians, Italians, Poles, and many others primarily of eastern European backgrounds. By the mid-1960s another ethnicity was struggling to carve its respective place in the city's makeup: African Americans.

Throughout the nation at that time whites and blacks were often at odds. Nowhere was this universal conflict more damaging or more public than in Cleveland where the black population had grown significantly in the second half of the century. By 1980 44 percent of Cleveland's population was black, rising dramatically from 16 percent in 1950. With so many other ethnic groups already having established their niches in the populace, there was widespread animosity and anxiety.

A perfect example of this racial change in the makeup of the population took place just outside of downtown in the small neighborhood of Hough, where in July of 1966 rising tensions and occasional violence snowballed into one of the darkest moments in Cleveland history. Four blacks were killed in a four-day riot that resulted in millions of dollars in property damage to an already deteriorating community. History repeated itself two years later when Glenville became a battleground in a fracas between black militants and police, leaving ten killed and dozens injured.

Ironically the "Glenville Shootout" occurred seven months after Carl Stokes took office. Stokes was the first black man to be elected mayor of a major American city. Many had voted for him in the hopes he would allay the city's obvious race problems, but he lost much of his support after Glenville. He was at odds with the primarily white Cleveland Police force. He battled with area businesses and city council, and after winning re-election in 1969 he chose not to run for a third term. But even had it not been for the riots and their aftermath, one man could not have been expected to solve Cleveland's deep-rooted racial problems. Racism by both blacks and whites would endure for decades, searing a city that had grown to prominence partly because of its diverse populace.

Race was also an issue in education. In 1976 a U.S. District court ruling stated that the city and state boards of education were responsible for the racial segregation of Cleveland's public schools and must desegregate them, which by 1980 cost the city $12 million in annual transportation costs, further exacerbating Cleveland's sorry fiscal status.

In addition to racial tensions during the late-1960s, industries were vacating the blue-collar town of Cleveland (and many others in the region), some relocating to the Sun Belt or overseas where overall costs and wages were smaller. In 1969 the National Screw and Manufacturing Company, which had owned a plant in Cleveland since 1889, closed up shop and departed for a more efficient factory in Mentor, taking a thousand jobs with it.

Downtown was crumbling. The city spent millions to demolish empty, decaying buildings but couldn't keep up with the growing number. Department stores like William Taylor and Son, Sterling-Lindner, and the Bailey Company were closing downtown. And even the city's professional basketball team, the Cleveland Cavaliers, wouldn't stay in downtown Cleveland. They moved to brand-new Richfield Coliseum in Summit County in 1974. Residents were also leaving Cleveland in hordes, departing at a rate of 20,000 per year by the early 1970s, dropping the city from among the fifteen most populated in the United States.

Cleveland's public parks looked like junkyards. The transit system was a joke, but it didn't really matter because there was no reason to go downtown. City streets, bridges, and water and sewer systems were falling apart because voters couldn't afford to raise their taxes to pay for improvements. Lake Erie was so contaminated that fish couldn't even live there, and the Cuyahoga River was so heavily polluted it actually caught fire multiple times. The most notorious fire occurred in the summer of 1969 and caused $50,000 in damage.

Not surprisingly a 1975 study said that Cleveland ranked second of fifty-eight large American cities in terms of having the worst social and economic problems. But when the residents of Cleveland tried to turn things around, they got worse. Desperate for cash during the 1970s under Mayor Ralph Perk the city borrowed heavily and sold many valuable assets. Cleveland sold its sewage-treatment facilities and its transit system to regional authorities in the civic equivalent of trying to earn a living by selling your own plasma. The city even turned over legendary Municipal Stadium to a private interest—in this case Browns' owner and well-known Cleveland philanthropist Art Modell—who then leased the Stadium back to the baseball Indians in a truly bizarre setup.

In 1977 young city councilman Dennis Kucinich was elected mayor as a champion of the underdog and the subjugated, promising to pull Cleveland out of its economic slump without raising taxes and without selling off any more of the city. But the confrontational style adopted by Kucinich and his appointees, also relatively young and inexperienced, antagonized many. They retorted by collecting enough signatures to force a special election to remove Kucinich from office in 1978, the first such recall election in Cleveland history. In an extremely close vote that resulted in two recounts Kucinich got to keep his job by a mere 236 votes. Nonetheless, Kucinich was swept out of office a year later by George Voinovich, and the city was certainly no better off following the Kucinich experiment. In fact in the midst of Kucinich's ragged term the city hit rock bottom. After a decade of scratching and borrowing, in 1978 Cleveland became the first major American city to default since the Great Depression when it couldn't repay $14 million in loans to six local banks. It would be nearly two years before the sides agreed to refinance.

Still the city was fighting back. In February 1980 Clevelanders approved a 50 percent income tax increase to help pull the city out of its fiscal hole, and with the development of the Flats, a lakeside bar-and-nightclub complex, and other urban renewal projects, progress was being made. But at the close of the 1970s Cleveland remained a mess. More damaging than the fiscal and physical appearance of the city, Clevelanders had been robbed of much by 1980. They had little reason to be proud of where they lived. There was little that united Cleveland's social and racial classes other than mutual disdain for the condition of their surroundings. They lived in a city that couldn't take care of itself. A city with citizens who couldn't live with one another. A city that was the laughing stock of a nation of which it had once been at the vanguard.

Though the cities were nearly identical in makeup and history (and suffered several of the same civic headaches) the industrial, blue-collar town of Pittsburgh, Pennsylvania, had one major advantage over Cleveland throughout the late 1970s. In January 1980 the Pittsburgh Steelers had become the first team in the National Football League to win four Super Bowls with a triumph over the Los Angeles Rams in Super Bowl XIV.

The importance of a winning professional sports team to the morale of a city is often overlooked when a city is without one. Many civic historians would argue that the great Steel Curtain (the nickname of the Steelers' ferocious defense) had gotten many natives of Pittsburgh through the dark times of the 1970s: the closing of steel mills, the poor economy, and the overall lack of nationalism. Cleveland had no such sports elixir. In fact it was quite the opposite.

The Indians, who had sloshed through the 1960s with little success in Major League Baseball, had continued to struggle in the 1970s, filing just two winning records in ten years as attendance dwindled to dangerously low levels. There was some excitement surrounding the Tribe that summer of 1980 mostly because of rookie outfield sensation Joe Charboneau, but the team still barely hovered over .500.

The Cavaliers joined the National Basketball Association as an expansion team in 1970 and aside from one exciting playoff run in 1976 had garnered little attention, particularly since the team moved from playing at the Cleveland Arena downtown to suburban Richfield. Through the late 1970s the Cavs had kept trading away their future draft picks for inferior players in mind-boggling deals, which were more often than not engineered by Cavs owner Ted Stepien. Things got so bad that just as the 1980–1981 Cavs season began that fall the NBA barred the team from making any more trades, marking a dubious historic distinction. Now it wasn't the fans; it wasn't the players; it wasn't the coach; it was the *league office* that felt Cavs owner Ted Stepien was incompetent. And then there were the Browns.

They had been the pride of the city for a quarter-century through the 1940s, 1950s, and 1960s, winning four NFL championships and posting an amazing .728 winning percentage with just one losing season in twenty-four years. "I was told when I first got there," said longtime Browns' safety Thom Darden, "that on Mondays the residents of Cleveland walk above the city or walk below the city based on whether the Browns win or lose. This town, more so than most towns, lives and dies with its football team."

But at the dawn of the 1970s the Browns began a new chapter in their history. As the NFL absorbed the upstart yet successful American Football League in 1970 and adopted its members, the NFL was split into two conferences: the American and the National. Though most of the AFL teams would join the AFC, for balance three existing NFL clubs would have to join them. The Baltimore Colts, the Steelers, and the Browns made the transition, with the latter two settling in the AFC Central Division along with NFL newcomers the Houston Oilers and Cincinnati Bengals.

Browns' owner Art Modell figured his team would be able to dominate the Central Division in the early 1970s just as it had dominated the short-lived Century Division in the NFL in the late 1960s. Pittsburgh had been one of the most embarrassing teams in the NFL over the previous thirty years, while Cincinnati and Houston had played in what most figured was an inferior league. It appeared that the Browns' reputation as being one of the NFL's titans would only continue.

It didn't. Instead it was the Steelers under young head coach Chuck Noll who quickly became the AFC's powerhouse. Legendary Browns' coach Blanton Collier, who had led the team to four NFL title games in eight years, retired after a 7-7 record in 1970, and assistant Nick Skorich was promoted to become the Browns' third head coach.

The Browns managed to win their first Central title in 1971 with a 9-5 mark but were overwhelmed in the divisional playoffs by Baltimore. The success continued the following year as the Browns went 10-4, finished second to Pittsburgh in the Central, but captured a Wild Card spot in the postseason. In the divisional playoffs they were matched with the Miami Dolphins, who were coming off a perfect 14-0 regular season, the first in the NFL's modern era. The Browns nearly pulled off the upset but fell just short as the Dolphins went on to win Super Bowl VII. Little did the Browns or their fans know that the Miami game would mark their final playoff appearance of the decade.

"When I joined the Browns, it was expected we'd make the playoffs," said veteran left tackle Doug Dieken, whom the team drafted in 1971. "Then all of a sudden, things got real sour. I remember listening to talk shows and they'd have funerals for us."

"They were guys who were used to winning," Darden said, "but they were on the down side of their careers. The energy, the excitement, the enthusiasm, the sell-all for the sake of winning was not there. They had already experienced all that. Then you start bringing in young guys and the Browns weren't doing a good job through the draft. Most of their picks didn't pan out."

Instead of watching their own team achieve success in the 1970s, Cleveland fans saw their archrival Steelers reach the playoffs eight times and capture a quartet of world titles. The Browns meanwhile compiled a record of 46-54-2 from 1973 through 1979. The Browns suffered the first double-digit loss seasons in team history in 1974 and 1975, which coincidentally were the first two championship seasons for the Steelers. "There was a very unpleasant atmosphere during those years," said Browns' quarterback Brian Sipe. "Things just weren't panning out. The team was dead. That's hard to explain, but you get a feeling about teams, and the team was dead."

But the 1980 season marked the beginning of a new decade, a decade in which anything seemed possible. The 1970s were over even if the reign of the Pittsburgh Steelers wasn't and following the thrilling 1979 season in which the Browns fell just short of the playoffs Cleveland was anxious to see what the 1980 team could achieve.

Most Cleveland backers would have agreed that many holes needed to be filled on the Browns' roster before the team could become a serious playoff contender. But most would also concur that they had the right man directing the troops.

Sam Rutigliano was entering his third season as head coach of the Cleveland Browns. He had succeeded Forrest Gregg who had led the team through three seasons before resigning with one game left in 1977. It was Rutigliano's first head-coaching job, and though he'd been coaching for more than twenty years, including twelve as an NFL assistant, at the time many fans were asking themselves, "Sam who?"

Rutigliano was born in Brooklyn, New York, in 1932, the son of an Italian immigrant bakery truck driver. He was an all-star end in high school and then attended East Central Junior College in Decatur, Mississippi, before transferring to the University of Tennessee. Rutigliano eventually graduated from the University of Tulsa in 1952, then began his coaching career at the high school level in New York and Connecticut over the next ten years. Rutigliano broke into the college game in 1964 when he joined the University of Connecticut's staff as offensive coordinator. Two years later Lou Saban offered him a job as Maryland's freshman coach, and within the year Rutigliano was promoted to the varsity squad's offensive coordinator. When Saban moved up to the AFL as head coach and general manager of the Denver Broncos in 1967 Rutigliano followed and served as pass-offense coordinator. Rutigliano debuted in the NFL when the Broncos merged into the senior league in 1970. In 1971 he joined the staff of the New England Patriots as offensive coordinator, then leapt at the opportunity to return to his roots in New York as defensive backfield coach of the Jets three years later. In 1976 Rutigliano joined longtime friend Hank Stram in New Orleans after the latter had been named head coach of the Saints. Rutigliano stayed with the Saints until the Browns came calling after the 1977 season concluded.

"What had happened before was not working," Modell said of the search for a new coach that December. "I needed a fresh perspective, a fresh slant, new ideas; not the same assistant coaches, not the same way of doing business." Modell's general manager, Peter Hadhazy, remembered Rutigliano after working with him in New England when Hadhazy was an administrative assistant. "Once you talk to this guy," Hadhazy told Modell, "you won't want to talk to anyone else."

Modell remembered Rutigliano. They'd had dinner in Denver following the Browns' 1970 season finale. Modell eventually invited the prospect to his Waite Hill home for an extensive interview just before Christmas 1977. During that three-day period Browns' history was changed forever. Rutigliano spent hours with Modell, his wife Pat, and Hadhazy. They watched films of the 1977 Browns in the Modell basement. Rutigliano, showing his extensive knowledge of the game, was impressed with the talent the Browns had. Conversely, Modell was impressed with Rutigliano.

"I was looking for someone I could be happy with," Modell said. "It's tough enough to be happy when you win, let alone when you lose. The greatest experience of all for me came in the Blanton Collier years. In Sam, my instincts told me I had a young Blanton Collier. Blanton was mentally and intellectually honest. Sam is, too." On Christmas Eve Modell called the Rutigliano home. Sam's wife Barb answered. The operator's voice was unusually cheery. "I have a person-to-person call for the coach of the Cleveland Browns," she said. By the time Barb handed the phone to her husband, she was crying.

At 3:00 P.M. on December 28, 1977, Rutigliano was officially introduced as the new head coach of the Cleveland Browns. During that first press conference members of the media and fans alike discovered that the new coach was nothing like Forrest Gregg, the man he had replaced, in terms of personality. Gregg was a taskmaster cut from the Vince Lombardi cloth of discipline.

Browns' center Tom DeLeone remembered Gregg's strict instructions prior to a game with Cincinnati to block big defensive tackle Robert Brown on every play.

During the game DeLeone broke his hand. "I never went out of the game, though," he said. "I was too afraid of Forrest Gregg. I just put some tape on it. I never even told him about it."

Rutigliano was more of a humanitarian, a players' coach who was much more relaxed and personable than his predecessor, "more like everyone's favorite uncle than a football coach," author John Keim would write. In contrast, "Forrest Gregg was more of your military-type coach, a screamer," Browns' running back Mike Pruitt said. "Sam was more laid back, more of a teacher." Browns' kicker Don Cockroft explained during the 1980 season that "one of Sam's best qualities is that he never gets uptight for a game and he creates that attitude among us." Furthermore, noted Cockroft, "he also treats everybody fairly, honestly, and openly and has a concern for us as family people as well as players. It helps everybody perform better."

The players and media seemed to like Rutigliano from the first. After three years of working with Gregg, who was not considered a good communicator by his players, the new coach was a breath of fresh air. Compared to Gregg, Rutigliano was Walter Cronkite. "My way is to somehow, someway reach a person," Rutigliano said at his introductory press conference. "That could come from putting an arm around one man and applying harsher methods to another."

"As football coaches go, he is unique," said Browns' cornerback Clarence Scott. "Sam makes no attempt to dominate the players. Most coaches always want you to know they are in control. To get you to do what they want, they think they have to make you afraid of them. That's how it was to some degree through high school and college until I met up with Sam."

"Sam injected a philosophy coming out of the Forrest Gregg era that was one of togetherness and trying to be a family rather than just a football team," Thom Darden said. "I think that type of atmosphere caught on with the players because that was a pretty close-knit team."

Rutigliano was articulate, a good public speaker, and intelligent. But most surprising he was a very funny and entertaining man. "I didn't really know who the head coach of the Browns was," Rutigliano later said. "I knew who Sam Rutigliano was, but this coach I kept reading about was a mystery to me." Added Browns' defensive end Lyle Alzado, "if you can't get along with Sam, then you'd better look in the mirror, because it's you, not him."

Rutigliano's football philosophy also differed greatly from Forrest Gregg's. While Gregg was old school and conservative, Rutigliano was more of a wide-open, offensive-minded coach.

"He made football exciting," Mike Pruitt said. "It wasn't the vanilla plays everybody else was running. It was something different. It was a tight-end reverse; it was a halfback option; it was a flea-flicker. Those things were around, but nobody really did them before Sam got there."

A player could suggest tinkering with a play on offense and Rutigliano would go for it. "Ozzie (Newsome) would say 'I can beat this guy one-on-one on an out,' and we'd do it even though that wasn't the play that was sent in," Pruitt said. "Then Sam would say, 'Hey, that was successful. Let's see if that works again.' You'd never hear that from Forrest Gregg. It was either his way or no way."

In addition to being somewhat of a cowboy in terms of offensive strategy, Rutigliano was also a gambler, quickly acquiring the nickname "Riverboat Sam." "Security is for cowards," he once said. "I believe in gambling. No successful man ever got anywhere without gambling."

For better or worse this would become his legacy as head coach of the Browns. Rutigliano won his first three games with the Browns to open the 1978 season, and the streak should have been four. But the officials incorrectly ruled that Pittsburgh had not fumbled on the kickoff in sudden-death overtime, which would have put visiting Cleveland in scoring position. The Steelers won, 15-9, and the Browns dropped four of their next five and six of their next eight games.

Though the 8-8 season ended with an embarrassing 48-16 loss in Cincinnati, Modell offered Rutigliano a three-year contract extension through 1983, demonstrating that he thought the team was on the right track. "I've got a good man," Modell said at the time. "He's a winner, and we shall win with Sam running the show."

The improvement continued in 1979 as the Browns won their first four games, the fourth a 26-7 stomping of the defending NFC champion Dallas Cowboys on *Monday Night Football.* It appeared as though the Browns under Rutigliano had arrived back in the spotlight of the NFL. A week later, though, the Steelers put Cleveland back in its place. The defending champs routed the Browns, 51-35, highlighting the primary weakness of the team that would rear its ugly head all season: a suspect defense.

Following another tough home loss to Washington the Browns rallied from a 20-7 third-quarter deficit to nip the Bengals, 28-27. An impressive win at St. Louis and another thriller in Philadelphia followed. Then an overtime win over Miami in mid-November put the Browns at 8-4 with four games to play. Suddenly they had a great shot of reaching the playoffs as a Wild Card. Instead, Cleveland dropped three of the four, including the heartbreaking loss in Cincinnati in the finale, to conclude the season at 9-7. But there was plenty of reason for optimism. United Press International named Rutigliano AFC Coach of the Year, the team was relatively young, and the Steelers couldn't win forever. 1979 had been the Browns' first winning season in three years, but more would be expected in 1980.

While the defense of the 1979 Browns was a sore subject, the offense was the pride and joy. "In football, people say you win with defense," Tom DeLeone said. "You could have the greatest defense of all time, but if you have no offense, it doesn't matter how good your defense is." Though Rutigliano's philosophy and style had helped resurrect an offense that had been dormant throughout the 1970s, it was another man who was directly praised for its success.

No one thought much of a brown-haired surfer from San Diego named Brian Sipe when the Browns selected him in the thirteenth round of the 1972 draft. A few days later when Browns' coach Nick Skorich was asked who he thought would be the surprise of that draft, he said it would be either eleventh-round pick Mel Long, a linebacker from Toledo, or Arizona State running back Hugh McKinnis, selected in the eighth round. Chuck Heaton of the *Plain Dealer* went out on a limb and said it would be Sipe. He had set several school records under Don Coryell at San Diego State, but few expected him to even make the Browns' roster, let alone ever become a starter.

Many thought Cleveland already had its quarterback of the future: Mike Phipps. The Browns had traded future Hall-of-Fame wide receiver Paul Warfield to the Miami Dolphins for the right to draft Phipps from Purdue in 1970. Phipps saw little action backing up Bill Nelsen in 1970 and 1971 but took over as full-time starter in the fall of 1972. The Browns expected Phipps to be their signal-caller for at least the rest of the decade.

Also Sipe didn't appear to have what it took to cut it in the NFL. He only stood at six-foot-one, 190 pounds, did not have a rocket arm, and certainly didn't look like a football player. After joining the team in September of 1980 offensive guard Joe DeLamielleure described his new quarterback to his wife. "This Sipe is built like a damn girl," he said. "He's got hips like a woman."

Sipe, however, was happy to be a Brown. "I wanted to go to Cleveland, probably more than anything else, as an experience," Sipe said in a 1980 interview. "I had never seen that part of the country, and I wanted to find out a little about professional football. I never pictured myself as a starting quarterback in the NFL. It was just part of a progression, of going on to the next step."

He didn't make the roster in 1972 but did earn a spot on the team's "taxi squad," on which players could practice with the team but never suited up for games. Despite a mediocre 1972 season Phipps led the Browns to the playoffs and kept the starting job again in 1973. Sipe, showing little progress, remained on the taxi squad for another season.

"It wasn't until that second year that I really applied myself because I wanted a spot on the club," Sipe said. "But I still wasn't thinking in terms of starting quarterback. I was still thinking, 'Well, shoot. Being a backup's not so bad. I'd get paid a pretty good salary and not get banged around and not be under the gun.' At the time, as a matter of fact, I thought that was probably the greatest job in professional football, because I would still be able to enjoy myself socially and do the things that I like to do and not feel that all the weight was on my shoulders."

He finally made the club in 1974 just as the team and the fans were beginning to run thin on patience with Phipps. In his fourth year in the league and his second year as the Browns' full-time starter in 1973 Phipps completed less than 50 percent of his passes with just nine touchdowns and a disturbing twenty interceptions. Things looked no better the following year with Phipps at the helm as the Browns dropped five of their first six. But on October 27, 1974, everything changed.

For the first three quarters of their game against the Broncos at Cleveland Stadium it was the same old story for the floundering Browns. They trailed Denver, 21-9, and were going nowhere. Almost out of desperation, five plays into the fourth quarter, Nick Skorich replaced Phipps with Brian Sipe. In his NFL debut Sipe completed four of six passes, including a critical fourth-down toss to wide receiver Steve Holden, and rallied the Browns for two touchdowns in the final 5:30 for a 23-21 win. Appropriately the game-winning score was a one-yard plunge by Sipe with 1:56 to play. Though no one knew it at the time, Sipe's comeback was the ultimate coming attraction.

Sipe started the next four games and directed the Browns to two more victories in an otherwise frustrating 4-10 campaign. Though the final statistics from his rookie year (54.6 completion percentage, one touchdown, seven interceptions, 47.0 quarterback rating) were not impressive, they were no worse than those of the veteran Phipps (45.7 completion percentage, nine touchdowns, seventeen interceptions, 46.7 quarterback rating). The guard had begun to change in the Cleveland huddle.

Phipps directed the team for much of the woeful 1975 season as the Browns compiled the worst record in their history at 3-11, but his numbers did not improve. In his sixth season he threw just four touchdowns along with nineteen interceptions and had a miserable 47.5 quarterback rating. Sipe's statistics were again comparable in limited action and not terribly impressive. 1976 looked to be a make-or-break year for Brian Sipe.

In the preseason Sipe threw just twenty passes as the Browns were once again going to give Phipps the job, still hoping for a return on their large investment. But Sipe had changed his mental outlook since his days as a rookie when he was just in Cleveland for the scenery.

"I don't think of myself as a backup quarterback," Sipe said at the time. "And I'm not going to consider myself a backup as long as I play in this league. I think I have the capabilities and the talent to be a regular." Two hours into the regular-season opener Sipe got the chance to back up his words. Early in the third quarter Mike Phipps left the game with a separated shoulder and Sipe took over. He threw two touchdown passes as the Browns rolled to a 38-17 win over the New York Jets at Cleveland Stadium.

Sipe started twelve of the next thirteen games and directed the Browns to one of the greatest turnarounds in NFL history. They improved their record six games from 1975 to 1976, and at 9-5 had a chance to make the playoffs up until the final Sunday of the season. The great Phipps experiment was over. Sipe was the Browns' new starting quarterback and knew his dark-horse status had played a major role in his eventual arrival. "With the exception of the money aspect of it," he said, "I felt that it worked to my advantage. I was not burdened with the great expectations that a lot of other quarterbacks had to deal with when they came in the league. Consequently, I feel I actually was given more time to develop and was able to do so without much pressure."

Phipps, who didn't have those luxuries, was traded to the Chicago Bears the following spring for a fourth-round draft pick in 1977 and a first-round choice in 1978—the latter of which would produce one of the greatest players in Browns' history.

Sipe and the Browns got off to a good start in 1977 and entered November with a 5-2 record. But after a tough loss to Cincinnati, Sipe was lost for the season with a fractured shoulder blade in a 35-31 loss in Pittsburgh. With Dave Mays at the controls the Browns dropped their last four games and finished 6-8, prompting Gregg's resignation in the face of certain termination.

As soon as Rutigliano took over the reins he set up a meeting with Sipe. "Sam called me in and told me I was going to be his quarterback," Sipe said. "He said we were going to throw the ball and throw it on first down and from anywhere on the field. He said I'd call all the plays, unless I showed I couldn't handle it. He told me what I wanted to hear, but there's a bit of an actor in Sam, and I got the feeling he told everybody what they wanted to hear. I didn't really believe him until I got on the practice field and started running that offense of his. He was for real."

As a result Sipe began to truly blossom when Rutigliano arrived. For the first time in his career Sipe enjoyed consistent coaching. "In my early years here," he said, "I played under five offensive coordinators. I felt like an Indianapolis driver stuck on a dirt track. I always felt there was a different way to play football than the way we played it."

"I was impressed with him right from the beginning," Rutigliano said. "I had talked to Len Dawson, Bob Griese, and Fran Tarkenton. They were similar quarterbacks. They said he will hit the open receivers. That's a very simple statement, but very, very important. When they're open, he'll throw strikes."

"He could thread the needle," said Tom DeLeone. "He couldn't throw far, but he could throw harder than people gave him credit for. He just didn't look like he could." Sipe attempted a team-record 399 passes in 1978 and threw for 2,906 yards and 21 touchdowns, the most in both categories by a Cleveland quarterback in twelve years. Things were even better in 1979 when Sipe hurled for a team-record

3,793 yards and twenty-eight touchdowns as the offense averaged 361 yards per game, the most since 1966.

"That's the kind of football I was weaned on at San Diego State," he said prior to the 1980 season. "It wasn't until I turned pro that I learned to play conservatively and got the reputation of a nickel-and-dime passer. Now I'm coming back to my old form again."

Sipe certainly had the physical skills to make it as an NFL quarterback, but what made him one of the league's best was his football intelligence, a quality that impressed his teammates: "Brian's ability to think on his feet and make plays was uncanny," said Doug Dieken; and his coach: "Why does a Mike Phipps fail?" Sam Rutigliano asked. "Why does a Brian Sipe succeed? It's from the neck up."

Plus in 1979 Sipe had proved that he was a maestro in crunch time. *Cleveland Press* sports editor Bob Sudyk wrote, "Telling Sipe there's 'two minutes to go' is like Popeye grabbing a can of spinach, Captain Marvel saying 'Shazam' or giving Frankenstein a couple of electric charges behind the ears."

If the Browns were down at halftime Sipe would comment to quarterbacks coach Jim Shofner, "We got 'em right where we want 'em."

"We were kind of like Pavlov's dogs in the fourth quarter," DeLeone said. "Maybe Sipe planned it, but we didn't plan it. Sipe liked to keep it exciting. I would have rather put 50 points on the board and sit on the bench in the second half, but that didn't happen."

When Rutigliano arrived Sipe was entering his prime. The coach knew that his job was to provide a supporting cast for Sipe to reach his full potential. "We got him just what he needed," Rutigliano said. "We surrounded him with five condominiums that could protect him. We got running backs, receivers and a tight end that were smart and very capable." The "condominiums" were the primary key, and when Rutigliano arrived the Browns were already in good shape at the important left-tackle position, which guarded a right-handed quarterback's blind side. Doug Dieken was only the third man in team history to hold that position, becoming the starter ten games into his rookie year, filling in for aging legend Dick Schafrath. Dieken was a 1971 sixth-round draft choice from Illinois, where he played tight end and left as the second-leading receiver in school history. Entering the 1980 season Dieken had started 121 consecutive games, often matching up against the opponents' top pass rusher. "You just put him on the field and forget about him," Rutigliano said of Dieken.

But Dieken was not the type of person you could ignore in the locker room. His one-liners and practical jokes had made him somewhat of a legend with the team and the media. Dieken had a particularly interesting relationship with *Plain Dealer* columnist Dan Coughlin, and the two would exchange barbs throughout the 1980 season.

Beside Dieken at left guard was veteran Henry Sheppard, a native of Cuero, Texas, selected by the Browns in the fifth round of the 1976 draft from Southern Methodist. Sheppard had started for the Browns at left guard throughout his first three years with the club and had switched to right tackle in 1979 before returning to left guard for 1980. When combined with Dieken the two formed an almost airtight seal on the left side of the line.

Sheppard was also cut from the same cloth as Dieken in terms of personality and was much happier being a part of Rutigliano's wide-open offense. "I was on a team in college that ran the wishbone," he said, "and it was boring as hell, quite frankly. On this team, it's like being a kid at Christmas. You never know what you're going to find under the tree."

Anchoring the middle of the line was another veteran, center Tom DeLeone. DeLeone was born in Kent, Ohio, and attended Ohio State, then was selected by the Cincinnati Bengals in the fifth round of the 1972 draft. After two seasons along the Ohio River he was traded to Atlanta, released because of a blood pressure problem, picked up by Houston, then released again, all in a two-week span. The following Sunday DeLeone was sitting at home with his wife watching the Oilers, the team that had just released him, play the Browns on television. He commented to his wife how great it would be to play in Cleveland since it was so close to where he grew up. A few minutes later the phone rang telling DeLeone the Browns wanted to sign him.

The Browns, unlike his previous three teams, grabbed hold of DeLeone and didn't let go. He succeeded center John Demarie six games into the 1975 season and held the starting position for the next four years. He was selected to the AFC's All-Pro team in 1979, marking the first time in nine years a Browns' offensive lineman had earned the distinction.

Robert E. Jackson expected to start the season at right guard just as he had the previous five years. Signed in 1975 as an undrafted free agent from Duke—where he had been recruited as a quarterback prospect—Jackson had been instrumental in paving the way for four individual thousand-yard rushing seasons for the Browns but would soon begin a new role with the team.

The final condominium was youngster Cody Risien, who would start the season at right tackle. Risien had taken over at left guard for George Buehler seven games into the 1979 season after being selected in the seventh round of the draft from Texas A&M that spring. He earned All-Rookie team honors from UPI but would now return to the position he'd played at college. At six-foot-seven, Risien was the tallest member of the unit, and it appeared that he could be an anchor on the line for several years.

"They're a very, very close bunch," Browns' offensive-line coach Rod Humenuik would say during the 1980 season. "One reason is that they're so similar. They've had to overcome the same things to get here."

"Our offensive line did some things pass-blocking-wise that allowed us to get more people out in pass routes," Dieken said. "If you keep your running backs and tight ends in all the time, that's two less receivers you've got out there for the quarterback to find. We were a capable enough pass-blocking team that we could get all our receivers out. The five of us played very well together. We really fed off one another. There was a lot of personal chemistry there that if one guy was having trouble, another would chip in and help him."

The combination of chemistry and talent made the Browns' line—nicknamed CLEBOL (short for Cleveland Browns Offensive Line) by its members and coaches—one of the best in the league as well as one of the finest and most unique in the history of the team. "Offensive linemen don't play for the glamour," DeLeone said. "They play because it's the only legal place they're allowed to hit somebody. Defensive guys are thinking, 'sack, sack, sack, sack.' What do offensive linemen think about? 'I hope my wife saw me make that block'? All you've got is each other watching the films patting each other on the back."

But this line had plenty to be proud of. When Humenuik, the only Browns' assistant to survive the Forrest Gregg–Sam Rutigliano changeover, went to New England as offensive-line coach in the mid-1980s, he tried to use the same kind of techniques he'd used with the Browns. The Patriots couldn't cut the mustard. "John Hannah, God bless him, was probably one of the best guards in the game," Dieken said, "but he couldn't do it. John Hannah was basically a run-blocking lineman, where we were more of a pass-blocking unit. We used the pass to set up the run."

"How the offensive line plays," said DeLeone, "is basically how the team plays." With the line serving as the foundation of the offense, the Browns had pieced together some lethal weapons Sipe could work with.

For starters the Browns had two of the best wide receivers in the business lining up on opposite ends of the line of scrimmage. Veteran Reggie Rucker began his career after being signed as a free agent by the Dallas Cowboys in 1968. Rucker, a versatile three-sport athlete at Boston University, finally cracked the Dallas offense in 1970. He started for the Cowboys in Super Bowl V but otherwise saw limited action. Dallas eventually released him early in what became a crazy 1971 season for Rucker. The New York Giants then signed him but released him after he made just one reception in four games. Shortly thereafter the New England Patriots became Rucker's third team in less than two months, but he made little impact in five games to close 1971. That would all change the following year.

Rucker burst into the Patriots' starting lineup, snagging forty-four receptions for 681 yards and three touchdowns. Rucker had finally arrived. His success continued over the next two years in a New England uniform, making an impression on a young Patriots' offensive coach named Sam Rutigliano. At the same time Rutigliano had made an impression on the previously struggling receiver. "There is no doubt in my mind that Sam saved my career," Rucker said prior to the start of the 1980 season. "If it weren't for him, I don't know what I might be doing today, probably not playing football. Sam taught me so many things, on the field and off. I owe him so much. I'm doing my best to show him I appreciate his influence."

The Patriots traded Rucker to Cleveland prior to the 1975 season for a fourth-round draft pick. It wasn't quite as disastrous as the Boston Red Sox selling Babe Ruth to the New York Yankees, but it would not go down as one of the better New England sports trades of the 1970s. Rucker became an instant star with the Browns, leading the team in receptions in 1975, 1976, and 1978 and in yardage in his first four seasons in brown and orange. Rucker became Cleveland's most consistent pass catcher, serving as something solid in the Browns' passing game as Brian Sipe slowly developed. If he could put together another season in 1980 like his previous five with the Browns, Rucker would surpass the 400-reception and 6,000-yard barriers, impressive territory for NFL wide receivers.

Though he wasn't quite as experienced as Rucker, Dave Logan brought a great deal to the Browns' passing game on the other side of the field. Logan, possibly the best overall athlete on the roster, had the opportunity to play football, baseball, and basketball professionally. He was drafted by the Cincinnati Reds while still in high school after an impressive scholastic career as a pitcher and first baseman, but Logan opted to go to college instead. He ended up second on the all-time reception list at the University of Colorado where he won four letters on the gridiron and three in basketball.

Playing two sports that overlapped often caused scheduling headaches for Logan. Once he played with the Colorado football team in the Bluebonnet Bowl on a December Saturday then flew to Kansas City that night to play a basketball game the following day.

As a senior he was an All-American wide receiver and averaged eighteen points per game on the hard court. But an ankle injury two weeks before the NFL draft dropped his stock. His lawyer sent letters to all twenty-eight NFL teams explaining Logan's injury and the prognosis for a speedy and full recovery, but he still slipped to the third round, where the Browns selected him in what would become one of the greatest draft steals in team history. Two months later the Kansas City Kings of the NBA also drafted Logan, who became the only man in Browns' history to be drafted by all three major American professional sports leagues.

He split time as a wide receiver and a tight end in his rookie season (after which both Colorado's coach and Larry Brown of the Denver Nuggets tried to lure him back to basketball), then Forrest Gregg tried to turn Logan into a backup quarterback in the 1977 training camp. Naturally (and fortunately for the Browns) it didn't work. He caught only nineteen passes that season but became a much bigger part of the Browns' wide-open offense upon Rutigliano's arrival in 1978. By 1979 he was the team's leading receiver with fifty-nine catches for 982 yards and seven touchdowns. A photograph of a dazzling one-handed touchdown catch that Logan made against the Steelers that October appeared on the cover of *Sports Illustrated*'s 1980 pro-football preview issue, making Logan the sixth Cleveland Brown ever to grace its cover.

The Browns' other primary downfield threat hadn't made any major magazine covers yet, but there was little doubt he would in the not-too-distant future. Following the long and frustrating Mike Phipps tenure from 1970 to 1976 the Browns and their fans were probably beginning to lose faith in the draft. Ironically when they finally traded Phipps, a draft bust, to the Chicago Bears following the 1976 season they received two draft picks in return: a fourth-round choice in 1977 and a first-round pick in 1978. In the first pick, the Browns selected defensive tackle Robert Sims from South Carolina State. In the second they picked Ozzie Newsome from the University of Alabama.

Newsome, who won nine letters in high school in football, baseball, and basketball, had played wide receiver with the Crimson Tide and done it so well that head coach Paul "Bear" Bryant called him the finest receiver in Alabama history. The Browns decided to switch Newsome to tight end, where in Rutigliano's two-receiver offense he could become a third downfield threat. He took to it like a fish to water, catching thirty-eight passes for 589 yards as a rookie and then fifty-five passes for 781 yards and a team-high nine touchdowns in 1979. In just two years in the pros Newsome was already living up to the nickname given to him by a Tuscaloosa sportswriter in his freshman year at Alabama: The Wizard of Oz.

"Offensively, you couldn't lose Newsome and you couldn't lose Sipe," Rutigliano said. "It would have been hard to lose anybody, but those were the most significant guys."

With Rucker, Logan, and Newsome serving as the deep threats, the Browns had another cadre of receivers who were possibly even more dangerous just by filling in the empty space between those three and Brian Sipe. "You knew you had good receivers out there," said fullback Mike Pruitt, "but probably 50 percent of Brian's passes went to running backs. You put us one-on-one with a linebacker, we'll beat him all day long. That really opened up the passing game. Now the defensive backs were worried about the running backs getting past the linebackers."

Under Rutigliano's offensive philosophy the running backs were usually used as much as receivers as they were rushers. And the Browns had collected some talented athletes who could both run and catch the football. "We had a well-balanced attack," Pruitt said. "People knew we could throw, but people also knew we could run. They couldn't stack the defense one way or the other. They had to be honest all the time."

And Pruitt was the most important factor in demanding opponents' honesty, leading the team in rushing in 1979 with 1,294 yards. The Chicago native attended Purdue and was chosen by the Browns in the first round of the 1976 draft. But Pruitt's role in the Cleveland offense was never truly defined in his first two seasons under Forrest Gregg. He only carried the football a total of ninety-nine times in 1976 and 1977, but everything changed when Rutigliano took over. At his first training camp in July 1978 the new coach pulled Pruitt aside. "I don't know what happened your first couple of years, and it's none of my business," Rutigliano said, "but I've looked at film and I don't know why you're not playing. First thing we're going to do is give you an opportunity. Then it's up to you."

It was the chance Pruitt had been waiting for. Rutigliano brought Pruitt into the Cleveland offense, and the move paid off as the former Boilermaker accumulated more than eighteen hundred rushing yards in Rutigliano's first two seasons. Pruitt's gradual improvement and larger role on the team were factors as his number of carries almost doubled from 1978 to 1979, but so was a key injury midway through the latter campaign. When running back Greg Pruitt (no relation) suffered a mild knee sprain in the Browns' Week Four victory over Dallas it didn't appear very serious. Pruitt missed the next four games but felt he was ready to start in Week Nine in St. Louis. On the first play of the game Pruitt tore a ligament in the same knee and was lost for the season.

In a way, Greg Pruitt's absence made the Browns' 1979 achievements all the more impressive. He had led the Browns in rushing for five consecutive seasons from 1974 to 1978 and had often been the lone star on a struggling offense. The Browns selected the University of Oklahoma product in the second round of the 1973 draft, and though he only had sixty-one rushes in his rookie year Pruitt averaged six yards per carry, and it was clear that he would soon become the heart of the Browns' running game. He topped the thousand-yard plateau three straight years (1975, 1976, 1977) and barely missed a fourth in 1978 despite sitting out four games due to a bruised calf. He was the third Brown to rack up three consecutive thousand-yard campaigns, following Hall-of-Famers Jim Brown and Leroy Kelly. He was one of the first "scatbacks" in the NFL, a relatively small runner (five-foot-ten) with dazzling speed, which inspired a line of t-shirts with "Hello" printed on the front and "Goodbye" on the back. But questions swirled around Browns' camp that summer as to the status of Greg Pruitt's knee. Rutigliano said early on that Pruitt would not appear in at least the first two exhibition games, but player and coach both expected him to be able to contribute in 1980.

Though he was entering his eighth year with the Browns, Greg Pruitt was not the elder statesman of the Cleveland backfield. That distinction rested with Calvin Hill, entering his eleventh NFL season in 1980. Hill, a Yale graduate, was a first-round selection of the Dallas Cowboys in 1969 and made an immediate impact on what had become one of the league's premier teams. Hill rushed for 942 yards in his first season and was named Rookie of the Year by *The Sporting News*. He helped the Cowboys reach the Super Bowl the following two seasons and was selected for the Pro Bowl in 1972 and 1974. In 1975 he defected to the newly formed World Football League with several other NFL stars but returned to the NFL with the Washington Redskins in 1976. After two seasons in the nation's capital, Hill was released prior to the 1978 season.

The timing worked out perfectly for the Browns. After Greg Pruitt bruised his calf in the season's second game they signed Hill to help fill in and provide depth at running back. Just before Hill joined the team he called his friend and former Dallas teammate Reggie Rucker, by this time a star on the Browns' roster. Though Cleveland had been the butt of many jokes around the nation Rucker told Hill not to make any hasty judgments about the city. "You know me and I'll tell you that I didn't like it when I came here," Rucker said. "And my first year I made quick judgments. But it is a good city with a lot of good people. Come on up. We need you, and you'll like it."

Hill did, and the team liked him as well. He became much more dangerous as a receiver out of the backfield, catching twenty-five passes in twelve games in 1978 and then thirty-eight for 381 yards in 1979. In some ways, whatever Hill brought to the Browns on the field was simply a bonus to what he provided off it. He was selected as the team's offensive captain, and his experience, leadership skills, and intelligence made an impression on many of the younger players. Brian Sipe called him "a thinking man's football player." Mike Pruitt said, "If the coaches tell us to run through a wall, we do, except Calvin. He wants to know why he can't run around, over, or under it."

Even if his career was nearing its conclusion, Hill still had a few matches left to fight.

"Calvin plays with the zest of a junior high school player who has just been given his first uniform," said Browns' running backs coach Jim Garrett. And though their respect for Hill was clear, the youngsters occasionally razzed the veteran about his age, which was thirty-three entering the 1980 season. "The guys kid me about being over the hill," Hill said, "but one thing about being over the hill, it means you were once on top of it."

The fourth member of the Browns' backfield expected to contribute in 1980 had just descended from the top of the hill in college football and now would try to do the same at the professional level. Rookie Charles White was coming off a dazzling senior season at Southern Cal culminated by his winning the Heisman Trophy. In four years with the Trojans, White accumulated 6,245 yards, and in his final collegiate game racked up 247 yards in a Rose Bowl triumph over Ohio State. Four months later the Browns picked him in the twenty-seventh selection of the draft with the hopes that he would someday replace both the Pruitts as the Browns' next dominant back. Coaches and fans alike would keep an eye on White all through camp, watching the progress of the team's highest draft pick. "In nine years as a pro I've never seen a rookie hit and run like Charles White," said offensive tackle Doug Dieken, the Browns' comic relief man, as he pointed to a small dent in his Mercedes that August. "Charles White backed into my car the other night and forgot to even leave a note."

"No doubt in my mind," Jim Garrett said on a more serious note, "he's a bona fide No. 1 choice. When you punch the cash register, there's never a no sale with him. He'll be a thousand-yard gainer one of these seasons." As it turned out, Garrett was half-right.

White was a topic of discussion that summer not only because of his college success, but because he'd already demonstrated what some feared would become a problem with authority a month after he was drafted. When the Browns' first-year players gathered for the team's annual rookie camp in May, White walked out, refusing to participate in the drills or even take a physical. His reasoning—or more appropriately his agent's—was that he had not yet signed a contract. Perhaps to dispel the idea that he would become a problem White arrived a week before his teammates were scheduled to report to training camp. He appeared eager to work and contribute to the team.

For that matter, from top to bottom, everyone in the Browns' organization was ready for the new season. "We had the running game and the passing game," Tom DeLeone said. "We mixed it up together and threw in the big play and things worked. We would run the ball and pass short to set up the big play. We were in the constant mode of setting the big play up." Rutigliano remembers that, "offensively, we were a very, very efficient football team. I knew we were going to get going. And I knew once we got going, it would be big."

Never one to back down from the grand statement, owner Art Modell said that summer, "the offensive team could be the best we've ever had, better than last year and even better than in the Jim Brown years. Time will tell."

There was no question that the offense would be the heart and soul of the Browns. "We were an offensive team," said Doug Dieken. "That made us tick. If we were going to win the game, it was going to be because we would outscore the other team, it wasn't going to be a case of us shutting anybody out. Offensively we just had a very good mix of people that were able to do a lot of things."

But if the team was going to be any better than it was in 1979, the defense would have to improve. "To win, you've got to have a good offense and the defense has to be sound and can't give up the big play," Tom DeLeone said. "If you've got an erratic defense, you've got a losing team." As impressive as the Cleveland offense had been the previous year, the defense had been shaky. In back-to-back games in October the Browns had allowed a combined eighty-two points in losses to division rivals Houston and Pittsburgh. The Cleveland offense had been good, scoring 22.4 points per game, but the defense had allowed 22 points a game. That margin was far too narrow if the Browns hoped to become a playoff team. And Rutigliano and his staff knew it.

When defensive-backs coach Chuck Weber left Cleveland for Baltimore following the 1979 season, the Browns hired Marty Schottenheimer as the first official defensive coordinator in team history. Schottenheimer, an All-American linebacker at the University of Pittsburgh, began his NFL coaching career with the New York Giants as linebacker coach in 1976, then was promoted to defensive coordinator. He had been the linebacker coach in Detroit the previous two seasons prior to coming to Cleveland. "He brought a different approach to the defense," said Browns' linebacker Dick Ambrose. "He was always probing, trying to find a weakness in the other team's offense."

"Marty was a hard driver," said safety Thom Darden. "Marty demanded obedience to discipline in your scheme of defense. There were times early in my career when we were more of a finesse defense. Marty was more aggressive and wanted to put pressure on people." Though a strongly offensive-minded coach, Rutigliano was eager to strengthen the Browns' defense. "There's no question but that we can move above mediocrity defensively," Rutigliano said. "We won't be the best, but we're going to get better."

One of the initial decisions Schottenheimer made with Rutigliano was to change the Browns' defensive philosophy. Throughout the Browns' first thirty years in the NFL they had primarily used a 4-3 alignment (four down linemen and three linebackers), but after their struggles in 1979 the team would try something new. They would, as many other NFL teams were doing, switch to a 3-4 alignment as their regular defensive set. The 3-4, which they had used with some success late in the 1979 season, seemed perfect for the Browns for two primary reasons. First, it was much more effective in stopping the run, which Cleveland had tremendous trouble doing in 1979 as they allowed 163 rushing yards per game. Second, it allowed the Browns to use another linebacker, a position at which they were relatively rich. In the 3-4 the defensive linemen were often sacrificial lambs, tying up the offensive linemen while the linebackers flowed to the football.

"We knew we weren't as good defensively as we were offensively," Rutigliano said. "We went into the season with the 3-4 and said 'We're just going to play solid defense. We're not going to confuse our guys. We're going to try to keep everything at a minimum, keep away from the big plays, just stay in the game and give the offense a chance in the fourth quarter to win it.' It's like basketball: you may not have a great night, but you can still play good defense." The heart of the unit had been playing good defense for the past decade.

Lyle Alzado, a native of Brooklyn and a graduate of tiny Yanktown College in South Dakota, began his NFL career with the Denver Broncos in 1971 and quickly became one of the league's finest defensive linemen. He started for Denver each of his first five seasons. After a knee injury sidelined him for the entire 1976 campaign Alzado returned in 1977 and helped lead the Broncos to Super Bowl XII. Though he was named AFC Defensive Player of the Year by the NFL Players Association in 1978, Alzado's days in the Rockies were numbered. In the middle of a contract dispute with Denver general manager Fred Gehrke, Alzado was traded to the Browns for a relatively small price: a second- and a fifth-round draft choice in 1980 and a third-round pick in 1981. "Bringing in Alzado," Rutigliano said, "told our players plenty about our intentions to build up the defense in a big way so we could get into the playoffs every year, which was our number-one goal. The players realized the importance of having Alzado as well. "It helped elevate the overall self-confidence of the defense from where it had been previously," Ambrose said. "Now we had a name star on our side. He was an inspiration to have on our team and helped motivate guys to a higher level of play."

Alzado made an immediate impact in 1979, collecting seven sacks and eighty tackles despite playing most of the season with a sprained knee. As the Browns discussed revamping the 1979 defense Alzado volunteered to switch from left to right defensive end, sacrificing his pass-rushing skills but making the Cleveland defense more balanced. "I don't care where I play, I just want to win," Alzado said prior to the 1980 season. "There is no room for selfish individuals or prima donnas."

"He's a throwback to 1950," Rutigliano said, "and it's very refreshing."

Not only was Alzado a tough defender and an unselfish player, he was also a loose cannon in the locker room. He verbally challenged his teammates and would accuse them of not working hard enough. His attitude toward life was probably best exemplified just a few days before he was traded to the Browns when he took on former heavyweight boxing champ Muhammad Ali in an exhibition bout. Needless to say, Alzado didn't win, but he wasn't carried out of the ring either. It was just about par for the course for the bearded, wild-eyed veteran. "I'm off the wall," Alzado once said. "I'm wacko. But I know it. How many people really know themselves?"

Appropriately Alzado nicknamed himself "Captain Wacko." No one disputed it. "I always thought Alzado would go into big-time wrestling," Joe DeLamielleure said. "That's what he was. He was a camera guy. But he was a great team guy to have. He had character and he *was* a character."

With Alzado anchoring one side of the defensive line the Browns were hoping veteran Jerry Sherk would be able to stabilize the other. But just as was the case with Greg Pruitt on offense, Sherk's health was a question mark entering the season. In a decade full of disappointment and mediocrity, Sherk was one of the Browns' few sparks of consistency. Drafted in the second round in 1970 the University of Oklahoma grad quickly became a starter and a dominant one at that. He was named the team's most valuable player in 1974, and by 1977 he'd reached the Pro Bowl four times. As Sam Rutigliano took over as head coach, Sherk was still going strong. He had recovered nicely from operations on *both* knees following the 1977 and 1978 seasons and was having another fine campaign in 1979. That is, until November 4.

During a Browns' victory in Philadelphia Sherk played with a boil on his arm. He scraped it and a staph infection entered his bloodstream, eventually settling in his left leg. He spent the next five weeks in the Cleveland Clinic while doctors determined whether Sherk would lose his leg or possibly his life. Though Sherk lost thirty-five pounds during his stay he recovered and hoped to return to the Browns' lineup come opening day. Like Greg Pruitt, Rutigliano said Sherk would not play in the first two exhibition games while he recovered.

Most members of the media agreed that if Sherk could not return to full strength the Browns had absolutely no shot at contending for the playoffs. It was hard to disagree with them. Sherk had been the team's best defender for ten years. Most figured he was all that stood between the 1980 defense being average or the worst in team history. If Sherk were to reinjure his knee, "the whole three-four scheme will self-destruct along with the season," conjectured *Cleveland Press* sports editor Bob Sudyk.

Sherk was concerned about his knee as well though not as distraught as Sudyk and other members of the media. "My knee is temperamental," Sherk said early in camp. "There's still some soreness in it. Some days, it feels pretty good. But some days, it doesn't. There's no way I want to kiss this season goodbye, mainly because I think we have a chance to go somewhere."

With Sherk a question mark, the other two spots on the line were wide open as the 1980 preseason began. But as camp wore on, a pair of newcomers began to emerge as the eventual starters.

At the ever-important nose-tackle position Henry Bradley showed the Browns that he was their man after an awkward 1979 season. Signed as an undrafted free agent he had performed well in the Browns' camp that summer but didn't make the final cut. For the next two months he drove a truck in Cleveland. Then when Sherk went down in November the Browns asked Bradley to come back. He did and played in the final six games of the season.

Bradley was no star, but his effort fit the nose tackle role perfectly. Dan Coughlin of the *Plain Dealer* called Bradley "an assembly-line worker on an assembly-line defense. If any one part breaks down, the entire operation shuts down." Bradley wouldn't rack up many impressive statistics playing nose tackle, but he would be a key factor in the Browns' defensive attack.

Beside Bradley at left end was another player who had experienced an odd 1979 season. Marshall Harris was an eighth-round draft choice of the New York Jets that year but left the team in training camp to pursue a career in commercial art. Later in the season Harris changed his mind and asked if the Jets would take him back. They said no but wouldn't stand in the way of allowing him to play elsewhere. He was dealt to the Browns for an eighth-round pick in 1981.

A pair of rookies was also expected to contribute on the line. The Browns had high expectations for second-round draft pick Cleveland Crosby from Arizona and hoped fifth-round choice Elvis Franks from Morgan State would provide some depth.

"Our No. 1 priority," Sam Rutigliano said as camp began, "is to find someone who can put pressure on opposing quarterbacks." In the 3-4 that task was usually left to the linebackers, a position at which the Browns felt they were loaded.

Left outside linebacker Charlie Hall had been with the Browns since they drafted him in the third round in 1971 and had been named the team's 1979 defensive player of the year by the Cleveland Touchdown Club. Entering the 1980 season Hall had been a model of consistency, starting 115 straight games.

At left inside linebacker would be Robert L. Jackson, who had been plagued by injuries thus far in his brief career. The Browns picked Jackson (who had grown up in the same Houston neighborhood as Greg Pruitt and played sandlot ball with him) out of Texas A&M in the first round of the 1977 draft, but a knee injury early in training camp knocked him out for the entire season. He came back strong as a role player the following year but missed much of 1979 to injury again. As the 1980 camp began Jackson was as healthy as he'd been in three years with the Browns, and his boundless on-field enthusiasm and kamikaze tackling style would prove to pay huge dividends.

Little was expected of right inside linebacker Dick Ambrose when the Browns selected him in the twelfth round of the 1975 draft, but he started several games in his rookie year. An ankle injury hindered him in 1976, but Ambrose won the middle linebacker job in 1977 and led the team in tackles in 1978 and 1979. In the 3-4 alignment Ambrose and Jackson would regularly be on the field together, something the Browns were excited to see.

Beside Ambrose at right outside linebacker was youngster Clay Matthews, who along with Ozzie Newsome (with whom, ironically, Matthews shared the same birthday), was picked by the Browns in the first round of the 1978 draft. The rookie from USC made an immediate impact, splitting time with veteran Gerald Irons, then won the position outright in 1979. Matthews's improvement was impressive in his first two seasons, and it would continue in 1980.

The Browns also had some depth off the bench at linebacker with the veteran Irons and a hard-working, intelligent youngster named Bill Cowher, signed by the Browns as a free agent after he failed to make the Philadelphia roster in 1979.

Though the Browns appeared set at linebacker, with the NFL stiffening its rules on pass defense in the late 1970s, the Cleveland secondary would also have to be able to hold its own if the Browns were to become a playoff-caliber team.

One position they didn't have to worry about was left cornerback, where Ron Bolton had been a regular starter since coming to the Browns from New England in 1976 in a trade for offensive tackle Bob McKay. In his first eight seasons, Bolton already had twenty-seven career interceptions and had the speed and tenacity to keep up with the league's best receivers. At the other corner spot, three-year veteran Oliver Davis was expected to start for the fourth straight year, while one-time corner Clarence Scott would start the season at strong safety. Scott, like Hall and Sherk, had been a mainstay of the Cleveland defense throughout the 1970s. He was drafted by the Browns in the first round in 1971 and spent eight years as one of the league's best cornerbacks. He then made a seamless transition to safety in 1978, filling in at corner when needed. He had twenty-eight interceptions in his career with the Browns, and over the previous three off-seasons had already begun preparing for his next career. Scott was attending John Marshall Law School in Atlanta and was halfway toward earning his degree.

Starting at free safety would be another longtime Browns' veteran: Thom Darden. The Sandusky, Ohio, native was a first-round pick from Michigan in 1972 and started as a rookie for the Browns in what would be their final playoff season of the decade. Throughout the late 1970s Darden had earned the reputation of a ball hawk, snagging a total of thirty-six interceptions in his previous five seasons. The streak included eight picks in 1974, then, after a knee injury sidelined him in 1975, rebounded with seven more in 1976 and a team-record ten in 1978. Darden entered the 1980 season tied with Warren Lahr as the Browns' all-time leading interceptor with forty.

The Browns' special teams looked much the same as they had in previous seasons. Don Cockroft, the oldest player on the team, had been the Browns' kicker since the legendary Lou Groza retired in 1968. The Adams State product, drafted in the third round in 1967, led the Browns in scoring from 1969 to 1979 and going into 1980 trailed only Groza on the team's all-time scoring list. But it was clear that Cockroft's career was winding down. He had missed twelve field goals and a career-high five extra points in 1979. With a team that liked to go down to the wire as often as the Browns did, a reliable kicker was a must.

Cockroft had also been the team's punter until 1977, when he was replaced by Greg Coleman, who was then replaced by Johnny Evans in 1978. Evans, also a backup quarterback, would boot for the Browns for a third straight season in 1980.

At the other end of the punting spectrum, wide receiver Keith Wright would handle much of the return duties in 1980, just as he had in 1978 and 1979, while tiny five-foot-seven running back Dino Hall took care of many of the kickoff returns.

Though no one knew it as the team worked through the preseason that summer, this cast of characters would star in the most thrilling single-season drama in team history.

The Browns' gradual track back to becoming a member of the NFL's elite in 1978 and 1979 had progressed just as Rutigliano had expected. "It's like raising a family," he said. "You get to a point in your life when you begin to realize things through experience and education. Our players were at a point where they had learned through themselves that they were good. They had to learn it for themselves."

"We believed we were ready to get over the hump," Thom Darden said. "We'd had two years of Sam's philosophy. We had a lot of offensive weapons and we felt we could compete with any team in the league. Our confidence level was very, very high."

Despite the question marks on defense, there was reason for optimism for the 1980 Browns. This optimism showed at the box office as season-ticket sales went up 20 percent, mostly because of the exciting 1979 campaign. The Browns' annual home game with the defending-champion Steelers in late October sold out on July 21, the earliest sellout in team history.

"The city is sky-high on the Browns and we don't want to let the fans down," said Browns' owner Art Modell.

The confidence was showing up on the practice fields as well when training camp began. "There is a change in atmosphere," Lyle Alzado said. "The intensity is there. The troublesome factors are gone; the positive factors remain. We should have won more last year and everybody knows it."

"I sense something, too," Dave Logan said. "Something different. I think it developed spontaneously last season when we had a little success."

But the learning process was still under way as the team gathered at Kent State University to prepare for the 1980 season. For the media and fans there were plenty of players and situations to watch.

On offense, most of the starting positions were already determined. Still many wondered if Charles White might win the starting halfback position over Greg Pruitt if Pruitt wasn't ready for action yet. Pruitt had no worries. "If my knee is 100 percent and White beats me out," he said, "it will mean the Browns got the best running back in the draft."

On the flip side of the ball, many were watching as new defensive coordinator Marty Schottenheimer introduced the new 3-4 system to his players. But the era of the Browns' 3-4 got off to a bit of a rough start. The Browns received a surprise on the second day of camp when veteran linebacker Gerald Irons unexpectedly retired, saying he wasn't in the team's future plans. The departure of Irons (who was working in the off-season as Ohio Senator John Glenn's assistant campaign manager) wouldn't affect the starting lineup, but it did rob the defense of some depth. It also assured that the right outside linebacker position belonged to young Clay Matthews, for better or worse.

Plus a pair of rookie linebackers also left camp, and Dick Ambrose didn't report on time because his lawyers were still negotiating a new contract with the Browns. Ambrose eventually joined the team a week later, causing no serious setbacks, but some wondered if the early problems forecasted the future of the 3-4.

After their first preseason game it appeared that there was no future for the 3-4. The Browns were blasted by the mediocre Kansas City Chiefs, 42-0, in what the local scribes quickly began calling the "Saturday Night Massacre."

"That is really not our football team you saw out there," Sam Rutigliano said afterward. "Training camp exists for one reason only, and that's to get 45 guys ready for the regular season. I've been involved in this game long enough to know that things like that are going to happen."

It was the worst defeat in franchise history, preseason or regular season, and the areas of concern everyone was worried about going into camp lit up like a Christmas tree. The offense had moved the ball but couldn't score. Don Cockroft had missed a chip-shot thirty-three-yard field goal in the first quarter. But most importantly, the Browns' defense was atrocious, giving up 198 rushing yards and 422 total to a team that had been 7-9 the year before.

Still Rutigliano managed to find the silver lining. "Start it in the obituary column," he told reporters, "and we'll try to work our way back to the front page."

In other words, it was not time to panic.

"Look at that exhibition game as though it were the New Hampshire primary," Dan Coughlin wrote in the *Plain Dealer*. "The open convention is a month away. Besides, Sam Rutigliano does not have a brother named Billy." But the Browns were hoping to fare better in the fall than many predicted President Carter would.

A week later the defense improved, but the offense did not in a 12-3 home loss to the Washington Redskins. The Browns committed eight turnovers, including five fumbles, while Brian Sipe completed only four of fourteen passes. Also, cornerback Oliver Davis went down with a separated shoulder and would be out for several weeks.

At Soldier Field in Chicago the next weekend the disturbing beat went on in the first half against the Bears. Sipe completed just one of his first six passes as the Bears built a 21-0 lead late in the second quarter, which swelled to 28-6 early in the third.

Instead of taking the first-team offense out in the second half, as was customary in the preseason, Rutigliano left it in to try and rebuild the dike. Sipe and

Company did just that, rallying for a 33-31 win on a touchdown pass to Dave Logan in the final two minutes. Sipe threw for 313 yards and five touchdowns as the Browns finally looked like the team that they had been in 1979. But as many pointed out, the success had come against the Bears' second- and third-team defenses. Also the Browns were guilty of eleven penalties, and Don Cockroft wasn't getting any better, missing two extra points.

Still the Browns had looked good overall, and maybe it was just a matter of getting some confidence under their belts before embarking onto the regular season. If the Browns could put together another solid performance in the exhibition finale against the Minnesota Vikings, most figured that they would be ready for the season.

Instead the opposite happened. The Browns were obliterated by the Vikes, 38-16, as the Minnesota offense racked up 405 yards and converted on twelve of fifteen third downs. In terms of point differential and arguably overall performance, it was the worst preseason in Browns' history.

2 · The Boston Massacre and the Monday Night Snooze

Though the 1980 Cleveland Browns had done nothing officially as the month of September began, there seemed to be a sense of panic surrounding the team. As is usually the case with panic in sports, however, it emanated from the press and the fans but not from the team itself.

Following the embarrassing loss to the Minnesota Vikings to close the exhibition season, the early optimistic hopes of the Browns being able to build on what they had established in 1979 and become a playoff team in 1980 were already circling the drain. "This is the worst defense in Browns' history," proclaimed Dan Coughlin of the *Plain Dealer*. "Anytime the Browns score 40 points or more, they have less than 50-50 chance of winning."

For instance, Coughlin said, if the Browns were to kick off at 1 P.M., the offense wouldn't see the ball until about 1:30. True the Browns' defense had been nothing short of atrocious in the preseason, allowing 123 points in four games, an average of nearly 31 per contest. Even more disheartening was that Cleveland had given up an average of 386 yards per game in the quartet of exhibitions. Even if Brian Sipe and Company could return to their 1979 form it was doubtful that they'd be able to average close to 400 yards and 32 points per Sunday. It was hard to believe that the 1980 Browns' defense could be any worse than its 1979 predecessor, but if the preseason was any indication, it was possible. Still Sam Rutigliano wasn't worried. "In pro football, preseasons are a misnomer," he said. "The preseason is to put in place all the people that you know are going to be the significant players and look at their backups and see if there's anybody who's going to fit into a slot that he didn't fit into the previous year. It's about just getting people playing time without having to worry about winning because the season is enough time to worry about winning. Get the guys in from the bullpen and get them a chance to play."

As the Browns prepared to open the season in New England, Rutigliano said that the defense was at about a 4 or 5 on a scale of 10, but he expected it to be at a 6 or 7 by midseason. "Our defense is improved, and we will continue to grow," he said. "What we've got to do defensively is stick with our solid first unit and keep working with it, developing it. If we get blown out in the regular season the way we did [against the Vikings], it will be time for concern, but not now. Not yet." Then in true Rutigliano fashion, "I am not trying to sound like Optimistic Ollie, but I don't want anybody to think I'm Doomsday Dan, either."

But as bad as the defense had been, it was the Browns' offense that was the primary cause for concern. Aside from the tainted thirty-three-point explosion in Chicago, the Browns had scored just nineteen total points in their other three games. Part of the problem was the absence of running back Greg Pruitt, who was still gimpy after a brief appearance in the Minnesota game, and he would not start against the Patriots. Rookie Charles White would get the call instead, and the Browns would get an early look at their investment.

While it was clear that the Browns' defense was hurting more than their offense, the latter was bolstered dramatically just days before the opener in what would turn out to be one of the wisest front-office moves in recent history. At 11:45 A.M. on September 1, just fifteen minutes before the NFL's trading deadline to begin the season, the Browns made a deal with the Buffalo Bills. Cleveland got All-Pro guard Joe DeLamielleure in exchange for two draft choices: the Browns' second-round pick in 1981 and their third-round choice in 1982. Though it sounded like a good trade, it was a risky one. If the 1980 Browns turned out to be a bust (as all evidence seemed to suggest in the sunshiny first week of September), this could prove to be a costly move. The worse the Browns could become in 1980, the more they would need that second-round pick in 1981. But the Browns were hoping this deal would ensure that 1980 wouldn't be a lost cause.

DeLamielleure, the Bills' first-round draft pick in 1973, had missed all of camp that summer because of a dispute with Buffalo head coach Chuck Knox that had begun the previous May. "I just didn't like Chuck and how he treated the guys," DeLamielleure said later. "Maybe I was a little immature at the time. I had played on five straight Pro Bowls, and they brought a bunch of guys in and were paying them 30, 40, 50,000 dollars more than me. I just felt that they didn't respect me, and I didn't want to play for the guy. He's a good coach; it was just a personal thing."

DeLamielleure had demanded a trade and held out but met with Knox the morning of August 31, and they reportedly ironed out their differences. DeLamielleure showed up for practice the next day prepared to stay in Buffalo for the season when he was told he'd been traded to Cleveland. "It was a bit of a surprise," DeLamielleure said. "Honestly, I think Chuck Knox wanted to punish me. He sent me to what he thought would be a bad team. Supposedly they had better trades lined up with other teams, and he never pulled the trigger. I think he traded me to Cleveland to get even with me."

The six-foot-three, 245-pound DeLamielleure was just twenty-nine years old and had started 103 consecutive games with the Bills. With this acquisition there was no question that now, if not before, the Browns had one of the best offensive lines in the NFL—possibly *the* best. Still the players' reactions to the deal were mixed. "I was happy about the trade on one hand, but I was stupid on the other being so happy," center Tom DeLeone said. "It meant that one of the guys that we had worked so hard with was going to be sitting down." Sure enough, Robert E. Jackson's starting job at right guard was in jeopardy.

"It was tough at first," DeLamielleure would say in a 1982 interview. "The linemen are a close-knit group, and I was taking somebody's job. But the Browns felt they needed me and although I wanted to play in Cleveland, I didn't ask to come here. It was just part of the business."

Though the trade may have affected the line's chemistry, it certainly bolstered its depth. With a proven starter as the odd man out, the Browns could survive an injury or two. "We'd always carry eight or nine linemen," said right tackle Cody Risien, "and there's only five starters, so there's always competition. But that's healthy. We still had a great group. People get banged up during the year, so you've got to have a bunch of linemen who can play, and we did."

Though one NFL official called it the "steal of the century," the DeLamielleure trade was not exactly a hit in Cleveland that week. "It seems to me this is like a guy with a weak right leg spending all his time exercising his strong left leg," wrote Bob Sudyk in the *Cleveland Press*. But, as with most matters in professional sports, there was more to the trade than appeared on the surface. A large motivating factor for Art Modell and General Manager Peter Hadhazy in pulling the trigger may have been Doug Dieken's holdout during training camp over a contract dispute. Dieken was only out a week and had returned long before September 1, but the deal appeared to serve as a bit of insurance to guard against future disputes. "All of a sudden, they make this trade," Dieken said. "We had good chemistry, the five of us. You bring somebody in from the outside and it can flirt with the chemistry. And to be honest, Joe D didn't really fit our style of play. Joe D was a run-blocker. We were pass-blockers. He was short and stocky, and other than DeLeone, the rest of us were long and lanky. We were more of a finesse style and Joe D was a thumper."

For example, in DeLamielleure's rookie season in 1973 the Bills attempted just 156 passes as O. J. Simpson rushed for a then-record 2,003 yards on 332 carries. In 1979 Brian Sipe had cocked his arm 535 times. "We felt that for a second-round draft choice we were going to get a quality, Pro Bowl offensive lineman," Rutigliano said. "We could upgrade something that was already upgraded. Obviously, we would have been better to get somebody of his caliber defensively, but we couldn't." To make room for DeLamielleure tackle Joel Patten was put on injured reserve.

That day the Browns also traded quarterback Mark Miller to Green Bay for a conditional draft choice, ensuring rookie Paul McDonald's job as backup to Sipe.

The defense got some good news as the week wore on when Rutigliano announced that Jerry Sherk would start at left end at New England after a tumultuous preseason. Clearly no one expected Sherk to be at the level he was throughout most of the 1970s when he was one of the most dominant defensive players in football, but any boost to a defense struggling as bad as Cleveland's was certainly welcome.

It was also the week for predictions, a tradition in NFL cities in early September as the start of the new season draws near. Rutigliano had told the Cleveland Touchdown Club on August 26 that he expected the Browns to make the playoffs, and he stood by his prediction even after the thrashing at the hands of the Vikings. "The day I stop thinking about 10 victories," he said, "is when we have lost seven games."

The local press was not as optimistic, though most did not share Dan Coughlin's apocalyptic view. The 1979 season seemed to be the baseline for measuring predictions: the Browns would either be better or worse but not the same. The *Plain Dealer*'s staff picks were one of each: Chuck Heaton forecasted the Browns to go 7-9, last in the AFC Central simply because of their defense, but Russ Schneider said 10-6 was within reach. Even if the double-digit plateau was achieved, Schneider warned, the Browns still could not dethrone the Pittsburgh Steelers. The *Press* picked the Browns third across the board, figuring the Cincinnati Bengals would be the only Central team the fans could count on the Browns beating. Writer Jim Braham put into words what most fans (and perhaps most of the Browns) had to be thinking: "Whoever decides these divisions should be flogged on Public Square at high noon."

In that spirit *Sports Illustrated* picked the Browns to finish third in the division with an 8-8 record. "Their biggest problem," *SI* football prognosticator Paul Zimmerman said, "is the division they're playing in. In the NFC, Cleveland would be a Super Bowl contender, but in the AFC Central it's just trying to survive against Pittsburgh and Houston."

Both Cleveland papers agreed, as did much of the football world, that the Steelers were the team to beat, not only in the AFC Central but also across the board. With the Steelers having essentially the same cast of characters returning, it appeared as though the road to the Super Bowl would once again go through Pittsburgh. And if there was a team in the AFC that stood a chance of ousting the Steelers from the conference's catbird seat, it was the Houston Oilers, the division's proverbial lady-in-waiting.

"Last year, we knocked on the door," Houston head coach Bum Phillips had said after his club lost to the Steelers in the 1979 AFC Championship. "This year we beat on the door. Next year, we're going to kick down the Steelers' door and win the AFC Central Division championship." Led by running back Earl Campbell and new quarterback Ken Stabler, whom Houston had acquired from Oakland in the off-season in exchange for its own quarterback Dan Pastorini, the Oilers were hoping for a third consecutive trip to the AFC title game. The Bengals, meanwhile, had limped out of the 1970s with 4-12 records in both 1978 and 1979, and it didn't appear that they'd be making any notable impact in the division to start the new decade. But the Browns-Bengals rivalry was as fierce as ever as evidenced by the previous two season-ending defeats Cleveland had suffered along the bank of the Ohio River.

But before the Browns could concern themselves with any of their division foes they had to prepare for the New England Patriots, a team that had narrowly missed the playoffs in 1979 and was coming off four consecutive winning seasons. Pats' starting quarterback Steve Grogan had thrown for twenty-eight touchdowns in 1979, tied with Brian Sipe for the league lead. With an offense similar to that of the Browns, New England would give the Cleveland defense its first test of the season.

It turned out to be a baptism by fire.

It's often difficult to gauge what kind of expectations coaches and players have for the first game of the regular season. It's unreasonable to anticipate everything to go as planned. After all, it is the first time out of the gate for a team after several weeks of practice and exhibition contests. Needless to say the bar is usually lowered for Week One, then raised with each forthcoming week until the team hits its stride, if it ever does. But it didn't take long for the Browns to realize that their bar at the start of the 1980 season hadn't been lowered; it hadn't even been lifted off the ground. Before the first quarter was over at Schaefer Stadium in Foxboro, Massachusetts, Dan Coughlin's woeful prediction about the defense started to look like reality.

The Patriots held the ball for eleven of the first fifteen minutes of the game, but luckily for Cleveland all they could manage was a thirty-five-yard field goal by John Smith. Browns' cornerback Lawrence Johnson, filling in for injured Oliver Davis, snagged his first career interception off Grogan on the first series of the game, but the Browns could do nothing with it. It wouldn't be their last blown opportunity on this day.

The Browns squandered several chances to take control of the contest in the first half. With the Patriots leading 6-0 in the second quarter and threatening to add to their lead, the Browns' defense stepped up and appeared to swing the momentum back in their favor. On third-and-two from the Cleveland four-yard line, Lyle Alzado stopped Patriots' running back Don Calhoun for one yard trying to go over left tackle. On fourth down Robert L. Jackson and Ron Bolton crushed Calhoun for no gain, and the Browns took over. But as was the case following the early Johnson interception, the Browns could not take advantage.

The Patriots' lead swelled to 13-0 on a ten-yard Steve Grogan–to–Harold Jackson touchdown pass with forty-nine seconds remaining in the half. But the Browns showed some sign of life as Sipe and Company marched fifty-six yards on six quick plays, including a nineteen-yard completion to Ozzie Newsome and a fifteen-yarder to Calvin Hill to set up a twenty-five-yard Don Cockcroft field goal with two ticks left. The Browns were finally on the scoreboard after a lackluster first half and trailed by only ten points.

As the second half began it appeared that things might be turning Cleveland's way. Two minutes into the third quarter New England wide receiver Preston Brown fumbled a Johnny Evans punt and Browns' tackle Gerry Sullivan recovered at the Patriots' thirty-eight yard line. After more than thirty minutes of mediocre-at-best football the Browns appeared poised to cut the Patriots' lead, but after a seven-yard Sipe-to-Reggie Rucker completion moved the Browns to the thirty-one, on second-and-three Charles White missed a block and Mike Pruitt was crushed by New England linebacker Rod Shoate and fumbled the football. Patriots' cornerback Raymond Clayborn recovered for the Pats, who cashed in a moment later when Grogan hit wide receiver Stanley Morgan on a sixty-seven-yard touchdown pass. Though there was still more than a quarter-and-a-half left to play, the lights had been turned out on the Browns, who now trailed, 20-3.

"We were hoping we could come out and probe a little, explore some of their weaknesses, and then attack them," Sipe said afterward. "But with so many mistakes, we had no continuity, and the next thing we realized, it was the middle of the third quarter."

The Patriots added two more touchdowns, first on a two-yard Calhoun run late in the third quarter and then a Grogan-to-Dan Hasselbeck seventeen-yard pass in the fourth that capped a twelve-play, eighty-eight-yard drive. As the day went on things just got worse for the Browns. Jerry Sherk was forced to leave the game after the first half when his knee tightened up. Greg Pruitt, still working his way back, did get into the game but only for three plays, and he didn't touch the football. Meanwhile, though Sipe may have been one of the best quarterbacks in the NFL, he never had time to prove it as the Cleveland offensive line was consistently disassembled like a cheap card table. The good news was that once Joe DeLamielleure entered the game the line began to stabilize itself. The bad news was that by the time he got settled in New England led, 34-3, in the fourth quarter.

Still the Browns showed some resiliency in the late going and managed two scoring drives. One ended when Sipe hit Dave Logan on a ten-yard touchdown pass, the other when he nailed Keith Wright from eleven yards out. Appropriate for what had transpired during the day, following his catch, Logan ran into the wall behind the end zone, separating the stands from the field, and twisted his ankle.

When the final gun mercifully sounded, the Patriots were victorious, 34-17. The Browns, who had not lost a season opener in five years, flew back to Cleveland to lick their wounds. They had many. It was one of those games in which the final score did not accurately reflect what had happened. True the Patriots had won by a comfortable seventeen points, but that margin didn't demonstrate their outright domination of most of the game statistics. Most notably, New England racked up a whopping 452 total yards—266 in the air and 186 on the ground—to the Browns' 263. In fact the Patriots punted only once all afternoon, late in the fourth quarter. "The defense is still adjusting but we've got to be able to play," said defensive coordinator Marty Schottenheimer, who had made an inauspicious Cleveland debut. "We've got to be able to play four quarters and we didn't do it."

New England also racked up twenty-seven first downs to the Browns' sixteen and had a pair of running backs over fifty yards rushing. "They played a hell of a game," Rutigliano said of the Patriots' efforts. "They put a lot of pressure on Brian early and took us out of synch. Then we had the fumbles, and you just can't beat a good team when you do that. And the defense has to stop the big plays—that's what it's all about."

Meanwhile the Browns individual yardsticks didn't look all that bad. Sipe completed twenty-two of thirty-five passes for 233 yards with two scores. Mike Pruitt led the team in both rushing and receiving, although he didn't truly excel at either with fifty yards on eleven carries and five receptions for forty-nine yards. Running back Calvin Hill snagged three passes for sixty-seven yards, while Charles White endured a frustrating afternoon at tailback. In addition to blowing the block that led to Mike Pruitt's critical fumble, he picked up only two total yards despite touching the ball seven times.

"I am frustrated," Sipe said. "I don't have any answers. I'm anxious to see the films because it's hard for me to figure out what happened, especially in the first half."

In case the Browns needed something else to feel bad about that evening, all they needed to do was to check out the scores coming in from around the league. Many teams, including their rivals, looked much stronger than they did on this opening day. First and foremost, the Pittsburgh Steelers were better than ever at Three Rivers Stadium as they blew out the only team most people felt had a chance to challenge them, the Houston Oilers, 31-17. However, the Oilers did their best to giftwrap the game with eleven dropped passes and five interceptions. It marked the Steelers' seventeenth consecutive home victory, and though there were fifteen weeks to go in the season, for many it appeared that the AFC Central had already been wrapped up.

Elsewhere in the division in Week One, the Cincinnati Bengals lost to the Tampa Bay Buccaneers in the waning moments at Riverfront Stadium. The Bucs scored the winning touchdown on a Doug Williams scoring pass to tight end Jimmie Giles with 1:47 to go for a 17-12 victory. The loss was particularly painful for the Bengals since the winning score was set up by a fumbled punt snap by Cincy booter Pat McInally.

Still for all the darkness that hung over the Browns following Week One of the 1980 season, Lyle Alzado reminded everyone that there was still a long way to go. "I just hope that you guys, the media and the fans of northern Ohio, hang in there with us, have faith in us, because we're going to be all right," he said.

As the Browns returned to Cleveland with their tails between their legs and started to prepare for Houston in Week Two, which couldn't come fast enough for either team, the fans and media believed they had already seen their worst fears for the 1980 season realized. "Even the Titanic made it out of port and stayed afloat for a week or so," Bob Sudyk of the *Press* riffed.

While most were ready to crucify the Cleveland defense, Rutigliano pointed out that it was the Browns' offense that deserved most of the blame. "If we had played according to our capabilities, we would have outscored New England, I honestly believe that," he said. "If it took 35 points, we could have put them on the board and beat the Patriots, 35-34. There's no excuse for it. It has to get better, and it has to get better immediately."

But as the Browns retreated back to practice, that didn't appear to be the case. Jerry Sherk was limping on his bad knee, which was still swollen. He couldn't practice but intended to continue to play. Greg Pruitt's knee was also hurting, while Logan was nursing a sore ankle from his introduction to the end-zone wall at Schaeffer Stadium. As the week wore on, Browns' kicker Don Cockroft pulled a muscle in his kicking leg in practice, and his availability for the Houston game was in doubt. Definitely out for Week Two was guard Robert E. Jackson, who also injured his knee. But that injury made the transition to Joe DeLamielleure, who would start against the Oilers, a bit easier.

But probably the most serious injury the Browns sustained in New England was to Chuck Cusick, the team's equipment manager. He broke his shoulder when Charles White's momentum took him off the playing field and slammed him into Cusick on the sidelines during a play. That was the kind of day it had been.

With all the injuries, plus the fact that even the healthy Browns hadn't looked very good, the Browns being able to bounce back to the .500 mark in Week Two didn't look likely, especially when one considered they'd be playing the Oilers, considered by what seemed to be everyone the second-best team in the NFL. Appropriately Houston was favored by three points.

But there were a few advantages in the Browns' corner. For one, Houston hadn't looked good in its opener either. For another, the game would be in Cleveland where a sellout crowd would be rooting the Browns on. Plus the game was to be televised on *Monday Night Football,* which seemed to bring out the best in most players. This boded well for Cleveland, but on the other hand, the Oilers would also be anxious to get into the win column since their expectations for the 1980 season were much higher than those of the Browns. "Two losses are not too many, unless they're the first two games you play," said Houston coach Bum Phillips. "Then you're in trouble."

Another plus for the Oilers was their new quarterback Ken "The Snake" Stabler, who held a record of 13-1-1 on *Monday Night Football* when he was with the Oakland Raiders. During his last appearance in primetime the previous December in New Orleans, he had rallied the Raiders from a 35-14 deficit for a 42-35 win over the Saints. To try to atone for Stabler's influence on the contest, the week before the game Browns' fans could buy noisy plastic rattlers so that they could "Rattle the Snake."

Even without *Monday Night Football* coming to town it was a big week in Cleveland. Presidential candidate Ronald Reagan visited the city on Wednesday, informing Northeast Ohioans why he was a much better choice for the Oval Office than his rival Jimmy Carter. And by Monday every one of the hotel rooms in downtown Cleveland was booked—some because of the game but most because of the annual convention of the Ohio Association of Realtors.

After a week of preparing for the Oilers the Browns could settle in and catch some NFL action on television on Sunday afternoon, and they saw that the Steelers' performance the previous week against Houston had not been a fluke. Though they didn't look as sharp, the Steelers knocked off the Baltimore Colts, 20-17, to move to 2-0 atop the Central. A Terry Bradshaw–to–Jim Smith thirty-two-yard touchdown pass turned out to be the winning score, and a Donnie Shell interception at the Pittsburgh four-yard line in the final moments sealed the Steeler win.

The news of the Pittsburgh triumph coincided with an odd notice in the *Plain Dealer* sports section on Monday: "The Terrible Towel, beloved leader and nationally known mascot of Pittsburgh Steeler fans, will be laid to rest on Sunday, October 26, 1980. Services will be held at Cleveland's Municipal Lakefront Stadium: visiting hours 1–4." It was an advertisement for Browns' fans' version of their own towel, which merchants were hoping fans would purchase before the Steelers came to town in October. But with the Steelers already at 2-0 and the Browns in danger of falling two games behind them, late October seemed like years away.

The good news for the Browns was that even if they were to lose to Houston, they would not be alone in the division basement since the Bengals once again blew a lead in the final minutes and lost to a team from Florida. This time it was the Miami Dolphins that took advantage after Cincinnati carried a 14-0 lead into the fourth quarter at the Orange Bowl.

After a Miami touchdown and a Cincinnati safety the Dolphins were forced to free kick from their own twenty, trailing 16-7 with just minutes to play. Miami head coach Don Shula called for an unorthodox onside kick, and the shocked Bengals watched in horror as the Dolphins recovered it. Shula's bunch then cut the lead to two when quarterback Don Strock hit receiver Duriel Harris (both of whom would don Browns' helmets before the decade was out) for a big gain to the Cincinnati twelve. Harris fumbled, but an alert Nick Giaquinto recovered for the Dolphins in the end zone. For the second straight week Pat McInally was the goat as a Miami blocked punt a few moments later led to the game-winning field goal by Uwe von Schamann with 1:55 to play. The Dolphins won, 17-16, dropping the Bengals to 0-2.

But by Monday evening all of Cleveland, as well as the entire football-viewing nation, turned its eyes to the North Coast as Frank Gifford, Howard Cosell, and Don Meredith settled in for the play-by-play of the first Browns-Oilers contest of 1980. "The scene speaks for itself," Cosell told his audience. "A city battling back and coming to life because of *Monday Night Football*. This city has been in distress and now they're fighting back."

Many fans fought back by downing some suds on the mall between City Hall and the County Courthouse during a pre-game "Party in the Park." Organizers sold beer for thirty-five cents a cup. An estimated 775 gallons were drunk. Meanwhile, much like cold beer, fans poured into Cleveland Municipal Stadium and created an electric atmosphere. The Browns hadn't played a regular-season home game since Week Fourteen of 1979 when they beat the Oilers, 14-7, to keep their playoff hopes alive. Banners, most dealing with the game but some endorsing political candidates for the upcoming election, adorned much of the Stadium as Cleveland welcomed *Monday Night Football* for the first time since the Browns buried the Dallas Cowboys the previous September. *Monday Night Football* would return less than two months later on November 3 when the Chicago Bears would come calling at the Stadium, marking the first time in Browns' history that they'd host two Monday-night games in one season.

Needless to say the Browns were just as anxious as their fans to take the field and erase any lingering memories from New England. "It's bad enough to be kicked around on the field as we were last Sunday," Brian Sipe said, "but then to be kicked around off the field as we have been all week is a little tough for our guys to take."

As this one got under way it became clear that if the Browns were to win they'd have to do it in a fashion they weren't accustomed to. The Oilers' defense, much like New England's the week before, was eerily effective at stopping the Cleveland offense. The Browns drove into Houston territory on their first two possessions but were unable to score. However, they did manage to get on the board early in the second quarter. Following a meek twelve-yard punt by Houston's Cliff Parsely after a bad snap and a remarkable fifteen-yard catch by Mike Pruitt of a Sipe pass deflected by Houston linebacker Art Stringer, the Browns cashed in. Sipe hit Calvin Hill on a three-yard flare pass for a touchdown and a 7-0 lead. The Oilers countered with a twenty-five-yard field goal by Toni Fritsch following a fifteen-play drive to cut the margin to 7-3 at the half.

Though the first two periods may not have included a whole lot of scoring, they did have their share of highlights. Most notably, a vicious hit by Browns' linebacker Robert L. Jackson on the second play of the game separated Houston fullback Earl Campbell from his bridgework. What went around came around for Jackson at the end of the half when he suffered a neck injury and was carried off the field on a stretcher, fearing he'd broken his neck. But remarkably Jackson returned in the second half as wild and enthusiastic as ever and ended up making the only Cleveland sack of the night.

If fans thought the first half wasn't very exciting, they had no idea what they were in for in the second. Many must have thought they were watching a Houston offensive practice, not so much for its scoring ability, but in its efficient monopolization of the football. After intermission the Browns ran just thirteen plays from scrimmage and held the football for just 3:47. Houston meanwhile simply kept grinding it out and moving the chains.

A one-yard scoring plunge by Houston fullback Tim Wilson on the first possession of the third quarter gave the Oilers a 10-7 lead. The turning point of the game may have occurred on this drive when Browns' defensive end Elvis Franks intercepted a Ken Stabler pass and returned it forty-eight yards for a touchdown that would have given the Browns a 13-3 advantage. But defensive end Lyle Alzado was penalized for lining up offsides, and Houston kept the football.

Soon after, weird things started to happen to the Browns, and not in a good way.

Just after the Oiler touchdown the Browns were faced with a third-and-one from the Houston forty-eight. Despite the fact that Mike Pruitt had just blasted over right guard for seven yards on second down, Sipe dropped back to pass on third down and fired incomplete on a long attempt intended for tight end Ozzie Newsome. The Browns punted and would not see the ball again until the fourth quarter. "Sam decided to gamble," Sipe said afterward. "Unfortunately, everybody was covered."

Opting not to give the ball to Pruitt seemed to symbolize the Browns' offensive mindset for the second half. Pruitt, who had rushed for nearly 1,300 yards in 1979, tallied just nine on two carries in the second half after Houston took the lead.

But that ill-fated third-down pass didn't turn out to be the most controversial decision Rutigliano would make on that night. In the fourth quarter, with Houston still leading 10-7, Stabler and the Oilers faced third-and-nineteen from the Cleveland thirty-seven. The veteran quarterback threw long for running back Ron

Coleman, but the ball bounced off his hands and was picked off by Browns' safety Thom Darden at the Cleveland three. It would have been the forty-first interception of Darden's career, putting him ahead of Warren Lahr on the Browns' all-time list, but there was a flag on the play, which the officials indicated was holding on lineman Conway Hayman of the Oilers. Instead of declining the penalty and taking the ball at the three, Rutigliano gambled and took the penalty, forcing the Oilers back to the Cleveland forty-seven for third-and-twenty-nine. "At that point, we felt the most important thing was field position," Rutigliano would say afterward. "We felt we could have gotten the ball as far back as our 20, or as far up as the 50."

"That was pretty nice of the Browns," Earl Campbell said, "letting us keep the ball."

Up in the booth Howard Cosell and Don Meredith backed up the decision. Even Bum Phillips agreed with Rutigliano's thinking. "If I was in the same situation, I would have turned down the interception," he said after the game. "I'd rather do that than have to go the length of the field. I guess it was a turning point in the game, but I thought it was a good choice."

It appeared that Rutigliano's strategy would work when Stabler completed a twelve-yard pass to tight end Mike Barber on third down, which would have set up fourth-and-seventeen from the Browns' thirty-five. But for the second straight play a yellow hankie changed everything. Lyle Alzado was flagged for roughing the passer, a fifteen-yard infraction and an automatic Houston first down. "I was actually trying to get away from the guy," Alzado said. "It's just that [Robert L.] Jackson's momentum took him into me and I hit Stabler."

Though it may not have been entirely his fault, this penalty, combined with his offsides call that wiped out the Franks touchdown, certified that Alzado was not having a good night. This latest Alzado flag gave the Oilers new life, and they responded with another Fritsch field goal, this one from thirty yards out, to cap a fifteen-play drive and increase their lead to 13-7 in the first minute of the fourth quarter.

No one knows what would have happened had Rutigliano declined the Houston penalty and let the interception stand, but Darden backed up his coach's decision. "It was the proper call, rather than take it at the 3," he said. "How are you going to know that you're going to get a penalty on the next play?"

In his weekly column in the *Plain Dealer* the following week Darden presented his argument in a more articulate albeit sarcastic manner. "I'll remember that the next time I'm flying through the air fighting two receivers for the ball," he said. "Next time I'll look down first to see what yard line I'm on. Maybe we could assign somebody on the sidelines to flash hand signals. They could indicate the yard line by holding up the number of fingers."

But even without the "gift" field goal Houston already had all the points it would need. After the Browns went three-and-out on their next possession, Fritsch added another chip-shot field goal with just over four minutes left following a sixteen-play, seventy-seven-yard drive that melted nearly ten minutes off the clock. It gave the Oilers an even more comfortable final margin of victory at 16-7.

As the final gun sounded and the Browns left the field, they were booed by what was left of a capacity crowd of 80,243.

The bottom line for many was that the Cleveland offense just couldn't get anything going when it counted for the second straight week. Aside from their lone scoring drive, the Browns did not move past the Houston thirty-five the entire evening and couldn't even get past the Oiler forty-four in the second half. But the offensive struggles were more painful this time since the defense did such a good job of keeping the team in the game. The Browns even stepped up for a goal-line stand in the fourth quarter, stopping Houston cold at the Cleveland one on three straight plays.

Following a performance in Week One in which it was burned for more than 450 yards, the Browns' defense did as well as could be expected against Houston. It kept the Oilers off the board as much as possible and "limited" them to 369 yards of offense, although the visitors did put together two drives of more than nine minutes in the second half. Earl Campbell rushed for 106 yards on eighteen carries, but that was in just over three quarters of work. He was forced to leave the game in the third quarter with a sore back. Still, Houston rolled up 192 yards on the ground.

One reporter noted after the game that the Browns' tackling had improved since New England. "Well," Rutigliano replied, "we had a lot of opportunities."

On the flip side of the offensive coin, though Ken Stabler threw for only 187 yards, he completed twenty-three of twenty-eight passes, many to keep drives alive. "Our defense bent a lot but it didn't break," Rutigliano said. "We needed to do offensively what they did, which was to keep the ball. They did a great job of controlling the ball."

Did they ever. Houston held the football for 42:20 of the contest and ran seventy-seven plays. "It's demoralizing for a defense when you control the ball for seven, eight minutes," Stabler said. "You sense what is happening to them when they are having the ball rammed at them."

The Browns meanwhile ran just forty-two plays, including a mere four in the third quarter (one of which was a punt), and Stabler threw for six more yards than the entire Browns' offense accumulated. Sipe was forced to warm up on the sideline to keep loose in the large gaps between offensive series, due mainly to the Browns' pitiful one-for-eight third-down conversion rate. "The offense made it easy for us," said Houston linebacker Robert Brazile. "Usually I have a slight head-ache after a game. Tonight, my head is clear."

Bum Phillips had avoided disaster. His team was now 1-1 and remained a game back of Pittsburgh. The Browns meanwhile joined Cincinnati in last place in the division.

To be down and out so early in the season was new for the Browns. Fans well remembered the 4-0 start the previous season and the 3-0 beginning in Rutigliano's first year in 1978. In fact, the Browns hadn't been 0-2 since the disastrous 1975 season under then-first-year coach Forrest Gregg. That team had gone 3-11, and just a three-win season, for the media and fans anyway, was beginning to look like a real possibility for the 1980 Browns.

"I'm not going to sell us down the river after two defeats," Sipe said. "The last couple years we came out of the gate really fast and all we got were respectable seasons. The bad start may be good for us. Who knows?"

3 · Silent Movie Days

It was very early Tuesday morning by the time Sam Rutigliano got to Art Modell's office at Cleveland Stadium for a postgame meeting following the loss to the Oilers. When he arrived he found a glum Modell sulking with general manager Peter Hadhazy. "They were flipping a coin to see which one of them would slit their wrists first," Rutigliano said.

This attitude was not unique to the Browns' braintrust.

"I think everybody was worried about the start," Mike Pruitt said. "When you start 0-2, there's always some doubt."

For many fans and members of the media it seemed the season was over. It didn't matter that there were fourteen games left. The Browns had just played two potential playoff teams and been embarrassed by both. If asked, most would probably have said it would take a miracle at this point for the Browns to reach the postseason. The real problem was that no one was asking; the seeds of apathy were already beginning to take root. Interest, let alone optimism, was hard to find.

And yet . . .

"I don't think there was any panic," said Doug Dieken. "Having brought in Joe D, we were still making adjustments up front. It was a big disappointment, but that made the resolve that much stronger."

"Being only 0-1 in the division, it wasn't time to panic," Thom Darden agreed. "There was just talk of shoring up what we were supposed to be doing. We had made some mistakes [on defense] we knew we shouldn't have made. With Marty coming in, there was a new mental education that had to go on to learn his system, learn his language, and know where to be and how to adjust. All of that was new. It took awhile for all of that to sink in and become a part of your everyday thinking on the field."

"We may have got out of the box a little slow, but we had our eyes on the prize," Ron Bolton said. "We knew exactly where we needed to go."

If the Browns' present didn't look good following the yawn-inducing loss to Houston, their future didn't look much better the following day. Six-foot-four, 252-pound defensive end Cleveland Crosby from Arizona, the Browns' second-round pick in the 1980 draft, was released as the team openly admitted making a huge miscalculation in selecting him and wasting such a high pick. Sam Rutigliano called it "addition by subtraction." "We have to admit we made a mistake," Rutigliano said. "We're letting him go in the best interests of improving this team."

The inside word on Crosby was that he was "lacking motivation," and accordingly he was the only healthy Browns' player who didn't see action in either of the first two regular-season games. Ironically one of Crosby's first post-draft comments may have foreshadowed his fate. "If I was doing something wrong in college football," he said the previous spring, "then I hope the pro coaches can correct them for me and I'll give 100 percent."

Crosby had signed a four-year $650,000 contract in June, but luckily for the Browns only his $50,000 signing bonus was guaranteed. Now just five months later he was unemployed. He said he was "shocked and disappointed, but not bitter." "I had a lot to prove and I had to do it quickly," Crosby said. "But I had no chance to do it. I don't think I was all that bad in practice. People said my problem was that I am not mean enough. But I could be tough in a game. I just didn't get enough of a chance to prove it."

The Browns, though obviously a bit embarrassed, weren't the only ones high on Crosby. After collecting seven sacks and fifty-four unassisted tackles for the Wildcats in 1979 Crosby was named to the All-PAC 10 team and was an All-American selection by the Associated Press. As surprising as his release was some felt it might have been because of his middle name, which incredibly was Pittsburgh.

Taking Crosby's place on the roster would be defensive lineman Jerry Wilkinson, just released by the Los Angeles Rams. Wilkinson was brought to Cleveland the week prior to Crosby's release for a workout and had been there since, which suggested that the Browns' brass had made this decision prior to the loss to Houston.

Crosby said he'd try to catch on with another team, but if he couldn't he'd go back to Arizona and get the six credits he needed for his degree. "There's nothing wrong with working for a living, is there?" Crosby asked hypothetically.

Ten days later the Winnipeg Blue Bombers of the Canadian Football League picked up Crosby. He would not play a down in the NFL in either the 1980 or 1981 seasons but appeared briefly with the Baltimore Colts in 1982. His career came to a close in the short-lived United States Football League in 1985.

The bad news just kept pouring into Cleveland that week as the Browns circled the wagons and tried to prepare for the Kansas City Chiefs the following Sunday at Cleveland Stadium. During surgery on right cornerback Lawrence Johnson's shoulder, which had been injured in the Houston game, doctors discovered the injury was worse than they thought. It wasn't just a fracture of the shoulder bone as doctors had diagnosed; the bone was shattered, and Johnson was out for the rest of the season. With Oliver Davis still recovering from a preseason shoulder separation, the Browns were suddenly vulnerable in the secondary. Taking Johnson's place on the roster would be Autry Beamon Jr., a defensive back the Browns signed after he was released by Seattle, but starting at right cornerback against the Chiefs would be 1979 sixth-round draft choice Clinton Burrell.

The Browns were also banged up at other positions. Linebacker Clay Matthews, who had a nice game against Houston after a shaky performance in New England, was doubtful for the Kansas City game with a sprained knee. Safety Clarence Scott had injured his ankle and tight end Curtis Weathers and Lyle Alzado both had strained knees. Linebacker Robert L. Jackson was diagnosed with a pinched nerve in his neck, and kicker Don Cockroft was still recovering from back spasms.

And probably the most damaging news of all was that defensive end Jerry Sherk had been placed on the injured reserve list for the next four weeks, still recovering from the surgery to remove the staph infection in his left knee the previous November. He was listed as week-to-week, but Sherk's 1980 season, and essentially his career, was over.

Another possible injury was one that the Browns denied but reporters kept questioning: the condition of Brian Sipe's right arm. Rutigliano and Sipe both insisted it was fine, but the question remained since Sipe hadn't looked anywhere close to his 1979 form in Weeks One or Two. And as they always do, members of the media started proposing solutions.

"If the offense doesn't start rolling soon, it would not be a surprise to see rookie Paul McDonald . . . get a chance at quarterback," wrote Bob Dolgan in a *Plain Dealer* column. "Usually they start fast and burn out in November. If they don't beat Kansas City on Sunday, look out below."

PD sports editor Hal Lebovitz went one step further. "Unless Sipe and Co. prove otherwise," he said, "this is going to be a boring season."

Add to all this delight the fact that the Browns were set to face a team that had emasculated them 42-0 a month earlier in the preseason, and Cleveland fans were tempted to turn their attention elsewhere that week. Some did because that Tuesday their hometown was the political capital of the world.

Jimmy Carter and Ronald Reagan's vice-presidential candidate George Bush were in Cleveland, debating through the press as to whether or not Reagan was a racist. Bush told his media gaggle that remarks Carter had made to black leaders in Atlanta inferred that Reagan was prejudiced. Carter naturally disagreed but was now fighting for his life as the polls said he trailed Reagan by anywhere from five to eight percent in Ohio. Carter was also being criticized for boycotting a debate with Reagan scheduled for that Sunday because independent candidate John Anderson would also take part. As September wore on and discussion of a Carter-Reagan debate continued, Cleveland was mentioned as a possible site for the potential forum.

But Election Day was still nearly two months away. Browns' fans couldn't help but wonder where their team would be when they pulled the lever in November. Would they be battling the Bengals for third place in the AFC Central, or could they somehow salvage something out of a season that had already been classified as a disaster by many in the media? "A more prudent Browns' game plan should be building toward the time when the Steelers and the Houston Oilers cave in with age," wrote Bob Sudyk in the *Press* that Thursday. "The Browns are not going to win it this year, not next year."

Not knowing what the future would hold the Browns pressed on, focusing on one game at a time. They opted to watch film from the exhibition blowout in Kansas City, "as pornographic as it is," Rutigliano admitted. "One thing I know," he added, "our people won't let their memory bank fool them in this one."

The key for the Browns would be stopping Chiefs' quarterback Steve Fuller, who had to be licking his chops after seeing what Steve Grogan and Ken Stabler had done to the Cleveland defense the first two weeks of the season. But Kansas City was also 0-2, and the Browns were favored by four points mostly because of their home-field advantage. Although as the Browns prepared for the Chiefs there seemed to be an air of desperation surrounding them. To be winless after two games was one thing, but to lose your first three, especially when two of them were at home, was quite another. Many wondered if this was the same team that started the season so well in 1978 and 1979.

Naturally the success of 1979 worked its way into Rutigliano's remarks to the team just before kickoff. "Let's open up today the way we did last year," he said in the locker room. "Let's get our fast break in gear and make them feel they have to stop our passing game."

And the blackboard behind him echoed that sentiment. Strewn across it was a collection of words that may not have looked like much but were the vital ingredients the Browns needed to turn the 1980 season around: BLITZ! ROVER! DOMINATE UP FRONT! FAST BREAK! PRESS! MAKE THINGS HAPPEN!

Ironically for all the praise and attention the Cleveland offense had received the year before and for as much criticism as the Browns' defense had undergone through the preseason, it was the Cleveland special teams that served as the alarm clock, rolling the Browns out of bed and into the 1980 season. After the Chiefs skated to a 6-0 lead in the second quarter on a pair of Nick Lowery field goals—the second of which was set up by a Frank Manumaleuga interception of Sipe—Browns' wide receiver Keith Wright reminded everyone present why he was one of the best return men in football. He took the ensuing Kansas City kickoff at the Cleveland nine and raced through the Chiefs' coverage, not to be brought down until he reached the Kansas City forty-one after a fifty-yard return. "He snapped us out of it," Brian Sipe said. "Suddenly, it was like last season again. Believe me, we missed Keith last year."

With as many weapons as the Browns boasted on offense in 1979, Keith Wright was often lost in the mix. Put simply the Browns started the 1979 season 4-0 with Wright going at full steam. He was lost for the season when he injured his knee in Week Five in Houston, and the Browns went on to lose seven of their next twelve. Other factors were obviously involved, but following Wright's fifty-yard return in the second quarter of the third game of the 1980 season, there was no doubt that he was capable of providing the kind of spark the Browns desperately needed. And Wright wasn't done yet.

The Browns eventually got on the board on a two-yard touchdown run on a sweep by Charles White, who was also in for a big day. Don Cockroft's extra point put the Browns ahead, 7-6, an advantage that would last into halftime despite a drive by the home team in the final minutes of the period which set up a thirty-eight-yard field-goal attempt. Cockroft missed it wide right and the lead remained one.

Despite the pick-me-up the Browns' special teams had provided in the first half, they nearly caused a disaster in the second. On the first possession of the third quarter Cleveland extended its lead when Sipe hit none other than Keith Wright for a twelve-yard scoring pass that made it 13-6, Browns. In celebration Wright heaved the football up into the upper deck, costing him $150 (the mandatory league fine for such an action), but in his opinion it was worth every penny. "I'd do it again," he said. "It was a special moment for me. It proved something. I knew I can play again. I've never felt better about a game in my life."

But just as the Browns were about to take a somewhat comfortable lead for the first time all season, Cockroft's extra point was blocked, keeping the Chiefs within one touchdown of the home team.

After the Browns stopped Kansas City on its next possession they were again given the opportunity to make their lead a bit more comfortable. But Mike Pruitt fumbled at the Cleveland thirty-eight, and Chiefs' linebacker Tom Howard recovered. Three plays later Steve Fuller hit tight end Tony Samuels for a sixteen-yard touchdown pass and Lowery's extra point equalized matters at 13. The Chiefs had now scored ten points off Cleveland turnovers.

The excitement was just beginning.

On the ensuing kickoff Keith Wright once again appeared to have given the Browns a huge boost. He exploded through the Kansas City coverage and broke free down the sideline, not stopping until he reached the end zone at the closed end of the Stadium, sending the crowd of 63,614 (noticeably smaller than Monday's turnout and not only because the crowd wouldn't be seen on national television) bonkers. But there were two problems. For one, the officials ruled that Wright had stepped out of bounds at the Cleveland thirty-four, and though after the game Wright would claim he hadn't touched the sideline, replays clearly showed he had. Even if he hadn't, a yellow hankie would have prevented the Browns from taking the lead back. Wide receiver Willis Adams would have been flagged for a clip at the end zone had Wright not stepped out of bounds some sixty-six yards earlier.

But as they had before, Wright's efforts seemed to spark the Browns. Three plays after his would-be touchdown return the Browns pulled off a critical play. From the Kansas City thirty-one Sipe swung a looping pass for rookie running back Charles White, who snagged it at the twenty. He juked past four Chiefs and then past strong safety Herb Christopher as he continued to mow his way toward the end zone. Incredibly Chief defenders who had position and appeared ready to bring White down were fooled by the crafty rookie and bit the dust. White eventually dove into the end zone for the touchdown that put the Browns ahead, 20-13, with 3:19 remaining in the third quarter following Cockroft's successful extra point.

White couldn't really describe how he got to the end zone; he was just happy he had. "That was just instinct," he said. "I don't want to remember that. When you do, it's time to get out of the game."

Instinct or not, it had a lot of people talking. "That was the best individual effort I've seen here in a long time," Sipe admitted.

"If he hadn't had No. 25 on his jersey," confessed Kansas City cornerback Gary Green, "I would have sworn that was Greg Pruitt out there."

"White didn't surprise me," Chiefs' head coach Marv Levy added, "but he did impress me."

But that one play wasn't all White contributed. He tallied 159 total yards on this sunny September Sunday on the lakefront: fifty-nine rushing on fifteen carries and one hundred receiving on seven catches. With those numbers, few would remember he began with just eighteen yards on eight rushes and no yards on three receptions in the first two games of his career.

"He just needed to play," Rutigliano said. "We had to show we had confidence in him, that he's a complete football player."

"It was my day today," White said. "I hope there are many more like this. I just want to be as helpful as I can when the chance comes up."

Browns' backup quarterback Paul McDonald had seen this before after being White's teammate at USC. "That's the Charlie White I knew," he said. "He just has to carry the ball, get it more than five times a game."

But White's touchdown hadn't brought the Browns out of the woods just yet, particularly with a whole quarter to play. Cleveland had an opportunity to extend the lead to ten early in the final stanza when it drove to the Kansas City twenty-one, but Cockroft was again wide right on a thirty-eight-yard attempt. The kicking team's failures had now cost the Browns seven very important points.

The Chiefs made a serious threat to tie the contest when they drove to the Cleveland eleven with nine minutes left. But fullback James Hadnot fumbled the football there and Browns' defensive end Elvis Franks recovered at the twelve, halting the drive and providing a bit of justice for the interception and touch-down Franks had called back against the Oilers.

In the following minutes the Cleveland offense looked like anything but the wild aerial show it had gained the reputation for over the previous two years. After failing to successfully hold onto the football earlier in the fourth quarter the Browns "moved well to the right of Ronald Reagan," in the words of the *Press*'s Bob Schlesinger, becoming "ultra-ultra-conservative." But it worked as the Browns took the Hadnot fumble and marched to the Kansas City thirty-three on an eight-minute drive. White ran for six, then reeled in an eight-yard pass from Sipe. The Browns' quarterback hit Dave Logan for fourteen yards on third-and-eleven, then scrambled for seven yards and another first down.

Then with fifty-six seconds left Rutigliano made an odd call that ended up working to the Chiefs' advantage. The Browns had the ball and were facing fourth-and-fourteen at the Kansas City thirty-three, and Rutigliano sent Johnny Evans out to punt. Instead of trying to pin the Chiefs back deep in their own territory and forcing them to go at least eighty yards to tie the game, Evans took the snap and ran to his right on an ill-advised fake punt. He was clobbered for a one-yard loss, and the Chiefs took over at their own thirty-four, now having to go just sixty-six yards in forty-nine seconds to tie the score. Rutigliano figured he would catch the Chiefs totally off-guard, but even if it didn't work, it was worth the risk since a punt from that distance would probably end up being a touchback and would only make a thirteen-yard difference. And a field goal was a bit too long to consider, particularly since Cockroft was not having a good day.

Fuller completed three of four passes in the waning seconds to move the ball to the Cleveland forty-two for a third-and-ten play with eighteen seconds left. Fuller's pass, intended for wide receiver Henry Marshall, was incomplete, which would have set up fourth down, but the Browns' just-acquired defensive end Jerry Wilkinson was penalized for lining up offsides. The infraction moved the Chiefs to the Cleveland thirty-seven for third-and-five with eleven ticks remaining.

Fuller lofted the ball into the corner of the end zone for wide receiver Stan Rome, but Browns' safety Thom Darden knocked it down with three seconds left. It brought up fourth down. Fuller dropped back and again lobbed the football into the end zone, this time shooting for Tony Samuels, and again, Darden and safety Clarence Scott were there to break up the play as time expired. The Browns appeared to have won the game—except for another yellow flag at the line of scrimmage.

Once again Wilkinson was called for being offsides, and Fuller was given another chance since the game cannot end on a defensive penalty. This time it would be from the Cleveland thirty-two with no time on the clock.

On the third desperation attempt Fuller aimed for wide receiver Carlos Carson, who was covered by his former college teammate Clinton Burrell, Cleveland's third choice to start at right cornerback. Suddenly thrust into the spotlight, Burrell would now determine the outcome of the game.

There was contact between the two former LSU Tigers as the ball fell incomplete, and the goal-line official tossed yet another yellow flag. For a few fleeting moments the Browns' worst fears seemed possible. Not only had they given the Chiefs two extra pops at pulling off the miracle, now it seemed they had given them a third plus interest. A defensive pass–interference penalty on Burrell would have given the Chiefs one more play from the Cleveland one, their second snap with no time remaining. But the Browns were let off the hook when it was Carson who was penalized for offensive interference. The game was finally over. "It seemed like that last minute took 10 minutes to play," said Thom Darden, whom Carson accidentally poked in the eye on the final play.

Though the Chiefs had taken advantage of the odd fake-punt call and ran nine plays on a shortened field in the last forty-nine seconds, the Browns had broken into the win column for the first time in nine months with a hard-fought—probably more so than necessary—20-13 win.

"Sam, your lucky number came up this time," wrote Schlesinger in Monday's *Press*, criticizing Rutigliano's fake-punt call in the final minute, which could have cost Cleveland the game. "But if you continue to throw boldness to the wind in that situation, your luck is sure to run out."

Lebovitz also pleaded with the Browns' head coach. "Sam, please don't come up with those poor percentage brainstorms," he wrote in a *Plain Dealer* column on Monday. "The only one you fool is yourself." Lebovitz also added a few words of advice for the sake of the owner's health: "I hope Art Modell tells Sam his contract doesn't call for unnecessary heart attacks." If so Modell may have had Charles White relay the message to his coach. After the game the Browns' owner called his first-round draft pick in the locker room from his private box to congratulate him.

"It could have been a lot easier," Rutigliano admitted. "It was really not an artistic game." Especially when one considered the Browns should have had at least seven more points on their final total had Cockroft and the kicking unit not been struggling. "I'll say it before you guys have a chance," the kicker told reporters after the game. "That stuff has got to stop."

The following week the *Plain Dealer* ran an article with the headline, IS COCKROFT WASHED UP? In it the thirty-five-year-old Cockroft confessed that he might have been kicking too much in practice. "I feel like I'm kicking better than ever," he said. "I have more pop in the ball. I'm getting good height and there's a lot of snap in my leg. That's why this is so frustrating."

Questions were also surfacing about the Browns' other kicker, punter Johnny Evans, who was averaging just 37.3 yards per kick in his first three games. Later in the week Rutigliano was presented with the age-old football question of trying to explain kickers. "Why are kickers strange?" he asked. "Well, take Brian Sipe. He can go out and throw 34 passes and 12 will be bad and everybody will say he had a great day. But *every* time the kickers go out there, they've got to do the job. No wonder they get a little nervous and they start seeing Harvey the Rabbit. You know, *I'm* starting to see Harvey the Rabbit, too! On extra points I used to feel I could go out for a drink of water. Now I'm saying the rosary."

Add to the Browns' kicking troubles against the Chiefs Sipe's interception that led to a field goal, Pruitt's fumble that led to a touchdown, and another cough-up by Ozzie Newsome, and you've got a narrow victory that should have been much more comfortable.

But a win is a win is a win as any true Browns' fan would agree following this one, and for the first time in 1980 there were signs of promise. First, there was good news filtering into the Stadium from around the league pertaining to the Browns' fortunes in the AFC Central. The most shocking score of the day came from Riverfront Stadium, where the Cincinnati Bengals had somehow come back to score seventeen points in the fourth quarter to knock off the Pittsburgh Steelers, 30-28, on a field goal by Ian Sunter with 2:15 to play. It marked Forrest Gregg's first win as Cincinnati's head coach. A fourth-down interception of Terry Bradshaw by Cincinnati cornerback Louis Breeden sealed the deal for the Bengals, who had obviously benefited from the absence of All-Pro wide receiver John Stallworth and a number of other key injured Steelers.

The only quasi-bad news for the Browns came from Houston where the Oilers had picked up where they left off in Cleveland and knocked off the Colts, 21-16, to tie the Steelers for first place. Just as they had done the previous Monday night the Oilers held the football for more than forty minutes. And once again Ken Stabler was the catalyst. In Weeks Two and Three combined he completed a remarkable forty-one of forty-nine passes.

The Browns and Bengals now stood just one game back of the frontrunners at 1-2.

All things considered, however, Week Three was a promising one for the Browns. Not only had Keith Wright stepped up and provided the kind of spark Cleveland needed, but Charles White appeared to have kicked off the kind of spectacular career the Browns hoped he would have. This was the kind of performance that won him the Heisman Trophy at USC in 1979 and why the Browns had invested so much in him.

A few days later the question naturally arose as to what Rutigliano planned to do when Greg Pruitt was healthy again. "I don't worry about it," Rutigliano said. "When Greg is ready to play, we'll see. In the meantime, this young man is doing a fine job." Ironically White's coming-out party as their No. 1 draft pick came just five days after the Browns had cut their losses with their second-round pick Cleveland Crosby.

Even more encouraging was the effort the Browns' defense put forth. The Chiefs were limited to just 251 yards of total offense to Cleveland's 352, and Fuller was sacked four times by four different Browns: defensive ends Lyle Alzado and Henry Bradley and linebackers Don Goode and Robert L. Jackson.

Offensively Sipe had his first truly solid game of the season, completing twenty-three of thirty-six passes for 295 yards with two touchdowns and an interception. More encouraging than those numbers was the fact that Sipe had spread his completions to seven different receivers after hitting just five different targets in each of the first two games. Included in the arsenal was wide receiver Willis Adams, Cleveland's top pick of the 1979 draft, who pulled down a thirty-nine-yard reception from Sipe, the Browns' longest completion of the season thus far. Add to that Newsome's six catches for fifty-five yards, Dave Logan's three for thirty-nine and Reggie Rucker's three for thirty-five, and it appeared this was an offense ready to get rolling.

And it all could be traced back to Keith Wright's fifty-yard kickoff return in the second quarter when the Browns were still mired in their moody, mediocre slump. "I felt that if I could do something big, we would get started," Wright said. "A big play can change the momentum of a game or a season."

In the days following the Kansas City win as the Browns prepared for 2-1 Tampa Bay, Lyle Alzado struck back at all the Doomsday Dans. "I'm tired of hearing the 3-4 won't work," he said. "It did in Denver and it will here. We're getting better and better every week. It's just a matter of going over things, learning them, and doing them right; executing and utilizing our strengths. We played this game with great intensity, and we're going to get better."

Alzado said that on a scale of one-to-ten, the Cleveland defense had earned an eight in the first half against New England but just a five in the second-half collapse against the Patriots. He gave the Browns an eight overall for the Houston game and said they had earned at least a nine against the Chiefs. In his mind there was no question that the Browns' defense had already improved dramatically, and he was tired of the negative attitude coming from the press and fans.

But Alzado's judging scale wasn't the only thing revealed that week. Brian Sipe admitted to the media that he had played the entire 1979 season and half of 1978 with a broken navicular bone in his left wrist. Sipe originally broke it late in 1978, and it healed in the off-season, but he refractured it in the 1979 opener and played with the injury for the remainder of the season. He didn't make a big deal about it because he didn't want the opposition targeting him.

Members of the media wondered if any nagging side effects from the wrist might have accounted for the sore-arm rumors plaguing Sipe in the first three weeks of 1980. "Sometimes it's a little sore, but not enough to affect my game," Sipe said. "It was kind of a freak injury to begin with, and it was another freak thing when it happened the second time. But I'm not worried about it happening again, and I'm fine now—and my right arm isn't sore, either."

Neither was the arm of Sipe's next counterpart: Tampa Bay quarterback Doug Williams, who had led the Buccaneers to a division title and an appearance in the NFC Championship in 1979. Williams worried Rutigliano, who said he reminded him of Steve Grogan and Steve Fuller, a talented pair of quarterbacks the Browns had already faced with mixed results. The Browns were also concerned with Bucs' tight end Jimmie Giles, who provided the same kind of threat that Ozzie Newsome did for the Browns.

But the Buccaneer who worried Rutigliano even more would be lining up on the other side of the ball: defensive end Lee Roy Selmon, an All-Pro capable of dominating an offensive line. An NFL Films crew would be on hand that Sunday to get footage for a piece they were doing on the heralded Selmon. Backed up by older brother Dewey Selmon at linebacker, Lee Roy had become the anchor of one of the best defensive units in the league—a unit that would no doubt challenge the Browns' offense, which still hadn't hit its stride.

The Cleveland defense took a blow when safety Thom Darden had to go to the emergency room early that Thursday morning. He woke up with severe pain in his eye stemming from the accidental poke by Carlos Carson at the end of the Chiefs game. Darden was listed as questionable for Tampa Bay. The good news for the Browns' injury-riddled secondary was that Oliver Davis, who had separated his shoulder in the preseason, had recovered and would return to his starting position at right cornerback.

It would turn out to be one of the most exciting—and most uncomfortable—Browns' games in recent memory. At sold-out Tampa Stadium temperatures reached ninety-five degrees, but with 74 percent humidity the heat index on the field registered over one hundred degrees. Making matters worse the Browns had packed the wrong jerseys. Instead of the lighter, mesh tops the players wore to combat the heat, they had to use their standard thicker jerseys.

While the heat may have taken its toll on the defensive units, it had little effect on the offenses as Sipe and Williams put on one of the greatest air shows in NFL history.

But things did not start well for the Cleveland quarterback as he misfired on his first six attempts, including an interception by Bucs' safety Mark Cotney, which set up a Tampa field goal. The Bucs led, 6-0, late in the first quarter on a pair of three-pointers by Garo Yepremian and threatened to add to the lead when they drove to the Cleveland seventeen and faced a fourth-and-short. Instead of going for the chip-shot field goal that would have given the home team a 9-0 lead, head coach John McKay opted to go for it. Williams's rollout pass intended for wide receiver Isaac Hagins fell incomplete, and the Browns got the ball back.

Sipe and Company, who had run just eight plays for five total yards in the first period, responded with an eleven-play, sixty-five-yard drive that ended with a thirty-five-yard Don Cockroft field goal that cut the lead to 6-3.

The momentum switched back to the defending NFC Central champions when Williams hit wide receiver Gordon Jones for a forty-one-yard touchdown pass less than a minute later, which gave the Buccaneers a 13-3 lead. It appeared as though the Cleveland defense was in for yet another long afternoon. But the Browns weren't pushing the panic button. "We weren't really concerned," Sipe said. "Some games just start that way. We weren't making the throws and the catches that were necessary. But we didn't panic and we didn't change anything." Instead the Browns went on an offensive tirade the remainder of that sultry afternoon that set the tone for the rest of the season.

A ten-play, sixty-six-yard march followed the Bucs' score, and Charles White got the Browns into the end zone with an eight-yard run around right end, which cut the lead to 13-10 with less than five minutes left in the half. After a key three-and-out defensive stop the Browns took the ball right back down the field, this time seventy-eight yards in six plays, keyed by a forty-two-yard pass from Sipe to Reggie Rucker and a critical roughing-the-passer penalty on Tampa Bay nose tackle David Logan (no relation to Browns' wide receiver Dave Logan.) The Browns capped the drive with a three-yard scoring pass from Sipe to running back Calvin Hill to put the visitors ahead, 17-13, with 1:34 to play in the half. The Browns were just warming up.

It wasn't just the backs and receivers who were feeling good either. The offensive line was playing great, and Joe DeLamielleure was feeling great despite the heat. On the bench following a series he told Tom DeLeone how good he was feeling. "You feel good because you didn't go to camp, you son of a bitch," DeLeone barked back.

"Maybe it's true," DeLamielleure replied. "I feel fresh as a daisy."

Meanwhile everything continued to come up roses for the Browns' offense in the third quarter. Sipe continued what would become a string of thirteen consecutive completions, breaking his own team record and coming within four of Baltimore quarterback Bert Jones's NFL mark. In the final minute of the third quarter Sipe hit wide receiver Ricky Feacher over the middle in the back of the end zone for a thirteen-yard score, putting the Browns ahead 24-13. Five minutes later the red-hot Browns' offense pulled off its most impressive play of the day.

With 10:20 remaining in the fourth quarter and the Browns at the Bucs' forty-three, still leading by eleven, Sipe dropped back to pass, and Tampa Bay blitzed the house. Ozzie Newsome picked up incoming safety Mark Cotney and gave Sipe just enough time to loop a toss down the sideline for Calvin Hill, who snagged it at the Tampa thirty, then out-raced the Buccaneer secondary into the end zone for a touchdown. Don Cockroft's point after gave the Browns a very comfortable 31-13 lead.

But if this game truly marked the return of the Browns to the kind of team they were in 1979, it was only appropriate that it also signaled the return of the Kardiac Kids.

Things were all but over moments later when Browns' cornerback Clinton Burrell intercepted Williams at the Cleveland forty-seven with 9:11 to play. The Browns' offense then began the process of attempting to melt some time off the clock. But after a pitch to Charles White on first down running back Cleo Miller fumbled at the Cleveland forty-nine, and Lee Roy Selmon, who was having a very quiet day, recovered with 8:19 left. Suddenly the Buccaneers awoke and did what they could to get back into the game.

Doug Williams, rising above a nagging ankle injury, led Tampa on a twelve-play, forty-nine-yard drive that ended when he hit Gordon Jones for another scoring pass, this one from three yards out, to cut the Browns' advantage to 31-20 with 5:09 left.

The Buccaneers attempted an onside kick, which was smothered by Burrell of the Browns at the Tampa forty-six. Aided by another roughing-the-passer penalty on linebacker Andy Hawkins, the Browns moved into field-goal range. Cockroft connected for the second time on the day, this time from thirty-six yards out, to give the Browns a 34-20 lead with just 1:56 remaining.

Believe it or not it was still far from over.

Williams drove the Buccaneers eighty-two yards in ten plays aided by an unnecessary roughness penalty on Browns' linebacker Don Goode and reached the end zone on a seven-yard pass to running back Jerry Eckwood to cut the lead to seven with forty-five seconds left. Naturally the Bucs attempted another onside kick. For a brief moment it looked like a reenactment of the previous one. The ball, spinning wildly, again bounded toward Clinton Burrell, who was in position and appeared to have caught the ball. Instead it bounced out of his possession, and Tampa linebacker Aaron Brown recovered at the Cleveland forty-eight with forty-two ticks on the clock. "I should have recovered it," Burrell said. "It hit my pads and bounced off."

Suddenly a game the Browns had dominated since the second quarter was in doubt. An eighteen-point lead had nearly vanished in four minutes. And a red-hot quarterback only had to guide his team forty-eight yards against an exhausted defense to force overtime. It was vintage Kardiac Kids football.

In the defensive huddle, as the Browns tried to rally the troops, the spirited Lyle Alzado urged the Cleveland defense. "C'mon guys," he barked, "think snow and let's have some fun!"

Tampa Bay, out of time outs, reached the Cleveland thirty-five with twelve seconds remaining. Williams dropped back to pass, and everyone in the stadium figured he'd fire to the end zone or at least to the sideline for a quick completion that would stop the clock. Instead Williams threw over the middle to tight end Jimmie Giles, who was tackled at the Browns' twenty after a fifteen-yard gain. Before the Bucs could reach the line of scrimmage, time expired, and the Browns, after an excruciating three hours and thirty-three minutes in the sultry sweatbox of Tampa Stadium, were finally victorious, 34-27.

"That's what happens when you have a young quarterback," Rutigliano said of Williams's ill-fated last-second decision. "Brian would never do a thing like that."

In the locker room after the game Rutigliano got a hug from Art Modell. Brian Sipe got a kiss from general manager Peter Hadhazy. "This was like the good old days," said Rutigliano. "The way we started, I thought we'd get blown out. But we came back, we never quit, and there's no telling what this team is capable of doing."

The exciting finish turned out to be a very disappointing ending for what had otherwise been a great day for Doug Williams. "It is idiotic, not knowing what time it is on the clock," said his coach John McKay, who had never been at a loss for words. "You've got to go to the end zone. It is non-concentration, which means we don't want it bad enough. All we want to do is talk about some other year. We ought to start talking about 1976, which will make them sick." McKay was referring to the Buccaneers' inaugural season when they went 0-14 and began an NFL-record twenty-six-game losing streak. McKay added to his spirited postgame critique, observing that, "Our offense was inept and our defense was terrible. We looked like we were playing in cement."

In the other locker room the Browns had plenty to be proud of. Not only had they evened their record with two straight hard-fought victories, but they had just defeated on the road a team that had almost reached the Super Bowl the previous season. The defense had dominated the game until the final seven minutes, and the offense looked even better that it did in 1979 behind the uncanny accuracy of Brian Sipe. After his first six incompletions Sipe completed twenty-two of his next twenty-six to nine different receivers for 318 yards and three touchdowns. It marked the first time anyone had ever thrown for three hundred yards against Tampa Bay.

"That was Brian Sipe's kind of game," Rutigliano said. "He sprayed the ball around to a myriad of receivers. It was another outstanding performance by Brian, the kind you come to expect from him."

Reggie Rucker paced the Browns' busy receiving corps with seventy-nine yards on four catches followed by Dave Logan's fifty on a pair. Willis Adams and Calvin Hill both caught two for forty-six, and both of Hill's were for touchdowns.

While Sipe was nearly flawless, a great deal of credit had to go to the Browns' offensive line, which allowed just one Tampa sack. "When I have time to sit back there and decide where I want to go, it's a lot easier," Sipe said. "When I get that kind of time, the defensive backs get antsy and start to move around in their zones, and I was able to throw into them." The line also paved the way for forty-eight yards rushing from Mike Pruitt, who was just as dangerous out of the backfield as a receiver with five catches for thirty-nine yards. Greg Pruitt even got back into the mix and ripped off a fourteen-yard run. However, Charles White couldn't find substantial daylight for the second straight week and was limited to twenty-seven yards on eleven carries.

But probably the most impressive performance in a day of impressive performances was that of Doug Dieken, who limited Lee Roy Selmon to just three tackles on the afternoon. "That Doug Dieken is something else," Selmon said afterward. "We try to force teams into passing situations but Cleveland pass-blocked so well it hurt us." After the game an NFL Films representative told Nate Wallack, the Browns' vice president of public relations, that they were doing a feature on the wrong guy.

The Browns' defense also put a hurt on the Tampa offense for much of the game until the final six minutes when they slipped into a deplorable "prevent" mode. They completely took away any type of running game the Buccaneers tried to establish, and Tampa picked up just eighty yards on the ground all afternoon. The Browns weren't too much better at ninety-two rushing yards, but Tampa also hurt itself with 115 yards on twelve penalties.

Somewhat lost in the excitement of the game's final play was that Giles's catch was just his second of the day and brought him to a total of twenty-two receiving yards. It was certainly a victory for the Browns' secondary led by Burrell's two interceptions and onside kick recovery. The Buccaneers were able to take advantage of a pair of one-hundred-yard games by Gordon Jones (seven receptions for 106 yards) and Jerry Eckwood (ten receptions for 101 yards), but of Williams's eight targets those were the only two that did any real damage.

Alzado said the Browns registered a season-high 9.5 on the "Lyle Scale" in the first half but dropped to a 7.5 in the second.

Despite the bad decision on the final play Williams was impressive, completing thirty of fifty-six passes for 343 yards with three touchdowns and two interceptions. It was the most passes ever attempted against the Browns at the time and a record that would stand for twelve years. Combined, Williams and Sipe attempted eighty-eight passes and completed fifty-two for 661 yards and six touchdowns.

The following week many Buccaneers voiced their opinions on what they thought was the difference. It wasn't that Cleveland was really better, they said, it was that Browns' defensive backfield coach Len Fontes knew the thinking of his brother, Wayne Fontes, Tampa's defensive backfield coach. "I believe it was Len knowing Wayne's thinking," said Bucs' safety Curtis Jordan. "I believe that Len was able to predict what our coverage would be in certain situations, and that information was given to Sipe."

Naturally the Browns passed that off as ludicrous.

"First, nobody asked me what I thought Wayne's tendencies would be; how he'd have his guys covering our receivers," Len said. "And if they had, I wouldn't have known what to tell them."

The Fontes brothers did have a bet on the game: the loser would have to pay for the winner's family vacation, two weeks in Lake Tahoe, the following June.

Despite their victory, which left both squads at 2-2, the Browns also didn't get a whole lot of respect from John McKay. "They aren't that good of a team; they aren't going to the Super Bowl," he said. "But the way we played today, we aren't even going to the Toilet Bowl."

Meanwhile in Cincinnati the Bengals put forth a wonderful effort in their attempt to climb out of the Central Division outhouse. They took the Oilers right down to the wire at Riverfront Stadium but couldn't quite pull it out. After falling behind 10-0, the Oilers fought back without the services of injured fullback Earl Campbell and tied the game in the fourth quarter. And for the third time in four games Cincinnati's special teams provided the difference. With 5:33 remaining Houston wide receiver Carl Roaches (who was driving an ice cream truck in 1979) returned a Pat McInally punt sixty-eight yards to the Cincinnati twelve to set up Toni Fritsch's game-winning twenty-nine-yard field goal. Veteran defensive back Jack Tatum intercepted Bengals' quarterback Jack Thompson at the Houston thirty-five to secure a 13-10 Oiler victory.

"We're getting better each week," Forrest Gregg said about his young Bengals, and it was hard to argue with him. "We can play with anybody. By the end of the season, we could be a real tough outfit."

Not the greatest news the Browns could hear since they would have to travel to Cincinnati to close the season for the third consecutive year, and it now appeared that the Browns making the playoffs as a Wild Card was a possibility. But there was a long way to go until December 21 at Riverfront Stadium.

At the same time nature simply took its course at Solider Field in Chicago, where the Steelers obliterated the Bears, 38-3. After four weeks Pittsburgh appeared ready to roll toward another division crown, and it was tied with Houston at 3-1 atop the standings. The Browns' two-game winning streak had kept them just a game back, while the Bengals were two back at 1-3.

"Until we stop making self-inflicted wounds, we can't be a real contender for the AFC Central Division championship," Rutigliano said after the win in Tampa. "But unless somebody has us thrown out, we're still in the race."

With a quarter of the season gone just two undefeated teams remained in the NFL: the Buffalo Bills and San Diego Chargers. Conversely, the New York Jets and New Orleans Saints were the only winless squads.

While the Browns knew they could do better in the remaining 75 percent of their schedule, the win over Tampa Bay seemed destined to turn the entire season around. With the victory over the Bucs and Week Three's squeaker over Kansas City, it appeared that the Browns had climbed out of the hole they found themselves in following their first two games. And they seemed to have picked up their flare for last-minute heroics right where they left off in 1979. Even the media, which had been so pessimistic in the first two weeks of the season, took notice. "This might be the day the Browns came of age in 1980," wrote the *Plain Dealer*'s Russ Schneider.

"This team is a throwback to the silent movie days," said Bob Sudyk of the *Cleveland Press*. "The girl tied to the railroad tracks with the train coming. The hero arrives in the nick of time."

While it was certainly a stellar day for the Browns, Sudyk pointed out that the team really could have used a killer instinct in the fourth quarter. "Every Browns' fan should take a course in heart resuscitation," he wrote. "This isn't the Kardiac Kids. This is Kardiac Arrest. The symptoms of a Browns' fan are chewed-off fingernails, sweaty palms, a tendency to jump at loud noises. Life insurance companies are canceling lifetime season-ticket holders."

But probably the most appropriate line in Monday's papers was penned by the *Press*'s Jim Braham, whose statement turned out to be far more accurate than he could have ever imagined. "Refill the digitalis, or whatever pill you pop to calm the nerves," he said. "The Kardiac Kids are back."

After returning from Florida the Browns got a live scouting report of their Week Five opponent when the Denver Broncos visited the New England Patriots on *Monday Night Football*. The Patriots won, 23-14, dropping Denver, the Browns' next opponent, to 1-3. With a struggling team coming into Cleveland after just five days' rest, it seemed like a golden opportunity for the Browns to extend their winning streak.

That Monday was also a big day for the Cleveland Public School district as it began to implement Phase Three of its desegregation plan, which included busing many students halfway across Cleveland. In the largest mass movement of students ever in Ohio, nine high schools were desegregated and about 39,000 of 85,000 students were entering new schools via 479 buses. School officials, expecting every conceivable problem, were pleased when Monday went almost exactly according to plan.

If all went as planned for the Browns the following Sunday they would be at 3-2 and still within arm's reach of Pittsburgh and Houston entering the middle portion of the schedule. After all the Broncos seemed ripe for the plucking. They were off to their worst start in three years under coach Red Miller, and young quarterback Matt Robinson was struggling. With the Cleveland offense just now shifting into high gear, it appeared that the only way to beat the Browns was to have an offense that could consistently carve through the Cleveland defense. Denver certainly didn't have that.

"Credit Marty," Calvin Hill said of the sudden resurgence in the Browns' fortunes. "[Schottenheimer] really has molded this group. Last season the offense felt we had to do it. Now we know the defense can win games, too."

One Brown on the defensive unit was a bit more motivated than usual to face the Broncos. Lyle Alzado had played in Denver from 1971 until he was traded to Cleveland prior to the 1979 season and was still peeved about how Denver general manager Fred Gehrke treated him just prior to and after the trade. After winning the 1978 AFC Defensive Player of the Year Award, Alzado had asked Gehrke for a guaranteed contract but not a raise. Gehrke told Alzado he couldn't do that because it was against team policy, a line Alzado knew wasn't true. Alzado walked out of camp, and after Gehrke publicly bad-mouthed Alzado, he traded him to Cleveland. Ironically Gehrke had played professional football in Cleveland as a member of the world-champion Rams in 1945. "Boy I wish Gehrke were still playing," Alzado said the week before the Denver game. "I'd beat him to a pulp."

Even with a fired-up Alzado, Sam Rutigliano figured that the Browns would need twenty-four points to win. It turned out that he was right.

As the first half wore on it looked as though they wouldn't have too much trouble getting the points. After Denver took a 6-3 lead on a forty-seven-yard Fred Steinfort field goal with 11:19 to play in the second quarter, the Browns rallied back to take command of the game. From the Denver forty Sipe looped a pass down the middle of the field for Reggie Rucker, who made a marvelous over-the-shoulder catch between two defenders for the go-ahead touchdown. In Monday's *Cleveland Press* Rucker's reception was compared to another a bit more famous, made in another October in another sport twenty-six years earlier, which Clevelanders never forgot. "I used to try and emulate Willie Mays with his basket catch," said Rucker, who also played baseball while attending Boston University. "That's how I played center field. If you can catch a baseball that way, you certainly ought to be able to catch a football, which is larger and softer. I had them both beat but the ball hung up a little. I decided the easiest way was over the shoulder. I just continued running and never turned around. You see, if you don't turn, the defenders don't turn, either."

They didn't, and Rucker's catch put the Browns ahead, 10-6.

After another Cleveland defensive stop the Browns appeared poised to really take the air out of the Broncos' balloon as they drove to the Denver one on a fifteen-play march in the final minutes of the half.

On third-and-goal with forty-eight seconds left Sipe rolled out on a quarterback option that Denver covered perfectly. Seeing his options were limited as he reached the Denver seven Sipe made a costly mistake. "I was going to try to run the ball into the end zone," he said, "but I saw I couldn't do it because the angle was cut off. I turned and looked for Ozzie and threw the ball, which was an absolutely absurd thing to do. I wanted to throw it out of bounds, and that's what I tried to do, but it was a very bad decision."

Denver linebacker Randy Gradishar blocked the pass and the ball shot downward, appearing to fall incomplete. But instead of hitting the ground the ball hit another Denver linebacker, Cleveland native Tom Jackson, who was lying on the ground, and bounced back up into the air. Neither player knew that the ball had hit him. It then landed back in the arms of Gradishar at the seven, and he had nothing but green grass in front of him. Gradishar took off and tried to ignore the pain in his side after his lowest right rib had popped out of alignment on the second series of the game. "I saw the referee running next to me so I kept going," he said. "The ribs were hurting, but the excitement of that run momentarily took all the pain away."

Several painful moments later (both for Gradishar and the Browns) the Broncos had taken the lead with just thirty-five seconds left in the half. It could have been 17-6, Browns, but thanks to two odd bounces it was 13-10, Broncos. The momentum of the game had changed dramatically.

"It was a 14-point or 10-point turnaround," Denver coach Red Miller said. "I never saw a play like that before."

"When you're supposed to go in and you don't, that's one thing," Rutigliano said. "But when you're supposed to go in and they take it and go in the other way, that's 14 points."

Thanks mostly to a thirty-two-yard kickoff return to the Cleveland forty-seven by running back Dino Hall, the Browns did manage to tie the game before the half on a forty-five-yard Cockroft field goal. But the interception was still a monumental turnaround that would haunt Cleveland for the rest of the game. "That play got everybody up," Gradishar said. "It seemed to give us new life. The defense felt particularly good. It was the turnaround we needed."

On the second play of the third quarter the Browns turned the lights out on Robinson when linebacker Robert L. Jackson intercepted him at the Denver twenty-three and returned it to the fourteen. The crowd was back in it, but the Browns squandered the opportunity. An untimely clipping penalty on Doug Dieken, who was not having a good day, stopped the Browns cold, and Cockroft was called on to attempt a twenty-five-yard field goal. A high snap from Gerry Sullivan to holder Paul McDonald threw off the timing of the entire kick and Cockroft missed it wide left. The unsuccessful attempt now brought the total number of points that the Browns had graciously given Denver to thirteen, and the contest was still tied at, for the Browns anyway, unlucky thirteen.

Although the Broncos were very much in the game, Miller decided to yank Robinson at quarterback and go with veteran Craig Morton, a move the Browns had expected if the Denver offense was struggling. Morton immediately took advantage of the Browns' second major gaffe. Following Cockroft's missed field goal Morton drove his team fifty-seven yards in ten plays, a drive capped by a forty-one-yard Steinfort field goal with 6:56 to play in the third quarter to give the visitors a 16-13 lead.

Not willing to succumb quietly the Browns took the kickoff and marched fifty-two yards to the Denver twenty-three, where Cockroft equalized matters with a forty-yard field goal with 2:01 to play in the period. For the third straight week the Browns would go down to the final minutes.

The Broncos were poised to take the lead back early in the fourth, but Steinfort's forty-two-yard field-goal attempt was blocked by Browns' tight end McDonald Oden.

Midway through the final stanza the Browns were attempting to drive for the go-ahead points. But a penalty on Dieken, his third of the day, for holding Denver rookie defensive end Rulon Jones wiped out what would have been a key first down at midfield and forced a Cleveland punt. Johnny Evans then proved that he was still in a slump when he shanked a thirty-five-yard boot that Denver wide receiver Rick Upchurch returned to the Cleveland forty-two.

Minutes later the Broncos had a first-and-goal at the Cleveland three, and things looked bleak for the home team. But for the fifth consecutive week the Cleveland defense came up with a stand, and this one forced Denver to kick a nineteen-yard field goal with 5:50 to play. The Broncos led, 19-16, but if the Kardiac Kids could manage just one more scoring drive they might be able to pull out what had turned into a nightmarish game.

Sipe and Company took over at their own thirty-eight and marched to the Denver forty, where Sipe hit Mike Pruitt for a fifteen-yard gain to the twenty-five. But the play was wiped out on another holding penalty, this one on Joe DeLamielleure, and pushed Cleveland back to midfield for second-and-eighteen. Sipe hit Mike Pruitt again for thirteen yards, then his third-and-five pass for Greg Pruitt fell incomplete with 2:38 to play. The Browns now faced a dilemma. Should they go for it on fourth down or call on Cockroft to attempt a fifty-four-yard field goal into the wind? The thinking process behind this decision led to one of the most confusing two-minute periods in Browns' history.

It all started with Rutigliano talking to Cockroft on the sideline. "I told him we hit on some fifty-three-yarders in the pre-game, and I felt I could make it if we got a good snap, a good hold, and a good hit," said Cockroft, who had kicked a career-best fifty-seven-yarder in 1972 and a fifty-one-yard field goal in 1978.

That was enough for Rutigliano, who wanted to play for the tie at this juncture. "The percentage of us getting the field goal was a hell of a lot better than making the fourth-and-five yardage, particularly when they knew we'd try to run or throw the ball short," Rutigliano said afterward. He sent the kicking team out onto the field.

Seeing Cockroft and the special teamers, Dieken and right tackle Cody Risien told referee Jerry Seeman that they were reporting as tight ends, as they usually did on field-goal attempts. But Sipe went over to the sideline and lobbied in favor of going for it. "Yeah, I was hoping to get another shot at making a first down," he said afterward, "but that's the way any quarterback would feel."

A moment later the Browns called time out and their brain trust gathered on the sideline to try to figure out what to do. With the combination of the time out and the sight of Sipe and the offense starting to go back out onto the field, it appeared as though the Browns had decided to go for it, and the crowd cheered its approval. But at the last second the offense was called back and the decision was final: the Browns would attempt a field goal.

"There seemed to be a lot of indecisiveness," Red Miller said. "They changed their minds twice. I thought they should have been called for too many men in the huddle."

"I felt a tie was what we wanted, that we'd be hard-pressed on the fourth down," Rutigliano said. "If we had gone for it and didn't make it everybody would have said we should have gone for the field goal."

Most in the stands seemed to think the field goal was a bit out of Cockroft's range, especially considering the Browns faced what seemed to be a very achievable fourth-and-five. But at the heart of the confusion were Dieken and Risien. As the Browns called time out Dieken asked Seeman if he and Risien could revert back to their normal offensive line positions if the Browns decided to go for it despite having reported as tight ends for the field-goal attempt. Seeman's reply was "By rule, no."

Despite all the confusion the Browns lined up for the field goal and Cockroft was confident. He got the good snap and the good hold he wanted and stepped toward the ball. "As soon as I kicked the ball," he said, "I thought it had a good chance to make it."

It was a solid kick, but then the stubborn Lake Erie breeze held the ball up. From fifty-one yards out it would have been good. But from fifty-four it was just short, and Denver took over at its own thirty-seven. Running back Jim Jensen plowed over left tackle for three yards on third-and-one at the Denver forty-six two plays later, and the Browns never saw the football again.

It was easily the most disappointing loss of the season. All the momentum the Browns had collected against the Chiefs and Buccaneers now seemed out the window as they had lost a game they not only could have, but absolutely *should* have, won.

"We played a better game than [the Broncos] did in a lot of offensive categories," Rutigliano said, "but we weren't opportunistic enough. They did some things to stop us, but we did more things to stop ourselves."

Naturally the coach was questioned about the Browns' fire drill before the field-goal attempt. "Nobody was involved but me," he said. "Initially, the field-goal unit went out because it was fourth down. Then I called time out because I wanted to think about it some more. Then the offensive team went out. But I was under control at all times."

At the same time there was still confusion over whether or not the Browns could have gone for it had they wanted to, following Dieken and Risien's adventures. "Yes, there was a decision to go for it," Sipe said. "I saw the field-goal team come out but I wanted to discuss the possibility of going for it. Sam called time out and there was a decision to go for it. Unfortunately, Cody Risien and Doug Dieken had already reported in as ends and so they couldn't come out. That committed us to that action. Thus, there was no decision to make."

But was that assessment truly accurate? Yes, the rule said that once a player reports at a certain position he must be at that position for that play. But things got a little cloudy in terms of whether or not that player could un-report after a time out. The referees didn't seem to be too clear either. In fact the following week Art McNally, supervisor of NFL officials, said that if he had been the referee Rutigliano would have had the option of un-reporting Dieken and Risien and going for it after the time out.

In the final analysis, however, Rutigliano wanted to try the field goal so that's what the Browns did. "A lot of players were shouting a lot of things," Rutigliano said. "There were a thousand things going on. The fact is, we had many opportunities in the first half to score, and if we had, it would have eliminated the melodrama of the second half."

The coach was certainly right about that. No matter how shaky the Browns' decision-making process in the final minutes, they lost this game when the football bounced off Tom Jackson and into Randy Gradishar's arms in the first half. There didn't seem to be much doubt in anyone's mind that was the play that turned the entire game around. "That play fired everybody up and in the end it was just what we needed to win," Jackson said amidst the raucous celebration in the Denver locker room afterward. Queen's latest rock hit, "Another One Bites the Dust," blared through the room, making postgame interviews a bit more difficult.

Naturally the local scribes jumped all over the Browns as the "killer instinct" question once again surfaced. "The Browns are nice guys," wrote Bob Sudyk in the *Press*. "There are too few brutes in the lineup. It is fair to wonder if the coach's personality subtly transfers his laid-back libido to his team."

Sudyk pointed out that the fourth-down conundrum was eerily similar to a play in the 1979 opener, which turned out to be a 25-22 Browns' win in overtime over the Jets in New York. Rutigliano had opted to go for it on a key fourth down in that game in order to "build confidence in his offense by giving them the gambling green light." That gamble paid off and, as Sudyk said, set the tone for the season. After the Denver game the light appeared to be amber at best.

In true Monday-morning quarterback fashion Sudyk suggested that the Browns should have faked the field goal and that McDonald could have thrown a pass to Dieken, who was flagged for holding three times against Denver after being penalized just three times in all of 1979. "Hell," he wrote, "Dieken was holding all day anyway trying to protect Sipe. Nobody had better hands on the field."

For the first time in 1980 there were also questions swirling about the Cleveland playcalling. Mike Pruitt only carried the ball nine times but racked up sixty yards, a good average that caused many to argue that Pruitt could have been better utilized. Sipe was basically sharp, completing twenty of forty passes for 258 yards with a touchdown and the costly interception, but to many it still didn't feel like the 1979 Sipe. The 1979 Sipe would have found a way to win this game, just as Craig Morton did. After replacing Robinson in the third quarter Morton may not have led the Broncos to a touchdown, but he certainly moved the Denver offense and kept the Broncos in the game, completing nine of twelve passes for 109 yards.

Then again no one person should have had to pull a rabbit out of a hat on this one. The Browns' offense had out-gained the Broncos, 358 yards to 239, but wiping out a good chunk of that advantage was the Browns' ninety-seven yards on twelve penalties. Encouraging signs for Cleveland were Greg Pruitt catching four passes for thirty-four yards and Reggie Rucker re-emerging as a deep threat with eighty-three yards on three receptions.

Though they had their share of misfortune on the field the Browns turned out to be pretty lucky on this day. That's because the Houston Oilers, even with Earl Campbell back in the lineup, were stomped at home by the lowly Seattle Seahawks, 26-7, in one of the biggest upsets of the season thus far. Adding to the Browns' pleasure was that the Bengals also failed to gain ground as they were handled 14-9 by the Packers in Green Bay in Forrest Gregg's first game as a coach at the old stomping grounds of his playing days. The bad news was that the Steelers just kept on rolling, jumping out to a 20-0 lead and holding on to defeat the Vikings in Minnesota, 23-17. Pittsburgh intercepted Vikes' quarterback Tommy Kramer five times, two by safety Donnie Shell, who sealed victory with his second with fifteen seconds to play. The victory improved the Steelers to 4-1 and gave them a one-game advantage over 3-2 Houston with the Browns in third and Cincinnati still in the cellar.

The Browns had failed to capitalize on a perfect opportunity to tie the Oilers for second place. What's worse is that they had lost in a fashion befitting their housemates, the Indians, who wrapped up their somewhat hopeful yet still-unacceptable 1980 season that day with a 7-1 loss to the Orioles in Baltimore. Despite the steady pitching of Len Barker and the surprising leap to stardom of rookie outfielder Joe Charboneau, the Indians could still do no better than 79-81, twenty-three games back of the New York Yankees in sixth place in the American League East Division.

Following this heartbreaking loss to Denver it appeared that the Browns were at the crossroads of their season. If they weren't careful they too might soon look back at the 1980 season, just as the Indians were, and wonder "what if?"

4 · The Old Magic

Their momentum gone, the Browns would once again have to start from scratch.

Any virility they gained from the win in Tampa Bay had now been lost with the frustrating defeat to Denver. Because of it, going into Week Six, 2-3 Cleveland once again trailed the Pittsburgh Steelers by two games and the Houston Oilers by one game. Considering what both the Steelers and Oilers had accomplished the previous two seasons, the Browns had to feel a little bit like their current president Jimmy Carter. On the Monday after the Browns' loss to Denver the *New York Times*, *Washington Post*, and NBC all predicted Ronald Reagan would comfortably win the forthcoming election, which was now a mere four weeks away. Many felt the Browns, like Carter, were running out of time.

"I don't think that team was ever really uneasy," Doug Dieken said. "I remember getting some pressure from the top, but pressure from the top is from people who never played the game. That was not uncommon to have those people start to gag up there. They had no clue how to handle the situation."

"We still had a lot of confidence because when we looked at the film, we saw we made mistakes that could be remedied," said Tom DeLeone. "It wasn't like we didn't have the players to do it. We just made mistakes that were correctable."

If Cleveland hoped to make a run for the playoffs, its upcoming match in Seattle loomed large. The Seahawks stood at 3-2 and had won three straight, including burying the Oilers in the Astrodome the previous Sunday as the Seattle defense intercepted Ken Stabler five times. Appropriately the Seahawks were four-point favorites over the Browns, who also had to overcome recent history. Seattle had defeated Cleveland all three times the teams had met, including a 29-24 Seahawks' win in Cleveland the previous November, which turned out to be crippling to the Browns' playoff drive. One consistent factor in all three of those losses was the Browns' trouble stopping Seattle quarterback Jim Zorn, who was quickly ascending toward NFL stardom. Sam Rutigliano called the southpaw "the most resourceful quarterback in the league" and noted that all he lacked to become a star was good talent around him. The Browns would also get a firsthand look at a coach as daring as their own in Seattle's Jack Patera. "Compared to him, I'm an ultra-conservative," Rutigliano admitted.

On offense the Browns would have to contend with Seattle's top draft choice in 1980. Defensive end Jacob Green was quickly making his presence known around the league, and it would be up to young right tackle Cody Risien to keep Green out of Brian Sipe's personal space. When one considered the Browns would also have to travel across the country to play in the palace of decibels known as the Kingdome, all the ingredients were on the counter for another Browns defeat. If Cleveland dropped to 2-4 with two games yet to play against Pittsburgh and another in Houston, the Steelers and Oilers would probably be off to the races for the division crown while the Browns would find themselves dueling Cincinnati for third. For the second time in four weeks the Browns were at the crossroads, but this time a wrong turn probably wouldn't include a second chance.

On the other hand there were signs of hope as the Browns jetted to the Pacific Northwest. Namely, for the first time all season, they would be facing a 4-3 defense, which meant Mike Pruitt would get more opportunities to shine. And Pruitt was eager for the opportunity. "For some reason we're always getting away from the running game," Pruitt said. "Against Denver, for instance, I felt I could have broken one if I had more carries."

There didn't seem to be much question that Pruitt would get more carries in Seattle. "The 3-4 is tough to run against because of all the stunting and blitzing," Rutigliano explained. "With that type of versatility, it virtually blows up the running lanes. It's true that establishment of a better running attack would give Brian Sipe better control of the game."

Speaking of controlling the game, the Cleveland defense had certainly done that to the best of its ability over the previous three weeks, and as the Browns prepared for the Seahawks, the brain behind the Cleveland attack unveiled his detailed grading system. After each game Marty Schottenheimer and his staff would carefully break down the films of each play. Each player would then be evaluated as to whether or not he did his job correctly on each snap, and the coaches would determine whether or not the Browns "won" that particular play. Schottenheimer believed if the defense won 65 percent of its plays, the Browns deserved to win. "If you fall below 65 percent," Schottenheimer said, "your defense is breaking down more than it should and exposing the team to getting beat."

In analyzing the Browns' first five games Schottenheimer's grading scale usually did represent the final result:

New England: the defense won 44 of 80 plays (55 percent) and the Browns lost, 34-17.
Houston: the defense won 44 of 81 plays (54 percent) and the Browns lost, 16-7.

Kansas City: the defense won 43 of 66 plays (65 percent) and the Browns won, 20-13.

Tampa Bay: the defense won 50 of 82 plays (61 percent) and the Browns won, 34-27.

Denver: the defense won 42 of 63 plays (64 percent) and the Browns lost, 19-16.

Some figured the Browns' defense would get another boost with the help of cornerback Autry Beamon, who had been a surprise release by the Seahawks six weeks earlier. Beamon did his best to tell his current teammates about the tendencies of his former ones.

But as Sunday's game began it didn't appear as though Beamon's advice was doing much good. Led by Zorn the Seahawks took the opening kickoff and began driving down the field. Aided by a twenty-five-yard scamper by Zorn to the Cleveland twenty-seven Seattle was poised to draw first blood. But two plays later Lyle Alzado stripped the ball from running back Jim Jodat and Henry Bradley recovered at the Cleveland eighteen. Though the Browns returned the favor three plays later when Mike Pruitt fumbled a handoff, and the Seahawks recovered at the Cleveland thirty-six, the visitors soon got rolling.

After Efren Herrera was short on a fifty-one-yard field goal the Browns took over and sailed down the field. Sipe and Company put together an eleven-play, sixty-six-yard drive that ended when Mike Pruitt scored on a two-yard scamper around left end to put the Browns up 7-0 on their first first-quarter touchdown of the season. When the Seahawks answered with another impressive drive, the Cleveland defense again rose to the occasion. It stopped Seattle at the Cleveland ten and forced the home team to settle for a short Herrera field goal to cut the advantage to four. It would be the last time Seattle would threaten the Browns' lead.

Cleveland was forced to punt on the following series, and after another time-consuming Seattle drive near halftime it was clear that the Browns needed some kind of spark to prevent this game from turning into what had happened the previous Sunday against the Broncos. And just as was the case when the Browns needed a lift against Kansas City, Keith Wright entered stage right.

The Browns marched from their own nine to the Seattle thirty-nine thanks largely to fifteen- and sixteen-yard completions to Dave Logan and Ozzie Newsome respectively. From the thirty-nine Sipe took the snap and dropped back but was flushed from the pocket and started scrambling in the backfield. Wright was running a post pattern but seeing his quarterback in trouble changed his route and tried to get open where Sipe, now nearly fifteen yards behind the line of scrimmage, could see him. "I saw Brian scrambling and all I tried to do was get loose," Wright said afterward, "[and] find an open spot so he could get the ball to me."

Wright maneuvered to the Seattle thirty where Sipe hit him with a bullet pass. Wright then whirled around, dodged cornerback Cornell Webster going for the tackle, and headed toward the end zone. He made it inside the ten, but it wasn't until Ozzie Newsome came through with a key block that Wright's path was clear. Though Don Cockroft's extra point was blocked by defensive tackle Bill Cooke, the Browns led, 13-3, following Wright's third catch and third touchdown of the season. "Given a chance, somebody on this team will come up with a big play," Sipe said afterward. "There's a lot of talent around here, and all we need to do is give it a chance to surface."

The second half was more of the same. With the Browns' defense frustrating Zorn and the Seahawks, the visitors continued to pile up the points. On Cleveland's second possession Sipe hit Newsome down the left sideline for forty-four yards on third-and-ten to the Seattle four. A play later Charles White scored on a three-yard run to make it 20-3 with 6:45 remaining in the period. On the ensuing series the Seahawks drove to the Cleveland twenty where they faced fourth-and-one. Trailing by three scores Jack Patera opted to go for it. Robert L. Jackson crushed Jim Jodat for no gain, and the Browns took over.

After they moved to the Seattle twenty-two on seven efficient plays, including a twenty-six-yard Sipe completion to wide receiver Ricky Feacher on third-and-seven, Mike Pruitt rounded out the scoring when he exploded off right guard for a twenty-two-yard touchdown run to make it 27-3 with 13:20 remaining. There would be no nail-biter this week. At one point in the third quarter a Seattle defensive back walked up to Dave Logan. "You guys are beating the hell out of us," he told Logan. "I'll be glad when this one's over."

As expected Pruitt finally got the opportunity to shine. He carried the ball twenty-four times for 116 yards and two scores as the Browns' ground attack rolled up and down the Kingdome carpet, collecting 176 rushing yards. "Our defense was very aggressive, but we didn't tackle as well as in the last two games we played, although I guess Mike Pruitt was as responsible for that as anyone," Seattle head coach Patera said. "He ran as hard as any running back we have faced this season."

And just as Rutigliano had predicted the improved running game allowed Sipe to make even bigger plays. He completed only twelve of twenty-four passes but threw for 221 yards, connecting with seven different receivers. Sipe was not sacked as the offensive line, particularly Cody Risien, did a marvelous job.

But as impressive as the offense was it was the Cleveland defense that stole the show. For the second straight week Schottenheimer's crew did not allow a touchdown and came up with three critical stands that prevented the Seahawks from staying in the game. The first came in the second quarter when Seattle settled for its only field goal. Then the Browns stuffed the Seahawks on fourth-and-one from the Cleveland twenty in the third quarter. But the most impressive stand came early in the fourth when Zorn and the Seahawks had a first-and-goal from the Cleveland two. Jodat was stopped for no gain then Zorn was sacked on two straight plays, first by Alzado and then by rookie linebacker Clifton Odom, pushing Seattle back to the Cleveland nine. Zorn's fourth-down pass then fell incomplete, breaking a string of fifteen straight completions.

Clearly Seattle's offensive woes weren't because the Browns caught Zorn on a bad day. He completed twenty-three of his twenty-nine passes, mostly of the short-yardage dump-off variety, for 222 yards. The Cleveland defense simply rose to the occasion when it needed to and sacked Zorn five times, three by Alzado. "It was like we knew exactly what they were going to do," Alzado said. "Everything we did turned out right."

And it appeared as though the Browns had thrown everything in their playbook at the Seahawks. At various times during the game they used an eleven-man defensive line, something hardly ever seen in the NFL. The Browns also occasionally strayed from their 3-4 philosophy and went with four linemen. And to prevent Zorn from hooking up for any long gains to his receivers, namely dependable wideout Steve Largent, the Browns used a nickel defense, employing five defensive backs, on fifteen plays after using it just six times over the season's first five games. "We went into the nickel because of Zorn," Schottenheimer said. "We felt we could get pressure on him with four linemen. Once we got the lead, we made him throw it short." The Browns' unpredictable defensive attack plus nine Seattle penalties for sixty-four yards helped keep the Kingdome quiet.

"This is the best we've played collectively in the three years I've been here," Rutigliano said. "It's the first time we've put together fine performances by all three of our units—the offense, the defense, and the special teams. We got our butts kicked [by the media and fans] from Monday through Saturday, and came back, which shows the character of this team. It wasn't a matter of outsmarting the Seahawks. There were no wondrous ideas. We just outexecuted them."

Following that sentiment, the four defensive coaches: Schottenheimer, Dick MacPherson (linebackers), Dave Adolph (defensive line), and Len Fontes (back-field) all received game balls. And the Schottenheimer Score for the game? It was actually a little below acceptable with thirty-seven "wins" out of sixty-three plays or 59 percent. But no one was complaining.

"We played reasonably well, but it was not as good statistically as a lot of people might have thought," Schottenheimer said. "We were somewhat fortunate in that some things went our way. It was the reverse of what happened in our game with Denver."

"This is the defense that was so suspect going into the season," wrote *Plain Dealer* sports editor Hal Lebovitz. "I think it is safe to say (knock on wood) that it has come of age."

"Basically, we're starting to react right away to things now, rather than taking time to think about what to do," Dick Ambrose said. "That just takes time with a new system."

Although the win was exactly what the Browns needed there were a few dark clouds hanging over the victory parade, or more appropriately, a few knee injuries. Newsome and linebacker Bill Cowher both had banged-up knees and were questionable for Week Seven against Green Bay as were Reggie Rucker with a sore back and Wright with a hip pointer. But even more critical, Brian Sipe had gone down late in the fourth quarter on a freak play.

With 3:44 remaining and the Browns ahead 27-3, Sipe handed off to Mike Pruitt and then was hit on the outside of his right knee by Seattle linebacker Terry Beeson. The hit strained Sipe's knee ligaments, but he said he was lucky. Had he not seen Beeson out of the corner of his eye and started to move away Sipe's knee would have taken a harder hit, which probably would have torn the ligaments. Before the team even left Seattle it was questionable whether or not Sipe would play against the Packers.

But it was six days until they had to face Green Bay, and since the Browns had played at 4 P.M. Eastern Standard Time they already knew the good news from elsewhere in the division earlier that Sunday. The lowly Cincinnati Bengals had completed a shocking season-sweep of the defending world-champion Pittsburgh Steelers with a 17-16 win at Three Rivers Stadium. This victory combined with the Bengals' 30-28 win over Pittsburgh at Riverfront just three weeks before had football fans from coast-to-coast scratching their heads.

But as was the case with the earlier loss to the Bengals, the Steelers had a chance to win late. With four seconds to go Pittsburgh lined up for a thirty-nine-yard field-goal attempt that if successful would have won the game. But the Steelers' young kicker, Matt Bahr (spelled B-A-R-R in Monday's *Plain Dealer*), missed it. The Bengals had pulled off their first win ever at Three Rivers and broke Pittsburgh's eighteen-game home winning streak. Forrest Gregg said it was his greatest coaching victory. It had been a bad day for Bahr, who had already missed a forty-eight-yard attempt and had an extra point blocked, which turned out to be the difference.

It was now clear to all the football world that there was something seriously wrong with the Pittsburgh Steelers, who stood at 4-2. To lose to the Bengals once and on the road was one thing. But to lose to a now-2-4 team twice? And at Three Rivers? "Maybe we *are* fat," said Pittsburgh linebacker Jack Ham. "I can't put my finger on it, but we're not playing with the intensity we should. There is no question we're not playing complete football games. We're not dominating from the word 'go.'"

In defense of the Steelers wide receivers Lynn Swann (broken rib) and John Stallworth (broken leg) didn't play. The rest of the Pittsburgh offense did the best it could to give the game away, coughing up six fumbles and an interception. Actually it was a minor miracle that the Steelers were even in the contest come game's end as the Bengals took a 17-0 lead by halftime led by quarterback Ken Anderson. But after Anderson re-injured his knee, Jack Thompson again took over the reins in the second half.

This game also caused quite a stir in Cleveland. Since it was a doubleheader weekend for NBC, WKYC in Cleveland carried the Cincinnati-Pittsburgh game at 1:00 P.M. with the intention of switching to the Browns-Seahawks game promptly at 4:00 P.M. per NFL broadcast rules. So when the switch was flipped with 1:30 remaining in Pittsburgh and the Steelers driving, WKYC was flooded with angry phone calls, as was (for some reason) the *Plain Dealer*.

In case the Steelers losing wasn't enough good news the Oilers were tripped up as well, dropping a tight 21-20 decision to the Chiefs at Arrowhead Stadium despite a career-high 178 yards rushing by Earl Campbell. Kansas City quarterback Steve Fuller scrambled for a thirty-eight-yard touchdown run with 2:51 remaining to propel the home team to victory and drop the Oilers to 3-3, tied with the Browns for second.

Even the formerly glum media were suddenly excited about the Browns. "Hold everything," wrote the *PD*'s Russell Schneider. "The Kardiac Kids are not dead. And there is a race once again for the Central Division championship of the American Conference."

The Browns' players, though, maintained the confidence they'd shown all along. "We had to win this one today, and we did, which should tell you something about the character of this team," Sipe said. "Now we're back in the groove—and we're back in the race. It's very exciting for all of us."

Some of the excitement was waning by Tuesday as it appeared Sipe would not be able to play against Green Bay. He was diagnosed with a second-degree sprain and a slight ligament tear of the left knee and was unable to practice early in the week. He started wearing a custom-made knee brace, but as of Tuesday afternoon, it looked like rookie southpaw Paul McDonald would get his first NFL start.

While the Browns certainly wanted Sipe in the lineup if possible, everyone expressed confidence in McDonald, who hadn't thrown a pass in relief in Seattle but had completed thirteen of twenty-three passes for 197 yards in the preseason. The only people who would be directly affected by McDonald starting were quarterbacks coach Jim Shofner, who would call all the plays with Sipe out, and center Tom DeLeone, who would have to spin the ball a half-turn before snapping it to McDonald rather than the right-handed Sipe. But things looked better by Wednesday. Sipe was still unable to practice but could move around. Furthermore Rucker was listed as questionable while Newsome and Cowher were labeled probable.

If Sipe's knee was the most important development Cleveland sports fans were following, then the World Series was the second as it began that Tuesday night. The previous Friday the Kansas City Royals had completed a three-game sweep of the New York Yankees in the American League Championship Series, and the Philadelphia Phillies joined them on Sunday when they nipped the Houston Astros in Game Five of what had been a marvelous NLCS. The Phillies took Game One of the Fall Classic on Tuesday in Philadelphia.

Despite the status of Sipe's knee the Browns were still decisive favorites over the Packers at 7½ points and with good reason. At 2-3-1, the Packers were struggling and it appeared as though head coach Bart Starr's days were numbered in Wisconsin. The Pack was coming off a frustrating 14-14 tie with the Buccaneers in which it rolled up an astounding 569 yards of offense but couldn't parlay them into points.

In addition one of the Green Bay wins had been a gift in overtime on opening day when Packer kicker Chester Marcol had his potential game-winning field-goal attempt blocked by the Chicago Bears. As luck would have it the ball bounced right back into Marcol's arms, and he turned and ran around left end and into the end zone for the game-winning touchdown. But since then things had not been going well for the Packers, particularly not for aging veteran Lynn Dickey at quarterback as he had already thrown for eight interceptions in six games. Dickey would try to improve his fortunes against the Browns on his thirty-first birthday.

On Friday, Rutigliano said that the decision would be made at game time whether to go with Sipe or McDonald. After not practicing all week, on Saturday Sipe ran a few plays on the wet Cleveland Stadium turf prior to a high school football doubleheader. Though the field would be in poor shape for the Green Bay game the following day the good news was that the Indians' season was over and the dirt portion of the infield had been filled in with sod the week before. But local television viewers wouldn't get to see the new field. For the third straight home date the game was not a sellout, at least not in time to meet the NFL's blackout deadline.

Before the Browns even took the field to face the Packers some fans were already looking ahead to the following Sunday when the Steelers would come to town. Whether it was because the game was now a week away or because Pittsburgh suddenly looked vulnerable, the Terrible Towel "death notice" surfaced once again in the Sunday *Plain Dealer*, this time with a cartoon depicting Browns' players as pallbearers. LET'S SHOW THE STEELER FANS WHY CLEVELAND FANS ARE NUMBER ONE! the ad proclaimed and informed readers how they could get a "Bad Rag," the North Coast's version of a rally hankie.

The Browns certainly seemed worthy of their own brand of Terrible Towel in the first half as they coasted to a 10-0 lead over Green Bay with Sipe at the controls, which wasn't much of a surprise to anyone. The forty-first interception of

Thom Darden's career—setting a new team record—led to a forty-yard Cockroft field goal, then a one-yard Mike Pruitt touchdown run with 1:55 left in the half gave the Browns the ten-point intermission advantage.

Gimpy knee and all, Sipe took off on a twenty-four-yard scramble early in the second quarter. When he had an opportunity to step out of bounds without getting hit he instead put his head down and plowed ahead for three more yards. When Sipe returned to the sideline Rutigliano asked his quarterback what he was thinking, risking more damage to his knee. "I've got to play the game," Sipe told his coach. "I'm not talking about it now. I'm playing the game. That's how I play."

Rutigliano shrugged. "He knew better than I did," he would say later.

Sipe looked good and so did the Browns through the first two quarters, but just as was the case in the Denver game the Browns made a critical mistake deep in their opponents' territory late in the first half. With fifty-three seconds left in the second quarter Browns' linebacker Charlie Hall intercepted a deflected Dickey pass at the Green Bay forty-seven. On the next play Sipe hit Greg Pruitt over the middle for a forty-three-yard gain down to the four where the Browns would have a first-and-goal. Instead of trying to muscle into the end zone Rutigliano decided to try and get there through the air. "Because of the footing, we were not able to move the ball well on the ground," he said.

Sipe's first-down pass intended for Calvin Hill fell incomplete, as did his second-down toss for Newsome. Sipe hit his tight end on third down for three yards to the one, and Cleveland called time out with fourteen seconds left facing fourth-and-goal. Instead of going for the chip-shot field goal, Rutigliano opted to roll the dice. Expecting Green Bay to be looking for Mike Pruitt to get a handoff, the play called was a draw to Charles White. White was buried at the line of scrimmage for no gain and the Browns' lead remained 10-0 at the half.

"That was the big play," Greg Pruitt said afterward. "We had a chance to put them away. No, we shouldn't have kicked a field goal. Even if we take a field goal, they can score two touchdowns and they're back in the game. If we score a touchdown, we've got them down, 17-0. Right there is when an easy game became a hard game."

When asked why he opted to go for the touchdown instead of the sure three points, Rutigliano replied, "Because 20 points [with a touchdown] is more than 16 [with a field goal]." The math of his reasoning added up since the Browns' lead increased to 13-0 on their first possession of the third quarter on a forty-two-yard Cockroft field goal. So, yes, had the Browns scored a touchdown prior to halftime their lead would have been 20-0 six minutes into the third quarter, while if they had kicked the field goal their lead would have been just 16-0. But without question either of those scenarios was better than 13-0, and the Browns were about to find out why.

For starters things had gotten very ugly by the third quarter. With the Packers blitzing as much as possible to take advantage of Sipe's questionable knee, the Cleveland offensive line was on red-alert status. Sipe's bodyguards protected him well but didn't always keep their cool in the heat of battle. Tom DeLeone was particularly fiery on this day. He got into a fight with Green Bay defensive tackle Mike Lewis and earlier was flagged for unsportsmanlike conduct for screaming at an official after he was penalized for holding. "That's the worst call I've ever seen!" DeLeone shouted after his number was called. "You couldn't even referee a high school game!"

His strong opinion cost him fifteen more yards.

Then a play later Packers' defensive tackle, Charles Johnson, was ejected for flattening Sipe belatedly. Naturally Johnson thought he got a raw deal. "I think the officials were overprotective because he had been hurt," he said. "Maybe I should have been penalized, but not thrown out of the game."

"They should put dresses on the quarterbacks if they're going to call them like that," Packers' defensive end Ezra Johnson said in defense of his teammate. "The refs knew Sipe had a knee problem and were trying to protect him. They called it because the play was close to the Cleveland bench and guys on the sidelines were screaming."

Charles Johnson also had some choice words about the Cleveland offensive line. "You can't believe what the offensive line of the Browns got away with today," he said after the game. "There were so many cheap shots, cutting from behind, that sort of thing. They are the worst dudes I ever played against, not just one of them—everyone. I don't usually complain because I know that football is a rough game, but this was too much to take."

The Browns' linemen agreed—that it was too much to take. "There was some dirty play on the line—on their part," DeLeone said and added that the Browns didn't so much lose their poise as they were forced to defend themselves. Once Johnson was tossed, DeLeone said, it was a clean game.

For example DeLeone said that on the holding penalty for which he was also given a side dish of an unsportsmanlike conduct foul, Johnson had grabbed DeLeone's facemask right after he snapped the ball and pulled the Browns' center to the ground. Henry Sheppard also testified to Johnson's dirty play as he defended his own personal-foul penalty. Sheppard said he was standing up for himself after Johnson tried to kick him while he was down. Sheppard added he'd already seen Johnson kick Robert L. Jackson in the face in a special-teams scrum. "It was your typical back-alley brawl on the line of scrimmage," Sheppard said. "Nothing big."

But the player who may have suffered the most from Johnson's ferocious play was Sipe, who injured his ribs on the play that earned Johnson a free pass to the locker room. If Green Bay's defensive game plan was to hurt Sipe and fluster the Cleveland offensive line, it worked nearly to perfection, and even with Johnson gone things started to click for the Packers in the third quarter.

A personal-foul penalty on Robert L. Jackson and a thirty-one-yard Dickey–to–wide receiver–James Lofton pass set up the Packers' first score, a seven-yard touchdown scamper by Dickey, which made it 13-7, Browns, with just under five minutes to play in the third quarter. It was the first touchdown the Cleveland defense had allowed in ten quarters. On the Browns' first snap following the Green Bay kickoff Mike Pruitt fumbled and Packers' linebacker John Anderson recovered at the Cleveland twenty-nine. Suddenly the visitors were very much back in it.

Five plays later running back Gerry Ellis scored on a one-yard plunge. After having been dominated throughout the first half and early third quarter, Green Bay was now in control. In just over three minutes the Packers had gone from trailing 13-0 to leading 14-13. And things would get worse for the Browns.

They drove to the Green Bay forty on their next possession but were forced to punt. After Clarence Scott stuffed Packers' running back Terdell Middleton for a three-yard loss on first down at the Green Bay twenty, Middleton was tripped up after a two-yard gain on second, which should have set up third-and-eleven at the nineteen. But Jerry Wilkinson was flagged for being offsides, and even worse the Browns were penalized for an unorthodox sideline infraction.

League rules stated that the coaches must stay two yards off the sideline and the players must stay two yards behind them. The officials gave the Browns three warnings before throwing a flag, which resulted in a fifteen-yard unsportsmanlike conduct penalty. During the last warning Rutigliano replied, "Look, why don't you just officiate the game and forget about the sidelines." If it sounds like a ridiculous penalty, it is, but it's only an infraction noticed if the players and coaches on the sideline are being particularly boisterous and vocally criticizing the officials. "My philosophy is that no judgment call that has nothing to do with the field of play should be made that can have something to do with the outcome of the game," Rutigliano said afterward. He added that with the rain that had swept through Cleveland during the week, the painted sideline markings had been almost entirely washed away.

One Brown who may have actually benefited from the lack of boundaries, thanks to the invisible sideline markings, was injured defensive tackle Jerry Sherk, who spent the afternoon on the Browns' sideline working on his second profession: photography.

Moments after the bizarre penalty that gave Green Bay a first down at its own thirty-seven the Packers extended their lead when Dickey hit Lofton—who was eating Browns' cornerback Clinton Burrell for lunch—for a twenty-six-yard touchdown pass. Tom Birney's extra point gave the Packers a comfortable two-score lead at 21-13 with 7:23 to play. Victory was in their grasp. But the Green Bay Pack-ers were about to make their acquaintance with the Kardiac Kids.

Ten seconds later Sipe dropped back to pass at the Cleveland thirty-one. He spotted Calvin Hill open on the right sideline and hit him at the Cleveland forty-five. Hill then slipped multiple tackles and was off to the races, weaving his way through the Green Bay secondary like a magician. Packer cornerback Estus Hood finally caught up with him and pushed him out of bounds at the Green Bay nine after a fifty-yard gain. The Browns had relit the pilot light. "That thing to Hill was a thing of beauty," Sipe said. "I was just hoping for a 15-yard gain. How he ever turned up the sideline I'll never know. Calvin's play ignited us."

On the next play Sipe found a wide-open Ozzie Newsome in the end zone for a nineteen-yard touchdown pass and Shazam! In a mere twenty-eight seconds the Browns had cut the lead to 21-20. "The pass to Calvin Hill ignited us," Sipe said, "and then when I hit Ozzie Newsome, I knew all we had to do was get the ball back and we'd win."

It was time for the Browns' defense to make a stop. The Packers took over at their own sixteen with 6:55 to play and did their best to run out the clock while moving the ball. Dickey hit Lofton on the sideline for ten yards on first down, then for fifteen more a play later to the Green Bay forty-two. The Browns ap-peared to be in good shape when the Packers faced third-and-thirteen from the thirty-nine a moment later, but Middleton scampered over right tackle for fifteen yards and a first down at the Cleveland forty-six with less than three minutes to play. The Browns' defense stood tall and forced Green Bay into third-and-seven at the forty-three with just over two minutes remaining. If Green Bay converted the Browns would have virtually no chance to win the game.

Dickey pitched to running back Eddie Lee Ivery who successfully turned around right end and appeared destined for a first down. But Robert L. Jackson and Charlie Hall recovered quickly and dragged him down one yard short of the marker. After the Green Bay punt the Browns took over at their own thirteen with 1:53 remaining.

Sipe hit Hill again, this time for a fifteen-yard gain, then scrambled for nine more to the Cleveland thirty-seven and in the process injured his left wrist. With 1:03 to play Mike Pruitt scampered for eleven yards to the Cleveland forty-eight, and after a time out Sipe hit Hill for sixteen more to the Green Bay thirty-six. Sipe then maneuvered out of the pocket and scrambled for a fourteen-yard gain to the twenty-two with forty-two seconds remaining, and it appeared as though the Browns had marched into Cockroft's field-goal range. But a yellow hankie on the ground halted everything.

Cody Risien was called for holding, and the Browns were penalized back to the Green Bay forty-six where it would be first-and-twenty. Suddenly the red-hot Cleveland offense fizzled like an Alka-Seltzer. Sipe's first-down pass intended for

Dave Logan fell incomplete, as did his next intended for Mike Pruitt. Now only twenty-five seconds remained, and the Browns needed at least fifteen yards to have a decent shot at a field goal. As the Browns came to the line of scrimmage for the critical third-down play—which was designed for Sipe to throw to Rucker over the middle—the Browns' quarterback couldn't believe his eyes.

"Everybody was coming, they were throwing the kitchen sink at us," Sipe said. "I just wanted to get us to the 30, that was the magic number, so that we could kick a field goal. But when I saw them dig in, I couldn't believe it."

The Packers were preparing to blitz the house on third-and-twenty.

Sipe looked over to his right where six-foot-four Logan was lined up on five-foot-eleven rookie cornerback Mark Lee. Sipe nodded. Logan nodded back. The Packers, not to mention the other nine Browns on the field, had no idea that the play had just been changed.

Sipe took the snap, dropped seven steps back, and then simply lobbed the ball downfield toward Logan. It was, as everyone agreed later, a "basketball pass." "I didn't want to lead Dave," Sipe said afterward. "I just wanted to throw it high and let him come back for it. I just wanted him to rebound."

Lee was running stride-for-stride with Logan, but the ball was underthrown. "I wanted him to be even with me," Logan said. "I looked back and at the last instant I cut back inside and jumped over him, really."

Logan, whose hoops abilities could have landed him in the NBA, recognized the situation a split-second before Lee did. He stopped in his tracks and leapt sideways behind Lee to catch the football at the Green Bay nineteen. "All I tried to do is get the ball at the peak of my jump," Logan said. "I don't think the defensive back timed his jump real well because I got to the ball first. I felt somebody grab my leg right after I caught the ball, but I wasn't about to be pulled down."

Lee staggered backward as Logan landed and took off running. Lee couldn't recover in time as Logan ran untouched into the end zone with sixteen seconds to play.

Cleveland Stadium nearly exploded.

All 75,548 fans went absolutely crazy as Logan literally skipped across the goal line at the open end of the field. He didn't have long to enjoy his moment of success before he was swarmed by his teammates in the end zone. "I almost passed out because I was getting mobbed," Logan admitted later. "I thought, 'Oh, no, don't let me get hurt here. It's going to be a hard thing to explain on Monday.'"

Cockroft's extra-point attempt sailed wide left, but nobody seemed to care. By the time Robert L. Jackson intercepted Dickey's desperation pass at the Cleveland forty-three to officially cap the victory a few moments later, Browns fans everywhere were delirious with joy following their team's 26-21 win. Without question it was one of the most exciting victories in franchise history.

As they celebrated some in the near-delirious crowd began chanting, "Bring on the Steelers!"

This win—and more importantly the fashion in which it came—seemed to make converts out of anyone left who didn't believe in the Kardiac Kids. "That's when I started to think fate was on our side," Joe DeLamielleure would say. "That never should have happened. In all the years I played, I never saw anybody go to an all-out blitz when you're ahead in that situation. It was ridiculous."

Even more ridiculous to some was how the Browns could go from playing so poorly to playing so well in such a short period of time. "We did everything in the world to lose, and then we did everything in the world to win," Rutigliano said after the game. "But I'll take the victory." Particularly after all looked bleak at the midpoint of the fourth quarter with the Browns trailing 21-13.

"I definitely felt it slipping away a little, and I won't say I didn't think 'What if,' a few times because it would have been such a shame to lose," Sipe said as he took turns soaking his knee, elbow, and ribs. "The old magic was there. This team has been through too much to let a game like this slip away."

It was hard to believe that Sipe had been playing injured. He completed twenty-four of thirty-nine passes for a career-high 391 yards, just ten yards short of the team record set by Otto Graham twenty-eight years before.

The Browns and Packers provided an interesting passing converse. James Lofton was everything for Green Bay's passing attack, snagging eight passes for 136 of Dickey's 230 passing yards. Sipe picked up his yards via a smorgasbord of targets. His leading receiver was Calvin Hill, who caught five passes for ninety-four yards. Sipe also hit Rucker five times for eighty-one yards, Mike Pruitt six times for sixty-one, and Newsome five times for sixty.

"He is a real pro, an exceptional quarterback," Bart Starr said of Sipe. "There was no doubt in my mind that he would play, and we were prepared for him. That Sipe is something special."

Lee would certainly attest to that. He hid in the showers and then the training room for a long time before finally facing the inevitable gaggle of reporters that wanted to hear his version of what happened on the game-winning play. When he appeared his eyes were red and he kept blowing his nose, telltale signs of the emotional duress he was experiencing. "I thought I had a chance to make the interception," he said. "I didn't play it right. I should have stayed behind him."

One reporter offered Lee a way out when he asked if Logan had pushed off. "If he did, I didn't notice it," Lee responded sincerely. "I realized too late that the ball was slightly underthrown. He just beat me." Sensing a comrade at the end of his rope, many of Lee's teammates began yelling at the reporters to back off and give him air.

But it really wasn't entirely Lee's fault. In retrospect the Packers' decision to blitz a veteran quarterback on third-and-long in the final minute was far too risky.

But Starr disagreed. "There's no way I'd ever second-guess a defensive call such as that," he said. "There was nothing wrong with calling a blitz, but it was very tough on the young man."

"When Brian nodded, I knew he was coming to me," Logan said. "There's no set play. Brian and I are timed in. He throws it to me and I go up and get it."

As miraculous as the last-second victory seemed, Doug Dieken had it all figured out. "I'll tell you why we came back and won the game," he said referring to a team party Art Modell was throwing afterward. "He sent word that if we didn't win it would be BYOB. You know all the liquor stores are closed on Sundays."

But as the players began filtering out of the Stadium to head over to the party Rutigliano issued them a warning. "After the game I told them to enjoy themselves at their party because I'm going to chew them out Monday," he said. "We lost control of ourselves and several penalties that were called for retaliation were extremely harmful. They could have cost us the game." In all the Browns were flagged for five unsportsmanlike-conduct or personal-foul penalties.

Many members of the media were doing their own chewing out of Rutigliano in Monday's editions, criticizing his ill-fated fourth-down decision late in the first half. Had it not been for Logan's jump ball the Browns would have lost by one point. How important would that field goal have been then?

"There was only one intelligent, percentage call to make," wrote Hal Lebovitz in the *Plain Dealer*:

FIELD GOAL. I don't care if the touchdown attempt would have been successful. Pro football is a numbers game. Don't be shut out when you get that close to the goal line.

To hell with what the crowd wants, Sam. The fans always like to live dangerously. But the coach should know better. Get the points, play the numbers game every time.

I'm making a big point of the highly questionable strategy because the same situation is going to come up again and somehow, someway it must be driven home to Sam that he can't walk away from a situation like that with NO points.

Bob Sudyk likened the Browns to an old joke about a man who tried to kill himself. He tries to do it in multiple fashions and is unsuccessful every time. He finally gives up and decides to accept his life as it is. The next day he inherits a million dollars. "Somehow, this team is able to reach back for something extra— usually a holding penalty," he wrote. "I mean this is Group Goof."

"Fans continue to search for reasons why the Browns, under Rutigliano, continue to win and lose nail-biters," he went on to say. "It seems to be a combination of Sam's sideline decisions and play-calling and endless penalties committed by the linemen."

At the same time, Sudyk praised Sipe for his poise under pressure. He called him "Clint Eastwood in pads," "like a guy who is going to the electric chair calmly because he is computing the voltage likely to be pulled," and "a man relaxed in a burning building because he knows his body's kindling point."

The win, which Lebovitz said, "they may have deserved on backbone but not on brains," allowed the Browns to remain tied with Houston, which held off Tampa Bay in the fourth quarter for a 20-14 win in the Astrodome. Earl Campbell rolled up 203 yards on thirty-three carries behind the Oilers' new double-tight end set with Mike Barber and former Oakland tight end Dave Casper, just picked up off waivers the previous week.

The Bengals meanwhile won their second straight and appeared to be coming together at 3-4. They shut out the Minnesota Vikings at Riverfront, 14-0, behind 270 passing yards from Ken Anderson and 115 rushing yards by fullback Pete Johnson. It was the first time the Vikings had been shut out in seven years. As the season neared its midpoint it was becoming clear that the AFC Central not only had two of the best teams in football but also was one of the toughest divisions, top-to-bottom, in the NFL.

And now, of course, the Browns would prepare for their biggest game of the season to date. Though the Steelers were still licking their wounds from the Cincinnati sweep no one in Cleveland had any doubt that the defending champions would come ready to play.

"Most assuredly we'll have to play better next week if we want to win," Logan said after the Green Bay victory. "If we had lost this one, it would have made it hard to get up for Pittsburgh next week, but that won't be the case now."

In fact some felt it was the Steelers who might have a hard time getting up for the Browns, especially since they would have a short week after hosting another bitter rival, the Oakland Raiders, on Monday night.

Without a doubt the 1980 Browns were starting to discover what it was like to be a playoff team: no matter how big your last game was your next one is even bigger. Or when it's the Pittsburgh Steelers, it's immeasurable.

"I salute the whole Cleveland team," Bart Starr said after the Browns' victory. "The Browns did it when they had to." They would have to do it again to defeat their archrivals and stay alive in what was quickly becoming a bitter division race.

"Hey Logan," Sipe hollered as his teammate prepared to leave the locker room for the party that Sunday night. "I've got to believe we're magic!" he said in reference to a popular Olivia Newton-John song besieging the radio airwaves that fall.

The magic was just beginning.

5 · Torn Curtain

Two days after the Browns' victory over the Packers many were still talking about the ferocity of the contest. Henry Sheppard said that Green Bay's tactics were "the roughest and dirtiest since the way Pittsburgh played us a few years ago."

And thus began the first Browns-Steelers week of 1980.

Cleveland Stadium had been sold out for this game for months, the eighteenth straight time that a Browns-Steelers contest was a sellout. Pittsburgh backers, donned in their traditional black-and-yellow gear, would fill a good portion of the 80,000 seats. About a thousand would be coming by the rails through a promotional package sponsored by a Pittsburgh radio station. For $68.00, Steelers' fans got a ticket to the game as well as a round-trip seat on a steam train owned by the B&O Historical Group. They called it the City of Championship Train. All told, about 15,000 Steelers fans would make the trek, and appropriately Stadium security would be nearly doubled.

Those Pittsburgh natives would enter hostile territory. The year before, when the Steelers came to Cleveland, several Pittsburgh fans planning on attending the game stayed at a Sheraton Inn in Beachwood that Saturday night. When they woke up Sunday morning they discovered all the cars in the parking lot with Pennsylvania license plates had their tires slashed. "I remember people telling me, 'We don't care if you don't win another game all year,'" said Cody Risien. "That was the mentality. They hated the Steelers."

Days before, the impact of the upcoming game began to sink in on those who had played in Browns-Steelers games before. "I could sense it as soon as the guys started coming in this morning," Browns' equipment manager Chuck Cusick said that Wednesday. "Everybody seemed more intense, more anxious. It was easy to tell this is the biggest week of the season for us."

"In your first Browns-Steelers week, you began to get educated in the history of the series," Risien said. "That's all the players, the coaches, and the media could talk about. There were all kinds of colorful stories about the Steeler game."

"You were indoctrinated as a young Browns' player to hate Pittsburgh," Dick Ambrose said.

Appropriately throughout practice all week Lyle Alzado would suddenly start shouting, "War! War!" Former Wolverine Thom Darden compared the Browns-Steelers rivalry to the Ohio State-Michigan one.

"The week we were going to play Pittsburgh was like in the 1940s and 1950s with Notre Dame and Southern Cal," Sam Rutigliano said. "It was a big, big game. Even though Cincinnati was important and Houston was important and all the rest of them were important, we played and prepared differently."

"As a rookie I wasn't really aware of it," Doug Dieken said. "But when they started winning Super Bowls, I was like, 'OK, I'm sick of hearing this crap.' They were a darned good football team. They probably had the best defense the NFL has ever seen."

It was a rivalry that dealt with more than just football teams. The cities of Cleveland and Pittsburgh were both heavy industrial towns with economies fueled by a blue-collar workforce. "Pittsburgh and Cleveland are almost clones," Rutigliano said. "From an ethnic, from a historical, and from a traditional standpoint—with the tremendous diversity and the people who followed those teams for years—they're very, very much alike."

"When you have people who share similar passions," Darden said, "such as drinking beer and being crazy, and you put that in a football stadium, it's combustible. I always said I was so glad I was playing because I wouldn't want to be in the stands. That was the worst place to be in that game."

"Every team has its rival," Joe DeLamielleure said, "but the difference here was that there were more fights in the stands than there were on the field."

Fighting through the recession of the 1970s both cities endured a rough decade in terms of growth and economics and had little to boast of. The Steelers had responded with four Super Bowl titles in six years, giving natives of Pittsburgh something to turn their attention away from the steel mills closing to take advantage of cheaper labor overseas. Plus the baseball Pirates had a prosperous decade, winning six division titles and a pair of world championships, with the first coming in 1971. But even more memorable was 1979 when, with Sister Sledge's disco anthem "We Are Family" playing in the background, the Pirates rallied from a three-games-to-one deficit to win a thrilling World Series over the Baltimore Orioles in seven games.

Cleveland on the other hand couldn't enjoy the luxury of sports success. The Indians and Cavaliers were regularly the laughing stock of their respective leagues. And the Browns, once donned "the New York Yankees of football," had failed to make the playoffs in seven years.

And all the while it had been essentially the same cast of characters for the Browns, matching up against the Steelers as the latter grew into the league's best team. "They basically had the same 11 guys on defense and we basically had the same 11 guys on offense for a good seven or eight years, which was unusual," Dieken said. "You really got to know and hate one another."

Cleveland was starved for a winner, and while it would take time for a dynasty like the Steelers' to develop, the natives of Northeast Ohio would settle for a short-term solution that week: beat the Steelers on Sunday.

It had been four years since the Browns had defeated Pittsburgh, and the Steelers had dropped seven consecutive losses on their rust-belt rivals. "I knew that if we were going to [win the division]," Sam Rutigliano said, "we were going to have to go through Pittsburgh. We knew we had to split."

But early in the week it was becoming more and more evident that the Steelers were ripe for the plucking. On Monday night at home against the Oakland Raiders the Steelers were picked apart, 45-34, to drop to 4-3 on the season. The score alone suggested this was not the same "Steel Curtain" defense that had led the team to back-to-back Super Bowl championships. In reality it wasn't. The Steelers were as banged up as they had ever been during their golden years, particularly on offense. They faced the Raiders without the services of wide receivers John Stallworth and Lynn Swann and running back Franco Harris; additionally quarterback Terry Bradshaw was forced out of the game twice. He first departed in the second quarter with a bruised shoulder and was replaced by backup Cliff Stoudt but returned in the second half. Bradshaw was then knocked out for good when he jammed his thumb in the fourth quarter, an injury that appeared might keep him out of the Browns' game.

Defensively the Steelers were better off but without their anchor, linebacker Jack Lambert, who left in the first quarter with a knee injury. Without his presence to contend with, Oakland quarterback Jim Plunkett, himself a replacement for injured Jim Pastorini, threw for three touchdown passes as the Raiders improved their record on *Monday Night Football* to an amazing 14-1-1. The loss dropped the Steelers into a three-way tie for first in the AFC Central with the Browns and Oilers, and while no one was panicking yet in Pittsburgh, there was still major reason for concern.

Following the loss to the Raiders a reporter asked Pittsburgh coach Chuck Noll if the Steelers' backs were against the wall. "I would say that's probably as good a description as you can find," Noll replied. "You might take a different piece of anatomy that might be more descriptive."

Steelers' fans were quick to point to the 1976 team, which lost four of its first five games, then won its final nine to capture the division and once again reach the AFC Championship. But there were questions floating about the Steelers' desire not being as insatiable as it had been as a result of winning four Super Bowls.

With Halloween just around the corner the *Cleveland Press* turned to superstition and omens to allay fans' fears of defeat. Though strained, the paper said there were several similarities between that week's contest and the last time the Browns had defeated the Steelers on October 10, 1976:

1. Both teams had the same records in 1976 at 1-3. They were now both 4-3.
2. The Steelers entered the 1976 game also having just lost on a Monday night.
3. The Steelers entered the 1976 game having lost two straight, as they did in 1980, and hadn't lost three straight since then.
4. The Steelers entered the 1976 game having won the previous two Super Bowls. They entered the 1980 game also having won the previous two Super Bowls.
5. The Steelers entered the 1976 game with Terry Bradshaw ailing, just as he was now.
6. Due to injury the Steelers started two new offensive guards in the 1976 game: Sam Davis and Mike Webster. Due to injury the Steelers would start two new guards in the 1980 game: Craig Wolfley and Tyrone McGriff.
7. As the Steelers prepared to battle the Browns in 1976 Jimmy Carter was fighting for his life in a presidential race less than one month from election day. The same was true in 1980.

Omens or not, Browns' fans hadn't forgotten that gray October day in 1976 when Brian Sipe was KO'd and backup Dave Mays entered the game to lead the Browns to a come-from-behind 18-16 victory. Despite the win over the defending world champions the game would always be remembered for the hit Browns' defensive end Turkey Jones put on Bradshaw. Jones, who claimed not to have heard the whistle blow the play dead, picked Bradshaw up off the ground and spiked him on his head. It was a truly frightening moment as Bradshaw lay on the ground with his legs twitching. Luckily it was just a spinal concussion, but Bradshaw, like Sipe, spent the night in the hospital.

The Steelers hadn't forgot Jones's hit either, even four years later. In 1976 Jack Lambert had said Jones deserved to get his neck broken for what he had done to Bradshaw. Though Lambert wouldn't play against the Browns in the teams' first meeting of 1980, the spirit of his words would be evident.

Regardless of motivation and injury the Browns knew victory would not come easy—especially if the Browns were too pumped up to play their archrival in what would be the biggest game of the season to date. "It can hurt you to want to win too badly if it interferes with your preparation," explained Brian Sipe. "I'd rather see things on an even keel. We'll all be high, that's for sure. But in terms of preparation, it's important to keep everything in perspective and we will. All we need to beat that team is a good blend of our offensive, defensive, and special teams, a good coordinated effort."

Some hypothesized that that's what had been happening in some of the Browns' previous losses to Pittsburgh in recent years. The two meetings in 1979 seemed to back up that thinking: in Cleveland in October the Steelers roared out to a 27-0 lead and held off a furious Browns' comeback in the second half for a 51-35 win. In Pittsburgh a month later the Browns led by ten with five minutes to play, but the Steelers rallied to tie it and send it to overtime where a Matt Bahr field goal won it, 33-30.

"We thought we could beat Pittsburgh every time we stepped on the field with them," Tom DeLeone said. "They had their weaknesses, but we had to play well."

"I've always thought of them as a super football team, but I think they're beatable," Sipe said, referring to the close calls the Browns had experienced with Pittsburgh in recent years. "I always thought so."

One factor from the losses in 1979 that was cause for optimism in Browns' camp that week was that the Browns had not had much trouble scoring on the heralded Pittsburgh defense. Now the Steelers' attack looked even weaker. Another bonus was that the Steelers used the 4-3 alignment, which the Browns had chewed up and spit out in Seattle. But the Browns kept reminding themselves that Pittsburgh is Pittsburgh. "I think if the Steelers lined up in a 2-9 defense, they'd give us trouble," quipped Sam Rutigliano.

As promised the Browns' coach did give his team an earful following their bouquet of penalties against the Packers, pointing out they could not afford those kinds of mental mistakes with the Steelers. "The biggest thing we should have done was kept our mouths shut and play football," Rutigliano said. "Against Green Bay, we won a split decision, but if we play the same way against Pittsburgh, it will end in a first-round TKO."

The condition of Sipe's knee was also questioned early in the week, but everything appeared to be fine. Rutigliano likened Sipe to an old story about former Browns' quarterback Otto Graham, who got socked in the mouth in the first half of a game and had thirty stitches put in at halftime. But Graham never doubted he would return for the second half and led the Browns to a victory, claiming he didn't have to play with his mouth.

Usually Browns-Steelers week is enough to carry the interest of Clevelanders from Sunday to Sunday. But this week there was a lot going on. For starters on Tuesday the Philadelphia Phillies won their first championship as they defeated the Kansas City Royals, 4-1, in Game Six of the 1980 World Series, bringing Major League Baseball's season to a close. But even more important to the city of Cleveland was the announcement by the League of Women Voters that Jimmy Carter and Ronald Reagan would debate in Cleveland the following Tuesday, just one week before the election. The format was still being ironed out at the time, as was the exact site, but by midweek area department stores were already selling debate t-shirts as if it were a concert.

Against this backdrop Browns' fans still managed to keep an eye on the news coming out of Pittsburgh concerning the health of the key Steelers. By Tuesday it was official that Stallworth, Swann, and offensive guards Steve Courson and Ray Pinney would not play. Lambert was also ruled out, and his replacement would be Dennis "Dirt" Winston. Franco Harris, who had missed the Raider game with a strained knee, and fellow running back Sidney Thornton, out with a bruised shoulder, were both listed as probable. And most important of all Terry Bradshaw said he would definitely play against the Browns. Steeler coaches and officials weren't so sure.

Though his team was as healthy as it had been all year, Rutigliano had his own problems in preparing for Pittsburgh. Namely, how to keep his team from becoming complacent by thinking they would win easily since the Steelers were so banged up. "If we don't beat the damned Steelers this time," said Browns' general manager Peter Hadhazy, "we might never beat them."

Still the Browns had to be cautious of provoking a wounded animal. The Steelers, who hadn't lost three straight games in four years, knew what was on the line Sunday. "We have to win in Cleveland," said Pittsburgh wide receiver Jim Smith, who had prospered with Swann and Stallworth out. "There are no two ways about it. It's plain and simple, we have to win and we all realize it."

Some figured it might come down to the Browns' mental approach to the game and how they dealt with the Pittsburgh injuries during the week. After all, the most recent injuries were just a continuation of what had gone on all year for Pittsburgh, which by that Sunday would see fourteen players miss a combined total of thirty-eight games in 1980.

"Stallworth and Swann are super receivers, and if you ask me if I would rather play against Stallworth and Swann, there's no way I could say I would," Rutigliano said sincerely. "Sure, they're 4-3, but they could put things together and go right on. Do you think something's wrong and they've slipped? Not that team. They'll be tough as hell on Sunday."

Thom Darden looked at it from another point of view. "To tell you the truth," he said, "I'd rather play against Pittsburgh's regular team, with Swann and Stallworth in the lineup, along with anybody else who's injured now, so that, if we beat them, they won't have any excuses."

"The players realize this is Pittsburgh," Rutigliano added, "and if you're going to the Super Bowl, the first tollbooth along the way is through Pittsburgh. So I am sure the players are very excited."

For the first time in years there was serious talk of the Super Bowl and the Browns in the same sentence. A win over the Steelers would officially register the Browns in the electorate of championship contenders. Accordingly the entire nation was turning its eyes to Cleveland not only for the upcoming debate but also for the game. WNBC-TV in New York City even announced that it decided to broadcast the Browns-Steelers game instead of the New York Giants-Denver Broncos contest. It was already Cleveland's biggest week of the year.

And then Charles White vanished.

At 9:30 A.M. Wednesday the rookie running back phoned Browns' headquarters and told a secretary he had overslept and would be late for practice, which had already begun. But instead of showing up late White never showed up at all. When practice was over the Browns tried to reach him at his Strongsville condominium with no success.

"I don't know where he is and I have no idea when he will be back," Rutigliano told the press. It wasn't the first time something like this had happened under Rutigliano's regime. The year before, defensive end Mike St. Clair had walked out of practice one day and returned the next. He was fined $500.

"It's unfortunate because White has been doing great in every department," Rutigliano said. "Talent is important, but dependability is critical. You miss a Wednesday or Thursday and you miss 40 to 50 percent of the game plan. And Pittsburgh is a tough team to prepare for." More than just concerned over a player skipping practice Browns' officials were worried White might have been in an accident or that something serious had happened.

Rumors swirled. One player mentioned that White had been depressed after being replaced by Calvin Hill in the Packer game. Another source said that White simply overslept and was too embarrassed to show up late to practice. Some assumed White had flown back to California to see his girlfriend, but even she didn't know where he was. In fact she called Paul McDonald, White's former USC teammate, and had him go to White's condo looking for him.

This marked the third time in five months White had up and disappeared. He had walked out of the Browns' rookie mini-camp in May because he wasn't officially signed yet. Then, following the Browns' loss in New England in the season opener, White had asked Rutigliano if he could drive to the airport with a friend and not ride the bus with the team. Rutigliano said okay, but White missed the plane and was absent from a light practice the following day. When he returned Rutigliano quietly fined him. The entire episode wasn't reported to the media for two months and even then Art Modell and Peter Hadhazy confessed they'd never heard about it. But this most recent disappearance was something else altogether. Even one of White's agents, a Los Angeles attorney named Mike Flanagan, didn't know where he was.

The *Cleveland Press* went on an all-out search for him all day Wednesday with no success. Finally early Thursday morning the *Press* reached White at home. The rookie running back had no real excuse. "It was just a mistake, a bad mistake," he said. "I just woke up late and I thought it was too late to show up. I didn't have any reason. It was just a mistake in not showing up.

"I didn't feel right about showing up late."

White, who said he overslept because he forgot to turn his alarm clock on, said he had been home all day. No one could reach him because he turned his telephone off.

Twenty-three hours after his last contact with the team White showed up in Rutigliano's office. He told his coach he had made a mistake and that he was sorry. "Everything has been resolved and I'm ready for Pittsburgh now," White told reporters. "Anything else you'll have to get from Sam."

But when their meeting was over even the coach said he didn't know exactly where White had been. The only thing Rutigliano really knew was that White would be fined an undisclosed amount. "If I thought the Cleveland Browns were wasting their time with White," Rutigliano said, "that we couldn't help him and he couldn't help us, I would have suspended him, not fined him."

Though not specifying the amount of the fine, Rutigliano said it would be more than St. Clair was fined the year before.

More than just the money White appeared to have also lost any hopes of starting on Sunday. Greg Pruitt was finally ready to return to active duty status as the one-year anniversary of his knee injury neared. Still Rutigliano said White would play against the Steelers.

The next question on everyone's minds was how disruptive White's day off was to the rest of the team. As it turned out, not very. "The only disruptive aspect of it is the attention it's getting," Calvin Hill said. "Everybody is trying to make more of it than there's in it. At this stage of the season, missing a day of work won't hurt, not even by a rookie. I've seen it a lot before, and there's no real harm done to the team. It's no big deal."

In fact when White did return to practice on Thursday he was not punished or isolated by his teammates but teased. "Most of us didn't even know White was missing until half the workout was over," said linebacker Charlie Hall. "But the kind of money Charlie is making, we knew he'd be back soon."

Through it all the Browns continued to prepare for the Steelers. Meanwhile, 137 miles away in Pennsylvania, Pittsburgh's injury status was becoming clearer.

Despite his pledge to the contrary, by week's end it looked like Bradshaw wouldn't play and that Oberlin native and Youngstown State grad Cliff Stoudt would get the start against the Browns, with the Pittsburgh offense being limited accordingly. It was reported that Franco Harris *would* play, and even if he wasn't 100 percent it was bad news for Cleveland. Harris had a history of eating the Browns for breakfast, gaining 1,454 yards and fourteen touchdowns, including seven one-hundred-yard rushing games in his career against Cleveland.

Still the mounting injuries started swinging the oddsmakers back toward the Browns. The Steelers were still favored going into the weekend, but instead of the five-point spread Las Vegas had laid down on Tuesday, it had shrunk to 3½.

The point spread wasn't the only thing that had changed during the week. By Friday Rutigliano seemed to have taken on a new personality. During his weekly phone interview with members of the press covering the opposing team it was obvious that this was not the same Rutigliano that the writers had dealt with in the past. He wasn't joking and tossing them one-liners as he usually did. This behavior, wrote Phil Musick of the *Pittsburgh Post-Gazette*, "led to the immediate suspicion that Sam finally has himself a football team."

As the warmth departed from Rutigliano's temperament, it also vacated Northeast Ohio when a weekend cold front swept through. The forecast for Sunday was a high of forty-three degrees with the possibility of pre-Halloween snow flurries on the lakefront. But the snow stayed away, and instead a slow and steady cold autumn rain soaked the Stadium turf on that dark Sunday afternoon.

The rivalry was stirred even before kickoff as Browns' and Steelers' fans crossed paths outside the ballpark. Pittsburgh rooters, feeling confident as only fans can who have seen their team beat another seven straight times, hollered chants and sang songs about their team as they trekked toward the Stadium. "Kardiac Kids? Hell, yes," one fan yelled at a group of tailgating Browns' backers. "If they ever beat us, half this town will have a heart attack."

Even before the game began extra security was on red alert. "All the drunks from Cleveland and Pittsburgh are here," said Cleveland Police Lt. William Stilnack, "but our drunks at least made it off the bus." By the end of the afternoon at least ten people would be arrested for disorderly conduct and fighting. Just your typical Browns-Steelers Sunday.

The teams, like the fans, matched one another blow-for-blow early in the first quarter as it was clear both were wired for a game that could be the fork in the road for both their seasons. The Browns appeared poised to take the lead midway through the period before Sipe was intercepted at the Pittsburgh seven by defensive back Ron Johnson, who returned it to the Pittsburgh twenty-six. From there the Steelers, led by Stoudt, began marching. Aided by a pass-interference penalty on Browns' cornerback Oliver Davis in the end zone, which gave Pittsburgh a first down at the Cleveland one, running back Greg Hawthorne bulled his way over the goal line for a 7-0 Steelers' lead.

Things appeared even worse after Pittsburgh forced a Cleveland punt on the ensuing possession. Gerry Sullivan's snap was low and punter Johnny Evans couldn't handle it. The Steelers recovered at the Cleveland thirty-two.

On the ensuing possession a key fourth-down pass from Stoudt to Jim Smith for sixteen yards kept Pittsburgh's drive alive, and the lead became 10-0 when Matt Bahr hit a twenty-seven-yard field goal in the final minute of the first quarter. Perhaps the Browns had been too wired for the game after all. But they quickly adjusted and got back in it—not that anyone doubted they would.

Following the Pittsburgh kickoff Sipe and Company drove sixty-four yards in eleven plays and cut the lead to three when the Browns' quarterback threaded the needle between linebacker Robin Cole and defensive back Mel Blount of Pittsburgh and nailed Calvin Hill in the end zone for a five-yard scoring pass. The play was called "85 Halfback Option." It wouldn't be the last time it was called on this day.

The teams battled throughout the remainder of the second quarter with limited success. After an exchange of punts the Steelers put together a sixteen-play, seventy-five-yard drive in the final minutes of the half, which ended with a twenty-two-yard Bahr field goal to make it 13-7 at the intermission. Though trailing it appeared that the Browns had weathered the storm and had the Steelers right where they wanted them. As it turned out the storm was far from over.

The Browns immediately dug another hole for themselves to start the second half when Mike Pruitt fumbled on the second play from scrimmage and linebacker Dennis Winston, filling in for Jack Lambert, recovered for Pittsburgh.

Displaying the killer instinct that had made them champions four times in the previous six years the Steelers cashed in on the costly mistake. After Clay Matthews dropped a sure interception along the way, on the eleventh play of the following drive Hawthorne scored his second touchdown of the day, this one from two yards out, to give Pittsburgh a 20-7 lead with 9:08 remaining in the third. Rutigliano's worst fears were coming true. The Browns were making more mistakes "than a guy on his first date," according to the *Press*'s Bob Sudyk.

The Browns' offense answered the bell with a drive of its own, marching deep into Pittsburgh territory sparked by a thirty-four-yard Sipe-to-Logan completion. Shortly after, the Browns faced fourth-and-three at the Pittsburgh eight. Rather than attempting a short field goal, which would have cut the Pittsburgh lead to ten, Rutigliano opted to roll the dice.

"We gambled," he said afterward, "because we needed seven points, not just three." Mike Pruitt got the call on a sweep around left end but managed only two yards. The Steelers took over at their own six with an opportunity to turn the lights out on the home team.

But the Cleveland defense rose to the occasion, kept the Steelers pinned deep, and forced a punt in a critical situation. The Browns' offense took over at the Steelers' thirty-five. They marched back to the six where the playcall was "85 Halfback Option." Sipe found Greg Pruitt in the end zone to pull the Browns to within 20-14 with 4:25 left in the period. The crowd went wild as the Browns had clawed back into it once again.

But the throng was silenced moments later when Stoudt connected with wide receiver Theo Bell on a seventy-two-yard pass on third-and-eight, which brought the Steelers to the Cleveland three. Less than two minutes after the Browns had cut the lead in half Pittsburgh doubled it once again when running back Sydney Thornton scored on a two-yard scamper. But the lead remained twelve when Bahr's extra point hit the left upright and fell away. It would prove to be one of the biggest plays of the afternoon.

As it had the entire game (and season) the Browns' offense responded quickly from setback and blazed its way down the field. Following a diving catch by Ozzie Newsome for a thirty-yard gain to the Pittsburgh seven, disaster struck. On the Newsome completion Pittsburgh left tackle Steve Furress leveled Sipe in the shoulder and his arm went numb. "My shoulder went one way and it stretched the nerves there and I lost the feeling in my arm," Sipe said later. "It cleared up but it took one play too many to recover."

Sipe had to be taken out of the game, and Paul McDonald entered for the first pressure snap of his young NFL career: first-and-goal at the Pittsburgh seven, trailing the world champions by twelve with less than a minute to play in the third quarter. Before he got a chance to prove himself or even attempt his first pass McDonald fumbled the snap from Tom DeLeone, and appropriately Furress recovered for the Steelers. "I really don't know what happened except that it wasn't a case of nerves," McDonald would say. "I was calm, I knew exactly what was going on and what we were going to do, which is what makes it so bad."

High above the field in the press box *Plain Dealer* sports editor Hal Lebovitz jotted in his notes, "It just doesn't figure today."

It appeared he was right. The Browns had now blown three golden opportunities to score and consequently trailed by twelve with a quarter to play. But as Lebovitz and the rest of the world were about to be reminded, you never, *ever* counted out the Kardiac Kids.

The Cleveland defense once again stepped up and forced a Pittsburgh punt, and the Browns took over at their own twenty-seven. Sipe regained feeling in his arm and returned to action without missing a beat as he wove his way through the Steel Curtain, completing five of eight passes to the Pittsburgh seven where Rutigliano and Company were again faced with another critical decision on fourth-and-two. If the Browns kicked a field goal they would still need two scores to catch the Steelers with less than ten minutes remaining. That was all the reasoning Rutigliano needed, and for the second time on the afternoon the Browns would go for it on fourth down deep in Pittsburgh territory. The playcall was "85 Halfback Option."

Sensing that this was an opportunity for the knockout punch the Steelers blitzed the house, leaving Greg Pruitt isolated by safety Mike Wagner. It was a similar defensive formation to what the Steelers had shown on Pruitt's first touchdown. On that play Pruitt faked Wagner inside and went outside. This time he faked outside and went in.

Sipe read it perfectly and released the football a moment before getting crushed by Robin Cole. Pruitt leaned forward to snag the pass for a touchdown, and the Browns had again sliced the margin in half. But Don Cockroft returned the favor Matt Bahr had granted the Browns earlier by missing the extra point wide right. The Steelers' lead remained 26-20 with 9:21 to play.

Once again the Browns' defense came up big, stopping the Steelers on a critical third-and-three with eight minutes remaining to force a punt. The Browns took over at their own forty, and with the crowd buzzing with anticipation, it seemed like nature was taking its course.

Sipe guided Cleveland into Pittsburgh territory with key completions to Dave Logan for twenty yards and Reggie Rucker for eighteen. The Browns reached the Pittsburgh eighteen, and the playcall of the day was once again dialed in the huddle: "85 Halfback Option." The offensive cast of characters took their places at the line of scrimmage as Sipe read the defense.

He and Ozzie Newsome saw it at about the same time. The Steelers were preparing to blitz and leave Ron Johnson all alone on the right side to cover Newsome. More importantly Sipe and Newsome noticed Johnson was lined up on the inside of Newsome, which gave the third-year tight end a clear path to the end zone angling right. Just as he had seven days before with Dave Logan, Sipe nodded at Newsome, and Newsome nodded back. Instead of running his intended route Newsome would take Johnson to the end zone.

Sipe dropped back to pass, knowing full well that this time there was no halfback option on "85 Halfback Option." The only option was Ozzie Newsome. After a four-step drop Sipe lobbed the ball toward the corner of the end zone where Newsome had already badly beaten Johnson. He caught the ball in full stride and brought down both feet for the touchdown right in front of an ocean of Browns' fans in the bleachers, who went absolutely crazy. The Browns had tied it at twenty-six with 5:38 remaining, but now came the critical part of the transaction: the extra point, of which two had already been missed on this day.

"It was crucial," Don Cockroft said. "I knew I had to make it. There was pressure, but it's not a scared pressure. If you know what you're supposed to do, the chance of success is pretty good."

Cockroft calmly stepped up and connected on the point after to give the Browns a one-point lead.

On the other side of the field where the Pittsburgh contingent of fans had purchased its block of seats one Steeler backer began banging his head against one of Cleveland Stadium's infamous metal pillars. One of his friends urged him to stop.

"Plenty of time, man," he said, "plenty of time."

"Yeah," replied a nearby Browns' fan, "you got until next year Pittsburgh, all the way to next year!"

Now it would be up to the Cleveland defense, which, other than the seventy-two-yard pass to Bell, had completely stymied the Steelers in the second half. That trend continued as the Steelers were once again forced to punt. The Browns took over at their own forty-nine with 4:52 left and had an opportunity to go for their own knockout punch. But the Steelers' defense showed why it had been the best in the NFL over the past six years by stopping the Browns on three straight plays. Following Evans's punt the Steelers took over at their own twenty with 3:53 remaining. Once again the ball was in the court of Cleveland's defense.

Suddenly all of their second-half success seemed to wash away as Stoudt connected on three straight passes which brought the Steelers to the Pittsburgh forty. With the clock ticking to the two-minute warning Stoudt and the Steelers only needed about thirty more yards before they could attempt a potential game-winning field goal.

After a six-yard gain on first down Stoudt's second-down pass was broken up by Ron Bolton, setting up third-and-four at the Pittsburgh forty-six. Stoudt dropped back to pass and tried to squeeze one through the Cleveland secondary to Jim Smith along the sideline. But Stoudt underestimated the quickness of Bolton, who recovered to intercept the pass at the Cleveland forty-one with 1:57 to play. It was Pittsburgh's first turnover of the day.

The Browns were a bit more successful in milking the clock this time. After a pair of short Greg Pruitt runs Sipe hit little-used wide receiver Willis Adams at the Pittsburgh forty-five for ten yards and a first down on third-and-six. After three more rushes Evans punted to the Pittsburgh eleven, and Theo Bell returned it six yards to the seventeen with sixteen ticks left. The Steelers would have one final chance.

The long shot grew even longer on first down when Stoudt was ruled in the grasp of Lyle Alzado for a four-yard loss, but in this case the ruling actually helped Pittsburgh. Stoudt had gotten off a pass while in Alzado's clutches, and it was intercepted by Bolton at the twenty-three and returned for a touchdown. Bolton might have become an instant cult hero had the whistle and the in-the-grasp call not blown the play dead.

With time for just one more play with four seconds remaining Stoudt dropped back and hit Smith upfield through the spread-out Cleveland defense. But Smith was tackled at the Pittsburgh forty-seven after a thirty-four-yard gain as the clock hit zero. As soon as Smith hit the ground the Browns and their fans went absolutely crazy—almost, as one Steeler fan had predicted earlier that day, as if they were all having simultaneous heart attacks.

"This is worth a million bucks to all of us," Brian Sipe said in an NBC post-game interview. "We're feeling like champions right now."

"They call us the Kardiac Kids, but I think we've been killing ourselves," said Newsome. "Still, I think we can come back even if we're down 21 points."

Once again the Browns had won the hard way. Had they not failed three times inside the Pittsburgh twenty or not spotted the Steelers three turnovers, this game probably would have been a washout. "I have been critical of the Browns' lack of 'killer instinct,'" Bob Sudyk wrote. "Hell, I give up. I like it better the way they do it. They are simply the most thrilling sports attraction, win or lose, that our town has seen in years."

And as Tom DeLeone pointed out, this was a win for the city of Cleveland. "Cleveland fans have been taking it [from Pittsburgh fans] for years," he said. "Now they can start giving it back."

"We just paid the first toll, but this was a milestone for us, especially for the guys who have been here longer than I," Rutigliano said. "The time you know you are pointed in the right direction is when you have to go uphill as we did today. And this is just the beginning for us. We've got a helluva long road ahead of us, and we've got to take them one at a time and savor this one."

"It has to be our most satisfying victory," Sipe said. "After an 0-2 start, we dragged ourselves back to the top. We struggled through adversity and now we just beat probably the best team in the NFL. Beating the Steelers is like getting something very important out of the way. It should make us an even better team."

There's no doubt that this was already a better Browns' team than had started the season, especially on offense. Sipe had his second straight career day, completing a team-record twenty-eight passes in forty-six attempts for 349 yards and four touchdowns. The Browns also set a team record for most first downs passing with twenty-six. It was the second straight game the Steelers' defense had been riddled through the air. When Sipe's and Oakland quarterback Jim Plunkett's numbers were combined Pittsburgh had surrendered forty-one completions for 596 yards and seven touchdowns in seven days.

But more important than the yardage Sipe had completed passes to seven different receivers led by Logan's eight catches for 131 yards, extending his streak of consecutive games with a catch to thirty-two, tying Rucker's team record. "We're so deep in receivers," Reggie Rucker said after the game. "Among ourselves we respect each other so much. We have confidence in each other's ability. This is better than making All-Pro or being on the cover of *Sports Illustrated*."

And it wasn't just the receiving corps. The Browns' offensive line had another super game and gave Sipe all the time he needed to find his talented cadre of receivers. "I don't want this to sound like bragging," Sipe said, "but I don't know too many teams that can stop us when we have time to throw."

The Browns' passing game was so effective that Rutigliano essentially set the tone for the remainder of the season with a postgame comment. After harping on the importance of establishing a running game all week, after the win Rutigliano articulated what many Browns' fans already believed. "Establishing a running game is for wishbone teams," he said. "We have to do what we do best, and that's throw the ball. Our pass protection was foolproof. You give Brian Sipe the opportunity to throw and he can beat the best."

Mike Pruitt still gathered eighty-two yards on seventeen carries, but only ninety-one of the Browns' 439 total yards came on the ground. With the Browns' emphasis on the passing plus his still-unexplained day off it was no surprise that Charles White carried the ball just one time for one yard and caught one pass for ten. "I think I'll take Friday off next time," White joked.

The slippery field conditions for the second straight week also helped the Browns as their quick receivers wreaked havoc on the Green Bay and Pittsburgh secondaries, which had a hard time recovering. "The Browns might reach the Super Bowl if they played in the Florida Everglades," Bob Sudyk suggested.

The Browns' players tended to discount the weather and field conditions and focused instead on their strength as a team. "Some teams have Olympic sprinters or one Earl Campbell," Rucker noted. "We're not a one-man gang. Nobody knows where we're going. We never let the defense know. I like to play this total team concept. It's a very important concept."

A concept the Steelers would certainly agree with especially since much of their team wasn't on the field. Naturally the questions arose about whether the Browns could have won this game had the Steelers been playing with a full deck. But as Sudyk wrote, "As in any war, you defeat the enemy's colors, their flag. The troops are faceless."

"They were hurting, but their defense is still the best," Newsome said. "They haven't lost a step, and don't believe anybody who says they did. But we have matured as a team. Everybody had a great day for us, and that's what won. Not that the Steelers have slipped."

"A lot of people will say, 'You beat Pittsburgh, but Bradshaw didn't play,'" Charlie Hall said. "But you want to know something? We don't care."

Other Browns' players, particularly those on offense, felt that they had faced down and defeated a basically intact Steeler defense, and they weren't buying the argument that it was injuries alone that had weakened and broken the Steel Curtain. "Could we have beaten them if Terry Bradshaw had played?" Rucker asked. "I think so. He can't play defense."

"In my mind, our victory isn't tarnished at all," Logan said. "They're still the best defensive team in the NFL."

Still the Browns understood how important players like Terry Bradshaw were to the Steeler attack. "Bradshaw makes things happen by himself," Ron Bolton admitted. "He makes the whole team go. Without him, they're not the same team." But Bolton was quick to add that the Browns' focus was not on beating individual Steeler players but rather on beating the Steeler *team*. "We practiced for Bradshaw. But we prepared for tendencies, not individuals."

Bradshaw had given it a go prior to game time, but his thumb was too tight and he couldn't keep it loose. "It would have been unfair to Terry to use him," Chuck Noll said. "He probably would have fumbled the ball with the thumb the way it is. Cliff played well. He got us 26 points, and how much more can you ask?"

For two more, evidently.

"It's tough to play a halfway decent game and lose, especially when you felt you had the game," said Stoudt, who completed eighteen of thirty-seven passes for 310 yards. "I'm going to spend the night thinking a lot about this game before I go to sleep."

"There's no denying that the Steelers weren't at full strength," Lebovitz wrote in Monday's *Plain Dealer*. "But the magnanimous Browns, with all their errors, nullified all physical edge they might have had." Lebovitz went on to compare the Browns to a fine racehorse that puts on some extra weight just to give the rest of the field an advantage. "What really has happened to the Steelers is not the result of injuries," he added. "It's that the Steel Curtain has rusted."

Rusted or not, bruised but definitely not broken, the Steelers remained defiant. "We haven't been in this situation very often," Steelers' center Mike Webster said. "It's time for us to put up and shut up. The end result is to win."

"People all over the world are celebrating now because they think we've won too much in recent years, but the situation isn't grim yet," Pittsburgh cornerback Ron Johnson said. "We still have eight games and we've got to pull ourselves together. We've got the personnel and the coaches to do it."

There remained a sense of confidence surrounding this Steeler team. Noll even joked, "We may go to the Super Bowl with the worst record ever."

"Wait 'till we get the Browns at home," Steelers' defensive end Dwight Evans said in that spirit. "We'll whip their tails."

While it appeared the Steelers' fortunes were descending in 1980 Greg Pruitt's seemed just ready to rise. He only rushed the ball five times for eight yards but caught eight passes for seventy-one and two touchdowns and felt good doing it. "I've had a lot of doubts about my knee," Pruitt said. "Now I feel like I've taken a big first step, to be totally involved in a game and come out of it okay. Oh, I hurt all over, and I know I will tomorrow. But that's the way it always was, and I guess it always will be."

The three-way tie atop the AFC Central became a two-team knot as the Houston Oilers buried the Cincinnati Bengals in the Astrodome, 23-3, behind 202 rushing yards from Earl Campbell, his second straight game with more than two hundred yards. Suddenly the Browns' November 30 meeting at Houston looked a lot bigger than it had two weeks earlier. With both Cleveland and the Oilers at 5-3, Pittsburgh at 4-4, and Cincinnati at 3-5, the division was certainly maintaining its reputation as the strongest in all of football. It appeared there would be a memorable race to the finish in the season's second half.

All made possible because of the Browns' first win over the Steelers in four years. "I knew then," Rutigliano would say years later, "that our guys knew what was on the line. No matter what was in front of us, they were going to be hard to beat. We felt that was a deciding moment in that maybe the guard was changing."

But before the Browns could start concerning themselves with the Oilers, or even the November 16 rematch with the Steelers in Pittsburgh, there was plenty of work to be done. First and foremost they would have to deal with the Chicago Bears on *Monday Night Football* as well as a city which was now bursting at the seams with excitement over its football team.

As the Browns' victory over Pittsburgh came to its conclusion, and Hal Lebovitz prepared to head down to the locker room for the post-game interviews, he paused and wrote one more word at the bottom of his notes: BEAUTIFUL.

"We have picked ourselves up after a rough start and we've earned the position we're in," Sipe said. "Now, I really don't think there's any team that can stop us."

6 · Sam's Glo-Coat Boys

In case the city of Cleveland wasn't still buzzing after the Browns' exciting win over the Pittsburgh Steelers there was still the little matter of a last-minute presidential debate being held downtown that Tuesday evening at Public Music Hall that would get the town humming again.

Monday, as Ronald Reagan had lunch with former President Gerald Ford and watched films of Ford's 1976 debate with Jimmy Carter, the Browns' coaching staff watched their own films of the win over Pittsburgh and agreed that even a day later victory was just as sweet. "Without question, beating the Steelers was the most satisfying victory since I came here," Sam Rutigliano said. "All I heard when I took this job was that we had to beat the Steelers. And now, since we did, all I am hearing is that we must beat them in Pittsburgh."

Such was life in the National Football League. The Browns would only get two weeks to enjoy the win over the Steelers before facing them again, this time in their personal house of horrors, Three Rivers Stadium, where Cleveland was winless in ten tries.

First the Browns would have to deal with the Chicago Bears the following Monday night and then travel to Baltimore to face the Colts, two deceivingly crucial games for the Browns' playoff hopes. As the NFL season hit its midpoint it was becoming clear that the two AFC Wild Card spots would be tough to come by. Buffalo and New England, tied for first in the East, held the conference's best records at 6-2, and with San Diego and Oakland tied for first in the West and Cleveland and Houston battling it out in the Central—all with 5-3 records—the margin for error in the final eight weeks would be very slim. Plus both the Browns and Oilers would play five of their last eight games on the road. "We have an uphill battle for the next eight weeks," Rutigliano said, "but we have the opportunity to control our own destiny and that is a position we've never been in before."

Another unfamiliar position the Browns found themselves in was worrying about a letdown after a titanic victory. After the coaches were concerned with the team being too pumped up for the Steelers game they now had to be wary of the team's energy and enthusiasm levels dipping after accomplishing a major milestone. "This is anti-climactic," said Reggie Rucker. "We reached our goals, what we were striving for. But you knew it would come. It's not a surprise."

"I don't think of the possibility of an emotional letdown as a problem," Rutigliano said. "Preparation is the key word, not the will to win. An emotional letdown is only a danger if you're not prepared, and we will be."

Another concern was that the 1980 Browns would soon be hitting the wall that the 1978 and 1979 teams had crashed into in mid-November after fast starts. In Rutigliano's first season in 1978 Cleveland started 3-0 and later improved to 4-2 before losing six of its final ten games to finish at 8-8. Things were even better a year later when the Browns roared to a 4-0 start, and following an exciting overtime win over the Miami Dolphins on November 18 they stood at 8-4 with a trip to the playoffs within reach. But the Browns dropped three of their final four games, including their last two to Oakland and Cincinnati, neither of whom made the playoffs, to finish at 9-7, missing a Wild Card berth. Many feared the 1980 Browns would suffer the same fate, but Rutigliano discounted the possibility, saying this Browns team was much better than the previous two. The statistics backed him up.

The 1980 team had scored more points, had better third-down efficiency, and was averaging more yards per offensive play than had the 1979 Browns after eight games. Sipe had only been sacked six times compared to fifteen the year before and his completion percentage was up 6 percent. On defense the Browns had allowed fewer points, and their opponents' rushing yards were down as was their average per rush by a dramatic difference of 1.2 yards per carry.

Plus, Rutigliano added, the 1979 Browns were playing without Jerry Sherk and Greg Pruitt down the stretch. The 1980 Browns were also without Sherk but unlike the 1979 team had been without him all year and had adjusted accordingly. And Pruitt, while still not quite 100 percent, was slowly getting better each week and figured to be a major component in the drive toward the playoffs.

"In recent seasons we started fast but were unable to sustain the intensity," Sipe said. "This year started out as a disaster but now Sam has this team just where it should be."

Meanwhile the 3-5 Bears would try to surprise the Browns before a national television audience on *Monday Night Football*. Led by young tailback Walter Payton, who was asserting himself as one of the best runners in the league, the Bears were capable of giving the Browns problems. Payton had already accumulated 762 yards on 172 carries and Rutigliano and the Browns' coaching staff essentially intended to ignore him in their game plan. Payton would almost certainly get his one hundred yards, but the key, the Cleveland coaches decided, was not allowing anyone else—like quarterback Vince Evans—to burn them.

The Browns' defense appeared up to the challenge after putting together its best statistical game of the season on the Schottenheimer Scale against Pittsburgh.

The unit scored a 67 percent by winning fifty-three of seventy-nine plays. Though the Browns were ranked thirteenth in the American Football Conference in yards allowed they were fourth in the only statistical category that really mattered, points allowed. "Overall, I'd say we're right on schedule," Marty Schottenheimer said. "We're progressing just about the way I expected we would."

The Browns' offense would also be in for a test as Chicago had quietly put together the Number Two pass defense in the league, evidenced by its twenty-eight sacks in eight games. It was certainly better than Pittsburgh's against which, Bob Sudyk commented, Jimmy Carter could complete passes to Ronald Reagan.

It would be the second time in less than three months that the Browns would face the Bears. Many fans remembered the Browns had picked up their sole win of the preseason at Soldier Field on August 23 when Rutigliano left Sipe and many other first-teamers in the game in the second half against the Chicago scrubs. Consequently the Browns rallied from a 28-6 halftime deficit and won, 33-31. Although it was a meaningless preseason game many Bears complained about Rutigliano's decision and were still grumbling about it in the first week of November.

In case that wasn't enough intrigue for the sportswriters on the North Coast leading up to the game, the contest would also mark a homecoming of sorts for one of the most disappointing draft picks in franchise history. Quarterback Mike Phipps, selected by the Browns in the first round of the 1970 draft, would make his first appearance in Cleveland since being traded to Chicago in 1977. Phipps saw very little action in his first two years with the Bears but became the starter in the fourth week of 1979 after Vince Evans went down with a staph infection. Phipps's 53 percent completion rate for just over 1,500 yards with nine touchdowns and eight interceptions turned out to be the best season of his career as Chicago reached the postseason for the first time since 1963.

Phipps had begun the 1980 season as the Bears' starter but was replaced by a healthy Evans after five games and didn't figure to see any playing time against the Browns. While his passing statistics certainly showed that Phipps turned out to be a bust for the Browns, other numbers were even more telling. In the ten years before the Browns traded Hall-of-Fame wide receiver Paul Warfield and drafted Phipps they held a record of 92-41. In the ten years after they were just 72-70. That Monday night it appeared that the Browns' past would meet its future.

As the Browns prepared for the Bears on Tuesday, Ronald Reagan and Jimmy Carter arrived in Cleveland for what many felt would be the ninety minutes that determined who would be the president of the United States for the next four years. With just one week remaining until the voters hit the booths it was an opportunity for Carter to gain ground and for Reagan to put it away.

At the conclusion of the debate, viewed by an estimated one hundred million across the nation, it didn't appear that either had accomplished his mission simply because neither candidate made any glaring mistakes. Each stuck to his guns on the primary issues: inflation, military spending, and the Persian Gulf crisis. The respective fears in each camp: the Democrats, that Carter would lose his temper; the Republicans, that Reagan would say something idiotic; were not realized. Still each candidate had his moments such as when Carter talked about discussing the issue of nuclear arms with his thirteen-year-old daughter and when Reagan praised the progress America had made since his youth—a time when, according to Reagan, the nation didn't know it had a racial problem.

But after the 1980 presidential election, when historians went back and studied the campaigns, Reagan's closing remarks on that October evening in Cleveland turned out to be much more significant than many realized at the time: "Are you better off than you were four years ago?" he asked rhetorically. "Is America as respected throughout the world as it was?"

An ABC telephone poll declared Reagan the winner of the debate by a two-to-one margin though it was later reported that callers trying to cast their opinion for Carter couldn't get through due to a busy signal or an operator telling them the number was not in order—an ominous omen for the week to come. Things looked even worse for the president when the polls showed Reagan holding a steady 45-to-40 percent lead after the debate. Many conjectured that unless the fifty-two American hostages being held in Iran were freed before Tuesday Carter didn't stand a chance.

As Americans mulled over the question of how different their lives were in 1980 compared to 1976, the Cleveland Indians were hoping to make a move that would make them better off than they were four years, or even twenty, years earlier. On Halloween Friday the *Plain Dealer* reported that Tribe owner Steve O'Neill was prepared to sell the club to a group led by New York theater tycoon James Nederlander and Los Angeles lawyer Neil Papiano. Though the deal wasn't official yet, O'Neill, who had owned the team since 1978, would keep 10 percent rather than the 60 percent of the team he currently possessed. The potential new owners forecasted a new era of baseball in Cleveland with a franchise not afraid to go out and get the big-money free agents, which would no doubt become evermore expensive in the 1980s.

While the Indians were hoping for a return to their glory days of the late 1940s and 1950s, that same day the Browns heard from a legendary voice from that same era. Following the win over the Steelers a letter arrived at Browns' camp addressed to Modell, Rutigliano, and Sipe.

Dear Art, Sam, and Brian:

I am writing the same note to all three of you—saving the taxpayers money.

That was a great victory last Sunday and I don't care if Pittsburgh had 20 guys sidelined. It is obvious that the ownership is letting the coach run the game. It is obvious that the coach is doing a great job. It is obvious that my prediction that Brian would replace me as the all-time Browns' quarterback will come true—but Brian—don't do it so damn quickly.

Seriously, congratulations on a great effort. I sure hope you go all the way. Best wishes,
Otts

"Otts" was none other than former Browns' quarterback and Hall-of-Famer Otto Graham, who was serving as the athletic director at the Coast Guard Academy.

Graham's reference to Sipe becoming the all-time Browns' quarterback was based on Number 17's proximity to Graham in the Cleveland record book. Going into the Bears' game Sipe was third on the Browns' all-time passing yardage list behind Graham's 13,499 and Frank Ryan's 13,361. Entering the Chicago game with 13,236 career passing yards, Sipe had a chance to become the all-time leader if not against the Bears then shortly thereafter. It was only appropriate that Sipe was poised to set the all-time team record at the same time he was the top-rated passer in the AFC with a 95.4 quarterback rating.

Another of the conference's best passers, Terry Bradshaw, returned to the lineup that Sunday and helped lead his Steelers to a much-needed 22-20 win over the Green Bay Packers at Three Rivers. Following Bradshaw off the injured list were running back Franco Harris and wide receiver Lynn Swann, and while Pittsburgh was victorious it was still clear that the Steelers weren't the team they were a year before. The difference in the game was a first-quarter safety the Steelers scored when a Green Bay punt snap went out of the end zone. But Pittsburgh fans weren't complaining since their team had kept their distant playoff hopes alive, moving to 5-4.

But the team the Browns were most interested in was the Houston Oilers, who ensured they would still be in first place in the Central following Week Nine with a 20-16 win over the Denver Broncos at Mile High Stadium. Earl Campbell rushed for "only" 157 yards and two touchdowns, unable to notch his third straight two-hundred-yard game. The Browns would now have to defeat the Bears in order to keep up with Houston, which improved to 6-3.

Rounding out the AFC Central action on the first Sunday in November, the Cincinnati Bengals were overwhelmed at home by the San Diego Chargers, 31-14. Cincy quarterback Ken Anderson reinjured his left knee and was forced to leave the game in the fourth quarter, with Jack Thompson once again filling in. The loss dropped Cincinnati to 3-6, and if the polls were accurate, the Bengals had become the Jimmy Carter of the Central Division.

But as testament to the power of positive thinking, with the polls set to open in less than twelve hours, several Carter campaigners were on hand at sold-out Cleveland Stadium that Monday night, passing out literature and buttons, as were Reagan and John Anderson supporters. Some fans, shut out at the Browns' box office, offered to trade their vote for tickets.

Almost as if sensing the intensity of the American political scene the Browns came out just as focused on that rainy Monday night. They stopped the Bears on their first possession, and then began marching down the field. Sipe and Company moved inside the Chicago twenty and twice appeared to have taken a 6-0 lead only to have both instances wiped out. First, from the fourteen Sipe hit Reggie Rucker in the end zone for a touchdown, but a holding penalty on Joe DeLamielleure nullified it. A few moments later Sipe connected with Ozzie Newsome on a six-yard touchdown pass, but the officials said the Bears had called time out just before the play started. With fate clearly not on their side in the early going the Browns settled for a twenty-three-yard Don Cockroft field goal and a 3-0 lead.

After another Cleveland stop it appeared that the Browns would add to their advantage as they once again drove into Chicago territory aided by a twenty-nine-yard Sipe completion to Newsome. But the Bears dodged another bullet when linebacker Jerry Muckensturm intercepted Sipe at the nineteen and lateraled to defensive back Lenny Walterscheid for an additional ten yards. Still the Cleveland defense was playing outstanding, and it wasn't until a fourteen-yard run by Walter Payton late in the second quarter that the Bears picked up a first down.

But things didn't look particularly rosy for the Browns either. Just prior to Payton's run Sipe had been intercepted a second time at the Chicago fourteen, this time by Walterscheid, who returned it to the Chicago forty-seven. The Bears finally put a drive together and reached the Cleveland nineteen only to have Bob Thomas's potential game-tying thirty-five-yard field goal sail wide right with 2:22 remaining in the first half. Now it was the Browns who had dodged a bullet and were ready to take control.

Sipe finally got them into the end zone with fifty-seven seconds left in the half when he hit a diving Rucker in the corner of the end zone for a touchdown and a 10-0 Browns' lead, which held up to the intermission. But the Bears had to feel fortunate only trailing by ten since Cleveland had outgained them 241 yards to sixty-two and had collected eighteen first downs to the Bears' two. By halftime Sipe had become the Number Two passer in Browns' history by throwing for 182 yards to leapfrog Frank Ryan but still needed eighty-one more to unseat Otto Graham. It didn't take long.

On the first possession of the second half the Browns drove to the Chicago seven, but a third-down sack of Sipe by defensive end Mike Hartenstine resulted in an eighteen-yard loss, and Cleveland was forced to settle for a forty-two-yard Cockroft field goal and a 13-0 lead.

Though the Browns were playing well things were going eerily similar to how they had in the Green Bay game when they had squandered numerous scoring opportunities early and held a precarious 13-0 lead in the third quarter. The Packers had come back to take the lead, and had it not been for the last-minute heroics of Sipe and Dave Logan Green Bay would have won the game. "I can't explain it," Sipe would say after the Chicago contest. "Maybe we just have to make mistakes to get ourselves going. I don't want to over-analyze it."

After an exchange of punts the Bears started to follow the same script. With just over a minute left in the third quarter Vince Evans scored on a seven-yard bootleg run to cut the Browns' advantage to 13-7. It once again appeared that the Kardiac Kids would be needed in the fourth quarter—especially when the Bears forced another Cleveland punt to close the third quarter. But as he had done the week before against Pittsburgh Ron Bolton came up with a huge play, ripping a deep pass out of wide receiver Rickey Watts's hands for an interception at the Browns' sixteen to end the threat. From there Sipe and the offense made things a little more comfortable.

The Browns drove eighty-four yards in thirteen plays on a march that took 7:14 off the clock, sparked by a Sipe pass to Newsome for twenty-two yards, which put the Cleveland signal-caller atop the team record book for all-time passing yardage with 13,500. With 7:29 remaining in the game Mike Pruitt scored from a yard out and Cockroft added the extra point to make it 20-7, Browns. It now appeared that the Kardiac Kids might be able to take the night off after all.

But anyone who had watched the 1980 Browns thus far knew better.

The Bears rallied with a quick sixty-two-yard drive that lasted less than three minutes and ended when Evans hit wide receiver Brian Baschnagel over the out-stretched arms of Clinton Burrell for an eighteen-yard touchdown pass that cut the lead to 20-14 with 4:45 to play. It all seemed so familiar to Cleveland fans: the Browns would punt, the Bears would score again with two minutes left, and it would be up to Sipe and Company to win the game with a desperation drive. After all, that was the way this team operated.

A minute later the Browns reached the Cleveland forty-four where they faced third-and-one, and a Chicago stop would almost certainly start that predication in motion. Accordingly the Bears lined up in a goal-line defense with six linemen and two linebackers. Sipe took the snap and tossed to Chicago native Mike Pruitt on a designed sweep around right end. But as Pruitt was waiting for the path to clear he saw a slight opening in the line just ahead of him. He cut back on the slippery turf and exploded through the hole for the first down, but there was even more real estate ahead of him. Thanks to key blocks by wide receiver Willis Adams and running back Cleo Miller, once Pruitt was three yards past the line of scrimmage he was gone. Fifty-six yards later he crossed the goal line to give the Browns a 27-14 lead with just 3:35 remaining. The crowd of 83,224—the largest at the Stadium in eight years and the largest that would attend an NFL game in 1980—went absolutely bonkers.

"I haven't seen an open field like that in eight games," Pruitt said. "I didn't know whether to stop and wait to be tackled or run. It's nice to see that again. I was overdue for a long run. It was about time I broke one."

"We must have missed a tackle on that play," Chicago coach Neill Armstrong said. "We felt it was crucial to stop them at midfield. That's an unfamiliar place on the field for us to be in a goal-line defense, and when you miss a tackle there, he goes all the way."

While Pruitt's touchdown seemed to have backbreaking potential, as was always the case with the Kardiac Kids the game wasn't over until it was over. After the kickoff the Bears took over at their own thirty and quickly marched back down the field. Ten plays and seventy yards later tight end Robin Earl scored on a six-yard pass from Evans and the extra point made it 27-21, Browns, with thirty-six seconds left. Just as had been the case in Tampa Bay five weeks before the outcome of the game was now resting on an onside kick.

But instead of flubbing it as Clinton Burrell had done in the final minute in Tampa to give the Buccaneers one last chance, the bouncing kick was smothered by cornerback Judson Flint, and a few moments later, at 12:27 A.M., Tuesday, the Browns were victorious.

"I would like a laugher, just once," Sipe sighed afterward, and most Browns' fans had to agree. Still there was something different about this Browns' win than the five that had preceded it. The play of the day did not involve Sipe or his cadre of receivers. It was a running play that made the difference. Mike Pruitt finished with a season-high 129 yards on twenty-seven carries with a pair of touchdowns, but the Browns really hadn't focused on running the football until they were draining the clock in the final quarter. Then everything clicked. "In the first half they weren't playing the run at all so in the second half we made some adjustments to make our running game work," Cody Risien said. "We narrowed down the plays essentially to inside plays. Traps and offtackle were our big plays in the second half."

"I think maybe we did wear them down a little bit," Sipe said. "They were concerned only about our passing. We milked the pass all we could. Then, when we saw that our offensive line finally was winning their battle it was the consensus of our coaches and myself that we feature Mike more in the second half."

Sipe still had another marvelous game, completing twenty-three of thirty-nine passes for 298 yards, and had reached the top of the charts in the Browns' record books. He saved the football with which he had broken the record, only the second time in his professional career he'd ever taken home a ball as a souvenir. The other instance was following his first NFL game in 1974 when he rallied the Browns to a win over Denver. "To tell you the truth, I was surprised, shocked really, when I heard the announcement," Sipe said. "But certainly I was pleased, flattered to be in such company. When you talk about Graham, you're talking about a Hall-of-Famer. And I am aware of how good Ryan was, too. They really are select company."

Logan also earned himself a spot in Browns' history as he caught a pass for the thirty-third straight game, surpassing Rucker for the team mark. Logan was one of eight different receivers Sipe connected with as the Cleveland attack once again topped four hundred yards.

"[Sipe] really hurt us hitting the backs coming out of the backfield, but he uses all his receivers extremely well," said Bears' safety Gary Fencik. "There's nothing you can do to defense that. We tried a lot of different things."

Unlike their opponents' reactions following previous wins over Tampa Bay and Green Bay, the Bears' players obviously respected the Browns. "We're not surprised," said Chicago defensive tackle Alan Page. "We let them move the ball. They've got a good team, an exceptionally good offense." Cornerback Allan Ellis remarked "It was tough out there. The Browns have so many weapons and they use them all. And their timing is so good. Cleveland is as good as any team we've played, and maybe better."

Probably the most impressive aspect of the success of the Browns' offense was that it had been done with a makeshift offensive line. Doug Dieken left the game early in the second quarter with a sprained left knee and spent the rest of the night on crutches on the sideline. DeLamielleure moved over to Dieken's left-tackle spot and not-quite-healthy Henry Sheppard—who had been replaced by Robert E. Jackson—limped in to replace DeLamielleure. Still the Cleveland offense was humming along as fine-tuned as ever, and, fittingly, Dr. Leonard Greenbaum, the team's osteopathic physician, was given a game ball for getting so many injured players ready to play.

But the story of the game was the Cleveland defense and the job it had done on Walter Payton. The Bears' talented young runner could only manage thirty yards on eleven carries, his lowest output since his rookie year in 1975. "It wasn't anything magic," Rutigliano said of the Browns' success against the man nicknamed "Sweetness." "We just did a great job of keeping him pinned inside."

Rutigliano pointed to the Browns' end-run force led by Clarence Scott and Clay Matthews, which prevented Payton from turning the corner on sweeps and forced him back to the middle of the field where the Browns' linemen and linebackers were waiting for him. Bill Cowher, making his first NFL start in place of injured Robert L. Jackson, stepped up to lead the team in tackles.

Evans ended up being Chicago's leading rusher with forty-six yards on six carries as the Browns limited the Bears to a mere eighty-six rushing yards and just 275 total yards.

The only bad news for the Browns was their usual penalty problem. They racked up ten for eighty yards. But it wasn't just the Browns that evening. The Bears were also flagged ten times as the game dragged on into the wee hours. In one five-play, twenty-two-second period in the second quarter, the teams combined for six penalties.

One reporter told Rutigliano after the game that it was an ugly win. "I don't know what girls you date," he replied, "but as a football coach, any game I won ain't ugly."

"It wasn't as artistic as we would have liked, but you've got to give great credit to Chicago," he added later. "They put more heat on us than anybody this year."

Though the Browns' victory may not have been perfect, it demonstrated that this was a playoff-caliber team. They'd come back from a huge emotional win over their archrivals the week before and beat a deceivingly talented team on a national stage to maintain a tie for first place. "This team is not riding an emotional high," Bob Sudyk wrote in Tuesday's *Press*. "It is winning on talent with as skillful a quarterback as there is in football. It has the makings of a Super Bowl contender, but not until the endless mistakes are eliminated."

And while several mistakes had already been eliminated since early in the season the Browns realized they had little margin for error in the final seven games. "We've already given up three ball games," Sipe said. "I don't think we can lose two more and make the playoffs."

In contrast to the Browns' narrower-than-it-should-have-been victory over the Bears on Monday night, less than twenty-four hours later word of a much more convincing victory was spreading around the globe.

As expected, Ronald Reagan rolled to a landslide victory over Jimmy Carter in the presidential election, 483 electoral votes to forty-nine, the largest margin of victory since George McGovern's devastating defeat by Richard Nixon in 1972. The sixty-nine-year old Reagan, the oldest man ever elected president, carried forty-three states. While the electoral vote was one-sided, the popular vote was less so, with Reagan getting twenty-five million votes for 50 percent, Carter twenty-one million for 42 percent, and John Anderson 2.9 million for six percent. Reagan's victory was so clear that in his national news broadcast at 6:30 P.M. EST, NBC anchor John Chancellor declared Reagan the winner.

Though the majority of Cuyahoga County voters had pulled the lever for Carter (246,779 to 192,784), the residents of Northeast Ohio could still feel their hometown had made a difference in the 1980 election. Shortly after victory was acknowledged Reagan officials highlighted the Cleveland debate as the turning point in the campaign that clinched the governor's victory. The debate certainly had an effect on Ohio voters, as Reagan took the state 53 percent to 40 percent for Carter after leading by a smaller margin in the polls prior to the debate.

Elsewhere in the state the Republican Party regained control of the Ohio Senate for the first time in six years, while Democratic U.S. Senator John Glenn was elected to a second term over James Betts by nearly a million votes. Glenn's win was one of few for Democrats across the nation as the GOP also took control of the Senate.

While many heated and competitive races ended when the polls closed Tuesday night, as the Browns showed up for practice Wednesday morning it was clear that their race was just beginning. Many figured the Browns would have to win a minimum of four of their final seven games and very likely would need five to make the playoffs, either as the division champ or as a Wild Card team. But the Browns also recalled what had happened the previous two seasons, with playoff hopes coming down to the final game of the regular season, and knew that they could avoid that do-or-die scenario with a strong finish to the month of November. "Each year, if you're in the race, the month of November is significant," Rutigliano said, "so we've got to do our Christmas shopping early and avoid the rush."

Trying to avoid the Browns' rush the following Sunday would be Baltimore quarterback Bert Jones, who despite having a mediocre season, could still light up opposing defenses, especially if given ample time to throw. And entering Week Ten Rutigliano was concerned about the Browns' pass rush, or rather lack thereof, against the Bears. But if there was a team in the NFL that could resuscitate a beleaguered pass rush it was the Colts, who had allowed twenty-one sacks of Jones in nine games, including an NFL record-tying twelve in a loss to St. Louis two weeks earlier.

For the second straight week the Browns would have a historical connection to an opposing team's quarterback. Jones was the son of former Browns' running back Dub Jones and said he was inspired to play football as a boy when his father, who later became Blanton Collier's offensive coach, took him to the Browns' training camp at Hiram College. The Browns would also be going against another specter of their own past in Baltimore head coach Mike McCormack, who had played on the offensive and defensive lines for Cleveland from 1954 to 1962.

Not only would the four-point-underdog Browns have to contend with Jones and the 5-4 Colts on the road, they would have to do so with one less day for preparation, the curse of *Monday Night Football*. What's more, for whatever reason, opponents of the Chicago Bears always seemed to have trouble the week after playing them. In 1979 Bears' opponents were just 2-14 in the game played after facing Chicago, and in 1980 their record was 2-5-1.

Things continued to look ominous for the Browns as the week went on. Doug

Dieken's status was up in the air after his knee was rolled on Monday night. By midweek Dieken was talking about starting, which would keep his streak of 130 consecutive starts alive, but most figured he would not be 100 percent. "Besides, a kicker [Don Cockroft] had the record for most consecutive games," Dieken said, "and we couldn't have that."

Anticipating he might not play, the Browns activated rookie offensive lineman Joel Patten and released defensive tackle Jerry Wilkinson, who helped the team get through the shock of cutting Cleveland Crosby. As it turned out Dieken was able to start on what would become a rainy afternoon in Baltimore but only played the first down to keep his streak alive. As Dieken jogged off the field, Henry Sheppard jogged on to take his place. "I softened 'em up for you," Dieken told Sheppard.

Sheppard's left-guard spot was taken by Joe DeLamielleure, whose right-guard spot was filled in by Robert E. Jackson. For all the criticism the Browns had taken in September for trading for DeLamielleure rather than trying to bolster the defense, the Cleveland offensive line was now without a doubt the deepest in the NFL.

Despite the vast changes on the line, in the first half the Browns looked as healthy as ever. They put together the best thirty minutes of football they'd ever played under Sam Rutigliano and probably dating back much further than that. Sparked by an offensive line that allowed Sipe seemingly an eternity to throw and opened holes the size of Buicks in the Baltimore defensive line, the Browns began what appeared would be a romp in the rain.

After forcing a Baltimore punt to open the game the Browns drove sixty-two yards in nine plays to take the lead when Charles White scored on a five-yard run over left tackle. After another Colts' punt Cleveland picked up right where it had left off with another scoring drive, this one fifty yards in five plays, capped by a thirty-nine-yard Sipe-to-Logan touchdown pass. In less than eleven minutes the Browns had built a 14-0 lead and looked unstoppable both on offense and on defense as Cleveland sacked Jones three times on Baltimore's first two possessions.

Things looked even better when the Browns got the ball back, but a Mike Pruitt fumble was recovered by linebacker Ed Simonini at the Baltimore forty-seven and took away some of the Browns' momentum. It appeared it would all shift to the Colts when Jones led his team to a touchdown two plays later on a twenty-three-yard pass to tight end Reese McCall early in the second quarter. But instead of cutting the Browns' lead to seven a bad center snap from Ken Mendenhall on the point after resulted in Steve Mike-Mayer's extra point sailing wide left to keep it a two-score advantage at 14-6. In a game that would turn out to be full of big plays and eight total scores, this flubbed point after would prove to be the biggest of the day.

The Browns atoned for the turnover by marching right back down the field after the Baltimore kickoff, paced by a twenty-yard run by Mike Pruitt. Just as they had before, the Browns turned to Charles White down close, and the rookie didn't disappoint, this time racing five yards over right tackle and scoring, thanks to a key block by Cody Risien. Any momentum the Browns had lost they now appeared to have back. They had grabbed a 21-6 advantage, which held up until halftime thanks to an interception by Ron Bolton that stopped one potential scoring drive and a missed thirty-nine-yard field goal by Mike-Mayer on the final play of the half.

At the intermission even the most positive thinker had to be surprised at how easy everything looked for the Browns. Granted, the Cleveland offense was one of the best in the league, but it hadn't enjoyed this kind of success all season. Sipe had completed fifteen of seventeen passes, including eight straight to start the game, for 150 yards. Meanwhile Mike Pruitt had rushed for seventy-eight yards in the first two quarters, and Charles White had picked up fifty-two as the Browns racked up nearly three hundred yards of offense in thirty minutes, leading Sipe to admit afterward, "that might have been as good as we ever played."

So why were the Browns so successful, especially playing on the road after a short week against a potential playoff team? The primary reason on offense was that the Colts came out playing the Browns man-to-man, which as Dave Logan said was "suicidal for any team to try to do against a guy like Brian Sipe."

On the other side of the ball the Browns were stopping the Colts because they were successfully mixing up their defenses much as they did to Jim Zorn and the Seahawks in Seattle. The Browns were playing the 4-3 85 percent of the time as well as many stunt and blitz variations. Everything, both defensively and offensively, was clicking.

In other words, it couldn't last.

The Colts realized their defensive mistake and switched to more zone coverages in the second half, which slowed down the red-hot Cleveland offense. Neither team could muster much through the third quarter. The Browns' defense hung tough, but Baltimore finally broke through with an eighty-three-yard drive capped by a five-yard touchdown run by rookie tailback Curtis Dickey with 3:17 to play in the period. Mike-Mayer's kick was good this time as the Colts cut the lead to 21-13. With the rain-soaked crowd beginning to show signs of life it appeared someone would have to shine a giant spotlight into the sky and once again call on the services not of Batman but of the Kardiac Kids.

But on the next drive the Browns suggested that maybe, just maybe, this team was beginning to get used to the idea of being a playoff-caliber squad. After Dino Hall returned the Colts' kick thirty-six yards to the Cleveland forty-one the Browns marched right back down the field where, at the Baltimore twelve, Sipe once again displayed why he deserved to be the top-rated quarterback in the AFC.

He dropped back and was immediately pressured by Baltimore defensive back Bruce Laird, who had cleared the Cleveland line on an outside blitz. Showing incredible poise, Sipe didn't panic and instead simply lobbed a pass over the outstretched arms of Laird and into the soft hands of Greg Pruitt on the other side at the seven. Pruitt tightroped the sideline and made it into the end zone for a Browns' touchdown with 13:22 to play. Cockroft's extra point made it 28-13 Browns, and it once again appeared that the Kardiac Kids would get a one-week respite.

Things looked even rosier as the Cleveland defense continued to play solid and kept the Browns' lead at fifteen through much of the fourth quarter. But the Browns blew an opportunity to add to their margin when Cleo Miller fumbled at the Baltimore forty-one after a seventeen-yard run on the possession following Greg Pruitt's touchdown. Though the Colts could do nothing with the Browns' second fumble, it kept them in the game.

After a Browns' punt from their own ten on their next possession gave Baltimore a first down at the Cleveland thirty-eight with 5:04 left, things, as they always seemed to with the 1980 Browns, got interesting.

Jones drove his team toward the end zone, albeit not very quickly. When he finally hit McCall for a two-yard touchdown pass to make it 28-20, just 1:27 remained after the Colts took nearly four minutes and ten plays to drive thirty-eight yards, another testament to the Cleveland defense.

On the ensuing kickoff everyone in the state of Maryland knew what was coming. Recalling Cleveland's botched onside kick in Tampa, Browns' fans were essentially expecting the Colts to recover the kick. Instead, Judson Flint snagged the bouncing ball, and all of Cleveland breathed a sigh of relief. Finally it appeared that the Browns would not take their fans down to the final gun and to the quick of their fingernails. Instead they would win a game the easy way. Or so it seemed.

A play later Mike Pruitt was hit from behind and fumbled the football. Colts' defensive back Reggie Pinkney recovered at the Baltimore forty, and just like that, what should have been a relaxing coast to victory again would become a bloody struggle.

On this drive the Colts wasted no time. Jones completed five straight passes while driving the Colts the sixty yards they needed to go in less than a minute. With nineteen seconds left he hit running back Don McCauley for a five-yard touchdown. Though Mike-Mayer's extra point was good, Baltimore fans couldn't forget that had his initial point after not been botched this kick would have tied the game. Still the Colts would have one more chance resting on one final onside kick.

Once again Browns' fans had to be having flashbacks to six weeks before when their team nearly cost itself the game by pooching an onside kick in the final minute. But with so little time remaining the Colts would have to pull off a variation of an onside kick that, if they recovered, would give them less distance to travel into field-goal range.

Mike-Mayer's kick was a chip shot that floated over the Browns' front line at the Baltimore forty-five and into Cleveland territory. As it started to come down,

Thom Darden was set to be the man who would either seal the victory or possibly give it away as he stood at the Cleveland thirty-six. "I was thinking just two things," Darden later said, "catch the ball and drop down. Obviously, I only did the one."

Darden did catch the ball, but then dropped it amidst a swarm of Colts' attackers. The sharp gasp of the crowd sent shivers up the Browns' spines as the ball hit the ground and a free-for-all followed. "I had the ball and it just popped out," Darden said. "I was scared to death." He wasn't alone. But instead of disaster striking once again, Browns' safety Autry Beamon saved the day for the visitors by outfighting several Colts for the football and sealing a Cleveland victory.

"I'm just glad it didn't take any funny bounces," Beamon said.

Paul McDonald, who filled in for Sipe on the Browns' final three plays after Sipe was shaken up by a Laird sack, knelt out the final seconds, and the Browns had won, though once again in a fashion that was much more difficult than it had to be.

The *Press*'s Jim Braham called the Browns "Sam's Glo-Coat Boys," since they simply detested a dull finish. "We can't seem to do things the easy way," Rutigliano said. "Maybe it's just that we have a propensity for wanting to line up for onside kicks. I really don't know how else to explain it. This team has to learn to take the melodrama out of the fourth quarter, or I won't be coaching much longer."

And it wouldn't have been a Monday without Bob Sudyk trying to figure out the mentality of the Browns. "It seems the Browns are powerless to prevent lapses just as much as some of us can't alter pattern baldness," he wrote. "There is no cure. You learn to live with it. They sure are fun when they keep winning. What concerns the diehards is that the near disasters continue to be self-inflicted."

While the obvious reasons for the near-comeback by Baltimore could be blamed on the Browns' offense, the Browns' defense was also not entirely innocent, allowing two touchdowns in the final minutes. "It seems that every week we feel we're in command, but then relax too much, or something," hypothesized Lyle Alzado. "What we've got to do is learn to play as hard in the fourth quarter as we do in the first."

But things would not have been so tight in the final minute had it not been for Mike Pruitt's second fumble, or his first for that matter, which led to Baltimore's initial touchdown in the second quarter. "The two fumbles I committed, especially the second one, takes something away from the pleasure I got in running the ball," he said. "I must protect the ball better, I know that."

"Every time we were stopped today," Sipe said, "we stopped ourselves."

Despite the two cough-ups it was a great day for Pruitt and the Cleveland running game. Pruitt racked up 103 yards on eighteen carries, marking his second straight one-hundred-yard game and third of the season. Using a tag-team philosophy at tailback the Browns employed Pruitt, White (who gathered seventy-seven yards on fifteen carries in his best rushing game of the year), and an unheralded Cleo Miller, who only carried three times but wound up with twenty-nine yards. The Browns ended up with a season-high 211 yards on the ground, almost matching to the letter their 212 yards passing.

"I feel real good," White said afterward. "I'll admit, I was getting anxious because I hadn't run the ball much the last couple of weeks. Being a running back, you want the ball as much as you can get it, and you get edgy when you don't. Maybe this game helped get me out of the doghouse, but then, I never really felt I was in one. Sam handled everything so well."

While Sipe and the passing game didn't have quite the success in the second half they'd enjoyed in the first, the attack was still more than adequate. Sipe hit on twenty-two of twenty-nine passes, including five to Logan for eighty-five yards.

The Cleveland offensive line, even without Dieken, played as inspired as it had all year, sparking a dominant running game and providing Sipe with protection that he called "a dream." Added Sipe, "They're a prideful group. They struggled some last Monday night, and were determined to prove they are better than they might have looked to some people in their last game."

Sudyk also commended the Browns' line, particularly Sheppard, who, despite playing with his own limp, "protected Sipe as if he were mom."

Appropriately—and ironically for Dieken—the line was given a game ball. "I played every game for 14 years, and in the majority of them I played at least three quarters," Dieken said. "That game I played one play and they decide to give the offensive line a game ball. I knew I was going to take a lot of pride in that. I played *one play*."

But once again the primary reason the Browns were victorious was the defense, which sacked Jones five times and only allowed one scoring drive of more than sixty yards. All of a sudden the Cleveland D, which in the preseason was considered to be the team's Achilles' heel, had directly won two games in the month of November. Thom Darden seemed to exemplify the new spirit of the defense in his weekly column in the *Plain Dealer* before the Baltimore game when he attacked *PD* columnist Dan Coughlin for calling it the worst defense in team history back in September.

With the improvement of the defense playing a major role in five consecutive victories, the Browns were bubbling with confidence. "This team is going places," Logan said. "We are gaining confidence, and that's very important. It might have been what we lacked before. Now the feeling is that we can win, and it's something everybody is getting, like a fever. One of the reasons for it, I believe, is because we have come back so well after losing the first two games of the season. A team of less character would have quit. But not this one. Instead, we got better, all of us, and now we believe."

Sipe agreed. "We did a lot of soul-searching after we lost our first two games and Sam handled everything just the way it should have been handled. Then, after we lost to Denver in a game we should have won, it was evident to all of us that we could do it."

The win in Baltimore gave the 7-3 Browns sole possession of first place, for a day at least, since the Oilers would host New England on *Monday Night Football*.

Elsewhere in the Central the visiting Bengals gave the improving Oakland Raiders all they could handle before a four-yard touchdown run by quarterback Jim Plunkett with 5:30 to play clinched the Raiders' 28-17 win. The Bengals not only dropped to 3-7 but also lost starting quarterback Ken Anderson to injury once again. Anderson left the game with a bruised chest and was replaced by Jack Thompson.

The Browns' thoughts now turned to Pittsburgh, where they would be traveling the following Sunday for what would be a much bigger game than most had figured following the teams' first meeting. Those who had written off the Pittsburgh Steelers after their loss to the Browns were rethinking those words following the Steelers' 24-21 win in Tampa Bay, which improved them to 6-4, just one game back of the Browns. Still Pittsburgh had not looked anywhere close to their Super Bowl form as Terry Bradshaw was yanked in the fourth quarter after a horrible game in which he completed just eleven of twenty-six passes for one hundred yards and was replaced by Cliff Stoudt.

The Steelers also received some help from the officials in the waning moments when the Bucs were driving for a potential tying field goal. With twenty-one seconds left and Tampa down three, a third-down pass from Doug Williams to Jimmie Giles was caught right at the first-down marker at the Pittsburgh forty-six. An official told Giles that he had the first down, and he relayed that to Williams, who rushed the offense to the line of scrimmage and spiked a pass into the ground to stop the clock. The problem was that Giles had been a foot short of the first down and Williams's intentional incompletion came on fourth down, ending the possession as well as Tampa Bay's hopes of forcing overtime.

Now that the Steelers were on a bit of a roll again they would enter their Week Eleven showdown with the Browns with an opportunity to tie Cleveland in the standings. "I am not going to think about next Sunday until tomorrow," Rutigliano said following the Colts game. "I've got all week to think about the Steelers. I just want to savor this victory right now."

With a trip to Three Rivers Stadium, where the Browns had never won, looming on the horizon, Rutigliano's desire for relaxation could certainly be understood.

7 · Part of the Journey

As the Browns prepared for their Week Eleven rematch with the hated Pittsburgh Steelers they began to notice a different aura surrounding this game. There was something that hadn't been present in the Browns' camp through much of the 1970s, not even prior to the Browns' narrow victory over the Steelers three weeks earlier.

"The interesting thing about this game," Sam Rutigliano said, "is we are in a position now where we are going in not with the hope of winning or the hope of playing well, but with the confidence knowing we have beaten them before and that we played well against them and can again."

"When we started taking a bus down there a few years ago, I thought it was a long ride," Thom Darden wrote in his weekly *Plain Dealer* column. "Now I'm sort of looking forward to relaxing on the bus and enjoying the scenery."

"This week it's what the *Steelers* have to do to beat the *Browns*—for the first time since I've been here," said Ozzie Newsome. "We always tried to find a way offensively to beat them. This week they've got to find a way to beat us."

It happened so gradually it may not have dawned on some, but the 1980 Cleveland Browns were looking and talking like a playoff team. Any remaining doubters could be silenced once and for all if the Browns could beat the defending Super Bowl champions at Three Rivers Stadium. A Browns' victory in Pittsburgh could also be doubly useful in paving the way toward an AFC Central Division title. First, it might be able to give them the motivation and confidence—not to mention the boost to the divisional record—to withstand the Houston Oilers, who defeated the New England Patriots in their Monday-night showdown after the Browns' victory in Baltimore. In their 38-34 triumph the Oilers' offense looked as sharp as ever as Earl Campbell ran for two touchdowns, and Ken Stabler threw for three more. The Houston defense had even stepped up to derail a fierce Patriot comeback when defensive back Greg Stemrick intercepted New England quarterback Steve Grogan in the end zone with thirty-five seconds to play with the Pats at the Houston nineteen. Heading into Week Eleven the Browns and Oilers were tied for first at 7-3, and their November 30 matchup in Houston was looking more and more like the game of the year in the division.

The other reason why a Cleveland win over the Steelers would be huge was it would all but eliminate Pittsburgh from the playoff hunt. If the Browns could beat them at Three Rivers, the Steelers' record would drop to 6-5, two games back of the Browns with only five games to play, and the Steel Curtain would almost certainly be drawn to a close, at least for the 1980 season.

A Browns' victory would extend their winning streak to six games. They hadn't won six in a row since 1972, the last time they'd made the playoffs. And a win in Pittsburgh would give the team a titanic lift—probably even more of a lift than their win over the Steelers in Cleveland, which was, for some reason, seen as globally important enough that an overseas Browns' fan had mailed Art Modell a clipping from The *Egyptian Gazette* containing a story about Cleveland's 27-26 win over Pittsburgh.

Following Pittsburgh's narrow victory over the Buccaneers the previous Sunday Tampa linebacker David Lewis put into words what many NFL observers (and Browns' fans) had been thinking all season. "The Steelers aren't the best team in their division," he said. "They didn't impress me as much as Cleveland."

Now the Browns would have a chance to prove that beyond doubt.

Still the Steelers weren't done yet. Pittsburgh defensive backs coach Dick Walker took issue with the notion that the Steelers' season was over and that the Browns had already proven they were the better team. "We're the Pittsburgh Steelers and we're at home," he said in an interview. "What makes you think the Browns are supermen?"

The oddsmakers seemed to side with Walker, making Pittsburgh a surprising 6½-point favorite.

But for as much motivation as the Browns may have had the Steelers would have just as much as they labored to stay alive in the playoff hunt. And instead of going into battle with several second-stringers as they did in Cleveland the Steelers would be as close to full strength as they had been all season. But they would again be without wide receiver John Stallworth, who had returned from a broken leg the week before only to break his foot in Tampa Bay, ending his season.

More importantly Terry Bradshaw would start at quarterback. Though he'd looked shaky in the two games since returning from his injury, the Browns knew Bradshaw was the guy Pittsburgh wanted in the huddle in the final minutes of a close game. After being replaced by Cliff Stoudt in the fourth quarter of the win over Tampa Bay, Chuck Noll admitted that if Bradshaw struggled early against the Browns he'd put Stoudt back in. Bradshaw agreed with his coach's thinking and refused to blame his thumb and rib injuries for his struggles. Rutigliano passed off the talk of benching Bradshaw as rhetoric, saying if anyone wanted to see Stoudt throw on Sunday they'd better get to Three Rivers really early for warm-ups.

Even if Bradshaw weren't 100 percent the Browns would still have to deal with wide receiver Lynn Swann, who also missed the game in Cleveland. The same was true for running back Franco Harris, who would also play in the rematch. But probably most important for the Steelers, at least defensively, was the return of linebacker and Kent State–alum Jack Lambert, which many felt was the most damaging of all the Pittsburgh losses. As important as Bradshaw was to the Steeler offense simply by being on the field, so was Lambert to the Steeler defense. "Jack Lambert was the best player on that team," Tom DeLeone said. "He could cover a wide receiver and he could stop a fullback. The guy could do both and he was good at it. That whole defense was built around him."

If the Browns were going to roll up four hundred yards of offense against Pittsburgh this time they'd have to be operating in their highest gear.

"But those things are all nebulous," Rutigliano said of the charges that the Browns only beat the Steelers because of their injuries. "We beat the Steelers last time, but anybody who has any concern about who played for them and who didn't, well, it can all be resolved in six days."

The Browns meanwhile would enter the game relatively healthy. Doug Dieken would be back, and the only noteworthy absence would be Keith Wright, who was out for at least two weeks with a sprained knee. The Browns had also dodged a bullet in Baltimore when it was reported Sipe's late-game "dinger" was a bit more serious than originally thought. On the play before he carved up the Baltimore blitz and hit Greg Pruitt for the eventual winning touchdown in the fourth quarter, Sipe took a shot to the head. As the fourth quarter progressed his peripheral vision worsened and reached a point where he had to be taken out of the game. After nursing a splitting headache on the plane ride home Sipe felt much better on Monday and showed no ill effects.

As the week wore on the Steelers revealed they would probably use a 4-1-6 defensive formation against Sipe and the Browns to try and take away the short passing game that had ravaged them in Cleveland. But Sipe's success against the Steelers three weeks earlier wasn't a one-time deal. In the Browns' previous three games against Pittsburgh they had scored ninety-two points, an average of nearly thirty-one per game, as Sipe threw for more than a thousand yards and twelve touchdowns. Of course, in losing two of the three the Browns' defense had surrendered 110 points, and many expected another shootout at Three Rivers between the second- and third-ranked offenses in the conference.

Whatever happened, both teams knew each other too well to pull any surprises. "We know what to expect from them, just as they know what to expect from us,"

Sipe said. "One thing is sure. There is no way they will be overlooking us, so it won't be easier. It will boil down to us doing the best thing we do, as well as we can do it. I mean why change the horses in the middle of the stream, you know?"

"There is no question," Rutigliano said, "but that the challenge of Cleveland, with us in first place, playing them in Pittsburgh and the position they're in right now, they will play the very best football they've played all year."

"But that's fine. Those are the kind of games we want to be involved in. The good thing about it from our standpoint is that there's nobody terribly concerned about it. We know we're going to play well and we'll find out whether it's good enough."

That seemed to be the spirit Rutigliano was preaching to his team all week. He refused to allow them to get caught up in the hoopla of the big game and instead kept them focused on the big picture. "I'll probably tell the players the same thing I told them in Baltimore last Sunday," he said. "I'll say, 'This is not the destination, it's only part of the journey.'"

Unlike the Steelers when they came to Cleveland, the Browns would have to essentially go it alone in Pittsburgh. Though about fifteen thousand Pittsburgh fans attended the Browns-Steelers game in Cleveland, only about six hundred Browns' backers would trek east to Pennsylvania simply because Three Rivers seated about 25,000 less than Cleveland Stadium and as a result fewer tickets were made available to the visiting team.

But despite the fans and crowd noise the site itself figured to have an impact on the game. Since its opening in 1970 Three Rivers Stadium had hosted some of the best athletes and teams in all of professional sports throughout the decade. It had been the home of six world-championship teams between the Steelers and Pirates, as well as twenty-five postseason games in both baseball and football. Going into the Browns' game the Steelers held a record of 70-15 at Three Rivers, including a 30-4 mark against AFC Central opponents. Prior to the Bengals' shocking upset in Pittsburgh two months earlier Houston was the only Central team that had ever tasted victory at Three Rivers.

But for the Browns Three Rivers was more than just a stage for a championship team. Over the previous ten seasons it had become their own private hell. "I think when you go into a game thinking that everyone expects you to lose, that negative thinking does affect you and your attitude," Dick Ambrose said. "If something goes wrong, you're thinking, 'Well, that was supposed to happen.'"

Between 1950 and 1969, playing either at Forbes Field or at Pitt Stadium, the Browns had won fifteen of their twenty games against the Steelers in Pittsburgh. When Three Rivers opened in 1970 the Steelers were coming off a 1-13 year, Chuck Noll's first as head coach, and there were no indicative signs of what lay ahead in the decade to come. By the time the Browns traveled east to Pennsylvania in late November 1970 the Steelers were already well out of the playoff hunt, while the

Browns were battling the Bengals for the first-ever AFC Central Division title. The Steelers dominated the Browns that day and won, 28-9, on their way to a 5-9 season. The loss prevented the Browns from capturing a share of the division crown, and they missed the playoffs.

In 1971 the Browns managed to win their first-ever Central title but were still skunked by the Steelers in Pittsburgh in early November, this time by a count of 26-9. In 1972, for only the second time ever, the Steelers finished with a better record than the Browns and won their first division championship. The Browns captured the Wild Card in spite of a 30-0 drubbing in Pittsburgh in early December. The teams would go in opposite directions for the next half-decade, and the Browns' losses at Three Rivers got no prettier.

In 1973 the Browns finished 7-5-2, while the Steelers tied the Bengals for the division crown and made the playoffs as a Wild Card. The Browns and Steelers met in Pittsburgh in September, and the home team romped, 33-6. Ironically, though the 1974 Steelers were the first of the four Pittsburgh Super Bowl champions, they endured the first truly tough game against the Browns at Three Rivers, with Pittsburgh narrowly holding off soon-to-be 4-10 Cleveland, 20-16. Pittsburgh rolled to its second straight world championship a year later and likewise rolled over the Browns at Three Rivers, 31-17. The most differential between the Browns and Steelers occurred in 1975 as the Browns struggled to a 3-11 season, at the time the worst in their history.

Though the Browns showed signs of improvement over the next two seasons their performances at Three Rivers didn't necessarily show it. A 31-14 loss in 1976 was followed by a 35-31 defeat a year later during which Dave Mays, filling in for an injured Brian Sipe, fell just short of rallying the Browns from a huge deficit.

When Sam Rutigliano took over as head coach for the 1978 season the Browns entered a new era of defeats at Three Rivers Stadium. After starting the campaign 3-0, the Browns in Week Four took the host Steelers into sudden death and appeared to have victory in their grasp when Ricky Feacher recovered a Pittsburgh fumble on the overtime kickoff. Although replays proved positive that it was, the officials ruled the fumble wasn't a fumble and gave the ball back to Pittsburgh. The Steelers won the game a few minutes later when Terry Bradshaw hit tight end Bennie Cunningham on a thirty-seven-yard "gadget" play.

The Browns and Steelers went to overtime at Three Rivers again in 1979, and both teams had opportunities to win early. Sipe was intercepted by defensive back Mel Blount at the Pittsburgh four; following that, Bradshaw was intercepted by Ron Bolton at the Cleveland twelve. The Steelers pulled out a 33-30 win on a thirty-seven-yard Matt Bahr field goal, and the Browns missed the playoffs by one game.

The incredible array of blowouts mixed with cruel heartbreaks during the Browns' numerous misadventures at Three Rivers led many to refer to it simply as The Jinx. "It was like, what can we do to win in this place?" Doug Dieken said. "We had some guys that didn't play well over there. I don't know if it was a mental thing or what. It could be that they'd had bad experiences over there and they started looking for more bad experiences, and when you start looking for negative things, they're going to happen. By the same token, they were a damn tough football team."

"That's the bottom line," Thom Darden concurred. "They had everything you need. They had a running back, they had two great receivers, but first and foremost, they had a great defense. You go down the line and there was not a weak link."

But 1980 was the start of a new decade, a decade that didn't appear would be dominated by the Steelers as the 1970s had. For the Browns it seemed like a perfect time to bring The Jinx to an end and to begin a new era of football for both the Cleveland Browns and the Pittsburgh Steelers. "Our players realize that Three Rivers is a myth," Rutigliano said the week before. "Hell, we could play in Ebbets Field and win." (A tricky task since Ebbets Field was demolished in 1960.) "If we play Carnegie Melon or the University of Pittsburgh [at Three Rivers]," he added, "we'd beat them. The problem wasn't The Jinx, the problem was they were very good. I never felt there was a jinx. We did everything we could."

But in the early going that Sunday it was clear that The Jinx wasn't going down without a fight. The tone may have been set before either team took the field. As the Browns came through the tunnel and onto the field for warm-ups a fan threw a can of Iron City beer from the stands and hit Tom DeLeone's helmet.

Though neither team scored in the first quarter the Steelers held the ball for 13:57 and looked more like the team that had won the past two Super Bowls. A Clinton Burrell interception halted Pittsburgh's first drive, and when he returned the football to the Pittsburgh thirty-three the Browns were poised to draw first blood. But the visitors couldn't move the chains and called on Don Cockroft for a forty-seven-yard field-goal attempt. When he missed it wide right none of the Browns could have known the eerie portent it represented.

The Steelers took advantage and drove seventy yards in fifteen plays and took a 7-0 lead when Bradshaw hit wide receiver Jim Smith for a ten-yard touchdown pass on the first play of the second quarter. In many of the Browns' previous ten games at Three Rivers such a turn of events would have been enough to cripple their hopes of winning. But these were the Kardiac Kids. The Browns took the ensuing kickoff and drove eighty-seven yards down the throat of the improved Pittsburgh defense, sparked by a twenty-five-yard run by Mike Pruitt and a thirty-nine-yard Sipe pass to Reggie Rucker to the Pittsburgh six on third-and-nine. With 8:40 remaining in the half Ozzie Newsome made a diving catch for a four-yard touchdown toss that cut the lead to one. But instead of kicking off in a tie game the Browns were forced to settle with a one-pont deficit as Cockroft's bad day continued. Gerry Sullivan's point-after snap cut through the crisp November air and through holder Paul McDonald's hands. "I just missed it," McDonald said. "The snap was a little high, but not too high. I should have caught it. Instead, it went right through my hands."

Cockroft picked up the bouncing ball and tried to run it into the end zone, but he was quickly smothered by the Steelers. Though it didn't seem like a big deal at the time, that flubbed snap would later turn out to have a huge impact on this brisk afternoon in Pittsburgh.

Four minutes later things began to turn around for the Browns. Burrell's second interception of Bradshaw gave the Browns a first down in Pittsburgh territory at the forty-four, but it appeared that they wouldn't be able to do anything with the takeaway when Johnny Evans was called on to punt on fourth-and-one at the Pittsburgh thirty-seven. But after all the talk the previous week about not being able to surprise one another the Browns pulled a fast one on the Steelers. Evans jogged up under center, quickly took the snap, and handed off to Dino Hall. Catching the Steelers off-guard Hall galloped for nineteen yards for a first down at the Pittsburgh eighteen, and the Browns were back in business. "I learned that in the school yard of P.S. 199 in Brooklyn," Evans said afterward.

A few moments later the Browns took the lead on one of the most impressive plays of the season. From the Pittsburgh fifteen Sipe dropped back to pass and spotted Dave Logan streaking down the right sideline, covered by safety Donnie Shell. Sipe lobbed the ball into the end zone, where Logan leapt up and over Shell, snagged the football with one hand, then came down with it in the corner of the end zone for a breathtaking touchdown. "Logan is a great athlete," Shell said. "I was in good position, but he just outjumped me." The snap and hold on the extra point were good this time, and the Browns led, 13-7.

The margin would stand up until halftime, but there were still some fireworks before the intermission. With less than two minutes to play in the half the Browns were faced with third-and-one from their own forty. Tailback Cleo Miller had injured his ankle a few plays earlier, and as the Browns prepared to break the huddle and line up several members of the offense were yelling at Charles White, who had replaced Miller. The Browns took their places at the line of scrimmage, but Sipe noticed White was lined up in the wrong place and hollered for him to move. When White didn't move, a frustrated Sipe called time out and went to the sideline to talk to Rutigliano. White joined him. "There were words between Charles White and everybody on the field," Sipe said. "It's something that needs to be resolved, and it's a good thing it's out in the open now."

When they returned to the offensive huddle there was more discussion taking place. The Browns took their formation once again, but it was thrown for a loop when both Mike Pruitt and White went in motion. "In that situation," Rutigliano said later, "Mike becomes the running back and White the fullback, but there was some confusion in Charlie's mind." Sipe tried to call another time out, but the officials disallowed it and penalized the Browns five yards for having two men in motion.

Now faced with a third-and-six at the Cleveland thirty-five, Sipe was intercepted by defensive back Mike Wagner, who returned the ball to the Cleveland thirty-one before being tackled with 1:02 remaining. Frustrated by the whole situation White got into a scuffle with defensive backs Mel Blount and Ron Johnson after the play.

Suddenly the Steelers were poised to take the lead. But after Bradshaw fired an incomplete pass on first down his second-down toss was deflected and picked off by Charlie Hall at the twenty-one, ending the threat. The Browns went to the locker room up by six.

Though the White controversy had no effect on the score there was reportedly a heated argument in the Cleveland locker room at the half. "Everybody lost his composure," Rutigliano said, "and I told them at halftime we could not afford to get involved in that kind of thing at any time on the field." Though the coach didn't blame White outright for the disruption the rookie was noticeably absent from the Cleveland attack in the second half even though Cleo Miller was unable to return.

The following week several Browns explained what happened in the huddle, though with varying points of view. One said that White just lost his cool and let the Steelers get to him.

"The only thing we were doing was trying to cool Charlie," the source said. "Nobody was giving him hell because he didn't know the play. That wasn't it, no matter how it looked. A couple of guys gestured to the sidelines because they thought Charlie was too mad at the Steelers to be effective."

White basically admitted as much. He said that on the play before he had made a good block on Pittsburgh linebacker Robin Cole, and the pair went down. It looked for an instant like they were fighting, even though they weren't, and Cole's teammates began yelling at White. They kept it up as White returned to the huddle, and White made the cardinal sin of yelling back at them. Then the fireworks began in the Cleveland huddle.

During the last play of the half, White said that he was punched in the neck by one of the Steelers, and tempers flared once again.

One thing that everyone who spoke of the incident agreed on was that the locker-room speech was not a berating. Rutigliano simply told the team not to get caught up in the Steelers' antics, because it would only cause them to lose their focus.

"It was a general team thing and then it was over," White said. "That's team unity. I wasn't looking for a fight. Nobody was. But our whole team was together on it." Still there were some strange things being said that suggested White was still a rookie in over his head. "This is something the players will handle," one player said. "Charlie has some maturing to do. He's got to learn this is a team sport and he's part of a team. He's no longer Charlie White, the big man on campus."

Also surprisingly missing from the second half were the two much-heralded offenses. Neither team could mount any kind of sustainable drive through the entire third quarter, though both had their chances. The Steelers drove to the Cleveland twenty-three on their first possession of the second half, but a ten-yard sack by Judson Flint and a delay-of-game penalty took Pittsburgh out of field-goal range. After a punt the Browns marched to the Pittsburgh twenty-eight where Cockroft was summoned for a forty-six-yard field-goal attempt, which fell short.

The Cleveland defense continued to entice Steeler mistakes and forced another punt after the missed field goal. A nineteen-yard run by Greg Pruitt and a twenty-yard Sipe-to-Newsome pass moved the Browns back into scoring range, but once again Cockroft missed a forty-six-yard boot short. Like a heavyweight fighter the Browns' defense kept getting knocked down but continued to get up.

Clarence Scott halted the next Pittsburgh drive when he intercepted Bradshaw at midfield and returned it five yards to the forty-five. But for as well as the Browns' defense was playing, the Steelers were even better and kept Sipe and Company from cashing in on yet another takeaway.

The teams traded punts, with both defenses rising to the occasion. But as the fourth quarter waned the Steelers appeared poised to pull out victory as they always did against the Browns at Three Rivers Stadium. With four minutes remaining Bradshaw hit Swann on a pair of plays in which the Steelers again showed glimpses of their former Super Bowl selves. After a twenty-three-yard completion moved Pittsburgh to the Cleveland twenty-four Bradshaw and Swann hooked up again, this time on a diving twenty-one-yard catch at the Cleveland three where Pittsburgh would have a first-and-goal. After an illegal-motion penalty, two short runs moved the Steelers to the one where they were faced with third-and-goal. Here they made a pair of decisions that appeared to cost them the game.

Instead of trying to power the football in from three feet out, the Steelers tried to finesse their way into the end zone. Still it very nearly worked. On third down the playcall was "sprint-out left," and Bradshaw fired a perfect pass to a wide-open Jim Smith in the end zone. But the ball bounced off his hands and fell incomplete. It brought up fourth down. The Steelers again decided to try to score through the air via "sprint-out left." But as the ball was snapped and the receivers cleared the line of scrimmage, Swann's feet got tangled up with wide receiver Theo Bell's, taking them both out of the play. Bradshaw ended up throwing to the wrong side of tight end Randy Grossman at the Pittsburgh three, where he was dropped for a two-yard loss with 2:44 remaining. The Browns had held and appeared to have victory in their grasp.

High above the field in the press box Hal Lebovitz wrote "Thank you, Steelers" in his notes. But as was the case with Lebovitz's comments in the first Browns-Steelers game, they were written a bit prematurely.

From the three the Browns ran Mike Pruitt up the middle for no gain on first down and Greg Pruitt around right end for two on second. Although the yardage was minimal, they kept the clock moving and forced the Steelers to take their final time out. On third-and-eight with two minutes left Rutigliano suggested the Browns run one more time, which, even if it didn't pick up the first down, would give the Steelers just over a minute to travel more than half the field with no time outs. But Sipe vetoed Rutigliano's recommendation and called for a screen pass to Calvin Hill, which was a high enough percentage play to at least keep the clock moving while still giving the Browns a good chance at converting the first down.

But when Sipe dropped back to pass from his end zone Pittsburgh linebacker Jack Ham read the play perfectly and covered Hill. Unable to zero in on his intended target Sipe quickly threw the ball out of bounds to avoid any incidents or accidents in the end zone. "I wanted to get the ball to Calvin Hill, and if I had, it would have been a first down," Sipe said. "We needed almost 10 yards, and I thought we had a better chance by doing what we do best, although I admit it was a gamble. I'd probably do it again. If it had worked, everybody would have called it a great play."

Now with just under two minutes remaining the Browns were faced with fourth-and-eight from their own five, and Rutigliano had another decision to make. Should he risk trying to have Evans punt from his own end zone? Had the Browns made the extra point after their first touchdown their lead would be 14-7 at this point, and there would be no decision to make. Evans would punt, and the worst thing that could happen was a block for a touchdown to tie the contest. But since the Browns only led by six, a block and a score here could cost Cleveland the game. So Rutigliano opted to have Evans take an intentional safety to cut the lead to 13-9. It avoided the possibility of a punt block, and the Steelers would still have to score a touchdown to win. But had the lead been seven instead of six . . .

Evans took the snap and waited for the Pittsburgh tacklers to swarm him but, as some criticized the next day, didn't run away from them to melt a few extra seconds off the clock. He was tackled with 1:51 to play, and the Browns would free kick from their own twenty.

Evans's kick was good, sailing to the Pittsburgh twenty-eight, but the Browns' kick coverage was not as Theo Bell returned it eighteen yards to the Pittsburgh forty-six where the Steelers would take over with 1:44 left. Once again it was up to the Cleveland defense.

After Bradshaw threw an incomplete pass on first down he connected with Bell for twenty-four yards to the Cleveland thirty with the clock running. Bradshaw's third pass of the drive fell incomplete, but Oliver Davis was penalized for defensive holding, giving the Steelers a first down at the Cleveland twenty-five with a minute to play.

Bradshaw rolled out of the pocket on the next play and past the line of scrimmage, then ran back behind it and completed a long pass to Swann inside the Cleveland five. But this time it was the Steelers who were penalized since Bradshaw couldn't throw a forward pass after crossing the line of scrimmage. It set up second-and-fourteen from the twenty-nine.

As he had done all day and throughout his brilliant career Lynn Swann came up big when he had to. He snagged a twenty-three-yard pass from Bradshaw at the Cleveland six with the Pittsburgh crowd going bonkers and the clock still running. The Steelers raced up to the line and Bradshaw, pursued by Lyle Alzado, fired an incomplete pass intended for Bell. But for the third time in four plays a yellow hankie changed the outcome. Clarence Scott was called for defensive holding, and the Steelers were given another first down at the three with seventeen seconds remaining. Pittsburgh did pay a price on that play as Bradshaw injured his leg on a hit by Alzado, who in turn took a shot to his ribs. But both stayed in the game since it was down to the final nail-biting seconds once again at Three Rivers Stadium.

For the second time in twenty minutes the Browns would have to stop the Steelers at the goal line. Out of time outs, Pittsburgh had no choice but to go to the air. Bradshaw and the offensive coaches all seemed confident that the "sprint-out left" play would have been successful on the fourth down at the one had Swann and Bell not collided. So for the third time in nine plays "sprint-out left" was the call.

Bradshaw took the snap and did just what the play instructed him to do: he sprinted to his left, angling toward the end zone as the clock ticked down. Ron Bolton was covering Swann, but as Bradshaw rolled out Bell cut between the cornerback and receiver, forcing Bolton out of the play. It was Thom Darden's responsibility to pick up anything that got past Bolton, but he didn't get there in time. In a flash, Bradshaw spotted Swann open in the corner of the end zone and hit him for the winning touchdown pass with eleven seconds to play—one second for each of the Browns' losses in Three Rivers Stadium.

With the crowd in a frenzy the Steelers kicked off and the Browns took over at their own thirty-one, but Sipe only had time for two passes. The first fell incomplete, and the second was a dump-off to Greg Pruitt that gained only ten yards. Steelers 16, Browns 13. The Jinx was very much alive.

So was the heated rivalry between the teams. Both Bolton and Darden argued that Pittsburgh should have been penalized for an illegal pick on the winning play.

"He couldn't beat me unless it was," Bolton said.

"It's illegal," Darden said, "but nobody called it so what good does it do to complain?"

"I think they are just looking for a reason to explain it," Swann countered.

But even Bell basically admitted he had broken the rules. "I bumped him intentionally on my part, but incidentally in the opinion of the officials," he said, "and that's what counts."

"It is incidental," Rutigliano said, "it's a play they've been doing for 100 years and is rarely called against them. They did the same thing a few plays before and it wasn't called either. When two talented teams play, there is going to be controversy. It just means we are getting more competitive."

The final play also stirred up the emotions of Swann and Bolton, who had both endured a long day going against one another. But Swann had gotten the better of the Browns' veteran cornerback as he put together the best statistical game of his career with nine receptions for 138 yards. Swann, who either purposely or unintentionally referred to Bolton as "Bolden," was glad to see his opponent get burned on the winning play. "Bolden has the reputation of doing a lot of cussing and other things on the field, trying to prove he's a tough guy," he said. "He throws an elbow here and there, and takes a shot at you when the ball goes the other way. I don't spike the ball very often, but I had a lot of steam and frustration to blow off after that catch. I wanted to spike the ball right in front of him, but I couldn't find him."

Bolton of course saw things differently. "Fuck Swann," he said. "Did he say anything about the illegal pick the Steelers pulled on me on the scoring play? No, he wouldn't. I'm through saying nice things about Swann. He can't beat me one-on-one and if we play them again this season I'll play him exactly the same way as today."

It was nothing new for the Browns-Steelers rivalry, which, even when both teams weren't playoff contenders, was always vicious and contentious. "There was some cheap stuff out there—hands in the face and that sort of thing," said Pittsburgh defensive tackle Joe Greene. "But it wasn't as bad as when Forrest Gregg was in Cleveland." Early in the game the Steelers accused Henry Sheppard of putting Vaseline on his jersey to keep defensive linemen from grabbing on to him. Though Sheppard denied it the officials made him change shirts.

Though the Steelers had pulled off a dramatic and much-needed victory, in the locker room after the game they seemed to realize that the Steel Curtain was officially dead and gone. Or as Bob Sudyk put it, that they were "A tottering dynasty with its very aging back against the wall."

This was a game the Super Bowl Steelers would have won in the third quarter. The malaise orbiting the dressing room was noticeable to all, to the point that one sportswriter hollered, "Hey, you guys, you won!"

"We've got a *chance* now," Bradshaw said of the Steelers' playoff hopes. "But we've got to win every game, that's all there is to it. It's tough, though. Everybody wants us. We're trying as hard as we can, and this will help give confidence to everyone."

Even Noll seemed to understand the message this game had sent. "A-a-g-h!" he said, describing his emotions. "I said that several times during the game. I don't remember having anything else to say."

The Browns meanwhile had plenty to say, mostly that they had just let victory slip through their clutches. "This was our game all the way," Alzado said. "They just came up with the big play at the end, and it killed us."

Sipe echoed Alzado's sentiments and added "I had the feeling we had the nails in their coffin. "I guess you can never assume you have these guys beaten, and this loss won't be easy to live with. We all need to do some serious soul-searching. But, as sure as hell, the sun's going to come up tomorrow, and we still control our own destiny. I'm still planning to be busy around Christmas time."

While the Browns' defense had done an admirable job of keeping the now-healthy Steelers at bay, Sipe and the offense had their worst game since the Monday-night loss to Houston. The Browns managed just 266 yards of offense with Sipe limited to fifteen completions in thirty-four attempts for 178 yards with two touchdowns and an interception. The Browns also struggled on the ground as Mike Pruitt picked up just fifty-five yards on fifteen carries. Though Sipe was only sacked once he was under pressure all day, and the Steelers felt that was the key to victory. "Overall, we put more pressure on Brian Sipe this time," Donnie Shell said. "That's probably what won the game for us."

As was the case following the victory over Kansas City in September, the Browns' biggest cause for concern was the performance of Don Cockroft. "A day like today and you wish you had another job," Cockroft said. "Today I got under all three of the kicks. I didn't hit any one of them solid."

He not only missed three field goals, any one of which could have won the game, but the Browns failed to add an extra point, which dramatically changed the complexion of the final two minutes. "To take the last eleven seconds out of the game, all we had to do was kick the extra point," Rutigliano said. "If we had, or if we had made one of the three field goals, our strategy would have been dramatically changed at the end of the game."

But to be fair the veteran Cockroft was not entirely healthy. "I won't offer it as an excuse," said the beleaguered kicker, "but my back has been bothering me since the Houston Monday-night game. The trouble is that I can't seem to give my back time to heal. It starts to feel better, and then it's Sunday again, although I'm not using it as an excuse." Technically, though, it wasn't Cockroft's back. It was a strain of the sciatic nerve that ran across his left buttock and hip.

Paul McDonald thought part of the problem also might have been the playing surface, since Cockroft was kicking on plastic for just the third time all year. "He might have had a little problem on the Astroturf," McDonald said. "He got under all the kicks too much, maybe because he wasn't accustomed to the Astroturf."

In case the Steelers tying the Browns at 7-4 wasn't enough bad news for Cleveland fans, more came out of Chicago. At Soldier Field the Oilers had overcome a 6-0 first-half deficit and nipped the Bears, 10-6, to improve to 8-3 and take over sole possession of first place in the Central. Though Earl Campbell rushed for a season-high 206 yards the Oilers needed a fake-field-goal pass for a touchdown late in the first half to turn the momentum around.

Meanwhile the Browns' next opponent, the Bengals, once again tasted defeat, this time 14-0 to the Buffalo Bills at Riverfront where quarterback Ken Anderson continued his 1980 custom of leaving games with injuries. This time it was to his chest, and once again Jack Thompson replaced him to no avail as the Bengals dropped to 3-8.

Despite their heartbreaking loss, with the Bengals on the horizon the following Sunday and the simple fact that they were still very much in the playoff hunt, the Browns were in relatively good spirits as they boarded the bus for their trip back to Cleveland. "I said, 'We'll have a helluva good meal on the bus going home, tomorrow is Monday, Cincinnati comes in next Sunday, and the beat goes on,'" Rutigliano said of his postgame comments. "The sign of what kind of character you have on the team is how well you play after you lose a tough game, not how well you play after you win a tough game."

"It was just one of those days," said Marty Schottenheimer, "a game between two great teams, and it just wasn't meant to be."

"This team has character, and all we can do is go on and try to win the rest of our five games," Lyle Alzado said. "Hopefully, we can and it'll give us either a division championship or a place in the playoffs. But regardless of what happens in the end, this team has come of age, offensively and defensively."

"If anything can be said for today, it is that we know we're on par with the Steelers," Sipe added. "We played them off their feet most of the game, and they know it."

Though a sign had been attached to a tollbooth on the Pennsylvania Turnpike reading CLEVELAND BROWNS CRYING TOWELS HERE, with a roll of paper towels beside it, it did not appear the 1980 team was ready to call it quits. The loss in Pittsburgh was certainly hard to accept, but the Browns were showing the maturity and level-mindedness of a champion with their thoughts and words.

Seven days later they would do so with their actions.

While the Browns-Steelers rivalry was without question the fiercest on the field in the AFC Central, the Browns-Bengals rivalry was the most vicious in the front offices.

Though the Cincinnati franchise was just twelve years old, as the Bengals prepared to face the Browns on November 23 the two teams already had a long, rich, and controversial history. "Paul Brown despised Art Modell," Sam Rutigliano said. "Art Modell despised him because he could never make friends with him. Paul Brown would have nothing to do with it. Art wanted to be friends, but it never happened."

"If the history of the Browns-Bengals rivalry were written in the form of a novel, there would be a subplot in every chapter," Thom Darden wrote in his weekly column, and he was exactly right. After Paul Brown was fired by Art Modell as head coach of the Browns following the 1962 season, it didn't take very long for Brown to once again be involved in establishing an NFL team. In December 1965 he met with Ohio Governor James Rhodes to discuss the possibility of bringing a second professional football team to the Buckeye State. Two years later the American Football League announced that Cincinnati would receive an expansion team to begin play in 1968 and take part in the AFL/NFL merger two years later. Brown served as the owner, general manager, and coach and was eager to enjoy the same rapid success with the Bengals that he had spearheaded with the Browns when they first took the field in 1946.

After struggling to just seven total wins in the 1968 and 1969 seasons the Bengals surprised many in their first year in the NFL. They went 8-6 and won the first-ever AFC Central Division title, partly on the strength of a 14-10 mid-November win over the Browns in Cincinnati. The victory atoned for a 30-27 Cincinnati loss in Cleveland in October, after which Paul Brown marched off the field without shaking the hand of Blanton Collier, his former assistant who took over as the Browns' head coach after his departure. (The story goes that Brown had spoken with Collier before the game and said he didn't like to shake hands after the game was over. But Collier, who had a chronic hearing problem, didn't hear him and ran out to midfield at the conclusion looking for Brown while his former boss marched to the locker room amidst the boos of 83,000 fans.)

Naturally the Browns-Bengals rivalry was a big one for the players, who always wanted to win division games. But it always meant more to the teams' ownership. "The players could care less," Rutigliano said that week. "They don't even know Paul Brown."

After leading the Bengals to two more playoff berths (though no postseason victories) Brown stepped down as head coach following the 1975 season and selected assistant Bill Johnson as his replacement. With Brown now strictly in the owner's box, the heart of the rivalry was off the field. Even though the teams were in the same division and the same state the on-field rivalry just didn't take off through much of the 1970s. Aside from the Bengals' AFC Central titles in 1970 and 1973 and the Browns' only crown in 1971, the Pittsburgh Steelers had completely dominated the division. From 1974 through 1979 the Browns and Bengals had combined for just five winning seasons and one playoff berth between them. The Browns won six of the first seven meetings but the Bengals rebounded to win six of the next seven through 1976 before the teams split the series in 1977, 1978, and 1979.

The 1980 matchup would not be much different on the field. As usual, one team—in this case the Browns—was challenging for the playoffs, while the other—in this case the Bengals—was foundering in or near last place. In the ten years they'd been playing each other only three times had both teams compiled winning records in the same season.

The close ties and numerous connections between the two teams also assured that there would be more to this Browns-Bengals contest than a simple football game. Cincinnati defensive coordinator Hank Bullough had been an assistant coach with Sam Rutigliano at New England in 1973. Cincinnati's backup defensive end Mike St. Clair had played with the Browns for four seasons, and Bengals' rookie guard Billy Glass was the son of Bill Glass, who had played defensive end for the Browns in the 1960s. But the most interesting connection was Cincinnati head coach Forrest Gregg, struggling through his first season along the Ohio River. Gregg had coached the Browns from 1975 through the second-to-last game of the 1977 season and was eventually replaced by Rutigliano.

So the Bengals entered this game with an owner who had once coached the Browns and had been fired by Art Modell and a head coach who had once coached the Browns and had been driven out by Art Modell. Needless to say there was a lot of pride and hard feelings involved, but no one was admitting as much. "I'd be either lying or stupid to call this just another game," Gregg said, though he did his best to avoid the Cleveland media all week, including canceling the customary conference call with reporters. "I'm sure they consider playing Cleveland an Army-Navy game," Rutigliano said. "The Bengals will come in emotionally high and ready to play, but so will we."

Gregg's tenure in Cleveland was a rocky one but one not without its share of success. He joined the club in January 1974 and quickly earned an impressive reputation coaching the Browns' offensive line, the area he'd played during a Hall-of-Fame career in Green Bay and Dallas from 1956 to 1971. After just one year as a Cleveland assistant he was promoted to head coach to replace Nick Skorich after a 4-10 1974 season. But Gregg could do no better in his first year as the Browns sloshed to their worst record ever, 3-11, in 1975. Ironically after a 0-9 start, Gregg's first victory was a 35-23 upset of the Bengals, who were on their way to the playoffs in Paul Brown's final year on the sideline.

But Gregg and the Browns turned things around dramatically in 1976. After dropping three of their first four games the Browns rallied to win eight of their last ten to finish 9-5 and were only kept out of the playoffs due to a tough loss in Kansas City in the final week. Gregg was named NFL Co-Coach of the Year by the Associated Press, and with Brian Sipe establishing himself at quarterback and several young players appearing to come into their prime, it only seemed natural that Gregg and the Browns would be ready to roll in 1977.

But a few months after receiving his postseason honors Gregg started the wheels of momentum turning against him in the front office when he demanded that Modell give him a raise and a contract extension. Modell eventually agreed to Gregg's terms, though reluctantly, and both sides were upset over the way the incident unfolded. Their already-rocky relationship became even more strained.

Nonetheless all went according to the expectations early that fall when the Browns started the year 5-2. But Sipe went down with a broken shoulder blade in a loss in Pittsburgh, and the season essentially became null and void. Cleveland dropped to 6-5 and then was blasted by the mediocre Chargers in San Diego in Week Twelve. Gregg then blasted his team in the locker room afterward. "You're cowards," he told them. "You quit on me. I don't even want to pray with you."

He didn't, and stormed out of the room.

One of the Browns' veterans suggested the team pray anyway and pray very loudly so that Gregg could hear them. They did, and the writing was on the wall. Looking back, Tom DeLeone wasn't sure what soured the relationship between Gregg and his players. "I don't know what happened with Forrest Gregg," DeLeone said. "Forrest Gregg was a good coach. I don't know whether it was a personality problem with the team or what. It just didn't click there for a couple of years. I can't put my finger on it."

After another loss to Houston a week later Modell decided to fire Gregg after the final game of the season. Word leaked to the press, and the week before the Browns were to travel to Seattle to close the schedule a *Plain Dealer* reporter called Gregg asking for a comment on a story revealing Modell's decision. "He's not firing me," Gregg told the reporter. "I'm resigning."

Gregg did, and assistant Dick Modzelewski stepped in to coach the Browns' final game, which turned out to be a 20-19 loss to the Seahawks, closing a 6-8 season. Rutigliano was hired later that month, and Gregg sat out the 1978 season before returning to coaching in Canada in 1979.

In vain, Gregg tried to distract the media's attention from his years in Cleveland. "I think I did a good job in Cleveland, but what happened to me is no different than getting traded," Gregg said the week before his first game against the Browns. "It's something that must be accepted as part of the business. The Cleveland papers can make it look like a vendetta. I am only one person and can't get in a battle with the media. They have the final words. The pen is mightier than the sword. It wasn't a pleasant experience in Cleveland. All anyone can ask is another opportunity. I have that here."

There was a rumor that Gregg's downfall ultimately stemmed from the fact that his wife and Pat Modell did not get along. It was also believed that Gregg and

Peter Hadhazy did not see eye-to-eye and that Gregg felt Hadhazy was nothing more than a meddler and Art Modell's errand boy. "My retort to that is this," a flustered Hadhazy said the day before the game, "if informing Forrest Gregg of certain waiver and personnel procedures, or correcting an illegal formation for him, or even advising him in strategical matters is meddling, then I am guilty. I meddled when he was here.

"I also plead guilty if meddling is insisting upon trading Mike Phipps, when Gregg did not want to, or preventing Gregg from trading two No. 1 draft choices for a guy who's no longer playing pro football.

"Ask Forrest if that's the kind of meddling he's talking about. If it isn't, then I don't know what he means."

There were also rumors that the Browns' brass was trying to spread the word that Gregg was "too dumb" to coach in the NFL, and Gregg threatened a lawsuit if a name was ever attached to that comment.

After Homer Rice was fired following two miserable seasons as coach of the Bengals, Paul Brown hired Gregg to take over in 1980, completing an odd circle and adding some pepper to an already spicy rivalry.

"There was unbelievable bitterness," Rutigliano said. "You could almost feel it. You could feel Art Modell during the Cincinnati week, even different than Pittsburgh. For as bad as he wanted to beat Pittsburgh, boy, he did not want to lose to Cincinnati."

Twenty Browns who had played for Gregg were still on the Cleveland roster, and the biggest questions of the week were directed to them concerning the differences between their current and previous coach. "I won't get into grading them," Brian Sipe said, "but I can categorize them by saying Forrest Gregg is a man who demands respect, and deserves it, based on what he has done with his life and career, and Sam Rutigliano is a man who has come in and earned our respect in a different way." Then he hesitated. "Oh, why do you guys ask me a question like that?" he asked the media gaggle surrounding him. "I really don't want to get into it any more than to say they are two different types of coaches."

"I got along with Forrest and the entire offensive line got along with Forrest," Doug Dieken said. "There was a faction of the team that didn't like his disciplined, Lombardi-esque demeanor. If you listened to him and then read Lombardi's book, you'd think, 'Been there, done that.'"

Mike Pruitt was probably the one man who benefited the most from the change atop the totem pole. Gregg felt Pruitt, the Browns' Number One draft choice in 1976, was a fumbler who couldn't be relied on. As a result Pruitt rushed for fewer than 350 yards in his two seasons under Gregg. That changed dramatically under Rutigliano, who saw Pruitt as an unutilized weapon. Pruitt rushed for 560 yards in 1978, then 1,294 in 1979, and appeared on his way to a second straight thousand-yard season in 1980 as the Bengals came to town in Week Twelve.

Pruitt said he harbored no ill will toward Gregg. In fact he was thankful he hadn't been used his first two seasons because it meant he now felt like he was only in his third year instead of his fifth. He said he planned on shaking Gregg's hand after the game.

"I know there are some of our players who feel strongly [about Gregg] but I am not getting involved in those things," Rutigliano said. "I want all our energies channeled in the right direction. The will to win is an over-used expression. Everybody has the will to win, but not everybody has the will to prepare. That's what I want our people to have, the will to prepare, because that's what keeps you involved in the task at hand."

And while the rivalry between the front offices may have been bitter, this game would still be played on the field where it appeared that the Browns would have a significant advantage. The 3-8 Bengals had lost four straight as well as several key players to injury along the way.

Quarterback Ken Anderson had started every game but finished few as he suffered from a rash of injuries. Fullback Pete Johnson, wide receiver Don Bass, tight end Dan Ross, punter-wide receiver Pat McInally, center Blair Bush, and tackle Max Montoya were all expected to miss the Browns' game. "We're trying to get up a team to come to Cleveland," Mike St. Clair joked. Not surprisingly the Browns were 7½-point favorites.

Though the Browns were relatively healthy they discovered the key to their offensive success wasn't completely so. Early in the week, after complaining of a run-down feeling and dizziness, Brian Sipe received treatment at the Cleveland Clinic for an inner-ear infection that had caused the peripheral vision problems that had begun in Baltimore and continued in Pittsburgh. It only made sense that something wasn't quite right since Sipe had his worst statistical game of the year in Pittsburgh after carving up the Steeler defense in Cleveland.

The Cleveland coaches knew that Sipe would have to play well for the Browns to win. Even the players, particularly the ones who had played under Gregg, knew that their former coach was capable of squeezing more out of his players than expected. "I know Forrest will have the Bengals sky-high Sunday, and the key for us is to bust their bubble by not letting them get off to a good start," Henry Sheppard said. "If they jump out early, they'll be even more keyed up and be tougher to beat."

Though the upcoming Browns-Bengals game and the annual Ohio State-Michigan clash would highlight a big sports weekend, most of America was more interested in what was happening in primetime that Friday night. At 10:00 P.M. CBS aired the episode of *Dallas* that millions of viewers had been waiting months for.

In the November 21 show it was finally revealed who shot the legendary series villain J. R. Ewing. Naturally the shooter wasn't identified until the final minutes of the program, and when it finally happened many fans were disappointed. Kristin Shepard, Sue Ellen Ewing's sister, confessed to shooting J. R., and most of the estimated eighty-three million who tuned in weren't very surprised. Various contests encouraged participants to "Guess Who Shot J. R.," and Las Vegas even took formal bets on fourteen suspects. The revelation made the front page of both the *Plain Dealer* and the *Cleveland Press* on Saturday.

The headlines of the sports sections the next day covered the Buckeyes' 9-3 loss to the Wolverines in Michigan, a defeat that cost Ohio State a trip to the Rose Bowl. The Browns were hoping they wouldn't be the second Ohio football team in two days to be denied its postseason destination because of a loss to a bitter rival.

But after one quarter things did not look particularly good for the Browns. They drove to the Cincinnati twenty-three on their first possession, but Don Cockroft missed his fourth field goal in five quarters when his forty-yard kick sailed wide right. Looking drained from its war in Pittsburgh seven days earlier the Browns' defense had trouble stopping the Cincinnati offense, which did have the services of Anderson, Ross, and McInally. An Oliver Davis interception of Ken Anderson halted the Bengals' first drive after they reached the Cleveland forty, but the Browns' offense could do nothing with the windfall.

A thirty-seven-yard pass from Anderson to Ross to the Cleveland nine set up the game's first score, a six-yard touchdown run over right tackle by Cincinnati running back Charles Alexander with forty-three seconds to play in the opening stanza. Paul Brown's second professional football team had taken a 7-0 advantage on his first.

"Our defense was a little stale," Rutigliano said of the early going. "I think we were still a little spent from the Pittsburgh game last Sunday. But we got it together and after they got their touchdown, we stopped them from making any big plays."

One reason the Bengals were having success was because the Browns' defense was getting burned on its angling. As the second quarter began Marty Schottenheimer told his crew to forget the angling and stunting and to just plow straight into the line. It worked.

Meanwhile the Cleveland offense started to heat up.

Following the Cincinnati kickoff, which ended with a personal-foul penalty on linebacker Ron Simpkins of the Bengals, the Browns began marching. They were aided by another personal foul, this one on linebacker Jim LeClair following a ten-yard Sipe-to-Mike Pruitt pass, and the down side of Gregg's fiery nature that was also reflected by his team was beginning to show. Less than a minute after the Bengals had taken the lead the Browns evened matters when Sipe hit Reggie Rucker for a sixteen-yard scoring pass twenty-two seconds into the second quarter.

Thanks to a block by Curtis Weathers of a forty-yard Sandro Vitiello field-goal attempt on Cincinnati's ensuing series, the score remained tied through the remainder of the period until the Browns began a long drive at their own sixteen with 1:47 left in the half. Aided by three straight passes to Rucker for eleven, twenty, and thirteen yards, the Browns took the lead with five seconds left when Sipe hit Calvin Hill in the end zone from five yards out. Cleveland led, 14-7, but if they didn't come out and make a statement quickly in the second half the Kardiac Kids might have to be called on once again.

That statement came following the second-half kickoff as the Browns marched forty-seven yards in six plays and scored when Sipe hit a wide-open and waving Greg Pruitt in the back of the end zone. Don Cockroft connected on his third consecutive extra point, and the Browns were in control, 21-7, but the Bengals weren't through yet.

Anderson drove his offense from its own fifteen to the Cleveland fifteen before leaving the game after reinjuring his knee, as was his custom. Though he returned one play later the Bengal offense stalled and was forced to settle for a field-goal attempt by Vitiello. The kick just barely cleared the line of scrimmage and fell short from thirty-three yards out with 3:09 left in the third quarter.

In case the Bengals weren't dead yet the Browns immediately went for the jugular. On first down Sipe connected with Greg Pruitt for a twenty-five-yard gain to the Cleveland forty-five. Then Sipe called for a post pattern by wide receiver Ricky Feacher, who had caught only six passes all season. Feacher found a seam in the Cincy zone and Sipe fired a pass for him at the Bengals' sixteen. Defensive backs Ken Riley and Bryan Hicks converged on Feacher, but the three-year veteran out of Mississippi Valley State outfought them both to catch the ball. In their efforts, Riley and Hicks collided and fell to the ground, and Feacher had a clear path to the end zone. He took it and raised his arms to the crowd in the closed end of the Stadium as he crossed the goal line. The Browns had landed the knockout punch they'd been unable to for more than a month. Cockroft's extra point made it 28-7, Browns, and it was all over but the shouting.

"That was the gamebreaker," Rutigliano said. "It gave us a lot of comfort. It made it uphill for them."

"We were looking for that play with Feacher all day," Sipe said. "We felt it was time to go on top with the ball, and Ricky made a great play of it."

Feacher called the play the "Shake and Bake." "The shake is getting loose," he explained. "The bake is to burn them."

But the reason Feacher was in the game was a bit disheartening for the Browns. Ozzie Newsome had sprained his ankle in the first half and was unable to return, forcing the Browns into a three-wide receiver look that brought Feacher into the mix.

There was still some exciting football to see in the final period as linebacker Clay Matthews pulled off a pair of the most exciting defensive plays of the season—on consecutive Cincinnati snaps. Midway through the quarter an Anderson pass bounced off the hands of running back Deacon Turner and into the arms of Matthews at the Cleveland forty-one. Matthews returned it six yards, then saw Oliver Davis running alongside him. Before being tackled he lateraled it to Davis, who took it another forty-seven yards to the Cincinnati six before being collared. The pick-and-lateral brought the crowd back to life and set up a thirty-one-yard Cockroft field goal that rounded out the scoring at 31-7.

On the Bengals' next offensive play Anderson completed a pass to running back Nathan Poole, but Matthews stripped the ball from Poole's arms and took off, leading another fast break. He saw Davis again and again tried to lateral the football to him, but Davis was in front of him this time, and Matthews was flagged for an illegal forward pass.

While Matthews was practicing his Magic Johnson impersonation, many Browns were keeping an eye on the Stadium scoreboard in the fourth quarter to see what was happening elsewhere in the division. Slowly but surely this was becoming a red-letter day for the Browns.

"Every time we heard a roar go up," Robert E. Jackson said, "we automatically looked at the scoreboard."

"It was tough not to," agreed Sipe, who sat out the final Cleveland offensive series in favor of Paul McDonald. "When I was looking at the scoreboard, I was a fan. But on the field, it was all business."

The first piece of good news came from Buffalo where the Bills overwhelmed the Steelers, 28-13, dropping Pittsburgh one game back of the Browns. Continuing their yearlong injuries, five more Steelers were forced to leave the game with injury, including Terry Bradshaw. "It's like buzzards are flying over Pittsburgh," Lynn Swann said, and he was right in more ways than one. The defeat dropped Pittsburgh to 7-5, and the Steelers would essentially have to win all four of their remaining games to have a shot at the playoffs. And with matches against Miami, Houston, Kansas City, and San Diego left on the slate, Pittsburgh's postseason hopes were in a coma.

With the Steelers losing, the Browns' attention turned to Shea Stadium, where the first-place Oilers were having all kinds of trouble with the 2-9 New York Jets. The Jets had raced to a 21-0 lead in the first half and appeared on their way to a shockingly easy victory. They took their advantage into the fourth quarter when Ken Stabler launched one of the greatest comebacks of his storied career. Stabler tossed four touchdown passes in the final fifteen minutes, the last of which, a five-yarder to wide receiver Rich Caster with 1:31 to play, tied the game at 28. But the

Above: Entering his third season in 1980, Browns' head coach Sam Rutigliano (left) brought in a key component: defensive coordinator Marty Schottenheimer (right), who quietly played a critical role in the success of the Kardiac Kids. Photo by Paul Tepley.

Below: Better known for his arm than his feet, Brian Sipe had the finest season of any quarterback in Cleveland Browns' history in 1980. Photo by Larry Nighswander.

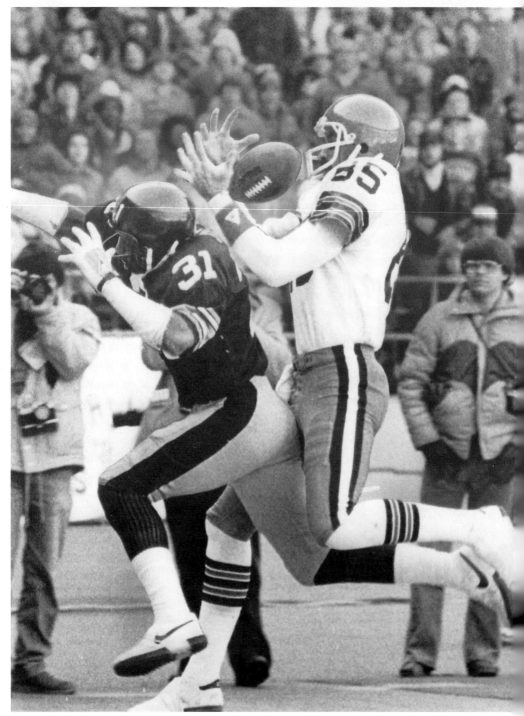
Versatile wide receiver Dave Logan makes another circus catch. Photo by Paul Tepley.

Browns' "Captain Wacko," defensive end Lyle Alzado. Photo by Larry Lambert.

Above: Fullback Mike Pruitt (right) plows through a hole created by center Tom DeLeone—a common sight in 1980. Photo by Paul Tepley.

Right: Wide receiver Reggie Rucker, one of the greatest pass-catchers ever to don the brown and orange. Photo by Paul Tepley.

ffensive guard Henry Sheppard departs the field with glory after an October victory over the Pittsburgh
eelers. Photo by Paul Tepley.

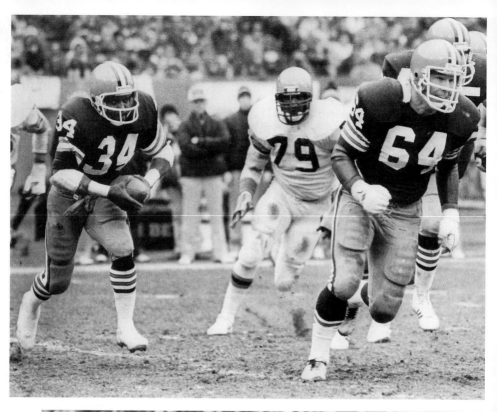

top: Though criticized at the time, the Browns' trade for All-Pro guard Joe DeLamielleure (right) turned out to huge factor in the success of the 1980 season. Here he paves the way for Greg Pruitt (left). Photo by Paul Tepley.

bottom: Greg Pruitt bounced back from a season-ending knee injury in 1979 to return to form as a danger-offensive threat in the Cleveland huddle. Photo by Larry Nighswander.

ve: Offensive tackle Doug Dieken: a stalwart on the offensive line and a jester in the locker room. Photo by Tepley.

Facing page: Linebacker Clay Matthews truly began coming of age in 1980—the third of what would become sixteen seasons with the Browns. Photo by Paul Tepley.

Left: Ageless running back Calvin Hill—the "thinking man's football player." Photo by Paul Tepley.

Below: Thousands of fans jam into Cleveland Hopkins International Airport awaiting the Browns' return after a 17-14 victory in Houston. Photo by Paul Tepley.

Another regular occurrence in 1980: Brian Sipe completing a pass to a running back. This one wound up being the game-winner in Week Fourteen against the New York Jets. Photo by Paul Tepley.

Above: Lyle Alzado carries Sam Rutigliano off the field after the Browns defeated the Cincinnati Bengals to win the 1980 AFC Central Division championship. Photo by Paul Tepley.

Left: Brian Sipe and team owner Art Modell are all smiles in the Riverfront Stadium locker room following the Browns' win over the Bengals. Photo by Paul Tepley.

Left: A policeman on horseback keeps an eye on the throng of fans at the Tank Plant gathered to welcome the Browns home after clinching the division in Cincinnati. UPI Photo by Jim Fetters.

Above: "Siper Bowl" fever grips the city of Cleveland. Photo by Larry Nighswander.

Below: Hundreds of Browns fans watch their team practice at Baldwin-Wallace College the week before the playoffs. Photo by Paul Tepley.

Left, top: From left: defensive end Henry Bradley, cornerback Clinton Burrell, cornerback Ron Bolton, and safety Clarence Scott celebrate Bolton's interception return for a touchdown in the second quarter of the Oakland playoff game. Photo by Paul Tepley.

Left, bottom: To combat a wind-chill factor of -36 degrees, electric benches were trucked to Cleveland from Philadelphia the night before the Browns' playoff game with Oakland. Photo by Paul Tepley.

Above and overleaf: "Red Right 88": Oakland safety Mike Davis intercepts Brian Sipe's pass intended for tight end Ozzie Newsome in the end zone on the final offensive play of the Browns' 1980 season. *Above:* Photo by Larry Nighswander. *Overleaf:* Photo by Paul Tepley.

Jets weren't surrendering victory yet. They drove to the Houston nineteen, and with two seconds remaining Pat Leahy was called on to attempt a thirty-six-yard field goal. Leahy missed it, the game went to overtime, and the mood in the Cleveland locker room darkened.

But four minutes into sudden death, Leahy got another chance, this time from thirty-eight yards, and he didn't disappoint. He connected to give the Jets a 31-28 win in one of the biggest upsets of the NFL season. It dropped the Oilers to 8-4, tied with the Browns for first, with the AFC Central's game-of-the-year coming up the following Sunday: the Browns-Oilers rematch in the Astrodome.

"As we heard the scores," said Joe DeLamielleure, "we were telling each other that everything was falling into place."

Everything had also fallen into place for the Browns at Cleveland Stadium as their offense was once again unstoppable after its frustrating afternoon in Pittsburgh. "It was our first easy game of the year," Rucker said. "Everybody figured in it as Brian sprayed the ball around. It's impossible for any team to defend against us."

"I could get used to doing it this way," Sipe said. "It was so unusual that Sam was almost at a loss for words. That is *really* unusual."

It was the Browns' first "easy" victory since the 27-3 triumph in Seattle in early October.

"This may just be a coincidence, but that Seattle game was the first of a five-game winning streak," Sipe said with a grin.

Sipe completed twenty-seven of thirty-six passes for 310 yards and four touchdowns, bringing his season total to twenty-five, four shy of the team record set by Frank Ryan in 1966. It was Sipe's fourth three-hundred-yard game of the season as he hit seven different receivers (Rucker led the list with seven catches for eighty-two yards and went over the four-hundred mark in career receptions) and carved up the Bengals "like you would dissect a Thanksgiving turkey—in short, steady strokes," wrote Dan Coughlin.

"Sipe picked us apart," agreed Cincinnati defensive end Ross Browner. "It is tough to get any rush with the three-man line, but he nickel-and-dimed us to death."

With the Browns' air attack proving to be almost unstoppable, there was no pressing need to establish the running game. Cleveland accumulated just thirty-one rushing yards, eleven of which came on Calvin Hill's only carry of the season. "When Calvin Hill carries the ball," joked Doug Dieken, "the play is listed in our playbook under 'deceptives.'"

Meanwhile the Browns' defense did a deceptively good job after the first quarter. Though the Bengals tallied 397 yards of total offense, including 150 on the ground, most of it came after the game had already been decided. More importantly the Cleveland defense didn't allow the visitors to cash in when they did move the ball. The Bengals had also run seventy-four offensive plays to the Browns' fifty-three and held the ball for thirty-seven minutes. But the only numbers that really mattered were "31" and "7."

It was as if the Ghost of Browns-Bengals Games Past revisited Cleveland Stadium after the game when Forrest Gregg ignored Rutigliano's attempt to shake hands. Gregg did shake hands with Mike Pruitt and offered him condolences for the death of his father earlier in the week. "I'm disappointed more in the way we played than the defeat," Gregg said. "Coming back here, I wanted to win, just like I want to win any game. There was a little extra meaning, this time, of course, playing in the Stadium and against this team."

Gregg and the Bengals would get one more shot at the Browns in the season finale December 21 at Riverfront, but that was the furthest thing from the Browns' minds. Next on the agenda was the Houston Oilers in what would be a knockdown, drag-out battle for first place.

"As I have been telling you all along," Rutigliano told reporters after the game, "the only thing I am interested in is being able to control our own destiny, and now we can."

As the Browns celebrated their win over the Bengals little did they know it would be the final time that season that the Kardiac Kids would not take center stage for a heart-pounding finish.

8 · In the Driver's Seat

If any Browns' players had any fond dreams the week before they were to play the Houston Oilers in the Astrodome, they probably would have gone something like this:

> The Browns, jetting back to Cleveland late at night after defeating the Oilers and capturing sole possession of first place in the AFC Central Division, would be sitting quietly in their seats, basking in the glow of their huge victory, when the pilot's voice would come over the speakers.
>
> "Gentlemen," he would say, "we are fifty miles from Cleveland Hopkins Airport. We are informed by the tower that a crowd of between 5,000 and 10,000 people is there to welcome you."

At that point the dream would probably end. In reality this sequence signaled the beginning of another dream.

It was shaping up to be the biggest game of the year, arguably the biggest regular-season contest of the past decade for the Cleveland Browns. They and the Oilers were tied at 8-4 atop the division, and the winner of their November 30 showdown inside the Houston Astrodome, the "eighth wonder of the world," would have the inside track to the title not to mention home-field advantage in the AFC playoffs.

While the Browns had also managed to be at 8-4 after twelve games in 1979, Week Thirteen had turned out to be the crossroads of the season. Trailing the Pittsburgh Steelers by one game going into the final quarter of the schedule the Browns went on to lose three of their final four, including the heartbreaking finale in Cincinnati that denied them the playoffs.

Injuries had played a huge role in the late-season collapse, but more than that, most assumed, was that the Browns weren't quite ready to be a playoff team. The 1979 Steelers, feeling pressure from both the Oilers and Browns, managed to win three of their last four and take the division crown with a 12-4 record. The end of the 1979 season seemed to be a perfect example of football nature taking its course.

But this was 1980. It was a whole new ballgame. The Steelers had dropped to 7-5 and were essentially one loss away from elimination. Either the Browns or the Oilers would take Pittsburgh's place atop the division. The showdown in the Astrodome would help determine which team would be the heir apparent.

It was a relatively unfamiliar situation for the Browns. They hadn't played in a battle for first place this late in the season since 1972, when they took an 8-3 record into Three Rivers to face the Steelers, who had an identical 8-3 record. Pittsburgh romped, 30-0 and went on to take the division title while the Browns settled for a Wild Card after two clutch wins to close the season. The Browns also came up big when necessary in 1971 when they won their final five games en route to the Central Division championship. But as the 1980 team prepared to face the Oilers that Thanksgiving week of 1980 it had been eight years since the Browns had come up with a clutch victory that paved a path to the postseason.

And with just four games remaining it was becoming clear that no AFC team was going to back into the conference playoffs, with several teams holding impressive records. The Buffalo Bills held the best mark and led the East at 9-3, followed closely by the New England Patriots, still very much in the hunt at 8-4. In the West, the Oakland Raiders and the San Diego Chargers were tied for first at 8-4, while the Denver Broncos had recovered from their shaky start to improve to 7-5. Add the tight Central race to the mix, and eight teams all within two games of each other were jockeying for five playoff spots.

By contrast the NFC playoff picture was much clearer. The Philadelphia Eagles were red-hot at 11-1 and had already clinched a place in the playoffs. The Detroit Lions led in the Central at 7-5 just ahead of 6-6 Minnesota, and the Atlanta Falcons topped the West at 8-4. Dallas at 9-3 and Los Angeles at 8-4 appeared to have the Wild Card edge.

But things in the AFC could become a bit more predictable if the Browns were to lose to the Oilers. A Cleveland loss would complete a Houston sweep of the Browns and give them the edge in any tie-breaking situation, either for the division crown or Wild Card possibilities. A Cleveland win on the other hand would propel the Browns into first place all by their lonesome and even the season series, wiping out the first tie-breaking advantage for Houston. If that proved to be the case, in the event of a tie, division or conference marks would determine the winner of the Central.

Neither team had forgotten the first meeting back in September when the Oilers controlled the ball for forty-two minutes and embarrassed the Browns on *Monday Night Football.* Even though it was accepted that the Oilers had improved in the following eleven weeks, the Browns believed themselves to be an entirely different team. "When we played the Oilers the first time, we were coming off a horrendous preseason," Sam Rutigliano said. "Our defense was bad and the best that could be said about our offense was that it was inartistic. All we were doing the first time we played was trying to avoid losing two games in a row. Now we're fighting for first place and, very possibly, the division championship."

If someone had told the sellout crowd filing out of the Stadium on that warm September evening after the Browns' loss that when the teams met again it would essentially be for the division title, it's doubtful anyone would have believed him. At the time the Browns were 0-2, the Oilers were 1-1 but looked incredibly better than the Browns, and the Steelers appeared to be on their way to a third straight Super Bowl at 2-0.

It proved what a difference eleven weeks could make. But the Browns were insistent that it wasn't just time that had made them a better team. "It's confidence," Rutigliano said. "We've grown each week in many ways and it has led to the belief we are a contender for the division championship. That's why I believe we had moved almost 180 degrees from where we were the last time we played the Oilers."

Then he said something that piqued the interest of Browns' fans everywhere. "We are going to make the playoffs this year," he added, "there is no doubt in my mind."

For a third-year head coach of a team that hadn't made the postseason since the Nixon administration to make a comment like that was bold, but it seemed to epitomize the feeling around Browns' camp that week. The players believed they were going to win, and they said so. They were talking and acting like a playoff team.

However, on the Tuesday before the game several of the Browns' rookies looked like something else altogether as they participated in an annual team tradition. Fliers were put up in the Browns' locker room informing the players that a local fan was offering them free Thanksgiving turkeys. Pete, owner of Pete's Poultry Palace, was a die-hard Browns' fan who gave the players a few of his gobblers every season. All the players had to do was go out to his farm located on state Route 43, "somewhere between Aurora and Ravenna," according to the flier. It was also customary for a designated rookie of each contingent of positions to be selected to go out on the team's day off and pick up turkeys for the veterans of the group. So on Tuesday afternoon several Browns' rookies set off to find Pete's Poultry Palace. It was the beginning of a very long day for the youngsters since Pete's Poultry Palace didn't exist. It was a long-standing ruse put on every year to make the rookies feel like rookies.

Joel Patten, out to pick up turkeys for the veteran offensive linemen, called the Cleveland locker room from a pay phone in Streetsboro and talked to Chip Falivene, administrative assistant to Rutigliano. Patten said that he hadn't found it yet, and Falivene gave him imaginary directions.

When tight end McDonald Oden and linebacker Clifton Odom went out on their voyage for their teammates, they returned to the Browns' training facility at

Baldwin-Wallace after finding no turkey farm. There they asked equipment manager Chuck Cusick for directions. Cusick told them not to feel bad because this sort of thing happened every year. He always told Pete to put a sign up, Cusick explained to the rookies, but Pete never did. The rookies were also warned they would be fined if they didn't bring back the turkeys, so they shouldn't give up. Instead of giving them directions to Pete's Poultry Palace Cusick told them to go to Hiram College to find a maintenance man named Joe Osako, who could tell them exactly how to get there. Naturally when Oden and Odom reached Hiram, Osako was nowhere to be found. Instead they met an elderly switchboard operator, who told them the whole thing was a joke. "We were the only turkeys anybody found," Oden said. "It was pretty bad, but I got to see a lot of the Ohio countryside."

Charles White got about halfway to Pete's when he realized something. He, along with all of the running backs, had been invited to coach Jim Garrett's house for Thanksgiving dinner, and several players would be going to coaches' houses to keep the holiday. So why did these players need their own turkeys? White stopped at a pay phone, called the locker room, and got a fellow rookie who had just returned from his wild turkey chase and let White in on the joke.

While the rookies of 1980 may have been given a hard time by their teammates, none topped the all-time rookie turkey story owned by wide receiver Willie Miller. In 1975 Miller drove all the way to Youngstown looking for Pete's Poultry Palace, then made another wrong turn and wound up in Bowling Green where his car was ticketed while he was out looking for Pete's on foot.

All the rookies eventually returned, wiser, and after a short practice on Thursday morning the players and coaches had the rest of Thanksgiving Day off. But in their leisure several Browns tuned in to the football games being played that afternoon, the first of which turned out to have one of the most memorable finishes in recent memory. Trailing the host Detroit Lions 17-10 in the final minutes Vince Evans drove the Chicago Bears eighty-four yards and scored the game-tying touchdown on a four-yard scramble as time expired. Then Chicago running back Dave Williams returned the overtime kickoff ninety-five yards for the game-winning touchdown. The shocking loss dropped the Lions to 7-6, now just a half-game ahead of the Vikings in the Central. The late game was far from exciting as the Cowboys slaughtered the Seattle Seahawks, 51-7.

Thanksgiving Day marked the first of two consecutive Thursdays with NFL football on the docket. A week later the Oilers would have to face the Steelers just four days after entertaining the Browns. The game would be nationally televised on ABC and was certain to be a ratings hit since it was bound to be huge in determining the AFC playoff picture. But few figured either team would be completely ready just a few days after playing games on Sunday.

The short turnaround time also concerned the Oilers, because Earl Campbell's health was now a question mark. He'd strained his knee during Houston's win over Chicago in Week Eleven and struggled in the Oilers' loss to the Jets, picking up just sixty yards on fifteen carries. Campbell was the heart of the Houston offense, and if he wasn't completely healthy the Oilers were very vulnerable.

Houston was also hit by several other injuries, primarily to backups, but one that struck a sensitive area was kicker Toni Fritsch. Fritsch's sore leg forced him out of the Jets game and linebacker Ted Thompson was called on to kick the Oilers' four extra points. With the divisional game of the year on the horizon, one could only wonder how effective Fritsch would be.

As the game unfolded in the first quarter it didn't appear that the Oilers would need to worry about Fritsch kicking in a critical situation come game's end. It didn't appear that there would be any critical situations in the fourth quarter.

The tone for the afternoon was set on the opening kickoff when Houston wide receiver Jeff Groth was hit, fumbled, and Browns' linebacker John Mohring recovered at the Houston eighteen. Two plays later Cleo Miller sprinted through the Oilers' line for a six-yard touchdown run that gave the visitors a 7-0 lead sixty-two seconds into the contest.

The Browns' defense also rose to the occasion and kept the momentum in the visitors' corner by preventing Houston from accomplishing anything on offense through the first period. As was usually the case in big games, Houston's defense did the same, and as the first quarter waned, Groth's opening mistake loomed as the difference in the game. But the Oilers made two more mistakes in the opening stanza that diverted attention away from Groth, if only temporarily. An interception by Houston defensive back Mike Reinfeldt gave the Oilers a first down at the Cleveland thirty-seven, but a play later Ken Stabler fumbled and Marshall Harris recovered for the Browns. This miscue didn't cost Houston, as Don Cockroft missed a fifty-yard field goal wide right.

But a play later Ron Bolton intercepted Stabler at the Cleveland forty-five and returned the ball to the Houston twenty-six. This time the Cleveland offense cashed in. Brian Sipe and Company took six plays and marched to the one where Miller scored his second touchdown of the day less than three minutes into the second quarter. Thanks to two costly Houston turnovers, the Browns led, 14-0, and the Oilers were in danger of getting in over their heads.

But this was a Houston team that had played in big games before. Though the Oilers had never won a division title they'd been to the playoffs the previous two seasons as a Wild Card and both times won two games to put them in the AFC Championship. A 14-0 deficit in the second quarter at home was nothing to panic about. And the margin was sliced in half on Houston's next possession as the Oilers drove seventy-five yards in eleven plays aided by a thirty-two-yard third-down Campbell run. Campbell put the exclamation point on the drive when he barreled into the end zone from a yard out midway through the period to cut the Cleveland lead to 14-7.

The defenses took center stage through the second quarter, and the score remained the same until halftime. But just as the Browns had notched a big play early in the first half, they'd begin the second with one just as vital. After Houston kicked off Mike Pruitt picked up four yards to the Cleveland thirty-four on the Browns' first play from scrimmage. Then Cleo Miller's number was called on second down. As he lined up he remembered seeing Greg Pruitt run the same play for short yardage earlier in the game. "I thought that if Greg had cut back, he might have broken it," Miller said. "That thought popped into my head when Brian called the play in the huddle." So Miller, who had carried the ball only eight times all season prior to this game, figured he'd give it a shot. He took the handoff and followed Joe DeLamielleure's block over right guard, then cut back across the field, where there was nothing but green plastic carpet shimmering in the incandescent light. Miller, after nearly stumbling at midfield, galloped down the left side with Dave Logan beside him. Houston linebacker Robert Brazile eventually squeezed between Logan and Miller and brought the seven-year veteran down at the Houston sixteen after a fifty-yard run, the longest of Miller's career.

"That was a fine run, maybe the turning point as it turned out," Houston head coach Bum Phillips said. "It didn't exactly surprise us because we've known all along that he is a fine runner and blocker. I guess he hasn't been used more because they have such depth of backfield people."

But the Browns' offense stalled, and facing a fourth-and-two at the Houston eight Rutigliano opted to go for the field goal. Don Cockroft connected from twenty-five yards out to give the Browns a 17-7 lead with 11:23 to play in the third quarter. Once again they had the momentum. But once again the Oilers would take it right back.

Ken Stabler and the Houston offense marched back down the field, covering sixty-two yards in just three plays. After Stabler hit tight end Dave Casper for twenty-seven yards on the second play of the possession, the heralded pair connected once again on the next snap. Casper caught a looping pass and barreled past Robert L. Jackson and Clarence Scott down the left sideline. Finally at the Cleveland two he spun out of a last-ditch tackle attempted by Scott and landed in the end zone, capping a thirty-yard touchdown play. Fritsch's extra point made it 17-14, Browns, with an eternity to play. It appeared that once again the Kardiac Kids would go right down to the wire in a shootout to be determined by who had the ball last and how much time remained when they did.

Instead the opposite occurred. Over the final twenty-five minutes of football the Browns and Oilers waged a titanic defensive battle as neither offense could muster any substantial drives. But as the fourth quarter progressed the home team had three opportunities to turn the game around. The first came with five minutes to play when the Oilers managed to move to the Cleveland twenty-one and called on Fritsch for a thirty-eight-yard field-goal attempt. But with his leg still ailing Fritsch's kick never had a chance. It sailed wide left and fell short. The Browns took over but, as had been the case for much of the second half, couldn't piece anything together and punted back to the Oilers with 3:23 left. Houston took over at its own twenty-seven, and moments later Opportunity Number Two presented itself.

Stabler hit wide receiver Mike Renfro for fourteen yards on first down, and things looked even better when Stabler hit Casper for twenty to the Cleveland thirty-nine a play later. But as Casper was going down, a hit by Thom Darden jarred the football loose, and cornerback Judson Flint recovered for the Browns and returned it to the Cleveland forty-three with 2:16 to play. As was the case in Pittsburgh, the Browns had the football and the lead with two minutes remaining. And as also was the case in Pittsburgh, they couldn't run out the clock.

Miller was stuffed for a two-yard loss on first down, then Sipe hit Reggie Rucker for ten to the Houston forty-nine on second down. On third-and-two at the two-minute warning Mike Pruitt was tackled for a yard loss, and Houston called its second time out. Johnny Evans punted to the Oilers' seven, but Carl Roaches returned it fifteen yards to the Houston twenty-two with 1:40 to play. This series would mark the Oilers' third opportunity to win or tie the football game. The Browns came out in a prevent defense and quickly learned why the prevent defense is so often blamed for losing football games. On first down Stabler connected with Casper again, this time for forty-three yards all the way down to the Cleveland thirty-five and the sellout Astrodome crowd reached jet-engine noise level. Houston called its final time out with 1:32 left.

For the Browns it looked and felt like 1979 all over again. They had already lost one divisional game they'd had in the bag two weeks earlier in Pittsburgh. To lose a second would not only hurt them in the standings but possibly wipe out any and all momentum they'd picked up in winning eight of their last ten games. For that one play the Oilers looked like the perennial playoff team, and the Browns looked like the pretender.

For the next play the Browns abandoned the prevent and returned to their 3-4 defense. Stabler tried to hit Renfro, but the pass fell incomplete. Then on second down Houston tried to go back to the Casper well one more time. "The play was the same one they ran the preceding time," the Browns' Clarence Scott said. "My guy was Mike Barber, but he didn't come out. That allowed me to free-up, to help the cornerbacks and the linebackers."

As Scott dropped back after the ball was snapped he moved in the direction of Barber but kept his eyes on Stabler. Understandably Stabler's eyes were fixed on Casper, who was running a crossing pattern over the middle. As Casper made his cut, Dick Ambrose, assigned to cover the tight end, lost him. Not seeing Scott, Stabler fired the ball toward his tight end. "That's their bread and butter," Scott said. "Casper had made the big play all day and it was about time to stop him."

After catching six passes for 130 yards and a touchdown on the afternoon there was nothing Casper could do to catch this one.

"The play was designed to get the ball to Mike Barber," Stabler said. "He was held up at the line of scrimmage and I tried to force the ball to Casper. He really didn't have a chance." Scott stepped in front of him and intercepted the pass at the Cleveland twenty-four as the capacity crowd hushed like a scolded five-year-old. Scott, making the thirtieth interception of his career, returned the ball to the Browns' thirty-three before being tackled. As he got up the Cleveland bench was ecstatic, spilling out onto the field. Just 1:17 remained, and with the Oilers out of time outs Cleveland was in control. The Oilers, despite being led by one of the best quarterbacks of the 1970s, had blown another chance.

"I tried to put the ball in a tight place," Stabler said. "We were out of time outs and had to make things happen. They were in a double zone that took away the sideline. The middle was our best shot."

"I'm certainly not going to second-guess Kenny," Phillips said. "When you put the ball in the air you open yourself to an interception. I guess you could say we went to the well once too often."

Two Sipe kneeldowns later the Browns had a 17-14 upset and, more importantly, first place all to themselves in the AFC Central Division. They marched, cheering and celebrating, into the locker room. Cries of "We're Number One!" could be heard in the adjoining tunnel.

"It was a game that was won by character," Rutigliano said, "and this is a team of oneness. It has been like this all year; somebody always coming in and doing something important."

On this day it was the Cleveland defense that provided that important something, limiting the Oilers to fourteen points and not allowing them to penetrate past the Browns' twenty-one after their second touchdown.

The unit had received some extra motivation the night before when several of its members saw Houston tight end Richard Caster on a local television show stating what the Oilers were going to be able to do against the Cleveland defense. "We were ready to tear into the TV set," Dick Ambrose said.

The first-place Browns needed every ounce of that extra effort since it was the worst statistical day of the season for the offense. Sipe completed just thirteen of twenty-one passes for a mere ninety-two yards, his lowest output of the year. His longest completion was just sixteen yards as the Oilers' defense shut down Cleveland's passing game. As a result of the weakened air attack Dave Logan saw his thirty-six-game reception streak end. Logan, however, was philosophical about the end of the streak. "If it had to end, I'm glad it did in a game like this," Logan said, "a game that we won and which puts us in the driver's seat for the division championship."

The Browns, who converted on just three of thirteen third downs, did manage 119 yards rushing, but nearly half of that came on Miller's long run. Still, Miller's power running on that play and his two touchdowns created just enough spark for the Cleveland offense, probably more so because it was fueled by an unexpected source. "Nobody said anything to me all week," Miller said. "I just went about my business of getting ready to do whatever they wanted me to do, as well as I could. I've always had confidence in my ability, but I also do what I'm told."

"We felt we needed Cleo to give us another dimension with his blocking," Rutigliano said. "But then he started running so well, we turned it around; we let him have the ball."

Miller matched his season total in carries with eight and compiled sixty-nine yards. Mike Pruitt collected fifty more on sixteen carries. Altogether the Browns managed just 193 yards of total offense, their lowest output of the year.

On the flip side of the ball Earl Campbell wound up with 109 yards on twenty-seven carries, but the Browns were tickled with that. They'd talked all week of just trying to "contain" Campbell, since no one really stopped him, and they'd done that. Especially in the second half when he carried the ball nine times for just nineteen yards. With the Browns ahead in the final two minutes and the Oilers forced to throw, Campbell was on the sideline as Stabler directed the last drive.

Despite most of the statistical advantages going to Houston, the difference in the game was the Browns' five-to-one victory in the turnover battle as they recovered three Oiler fumbles and picked Stabler off twice. And none was any bigger than Scott's, which now had to rank as the biggest play of the season.

Rutigliano was especially pleased with his defense, which had come a long way this season. "I really thought we'd need 24 to 30 points to win," Rutigliano said, "but we didn't because the defense keeps getting better and better, like good wine." And the improvement of the Browns' defense was evident to the Oilers as well.

"The Browns have improved a lot since we saw them in Cleveland," Phillips said. "Particularly on defense. They made some big plays today and we didn't. They have a right to be proud. I'd rather say that they won than we lost. These teams are very close in talent and that's why the breaks often decide our games."

The Oilers, now 8-5, would have to defeat the Pittsburgh Steelers the following Thursday to avoid putting themselves in a world of hurt. Just to make things even more interesting Pittsburgh had avoided elimination with a 23-10 victory over the

Miami Dolphins at Three Rivers. Had it not been for a good break of their own, though, the Steelers may very well have kissed any hopes of the playoffs good-bye before the first of December. Trailing 16-10 early in the fourth quarter, the Dolphins drove to the Pittsburgh one and were poised to take the lead. A Tony Nathan dive for a touchdown backfired miserably as Ron Johnson knocked the ball loose and Jack Ham recovered for the home team at the two. Terry Bradshaw and the offense then went on a ninety-eight-yard touchdown drive that sealed the deal and forced a second-place tie with the Oilers.

While that wasn't necessarily good news for the Browns, other scores filtering in from around the league that day were. In San Francisco, second-year quarterback Joe Montana threw three touchdown passes as the 4-8 49ers upset the Patriots, 21-17, damaging New England's chances for a Wild Card. In Baltimore, the mediocre Colts had upended the first-place Bills, 28-24, ensuring that the Browns' 9-4 mark was now tied for tops in the AFC with Buffalo and San Diego, which had handed the Eagles their second loss of the year.

Though it didn't seem important at the time, another score would prove to have a huge impact on the Browns' playoff fortunes. In a seemingly meaningless game the Cincinnati Bengals scored two fourth-quarter touchdowns and defeated the Kansas City Chiefs at Arrowhead Stadium, 20-6, to snap a five-game losing streak and improve to 4-9. Little did the Browns know what that seemingly meaningless game would set into motion.

But as the team boarded its flight back east the Browns' coaches and players weren't concerned about what the future held. They were basking in the moment of the biggest victory the franchise had experienced in at least eight years. "You're damned right this is our biggest win in a long time," Art Modell said. "Until next Sunday."

"I'm not going to say this game was *the* most important one we've won, because every game since our first two losses this season has been very important," Sipe said. "But obviously, it was critical for us, and if things turn out the way we want them to turn out, it could be that this one was the most important. We're thinking championship now."

"From here on in we're going to play like hell," Rutigliano said. "I don't see how we will let anybody stand in our way."

Meanwhile thirteen hundred miles away in Cleveland thousands of Browns' fans were mobilizing.

Following the conclusion of the game telecast WKYC in Cleveland ran two notices across the bottom of the screen announcing the time and location of the Browns' return to Cleveland. With the team set to arrive at Hopkins Airport around 11:10 P.M., fans started arriving at the airport at 9:00, waiting to welcome their heroes.

Within an hour the airport was jammed with thousands of people and concourses were essentially shut down, forcing many passengers to miss their flights.

Police rope that had been set up to contain the masses was ineffective. With so many people packed together in such a small area, temperatures rose to nearly one hundred degrees, and dozens fainted. Airport bars ran out of glasses. Regular passengers exited their planes via special security hallways because the concourses were jammed wall-to-wall with people.

Outside traffic looked as though it were a Friday rush hour rather than a typical Sunday night. Cars throttled Interstate 71 for miles, and by 11:00 P.M. traffic was backed up from the airport to Brookpark Road. Cars lucky enough to reach the airport could find no parking spaces so drivers simply abandoned their automobiles wherever they could find empty space, be it in the grass or mud.

Longtime Browns' trainer Leo Murphy later confessed the only thing he'd ever seen that even came close to this was in December 1964. Then the team had returned from a 52-20 win over the Giants in New York that clinched the Eastern Conference title and propelled the Browns into the NFL Championship against the Baltimore Colts. But Murphy said this airport display was bigger. Many agreed that the city of Cleveland hadn't seen anything like this since the Indians won the 1948 World Series.

On the surface it may not have seemed like much. Yes, it was a big game, but it was still just a regular-season contest. The Browns had not played particularly well, had clinched nothing, and still had three games to go. They could still miss the playoffs and break their fans' hearts once again. So why was Hopkins a Mecca for Browns' fans that cold November night? "This is a suspicious old factory town, finding comfort in 'knowing all along' that things won't turn out right," explained Bob Sudyk the next day in the *Cleveland Press*. "Well, Our Browns are making us believe in something once again."

When the team finally arrived shortly after midnight, they exited the plane knowing of the throng that awaited them. When the pilot made his dream-like announcement, Modell had jokingly told an adviser to quickly open the ticket office. The players were given the option of departing through one of the security hallways to avoid the chaos, but most of them turned it down. This was the stuff of dreams, the kind of thing that comes along once in a lifetime. They weren't about to pass it up. After some hesitation Rutigliano led the team off the plane and into the terminal. Rutigliano wanted the players to go first, but when they urged him to take the lead and Modell good-naturedly informed him this was a designated duty in his contract, Rutigliano agreed. The flight attendants opened the boarding door.

"You could feel the heat from all the people rush down the gangway and into the plane," Ron Bolton said. "It was unreal."

When the team entered the terminal the crowd went crazy. They screamed at, chanted for, and sang to the players, many of whom stopped for pictures and autographs on their way through. Appropriately Brian Sipe marched into the chaos with several offensive linemen in front of him. "That was the best protection I got all day," he joked.

"Even Earl [Campbell] could not have gotten through the crowd," Rutigliano said. It took nearly two hours for the players to get from the terminal to their cars.

"We were thinking, 'What are these people doing?'" Doug Dieken said. "It was amazing. It was an unbelievable scene to get off that plane and see all those people in the heat and the adulation they had."

"I had never experienced anything like that and I'd played at Michigan and gone to the Rose Bowl," Thom Darden said. "To see the enthusiasm and the way people responded was indescribable."

The players were escorted through a side exit by airport security and led to the baggage-claim area, where it would be easier to board the buses that would take them to their parking lot. But shortly after they made their "escape," they heard someone yell, "Look! There they are!" and another swarm of fans came running down the concourse toward them. When the players finally piled into the buses, fans were jumping onto the roof and hanging onto the windows, not wanting to let their heroes get away.

Modell had tears in his eyes as it all unfolded. After nearly a decade of sheer ineptitude and disappointment, both on the athletic fields and in the court of public opinion, Cleveland had finally fallen in love with one of its teams. The Woodstock-esque feeling in the airport that night—"like being in the middle of a Fellini film," as Dick Ambrose described it—was one the city hadn't experienced in more than thirty years.

"It wasn't earning a spot in the Super Bowl," wrote Bob Sudyk. "It wasn't clinching a pennant. It was merely that the Browns, for the first time in almost a decade, were leading the high-quality Central Division with three games to play."

"I've been saying all along that the road to the big one is through Pittsburgh," Rutigliano said. "Now, it's through Cleveland! We've got a full tank of gas and *we're* driving the car!"

But on its way through the terminal the car suffered a few dings. Two thousand dollars worth of damage was done to the airport, mostly to ceiling tiles by fans sitting on other fans' shoulders. Calvin Hill lost the checkbook he had in his pocket. Dave Logan had his shirt torn. As he entered the terminal Thom Darden set his suitcase down beside him to survey the scene. When he went to retrieve it a few moments later it was gone. Ironically, along with a cassette player and credit cards, one of the items in the suitcase was a booklet containing the Browns' game plan for Houston. When Darden reached the parking lot a fan ran up to him and returned the suitcase.

The Browns' players labored in one of the toughest divisions in the NFL. Each game was a brutal, physical battle. If Jack Lambert wasn't after you, then Earl Campbell was out to run you over. Yet for a number of players, true fear was found, ironically, when they faced their own adoring fans. "From the time we left the plane and walked through the gate, there was nothing but a sea of people," Darden said. "There was no supervision. I kept thinking about what happened at that rock concert in Cincinnati [On December 3, 1979, eleven people were killed when a disorganized crowd tried to force its way into Riverfront Coliseum prior to a Who concert]. I was scared."

"When I got about halfway down the corridor," Cody Risien said, "all I could think is to make sure I kept my feet because if you fall down, nobody will ever know you're down there. It actually then became a little scary. People weren't ugly or tearing things up, it was just kind of frightening."

Even against this backdrop the Browns were willing to share the spotlight. Abraham William Abraham, the seventy-two-year-old Cleveland icon better known as "The Man in the Brown Suit," was at the airport that night to have Modell's and Peter Hadhazy's cars ready. Abraham, who had also done airport maintenance work since 1967, was as much a part of the Browns as any non-football man ever could be. After getting hit by a football on a Lou Groza field-goal attempt while walking behind the end zone in 1946, Abraham (a pass-gate employee who happened to be wearing a brown suit) had been at every Browns' home game since, catching the footballs on extra-point and field-goal attempts. When he met Modell in the terminal that night, Modell handed him a game ball, which the players had decided to give to him.

"I cried!" Abraham exclaimed a few days later. "It was so nice of them. It was the biggest surprise I ever got in my thirty-four years."

The players also decided to give a game ball to Jerry Sherk, who had meant so much to the team for so many lean years. "It's our way of telling Jerry we want him to share in our pride," Lyle Alzado said, "as we will share with him any accomplishments we achieve in the future."

Sherk, not at all bitter about the injury that was depriving him of participating in this experience, was grateful but made an interesting observation. "It does seem a little ironic that before I came to Cleveland, the Browns were in their heyday, then we didn't do much while I was here," he said. "And now that I may not play again, it looks like they're in the thick of it."

A year before being in the thick of it would have seemed impossible. Then the best the Browns could be was third place in the division. The Steelers were still the world champs, and the Oilers were waiting in the wings if they stumbled. Even if everything did roll the Browns' way in 1980, there seemed to be no way they could ever go into Houston and pull an upset that would put them in the driver's seat for the division crown.

When all of it was put together it seemed like a dream.

But the dream, for the Kardiac Kids and the city that was now head-over-heels in love with them, was just beginning.

9 · It's Worth Living Here

The Cleveland Browns would now have to overcome an obstacle that hadn't stood in their way in a very long time.

The victory over the Houston Oilers had introduced them to the rest of the sports world and national media. *Sports Illustrated*, *Sport Magazine*, the *New York Times*, and *Newsweek* would all visit Browns' headquarters the following week, as would the cable channel Home Box Office.

"The Browns' movement toward a world title is a possibility for the first time in more than a decade," Bob Sudyk wrote. "It can be compared to the Indians in first place in their division in early September." And anyone who knew anything about the recent history of Cleveland athletics knew that statement meant Northeast Ohio was truly entering a fantasy world.

"They had a lot of hopes, but they never had been fulfilled," Sam Rutigliano said of the fans' frenzy. "The town was absolutely on fire. You just couldn't believe the response. It's an unbelievable town when you win. They all are, but this one is more so."

"It was downright euphoric to see people jump on the bandwagon," Thom Darden said. "I can't even put into words how the guys felt, especially those of us who had been around for a while and hadn't experienced winning."

"Some of the guys hadn't been around that long," Doug Dieken said, "but those who had had seen the town take its lumps. It was like the place was dying. Then all of a sudden, you get a heart transplant. They were looking for a light at the end of the tunnel. It wasn't an oncoming train. It was us. There was just something magical about it."

Clarence Scott got a taste of that magic Monday morning when he made a quick run to a nearby supermarket. Shoppers and employees swarmed him, congratulating him on the game-winning interception and asking for autographs. When he finally got home he received a phone call from his mother, asking him to give her the ball he'd intercepted the day before and kept as a souvenir. "I don't know about that," Scott said, contemplating his decision. "That will take some real soul-searching. I think she may have been kidding. At least, she wasn't really insisting. If it comes right down to it, I just may have to slip her another ball."

Mobs at the airport? Groupies at the supermarket? Mothers asking sons for prized possessions? It was clear there was something a little bit different going on in Cleveland that week. The question was how would the team handle the on-slaught of attention, coverage, and expectations. "It's like poison," Rutigliano said. "It only hurts if you swallow it."

The Browns couldn't afford to swallow any poison if they wanted to stay in the driver's seat toward a playoff berth. "We would not be in first place today if the team we play next did not beat Houston," Rutigliano pointed out. "The will to win is not as important as the will to prepare." Many fans, still basking in the glow of the Houston triumph, had already declared victory over the 3-10 New York Jets the following Sunday. Others were worried. After all just two weeks before the Jets had defeated the Oilers and earlier in the season had knocked off the now playoff-bound Atlanta Falcons.

Mike Pruitt called the Jets the best 3-10 team he'd ever seen. Though New York had struggled defensively in 1980—ranked dead last in the AFC in yards allowed—the Jets' offense had showed signs of life. The Browns were particularly worried about speedy wide receivers Wesley Walker and Johnny "Lam" Jones, both of whom could give the Cleveland secondary trouble.

Even if the Browns, made 9½-point favorites, did beat the Jets, a postseason berth was not assured despite what many fans were assuming. On Monday morning the Browns' ticket office was flooded with calls about playoff tickets.

"Please tell the fans we are not taking orders yet," Browns' public relations director Nate Wallack told the *Plain Dealer*. "Ask them to be patient because we will make an announcement sometime next week as to the procedure to follow."

"But don't get involved in trying to figure out the playoff situation," Rutigliano warned his team. "Let everybody else worry about that. For now, let's just think about the Jets, and nothing beyond the Jets."

On that note a word of warning came from Bum Phillips as the Oilers licked their wounds following their heartbreaking loss. "This thing isn't over yet," he said. "It will be a dogfight to the finish. I don't expect the division title to be settled until the Browns play the last game in Cincinnati."

The good news for the Browns was that on Thursday the three-team race in the Central would be narrowed down to two without their even taking the field. The Oilers and Steelers, both 8-5, would square off before a national television audience in the Astrodome, and the loser would almost certainly—though not mathematically—be eliminated from the playoff picture with two games to play.

The Oilers' players meanwhile were frustrated with their current two-game losing skid. Tight end Mike Barber said that Houston had lost two straight to teams inferior to the Oilers and that the Browns weren't good enough to win the division. Naturally his comments evoked strong reactions from Berea.

"I don't care what Barber says," Rutigliano said. "Send him our newspapers."

The Browns couldn't afford to show the same kind of disrespect to the Jets, who were coached by Walt Michaels, a Browns' linebacker from 1952 to 1961. In each of the previous two seasons the Browns and Jets had gone right down to the wire in true Kardiac Kids fashion. In Week Fifteen in 1978 the Browns led visiting New York 27-10 after three quarters, but a furious Jets comeback gave them a 34-27 advantage with 1:16 to play. Not to be outdone Brian Sipe drove the Browns seventy-three yards in sixty-two seconds and sent the contest to overtime with an eighteen-yard touchdown pass to Calvin Hill. The Browns took the opening kick-off of sudden death and marched down to the Jets' five where Don Cockroft ended it with a twenty-one-yard field goal.

It was an eerily similar backdrop on the opening Sunday of the 1979 season at Shea Stadium. The Browns trailed the Jets 22-19 with thirty seconds to play and had the ball at their own sixteen with no timeouts. Sipe and Company marched sixty-six yards in just twenty-six ticks this time, and Cockroft sent the game to overtime with a thirty-five-yard boot. Neither team could do much in sudden death, and with less than a minute to play it appeared that the Browns would open the campaign with a tie. But an interception by Oliver Davis and a thirty-three-yard runback set up a twenty-seven-yard Cockroft field goal with fifteen seconds left, giving the Browns a hard-earned 25-22 victory.

But there was much more on the line for the Browns in this meeting than in their previous two with New York. With two road trips looming in Weeks Fifteen and Sixteen they really couldn't afford a loss to a losing team in their final home game of the regular season.

But Cleveland seemed to be exuding confidence all week. It seemed that finally after nearly a decade of strife that the gods of fate were smiling on the North Coast—in multiple sports. The Browns were in first place in December for the first time in nine years, and that Tuesday an Indians' player was selected as the American League Rookie of the Year for the first time in nearly a decade. As many expected, outfielder Joe Charboneau took the award after his dazzling 1980 debut. Charboneau, who hit .289 with twenty-three home runs and eighty-seven RBIs, was the first Indian to win the award since first baseman Chris Chambliss in 1981. Following a near .500 season, with several players full of potential, it appeared that the Indians were ready to roll. "I plan to skip over the sophomore jinx and go on to my junior year," Charboneau joked at the press conference announcing the award. The next day the Indians gave the twenty-five-year-old from Belvidere, Illinois, a $900,000 contract for 1981, and it appeared that the city had a new sports hero who would be a fixture in Cleveland for a long time.

As the legend of Charboneau ascended, a day later the dynasty of the Pittsburgh Steelers appeared to fall. In their Thursday night contest of survival the Oilers had lived to die another day with an intense 6-0 victory in one of the best-played defensive contests of the season. Terry Bradshaw was limited to ten completions in twenty-six attempts for just 138 yards, while Earl Campbell picked up a mere eighty-one yards on twenty-one carries. Franco Harris also fumbled twice, as the Steelers were shut out for the first time since 1974–their first championship season.

"We will miss not playing them in the playoffs," Bum Phillips said.

Two Toni Fritsch field goals in the second half made the difference on the scoreboard, while a pair of Mike Reinfeldt interceptions of Bradshaw kept the Steelers at bay. Reinfeldt's first pick came in the end zone after Pittsburgh had taken the second-half kickoff and marched to the Houston one. From that point on it was all Oilers.

Following the Oilers-Steelers game the Browns were slurred for the second time in four days. This time the slight came from the lips of Bradshaw, who said he felt that the Browns weren't as good as the Oilers. Again the comment did not go over well in Cleveland. "Terry should have concentrated more on beating the Oilers instead of worrying about coaching the Browns," Rutigliano said.

"Tell Terry we felt the same way the last two years about Houston and Pittsburgh," Ron Bolton added.

"All I know is that Bradshaw will be watching the playoffs on television and he might be seeing us," said Thom Darden.

That Friday, Browns' fans learned that they would be watching one of Rutigliano's assistant coaches on the college sidelines the following fall. Linebackers coach Dick MacPherson announced that he would leave the team after the season to take over the head coaching position at Syracuse University. "Syracuse is fortunate to get a man of MacPherson's caliber and I wish him well," Rutigliano said, "but I hope Mac is here for a while."

MacPherson wasn't the primary focus of attention on the Browns' coaching staff that week, however. The talk of the town was Marty Schottenheimer and the job he was doing in transforming the Cleveland attack from one of the worst in the league in 1979 to one of the better units in the AFC in 1980. The consensus was that the Browns' victory over Houston would not have been possible the year before simply because it was the Cleveland defense that made the difference. "That's the sign of a maturing team," Rutigliano said, "when the big gun comes in and doesn't have the kind of game you want, and somebody else picks you up. In the past it didn't happen that way for us."

The Browns had scored a 60.3 percent on the Marty Scale in the Houston victory, winning thirty-eight of sixty-three plays, which was right on course with their overall season percentage of 60.2. If there was any truth to the football cliché of offense winning games but defense winning championships, it was beginning to look like the Browns were for real after all.

Sunday, December 7, 1980, an unseasonably mild day, felt like a holiday in downtown Cleveland. In addition to the 78,454 who ventured to the lakefront for the Browns-Jets game, thousands of others flooded downtown to show their holiday spirit. The *Plain Dealer*'s Holiday Gift Show drew a big crowd at Public Hall, as did a pair of performances of *The Nutcracker* at Public Music Hall.

Make no mistake about it, though, the Browns were the talk of the town.

"When they lost 42-0 in the preseason, I thought they were going down the tubes this year," said fourteen-year-old Brian Donovan on his way to the game. "Now WE'RE going to the SUPER BOWL!"

Donovan's feelings may have been fueled more by youthful enthusiasm than reality, but his good spirit was shared by many. "People smell a winner," said Richard Pavol, a ticket-taker at Cleveland Stadium since 1970. "A few years back, the fans were almost mean. Now they're nicer. They smile and say thank you. They're in a better mood."

"There is no greater remedy for an ailing town than a winning sports team," Art Modell said. "It has a binding effect."

That effect was displayed in the various banners hung along fences and concourses inside the Stadium as the Browns and Jets prepared for battle: "Luv Ya Orange," "Who Says it's Lonely at the Top?" and probably the most appropriate one for the atmosphere of this day, "It's Worth Living Here."

"We have to keep things in perspective, though," Modell warned. "We've been let down too often by sports teams and politicians in this town. We have a long way to go. I hope there's no stumbling."

As the game wore on it didn't appear that there would be. Although the Jets took the opening kickoff and marched to the Cleveland thirty-seven, Pat Leahy's fifty-five-yard field-goal attempt seemed to foreshadow the events to come. The kick was right on the money but didn't have quite enough juice. The ball hit the crossbar and bounced three feet up into the air as the capacity crowd leaned forward to see which side of the bar it would land on. Much to their delight the football came down in front of the bar, signifying a missed attempt. Though Cockroft also left a fifty-two-yard attempt short seven plays later, it seemed that good fortune and luck would be on the Browns' side on this day.

The Cleveland offense was clicking through the first half but key mistakes and penalties prevented them from cashing in. A Ron Bolton interception of Richard Todd halted the Jets' second drive at the Cleveland nineteen, but the Browns returned the favor when Sipe was picked off by defensive back Donald Dykes at the

New York seven four minutes later. After a Jets punt, a Browns' drive resulted in a thirty-four-yard Cockroft field goal midway through the second period that would be the only score for either team in the first half. The Browns' defense continued to frustrate Todd when Clinton Burrell picked off a pass intended for Wesley Walker at the Cleveland thirty-two with 2:21 left in the half.

The only true bad note of the first two periods for the Browns was when Lyle Alzado suffered a left hamstring injury midway through the second quarter. He limped off the field and to the locker room where doctors examined him and said it was doubtful he would return.

"The first half was kind of tough to swallow," Sipe said. "I'm just thankful the defense gave us some breathing room. The Jets made some tactical changes that screwed us up until we were able to make some changes of our own."

Those changes resulted in an impressive opening drive to the second half. The Browns milked nearly seven-and-a-half minutes off the clock as they marched seventy-seven yards in fourteen plays. Cleveland's good fortune continued on the thirteenth play of the drive as the Browns faced a fourth-and-inches situation at the New York ten. Figuring his team needed the extra boost of confidence only a touchdown could provide Rutigliano opted to go for it. It proved to be a wise decision. Mike Pruitt blasted up the middle for a first down, then capped the drive on the next play with a nine-yard touchdown run, carrying two defenders the final four yards into the end zone. Pruitt's explosion and Cockroft's point after gave Cleveland a 10-0 lead as the sellout crowd finally had something to celebrate.

"I haven't gone for it for a few weeks and there are a few judges I haven't heard from for a while," Rutigliano joked. "I was concerned with the fact that we had been frustrated so much before that, and we had to have seven points as opposed to only three.

"Besides, as I've said before, if we can't make one yard when we need it, we shouldn't be involved in this game."

Now the Jets were in danger of not being involved in the game–on the road trailing a hot team by ten points in the second half with a rocking crowd behind it. It seemed a Cleveland defensive stand and another score by the offense would all but turn the lights out on the New York Jets.

But that scenario would not have made for good theater.

Just over two minutes after the Browns kicked off the Jets struck back. Richard Todd drove the visitors from the New York thirty to the Cleveland thirty-nine in three plays, then hit Johnny "Lam" Jones with a pass at the Browns' twenty. Jones sidestepped Clinton Burrell and streaked into the end zone for a touchdown that cut the lead to 10-7 with 5:09 remaining in the quarter.

After Dino Hall returned the Jets' kickoff forty yards to midfield, Sipe hit Dave

Logan for ten yards, then Reggie Rucker for nine to the New York twenty-nine. The drive appeared to stall two plays later when Sipe was sacked at the New York thirty-seven, and the Browns were faced with a fourth-and-eighteen. But Riverboat Sam reached into his bag of tricks again. He sent Johnny Evans in to punt, but just as he had three weeks earlier at Three Rivers the former college quarterback slowly walked up beneath center and took the snap. The play was an end-around run to wide receiver Willis Adams, who found daylight around the corner and for a brief moment looked like he would pick up the first down. But Adams was dragged down at the twenty-two, three yards short of moving the chains, and the Jets took over with 1:35 to play in the third quarter.

Once again New York wasted little time in taking advantage of the presented opportunity. A short Todd flare to running back Bruce Harper on third-and-six burned a Cleveland blitz and resulted in a thirty-one-yard gain. Suddenly the Jets were poised to take the lead. A personal-foul penalty on Marshall Harris made it easier for the visitors, who wound up at the Cleveland five, ninety seconds into the final period.

Though the fans may have been used to this type of anxiety, Lyle Alzado wasn't, at least not while watching it from the sideline, unable to play. "I was going crazy," he said. "I couldn't stand it on the sidelines. I had to go back into the game. I also was scared. This was a very important game for us, and an important game like that, you have to play."

As the Jets were driving Alzado tried to check into the game, but Schottenheimer pulled him back. "The doctors were afraid that if Lyle hurt his leg worse, he might tear the hamstring muscle and possibly he would be out for the rest of the season," Rutigliano said. "We didn't want to take any chances." But Alzado was not a particularly cautious man. He moseyed down to the other end of the sideline and when Schottenheimer wasn't looking "snuck" into the game, sending Elvis Franks out when the Jets reached the five. Ironically Alzado's courageous effort appeared in vain.

On his first play back, Todd faked a handoff, then looped a pass into the end zone to wide-open tight end Mickey Shuler who snagged it for a Jets lead. Pat Leahy's extra point made it 14-10, New York, with 13:26 remaining. Alzado wasn't through, however. Neither were the Browns.

After all the work they had done to climb into the driver's seat in the AFC Central Division, a 3-10 team (from New York City no less) was now trying to spoil their fun and all the enjoyment that the city of Cleveland was experiencing. It was time for the Kardiac Kids to come to the rescue once again.

"When they scored, we huddled on the sidelines and said, 'Hey, they haven't stopped us yet. Let's not stop ourselves. Stop holding, dropping passes, and get together,'" Dave Logan said. "I just knew we would go down and score."

"When we're behind in the fourth quarter, I feel the advantage goes to us," Sipe said. "Don't ask me why. It just does."

After Hall returned the kickoff to the Cleveland thirty-two the Browns made a key observation that turned into the play of the game. New York starting cornerback Bobby Jackson had injured his shoulder early in the second quarter and had now been taken out of the game. His replacement was rookie Jesse Johnson, who ordinarily played safety.

"Jackson is a good player," Reggie Rucker said. "It was the first thing I noticed and I told Sam that Jackson was out of the game. Whoever comes into the game in his place is not that good. You have a twelve-year guy on a rookie. This play was going to make everything happen."

Sipe agreed. "You have to test a guy like that right away," he said.

Test him they did. On first down Sipe called the play "80 Dig Wing Go," targeting Rucker, who ran it perfectly. He took Johnson inside, then lost him with a sharp cut outside and streaked down the sideline. Johnson was turned inside-out and Sipe lofted a perfect pass that Rucker snagged for a forty-five-yard gain to the New York twenty-three.

Ironically after the game Johnson wasn't even sure who it was who had burned him so badly. "Whoever it was put a good move on me," he said. "I thought I had a chance to knock down the ball, but I was a little late."

It took the Browns five plays to march the remaining twenty-three yards, and they took the lead back when Sipe hit Greg Pruitt on a five-yard scoring pass. Don Cockroft's extra point made it 17-14, Browns, with 9:27 to play. As usual, however, the game wasn't over yet.

Despite Alzado's return Todd and the Jets' offense picked up where they'd left off on their previous two possessions, marching to the Cleveland forty in six plays. Then Todd, who had been burning the Browns with short screens and flare passes throughout the second half, might have gone to the well once too often. On first down Charlie Hall read Todd's designed screen for running back Scott Dierking perfectly and dropped him for a six-yard loss.

"I knew it was coming," Hall said. "I widened out a little bit and paid no attention to what the tight end was doing. On the sidelines just before we came back out, we said we would forget about playing the tight end inside and just jump in. I played the man coming out and beat the guards. They didn't have a chance to come out and block me."

Then, perhaps displaying why the Jets were a 3-10 team, Todd called the same play, this time for Bruce Harper. Once again Hall crashed through the line and broke up the short pass, setting up third-and-sixteen. Those plays had been successful throughout the second half with Alzado on the bench. With the Browns' spiritual leader back in the game, suddenly they weren't working. Most Browns' fans would argue that it wasn't coincidental.

After another incompletion the Jets opted to punt on fourth-and-sixteen with 5:51 to play. The question arose afterward whether Walt Michaels had considered going for it in that situation. "Not for a second," the Jets' coach replied. "No matter what your problems, you have to show your defense you have confidence. I had to believe that we could get the football back."

It also seemed like a sound decision to anyone who had watched the Browns eschew the easy path to victory numerous times earlier in the season. While the members of the capacity crowd were roaring at the defensive stand, most of them probably had the final five minutes scripted in their mind's eye: the Browns would punt back to the Jets, who would then march down the field and score with two minutes to play, and it would be up to Sipe and Company to pull off another last-minute miracle.

Though anyone who thought it had good reason, he turned out to be wrong. The Browns took over at their own eight, and the Jets never saw the football again.

The reason the Browns were so successful in running out the clock is that they didn't appear to be trying to run out the clock. In the next four minutes the Browns ran eight plays, four rushing and four passing, and did not face a third down. All four passes were short flares to either Mike or Greg Pruitt over the middle. All four were completed, kept the Browns moving, and kept the clock running.

When the Browns reached the Jets' forty-nine with 1:28 to play after a nine-yard completion to Greg Pruitt on second-and-seven, Sipe kneeled three times and the Jets, now out of time outs, were helpless to do anything. The clock hit zero and New York's eleventh loss was in the books. The Browns meanwhile had reached double-digit victories for the first time in eight years and marched off the field chanting, "Two more to go!"

Though the Browns' offense scored only seventeen points, Sipe and the passing game had turned in one of their finest performances of the season. The NFL's top-rated quarterback broke the team record he had set six weeks earlier for completions in a game by hitting on thirty of forty-one passes for 340 yards. Sipe now had 293 completions for the season, seven more than he had in 1979 with two games yet to play. It was the fifth three-hundred-yard game of the season for Sipe and the tenth of his career.

Ten of Sipe's completions went to Greg Pruitt for seventy-five yards as he came one catch shy of tying the team record set by wide receiver Mac Speedie in 1952. Pruitt, who had baffled the New York linebackers all afternoon, appeared to be as recovered from his 1979 knee injury as he would ever be. The primary question asked him after the game pertained to his possible future as a wide receiver instead of a running back in 1981, as some rumors had suggested. "I never said I would like to be a wide receiver," Pruitt said. "I said that during rehabilitation I *could* be one.

"I still would like to come back and play at 100 percent and do the things I did before just to prove to myself I can. If they want to switch me to wide receiver, then fine. I enjoy catching passes out of the backfield because that's another way I can get my hands on the ball."

While the Cleveland offense had put together another sterling effort, the defense also deserved kudos for keeping a deceivingly talented Jets offense at bay. The speedy receivers the Browns had been so concerned about, Walker and Jones, were held to one catch apiece. The Jets only ran forty-eight offensive plays, and Richard Todd was intercepted twice. It was the Jets' final drive, however, that burned brightly in many minds as the Cleveland defense's finest moment.

Some felt Alzado's heroic shenanigans inspired the team in the final minutes, and Rutigliano was asked whether his defensive end would be punished for manipulating his coaches. "I get no respect from that guy," Rutigliano said, comically pretending to be annoyed. "But tell me, where are you going to find guys in this business like that anymore? If I were a real disciplinarian, I suppose I would have to say Lyle was wrong.

"But it was a matter of intention rather than judgment. Lyle wasn't intending to be disrespectful. He's a great kid. A great man. Oh, okay, a great man-kid. Maybe I'll fine him just for appearances. But if I do, it'll only be a chin strap, or something like that."

The other major query circulating through the Cleveland locker room was whether or not the Browns had suffered a letdown after the huge win in the Astrodome. "There was no letdown," insisted Rucker, who led all receivers with 108 yards on five receptions. "The Jets beat Houston two weeks ago. And when you beat Houston, you beat one helluva team. But this game was tougher than I thought it would be. The Jets did not come in and lie down."

"It was a struggle for us, but that's a good sign because good teams struggle and win," Rutigliano said. "It took a lot of character and execution—and yes, guts, to come back the way we did and win."

However, some sensed that the Browns might have been playing mind games with themselves either because of the added pressure of a playoff run or because of the media blitz that came with it. "Some of the new guys were overwhelmed," Alzado admitted. "Instead of reading the playbooks, we were reading the press clippings."

"I got the feeling they had put enormous pressure on themselves," wrote Hal Lebovitz, "especially on defense, worrying so much about mistakes they fretted themselves into making them."

"If any of us is feeling any pressure, it's only the result of everybody saying we're already in the playoffs, that we've got it locked up," Sipe said. "But this business about us being a shoo-in is a bunch of bull. Nobody is going to give us any-thing and we know it."

Statistically the home team certainly deserved the victory. The Browns accu-mulated 398 yards of total offense, exactly one hundred yards more than they allowed the Jets. Cleveland also ran seventy plays to New York's forty-eight and only punted twice. It wasn't going unnoticed that the Browns' statistical domina-tion was eerily similar to the way they had been dominated in the preseason and first two games of the schedule.

Still, as was the case with many of the teams that had lost to Cleveland in 1980 the Jets didn't seem all that impressed with the Browns. "I thought we could win today," Walt Michaels said. "Cleveland has a lot of room for improvement."

"The Browns are a good team, but not that good," Richard Todd agreed. "We've played some better teams. Houston is one."

To their credit the Browns held back from retaliating against the words com-ing from a 3-11 team. "I don't get involved in that kind of stuff, but I will say this," Rutigliano said. "We're 10-4 and it must be one of two things. Either I'm the great-est coach in the NFL, or our players have a great deal of character. I'd like to buy both of them. But frankly, Scarlet, I don't give a damn."

Following the same spirit that spread forth after the win in Houston the Browns presented ten game balls to nonplayers after the Jets' win, mostly to members of the front office.

Now just two games remained: at Minnesota the following Sunday and then a rematch with the improving Bengals at Riverfront Stadium on December 21.

While the Browns were toiling with the Jets, Forrest Gregg's squad was in-volved in a heart-stopping finish of its own downstate against the Baltimore Colts. After Cincinnati led 31-6 going into the final quarter Bert Jones led Baltimore on a furious comeback that saw the Colts take a 33-31 lead in the final two minutes. The Bengals then drove seventy-seven yards with no time outs and just-signed kicker Jim Breech kicked the game-winning twenty-one-yard field goal with twelve seconds to play to give the home team a 34-33 victory. Cincinnati now stood at 5-9 on the season.

The Browns' playoff hopes grew stronger as more scores came in. The Oakland Raiders had lost to the Dallas Cowboys, 19-13, and the San Diego Chargers had been blown out by the Washington Redskins, 40-17. The defeats dropped both the AFC West co-leaders to 9-5, a game behind the now 10-4 Browns. The Denver Broncos had also been eliminated with a 31-14 loss to the Chiefs—a good sign for the Browns, whose October loss to Denver could have caused tie-breaking problems. As it was the opening-day defeat in New England looked like it might do damage.

The Buffalo Bills had managed to squeak past the Los Angeles Rams in over-time, 10-7, and were tied with Cleveland for the best record in the conference.

After a month-long preseason and fourteen grueling weeks of football, nothing had been settled in the AFC playoff picture. It would all come down to the final two weeks.

"The town is behind us," Art Modell said that Sunday. "This team knows that. This team is made up of a lot of character and determination. I don't think we will disappoint this town."

Disappointment was hardly the word for what millions were feeling around the world the night after the Browns defeated the Jets.

At about 11:00 P.M. EST forty-year-old singer-songwriter John Lennon was shot to death outside his apartment on Manhattan's Upper West Side. Police arrested twenty-five-year-old Mark David Chapman, whom they described as a "local screwball," and charged him with second-degree murder.

Lennon, one of the most famous men in the world, had just begun a comeback into the music industry after taking several years off to be with his family. Beatles' and Lennon fans around the globe wept openly, organized candlelight vigils, and stampeded record stores for his albums. Radio stations temporarily changed formats to all Lennon and Beatles music. Yoko Ono said there would be no funeral for her slain husband but asked for everyone to observe ten minutes of silence at 2:00 P.M. the following Sunday in his memory.

Any Lennon fans on the Browns' roster would have to observe their ten minutes of silence at another time since they would have their hands full with the first-place Minnesota Vikings on that Sunday afternoon at frosty Metropolitan Stadium, where the Browns had never won. As the week wore on, however, some in the media suggested that the Minnesota game wasn't as important as it initially appeared.

In a surprising turn of events the Miami Dolphins had upset the New England Patriots on *Monday Night Football* (the broadcast incidentally had been interrupted by Howard Cosell, who broke the news of Lennon's murder.) The Patriots, who dropped to 8-6 with the 16-13 overtime loss, had an opportunity to win the game at the end of regulation, but John Smith's thirty-five-yard field-goal attempt was blocked by Miami guard Bob Baumhower. The game entered overtime, and an Uwe von Schamann field goal won it for the Dolphins three minutes later. The New England loss simultaneously dealt a serious blow to the Pats' postseason hopes and improved the Browns' chances. The down side for Cleveland was that the Patriots' loss also kept the Steelers' slim Wild Card hopes alive.

Everything was up for grabs in the AFC where seven teams were fighting for five spots: Buffalo, Cleveland, Oakland, San Diego, Houston, Pittsburgh, and New England. A Cleveland victory in Minnesota would clinch a Wild Card spot for the Browns and eliminate the Patriots. But even if the Browns were to fall to the

Vikings, Sunday could still be a red-letter day. If the Bills defeated the Patriots on the road, the Browns would be assured of a Wild Card spot regardless of what they did in Minnesota. Plus Cleveland could still win the AFC Central with a triumph in Cincinnati in Week Sixteen even if Houston won its final two games—at Green Bay and home to the Vikings. Assuming the Browns lost to the Vikings and defeated the Bengals while Houston won its final two, they'd have the same overall record (11-5) and division record (4-2) as the Oilers, but they'd have a better conference record (8-4 to 7-5).

But if the Browns were to beat the Vikings and lose to the Bengals, while the Oilers won their last two, the deadlock atop the Central would go to a fourth tiebreaker, winning percentage against common opponents, which would give Houston the division crown.

Since the Minnesota game wasn't a clear-cut must-win situation local writers asked the Browns how important it really was. "Those guys in there don't want to lose another game, not one," Rutigliano said outside the Cleveland locker room on Monday. "They want to go 12-4. It is a matter of pride and they are proud guys."

Rutigliano's statement made sense to Greg Pruitt. "Mainly it's a matter of pride," said Pruitt. "We didn't come this far to let down now."

Playoff and Super Bowl veteran Calvin Hill (who played on the 1971 Dallas team that won the title) also wanted to avoid a letdown. "If we don't win, we're in trouble," the Yale grad confessed. "Every playoff team I ever was on did well at the end of the season. This is a time to get everything together, to get our rhythm together, and math has nothing to do with it."

Probably more important than pride, however, was the reward of home-field advantage throughout the conference playoffs that a 12-4 mark would almost certainly bring. "I don't really care who else makes the playoffs, the only thing I really want is to play our first game in Cleveland," Rutigliano said. "We could draw a southern or western team into our weather, which could be a problem to them."

On the other hand pride would certainly be a motivating factor for the Browns, who hadn't forgotten what the Vikings had done to them in the final game of the exhibition season nearly four months earlier. Both teams had stumbled out of the starting gate in September but improved just in the nick of time. The Vikings began the season 3-5 but had won five of their last six and stood one game up on the Detroit Lions in the mediocre NFC Central. A Minnesota victory over the Browns would give the Vikes the division title, which Minnesota would have to win to get into the playoffs.

With two weeks of action remaining the NFC playoff picture was almost entirely in focus. Philadelphia and Dallas were both in from the East regardless of who won the division. Atlanta already had at least a Wild Card spot locked up and would almost certainly win the West. That left either the Vikings or Lions from the Central and the Los Angeles Rams as the second Wild Card. Clearly the Vikings had a very small margin for error, much smaller than that of the Browns, at least entering Week Fifteen.

Rutigliano was also presented with the question of whether the Browns would be better off facing a team that didn't have its back against the wall as the Vikings did. "Hell no," he responded frankly. "I feel better about the game coming up because the Vikings still have a chance, I really do.

"When you get to this stage of the season, a team that comes in with a 3-11 record doesn't have anything to lose. I'd much rather be playing the Vikings than, say New Orleans."

The 0-14 Saints, by the way, would be taking on the Browns' latest victims, the Jets, at Shea Stadium, trying to prevent becoming the first NFL team to lose fifteen games in a season. Before the game Jets' officials had arranged a musical tribute to John Lennon, who as a member of the Beatles had drawn nearly 100,000 to a concert at Shea in 1965.

Ironically airport officials said that the throng that greeted the Browns at Hopkins following the win over Houston eight days before Lennon died was the second-largest crowd that had ever formed there. The first was in 1966 when the Beatles arrived for a concert.

Almost in tribute to John Lennon, the Browns were becoming very Beatle-esque around Cleveland that week. To prevent another costly mob scene upon the Browns' return from Minnesota airport officials and police designed an alternate plan. Instead of arriving at the terminal the Browns would disembark at the old Tank Plant just south of the airport, renamed the Park Company complex. Any fans wishing to greet them would do so in Beatle fashion: behind an eight-foot tall chain-link fence. The plan would also be implemented for the Browns' return from Cincinnati the following week.

What's more, Lyle Alzado neared rock-star status that Thursday night at the Cleveland Touchdown Club's annual awards dinner. "We're going to bring the world championship to Cleveland where it belongs," he said to raucous applause. Then when presented with the organization's most valuable defender trophy, he refused to take it. The man who deserved it, he argued, was Marty Schottenheimer. Dan Coughlin went one step further, suggesting that Schottenheimer deserved a Nobel Prize for physics for what he had done with the Browns' defense.

That week both *Newsweek* and *Sports Illustrated* featured stories on Cleveland's gridiron heroes. "What are these Browns, anyway?" asked *SI*'s Paul Zimmerman. "For one thing, they're a breath of fresh air—a refutation of all the clichés."

As if gracing the pages of two of the most famous magazines in America wasn't enough for one week, a song about the Browns was quickly becoming legendary along the North Coast. With the team closer to the postseason than it had been in eight years Cleveland radio stations began playing "The Twelve Days of a Cleveland Brown Christmas" seemingly nonstop. Record stores were flooded with 45s of the tune. By midweek fans had purchased forty thousand copies and ordered 100,000 more.

The lyrics, sung to the tune of "The Twelve Days of Christmas," went through each day of the Yuletide season and rattled off what Art Modell had given to them. From Alzado attacking to Doug Dieken blocking to Brian Sipe a-passing, it hit on every major contributor to the Kardiac Kids "a-winning" on a Rutigliano Super Bowl team. Most inspiring was its final line promising the Browns would indeed make the playoffs.

For as intimate as the song was for Browns' fans, it was actually more of an assembly-line production. The tune, written and produced by Progress Records in Houston, was one of eleven recorded, each for a different NFL team in contention for the playoffs. While clearly it was worth their while to create the Cleveland version, the enterprise's creators should have done their homework a bit more on Buffalo's version. In "The Twelve Days of a Buffalo Bill Christmas" was a lyric about Joe DeLamielleure a-blocking. Oops.

The records, along with the thousands of dollars fans were spending on Browns' paraphernalia for the Christmas rush, reminded many of the last time a sports team had captured the imagination of the city the way this one had. Long-time Cleveland residents hadn't seen anything like this since 1948 when the Cleveland Indians were involved in a four-team race for the pennant all summer long. Nearly eliminated by Labor Day the Tribe made a furious comeback, tied the Boston Red Sox for the pennant, then defeated Boston in a one-game playoff to get to the World Series. In what was almost an anticlimax, the Indians beat the Boston Braves four games to two for Cleveland's first world title in twenty-eight years.

Thirty-two years later the city had once again fallen in love. Brian Sipe's locker at Baldwin-Wallace was jammed with thousands of letters from adoring fans. Players were besieged with public appearance and endorsement offers. WKYC, Cleveland's NBC affiliate, was getting much higher ratings than in previous years, as local fans lived and died with the Kardiac Kids at every turn in the road.

But some of that living and dying may not have been especially good for the viewers.

"Watching the Kardiac Kids might be a hazard to your health," concluded Dr. Herman K. Hellerstein, professor of medicine and cardiology at Case Western Reserve University. True enough, moments after Clarence Scott's game-clinching interception against the Oilers one local woman watching the game began having chest pains. She was rushed to the emergency room and was successfully treated. In fact during her visit doctors determined the woman had a minor heart problem she hadn't known about. As it turned out the Kardiac Kids might have saved a life.

Still the Kardiac Kids were appropriately named, as many ordinarily healthy fans would appear riddled with disease while watching the final moments of a Browns' game. Bob Sudyk called it the "Kardiac Kondition," which included symptoms such as "perspiration, rapid heartbeat, trembling fingers, shortness of breath, inability to sit still, ravenous appetite, compulsion to gulp down martinis."

As a result Dr. Hellerstein offered tips to those wanting to watch the Browns and stay in good health: "Before a game, eat lightly and avoid fatty foods," he said. "Don't drink until it ends. Actually, screaming and cheering the team is healthful. It is a positive release of emotions." Still . . .

"If you have suffered heart disease, take an extra dose of whatever medication you take before you exercise.

"The Kardiac Kids can be healthy. They can also be dangerous."

At the center of most of the merchandising ideas swirling around Cleveland's latest cash cow was John Minco, director of programs and advertising for the Browns. Local businesses and would-be entrepreneurs pitched all kinds of ideas to him, many of which would have seemed downright ridiculous had the team not become the center of Cleveland's universe. Even so some were still ridiculous. A group of local florists had offered fifteen thousand orange mums to give away to the first fifteen thousand women attending a Browns home game. One person came up with a recipe for the "Official Browns Cocktail," better known as the "Super Sip(e)," with just the right mix of orange juice, vodka, and brown sugar. Remarking on the regional craze the Browns had become, Rutigliano said, in what might have been the understatement of the year, "We've created a MONSTER!"

Minco's biggest task that week was selling ads and putting together programs for two potential playoff games to be held at Cleveland Stadium. He'd already fallen victim to the Browns' surprising success in one fashion: since he had to order the printing of the programs for all games in June, he'd requested only fifteen thousand for the Jets game, not expecting it to be the cultural event it was. "Usually I'm stoking my furnace with the programs I have left over in December," he said.

Though Minco didn't say as much, regardless of how well the team started or how well it was playing in November in recent seasons, many fans had just come to expect the Browns to fold near year's end. Many expected it to happen in 1980 as well since they had done it each of the seven seasons since Cleveland's last playoff berth. From 1973 through 1979 the Browns held an overall December record of 5-14-1.

But 1980 was different. It didn't appear that there would be any fold this time. One of the biggest reasons was that the Browns were unusually healthy going into Week Fifteen. No one was ruled out of the Vikings game, not even Lyle Alzado, who said he would find a way to play through his painful hamstring injury.

The Browns' good-health fortune even transcended off the football field when hours after the Jets win Ricky Feacher was only slightly injured in a car accident in Westlake that totaled his 1979 Caprice Classic. Feacher's injuries required twenty-three stitches on his chin and six on his knee, but doctors said he would be able to play in Minnesota.

The Vikings on the other hand were a bit more banged up. The most serious injury was to wide receiver Ahmad Rashad, who had strained ligaments in his knee and was unable to practice all week. On Saturday night, Rashad didn't sleep well worrying about the condition of his knee. When he woke up it felt no better—"sort of mushy," he would say later—and he nearly resigned himself to not playing. He drove to Metropolitan Stadium and parked at the far end of the players' lot, thinking a long walk would give him a better idea what kind of shape his knee was in. As he marched through the frosty morning air toward the ballpark Rashad decided he'd give it a shot.

His decision would have a dramatic impact on the 1980 season and alter the course of history for the Cleveland Browns.

Despite Minnesota's reputation for brutally cold winters, December 14, 1980, was surprisingly "mild" under the circumstances. Temperatures only reached the mid-twenties by game time, but considering the highs in Minneapolis had been in the single digits all week none of the Browns were complaining.

Even those that didn't appreciate the cold weather warmed up in a hurry when the Browns took an early lead. Rick Danmeier (who along with Don Cockroft was one of just three straight-ahead kickers remaining in the NFL) missed a forty-five-yard field goal short on the Vikings' first possession that set an ominous tone for kickers for the rest of the afternoon. The Browns then marched seventy-three yards in ten plays. They drew first blood when Sipe hit Calvin Hill over the middle for an eighteen-yard scoring pass that, with Cockroft's point after, made it 7-0, Browns.

But the cold seemed to stifle both teams' high-potent offenses for much of the remainder of the first half. The Vikings had another opportunity to score late in the second quarter, but Danmeier missed again, this time from forty-one yards away, and as they had before the Browns took advantage. Bolstered by a twenty-two-yard pass from Sipe to Mike Pruitt and then a forty-one-yarder to a leaping Dave Logan at the Minnesota nine, the Browns traversed seventy-seven yards in just five plays. Sipe capped the drive with 1:12 left in the half with a two-yard touchdown run around right end that gave Cleveland a 13-0 lead. However, Cockroft's second extra point of the game was no good, the third missed kick of the day.

The thirteen-point margin stood until halftime but only with some good luck. After the Vikings drove to the Cleveland twenty-five with ten seconds left, quarterback Tommy Kramer hit wide receiver Sammy White for twenty-one yards to the four, but out of time outs Minnesota couldn't get off another play.

So far, so good, for Cleveland. The Browns were in control on the road and a playoff berth was within reach, just thirty minutes away.

The Vikings made the reach a bit further on their first possession of the third quarter when Kramer hit tight end Joe Senser with a lobbed screen pass that turned into a thirty-one-yard touchdown, capping a ninety-eight-yard drive. Unfortunately for Minnesota, Danmeier's bad day continued as he plunked the extra point off the left upright. Thus the Browns' lead was 13-6.

They extended it to ten points when Cockroft atoned for his earlier miss by connecting on a thirty-two-yard field goal with 5:52 to play in the period. Minnesota answered that score with one of its own as Danmeier finally made good on a twenty-four-yard attempt with ten seconds left in the third. The Browns led 16-9 as they entered what would be one of the craziest fourth quarters in franchise history.

After the Vikings kicked off it appeared that the Browns had picked up right where they'd left off the week before in terms of fourth-quarter clock management. Taking over at their own seventeen, Sipe and Company embarked on their most impressive drive of the afternoon. Traveling primarily on the ground, the Browns marched down the frozen turf of Metropolitan Stadium a little bit at a time, with no one play of the drive covering more than thirteen yards. After sixteen plays and nearly eight minutes melted off the clock Cleo Miller scored on a one-yard plunge with 7:16 remaining. Cockroft's extra point made it 23-9, Browns, and for many fans back in Cleveland it was time to start getting in line for playoff tickets.

But Kramer and the Minnesota offense did what they could to slow down the premature sales on their next drive. The Vikes marched seventy-two yards in five plays helped by a personal-foul penalty on Elvis Franks following a Kramer run and a twenty-four-yard completion to White. Kramer eventually hit running back Ted Brown for a seven-yard scoring pass to cut the margin to 23-15, but Danmeier's extra point, after a high snap, was blocked by McDonald Oden. That meant the Vikings would still have to score twice to take the lead, and with just 5:01 remaining and the Browns' offense humming, it didn't look likely. Browns' fans again began to turn their attention to the postseason.

Then things got a little hairy. The Browns took over in their own territory following the ensuing kickoff and shortly after picked up a first down at the Cleveland thirty-nine. Then after the Vikings took their first time out with 2:18 to play the Browns' brain trust decided to roll the dice in the manner that had been so effective in the final minutes against the Jets the week before. The coaches allowed Brian Sipe to go to the air on second down.

The play called included an optional screen to a halfback—in this case Cleo Miller—or Sipe could choose to shoot for Reggie Rucker upfield. Minnesota linebacker Fred McNeil blanketed Miller in the flat, so Sipe opted for Rucker and just barely got the pass off in the face of a Viking blitz. Sipe was hit as he threw and didn't see the end of the play. "I just heard the crowd and I figured the worst had happened," Sipe said. "Under the circumstances, it was a bad decision to go to Reggie. But it worked last week."

This time it didn't. Minnesota cornerback Bobby Bryant stepped in front of the pass and intercepted it at midfield. He returned it three yards to the Cleveland forty-seven, and the Vikings were back in business with 2:12 remaining. "You can only second-guess that play if you are a sportswriter, I am not second-guessing anything," Rutigliano would say later. "He chose to throw it upfield, and it was intercepted. That's all."

After an eleven-yard pass to tight end Bob Tucker, a seventeen-yarder to Rashad, and a seven-yard toss to Ted Brown, things got even more interesting when Kramer hit Rashad on a crossing pattern past Clarence Scott for a twelve-yard touchdown. Danmeier's extra point was good this time, and with 1:35 to play the Vikings had cut the lead to 23-22. It was becoming just another day at the office for the Kardiac Kids.

Next came an almost ordinary event in a Browns game: an onside kick. Danmeier's boot was recovered by Scott at the Minnesota forty-four, and once again the Browns were in control. If they could pick up just one first down the contest would be over. On first down Cleo Miller went up the middle for three yards. Minnesota called time out. On second down Mike Pruitt scampered around left end for a critical five-yard gain, but it was wiped out on an illegal-motion penalty on Cody Risien, bringing up second-and-twelve at the Minnesota 46 with 1:23 remaining.

Mike Pruitt ran around right end for three more, and the Vikings called their final time out with 1:15 left. Not willing to repeat the same mistake on two straight possessions the Browns kept it close to the vest on third-and-nine, sending Pruitt up the middle. It very nearly worked as he rushed for seven to the Minnesota thirty-six and kept the clock running. The Browns now had another decision to make on fourth-and-two: go for it or punt. Critics would later point out that on the Browns' last scoring drive they had gathered sixty-one of their eighty-three yards via the ground game, so it was conceivable, if not expected, that they could pick up two yards when they absolutely needed them.

Again the Browns decided to play it conservative. With twenty-three seconds remaining Johnny Evans booted the ball high and deep and it carried into the end zone for a touchback. Those same critics would later argue that had the Browns gone for it and not picked up the game-ending first down, the Vikings would have only been fifteen yards closer than they were following the touchback. That was a small price to pay for a high-percentage gamble, they argued.

Still with the Vikings at their own twenty they would now have to drive eighty yards in fourteen seconds with no time outs. At best the Vikings would have time for two successful plays.

The first one was so ridiculous, the Vikings would later say, it was almost laughable.

"It's the kind of thing you see the kids on the sandlots doing all the time," Minnesota head coach Bud Grant said. "I don't know if we've ever worked on it in practice." It almost didn't work at all. Tight end Joe Senser, Kramer's intended target, was held up at the line. Kramer took two more steps back, knowing if Senser couldn't get open he'd have to go to his second—and even less likely successful—option. But at the last moment Senser broke free and Kramer hit him with a short pass over the middle at the Minnesota thirty. The Browns' linebackers, knowing the game was over if they could just tackle Senser in bounds, took the bait and swarmed to him.

But Senser lateraled the ball to Ted Brown, who scampered down the left sideline. Brown eventually ran out of bounds at the Cleveland forty-six with five seconds to go after twenty-four additional yards following the lateral. Now the Vikings at least had a glimmer of hope. The sandlot play had worked.

Out of time outs the Vikings had one play to reach the end zone. The play they called was titled "Squadron Right." Wide receivers Terry LeCount, Sammy White, and Ahmad Rashad all lined up to the right side and were to streak down the field. Kramer would loft the ball down to the end zone and pray. The Vikings would hope for either a tip that someone might come down with or a pass-interference penalty on the Browns that would give them one more snap. If the latter happened they'd have a chance to win the game with a field goal since the game couldn't end on a defensive penalty.

"Tommy throws it into the end zone," Grant would say later of the designed play. "We get an interference call, a touchdown, or nothing. We have nothing to lose." The Browns, knowing exactly what was coming, dropped eight players back and rushed just three. "We had three layers," Rutigliano said. "The first layer was our line, but there was no real rush. The second layer was trying to hold up the receivers and the third layer was all our experienced guys [in the secondary.]"

One of the three up front was Lyle Alzado, who had been hobbling on his sore leg all day and was playing more on guts than on strength. With the numbers against them the Browns could get no pressure on Kramer after he took the snap. He faded back, then stepped up and released his forty-ninth pass of the afternoon. It was right where it needed to be. Alzado didn't see any of the play in his attempt to get to Kramer. With his back to the action he heard the crowd's reaction a few seconds later and knew what happened.

LeCount and White slowed down at the five as the ball neared them, as did several Browns' defenders. Rashad knew this would happen as he sprinted down the field, so he slowed up as he neared the ten to get some distance between himself and the group.

As Kramer's throw neared the end zone Thom Darden appeared to have timed his leap perfectly. He rose up over the bunch just as the ball neared them and reached for it. For a split second it appeared he would intercept it and send the Browns to the playoffs. The problem was that Ron Bolton was doing the exact same thing. He had his eye on the ball and had its flight path timed. He left the ground at the same instant Darden did. Both were veteran defensive backs doing the right thing at the right time. The problem wasn't their thinking or their technique. The problem was that there was one too many veteran defensive backs in the picture.

Bolton touched the ball first, getting both hands on it. For one fateful half-second he knew he had the game-winning interception. Then Darden's left hand tipped the football as he collided with Bolton. The ball ricocheted into the air as Darden and Bolton both returned to Earth.

It was just the break the Vikings were hoping for. The cluster of Browns and Vikings came down, no one within it able to catch the ball, which spiraled down toward the right sideline—right toward Rashad, who had snuck in behind the pack.

Before the ball could land out of bounds at the one Rashad reached back with his left hand and snagged the football as if it were an apple falling off a tree. He pulled it into his chest. Dick Ambrose tackled him immediately, though he knew it was in vain. "I didn't want him to spike the ball or anything," he said. "I wanted to take that little pleasure away from him."

Ahmad Rashad, who hadn't practiced all week, who six hours earlier wasn't going to play in the game, had caught a game-winning forty-six-yard Hail Mary pass to defeat the Browns with no time remaining. The Kardiac Kids had received a taste of their own medicine.

"It was like five fans under a pop foul at the stadium, grasping for the falling object," Bob Sudyk wrote in Monday's Press. "After everyone misses, it is always the guy standing nearby who gets the souvenir."

"I just waited and played the rebound," Rashad said. "It came to me and I hugged it with all my might. It was a beautiful way to win."

"It was a freak play," Darden countered, "and we just made a hero out of Rashad."

"Everybody was going for the ball," Ron Bolton said. "I don't even know who got his hand on the ball or what happened, except that Rashad is a great receiver. The worst thing that could happen for us is exactly what did."

"It was nobody's fault," Rutigliano said. "There were a bunch of guys there, and because of Rashad's great concentration, he was able to make a great play, which is what makes this such a great game."

Since Metropolitan Stadium was designed so that both teams' benches were on the same sideline, what followed was a fascinating study of the thrill of victory and the agony of defeat, all along the same sight line. The Vikings' half of the sideline, including ordinarily stoic coach Bud Grant, exploded out onto the field and flooded the corner of the end zone. Though many of the players didn't even know who had caught the football, they piled on top of one another like children in the back of the end zone, knowing they were on their way to the playoffs.

The orange-and-white half of the sideline was a stark opposite. Sam Rutigliano turned away from the end zone and marched the opposite direction across the sideline, as if by refusing to look at the celebration he could erase its reality. Brian Sipe ripped off the sideline parka he was wearing and flung it to the ground. But most players stood completely still, shocked beyond justifiable movement.

"Everybody was stunned," Mike Pruitt said. "Even the water boys were stunned."

"We had been winning that way. We'd do that to other people. We didn't expect anybody to do it to us."

After a lengthy celebration the Vikings finally began to peel themselves off one another and headed down the tunnel to their locker room so overjoyed they even hugged and kissed sportswriters as they went. Just after both teams had reached their respective locker rooms, however, they marched right back out to the field since the officials demanded the extra point be attempted. Though it would make no difference in the outcome, since total points was something that could be factored into a tie-breaking situation, the attempt was mandatory. Appropriately Danmeier's kick was blocked by Henry Bradley, marking Danmeier's third missed point after of the afternoon.

"It was kind of symbolic," Dieken said of the block. "We lost the game, but we ain't quitting yet. That just sent a message."

Still the Browns, as well as their fans back in Cleveland, were in shock. At the Gristmill Tavern on South Woodland, the play unfolded on television before dozens of fanatic Browns' fans. *Plain Dealer* columnist Doug Clarke described the scene as Rashad reeled in Kramer's prayer of a pass: "There came agonizing groans, a screamed curse . . . and then nothing. Only stunned silence."

"In all my years," a jubilant Grant said, "I've never seen two crazy plays like that work."

It was the most stunning, most sudden loss in Browns' history. In five seconds the Browns had gone from a team that had clinched a playoff spot to a team that now could very well be spending the holidays in front of the television. The Browns would now have to win in Cincinnati in Week Sixteen to win the division and make the playoffs.

"I'll never forget this finish as long as I live," Rashad said. "The Browns got to be down after this one." And there was no doubt they were as the players and coaches made their long walk to the locker room.

"I've always felt it's at that time that you really have to be a coach," Rutigliano would later say. "No matter how rocky the water is, my job as the captain is to get the ship into port."

Still it was not one of the coach's happiest moments. As Rutigliano departed the field a Minneapolis television reporter requested doing a live interview. "There's no way to do a live interview with a dead man," Rutigliano replied.

Though still flabbergasted, the Browns tried to remain upbeat. "Don't forget, we beat Green Bay this way earlier this season, and Kansas City and Miami last year on plays that were similar to the one that won for the Vikings today," Rucker said. "Sooner or later the dice comes up craps, which they did for us today. But this does nothing more than increase the drama."

While Rucker's statement was certainly true, Browns' fans were wondering how much more drama they could take. "This was too much, too exciting," Ted Brown said, echoing that sentiment. "My heart is still pumping way too fast. I thought I might have a heart attack."

Marty Schottenheimer could have justifiably had a heart attack when he saw the final statistics. Tommy Kramer had lit the Browns up for 455 passing yards as the Vikings rolled for 530 yards of total offense and scored on all five of their second-half possessions. Granted, a large chunk of both totals came on a pair of freak plays at game's end, but it was still very disturbing for a defense that had showed so much improvement over the course of the season. To allow an unproven quarterback like Kramer to set a new Browns' record for most passing yards against—breaking the previous mark of 418 set by Washington's Sonny Jurgensen in 1967—was unacceptable. Rashad, playing injured, ended up with 142 yards on nine receptions, one of four Vikings to catch seven or more passes.

Sipe had set a team record of his own, though it drew little attention in the aftermath. His 232 passing yards gave him 3,824 for the season, breaking the mark he set the year before.

The field day enjoyed by the Minnesota offense further underlined the importance of a healthy Lyle Alzado to the Cleveland lineup. With Alzado only able to rush on one healthy leg, he was essentially a nonfactor. And with Alzado contained, Elvis Franks and Henry Bradley were unable to make anything happen. The Browns' lone sack was by Clay Matthews for a loss of one yard as the Cleveland linebackers spent much of the day chasing the Vikings' running backs.

Art Modell went into the locker room after the game embracing and consoling the players, ensuring them they'd get the job done in Cincinnati. "I know this club has the character, the quality, the ability, and the talent to do what has to be done next week," he said. "It was a terrible way to lose today, but we still have control of our destiny.

"We will do it next Sunday, and everything that happened today will be forgotten."

As was usually the case the local media was not so kind toward the Browns. The primary focus of the criticism was Sipe's interception that gave the Vikings new life and turned the game around.

"What did you expect from the Browns?" asked Bob Sudyk. "Certainly not a casual clinching of a playoff spot a week early."

"They should have had it wrapped up," Hal Lebovitz wrote, "and then they cut the ribbon themselves and let the insides fall out."

"On the 13th day of Christmas Art Modell gave to us," Doug Clarke callously reported, "Rutigliano a-chokin'."

Clarke criticized Rutigliano for trying to win in his own way rather than grasping victory any way he could get it. Instead of simply running the ball and milking the clock, Clarke argued, Rutigliano was "going to wrap the game up in style; doing the unexpected and going against the book he loves to eschew. The pass would be the coup d'etat, the final arrogant stroke of genius at work."

Naturally the Browns defended the call.

"There are some 70 offensive plays in a game, 70 defensive, and 30 by the special teams, and no one play wins or loses," Rutigliano said.

"What can I tell you?" said Sipe. "Last week we did it the same way and we were heroes. But it didn't work today, that's all. I didn't think it was a great risk, because we were up two scores. But it turned out to be critical.

"Looking back at it, I guess we were wrong. I guess I tried to force the ball to Reggie and I probably shouldn't have. But again, it worked last week and everybody thought it was great then."

"We thought we had the element of surprise," argued running backs coach Jim Garrett. "They expected us to stay on the ground. It was a safe call. Rucker should have been wide open. That call could have gone for a touchdown.

"We consider Sipe on a pass play, like this one, as safe as a run. He has as much chance being intercepted as a runner fumbling. It's like a three-foot putt in golf."

Statistically Garrett was right. Sipe had now thrown 510 passes on the season with just twelve interceptions. The Browns had executed 417 running plays and fumbled thirteen times.

The Vikings were as surprised as the scribes at the Browns' decision to throw. "I didn't think he would throw it then," Grant said, "at least that type of pass."

"That's his type of game," said Minnesota linebacker Matt Blair. "I expected him to throw the ball. Perhaps the type of pass was unexpected."

Beyond the interception Clarke also slammed Rutigliano for not going for it on fourth-and-two from the Minnesota thirty-six with twenty-three seconds left.

"Now it comes down to what none of them wanted—an absolute 'must-win' game in dreaded Riverfront Stadium against a Bengal team with momentum—a game in which anything can happen. Anything at all," wrote Clarke.

Not that the Browns had been doing much scoreboard-watching down the stretch in Bloomington, but if they had they would have noticed the Oilers coasting to an easy 22-3 victory over the floundering Packers at Lambeau Field. Earl Campbell rushed for 181 yards and two touchdowns as Houston tied the Browns for first place atop the AFC Central, both with 10-5 marks.

Elsewhere that afternoon the Steelers kept their slim Wild Card hopes alive with a 21-16 victory over the Chiefs at snowy Three Rivers Stadium. Appropriately running back Rocky Bleier, playing in his final home game before retiring, scored the winning touchdown on an eleven-yard run in the fourth quarter. Pittsburgh was still a long shot at 9-6, especially after the Patriots rebounded from their Monday-night loss to bury the Bills, 24-2, to keep the Browns from backing in to the playoffs.

Bad news for both the Steelers and Browns was a 24-21 victory by Oakland over Denver and a 21-14 Chargers win over Seattle the day before.

It all added up to a mess. Going into the final week of the regular season no AFC team had clinched a playoff spot, and all seven that had been alive going into Week Fifteen were still mathematically in the mix. The Browns, Oilers, Bills, Raiders, and Chargers all stood at 10-5 with the Patriots and Steelers at 9-6. The latter two would need to win their final games and get some help. The former five simply needed to win their final game to get into the postseason. But that was easier said than done.

Particularly for the Browns, who would now have to crawl into the lion's den to face the suddenly red-hot Bengals. Shortly after Rashad's miracle beat the Browns, Cincinnati won its third straight, this time over the Chicago Bears in overtime at Soldier Field, 17-14. For the second straight week it was a Jim Breech field goal that provided the difference as Cincinnati improved to 6-9. The Bengals would now without a doubt be charged up for the Browns the following Sunday at Riverfront, where Cleveland had lost six of its last seven contests. With Paul Brown and Forrest Gregg both in a position to keep Art Modell from getting what he really wanted, the Browns knew nothing would come easy in the Queen City.

"After the game I told the squad the most important thing we have now is hope," Rutigliano said. "We certainly do have a flair for the dramatics; we never do anything easy."

"Rutigliano didn't bat an eye," Joe DeLamielleure said. "He made it like it would be too easy if we won this one. He was always the showman."

Like professional entertainers the Browns pushed the heartbreak and disappointment out of their minds as fast as they possibly could. And looked forward to the next show. "On the way to the airport, everybody was already talking about Cincinnati," Dick Ambrose remembered. "We had already kind of filed Minnesota away. It was the shortest we had ever let a bad taste like that stay in our mouth. We were on a mission."

"Maybe this will have a good effect on us," Henry Sheppard said in the locker room. "Our mood is that we want to play *tomorrow*. We don't want to wait until Sunday."

"We can do it, we just have to pull ourselves together," Mike Pruitt said. "Losing makes it tough going into Cincinnati and having to win the division. But we can do it. We've got until Wednesday to sulk about the way we lost, and then we've just got to get ready for the Bengals.

"We're going to rebound from this. This loss is not going to hurt us. We just made it tougher on ourselves, that's all. We're going to win next week."

Also believing that was a group of about a thousand Browns' fans who greeted the team at the old Tank Plant upon their return that evening. Signs like "We Still Believe You Will Do It" and "So What! We Believe Number One!" adorned the chain-link fence as the diehards weathered a wind-chill factor of five degrees. After disembarking some of the players walked over and exchanged high fives with the fans through the fence.

However, one Brown wasn't there. Thom Darden was so distraught over his failure to break up the Hail Mary that he couldn't travel back to Cleveland with the team. Instead the former Michigan Wolverine went back to Ann Arbor and sulked before returning to Cleveland on Tuesday. Adding insult to injury, a friend of Darden's who worked at a Detroit television station talked him into an on-air interview about the play, which wound up costing the hometown Lions the NFC Central title. For Darden and the Browns there was no escape. "It was probably one of the more devastating times in my career," he said. "It was embarrassing. More than anything else, I felt I'd let my team down and that I had caused the loss that would have given us the playoff berth."

Though players, coaches, and fans alike put on their best faces, everyone was heartbroken. The Browns were literally inches away from their ultimate eight-year-old dream, only to have it ripped away.

"This game was a tough one to swallow," Sheppard said. "But I guess that's why they call us the Kardiac Kids."

"One thing is certain," Paul Zimmerman had correctly predicted in *Sports Illustrated* the week before the Minnesota game. "Whatever happens, it will happen the hard way. Cleveland never makes things comfortable."

Thus the Kardiac Kids and all who had fallen in love with them were about to experience the ultimate climax to the most memorable regular season in Cleveland Browns' history.

10 · The Maximum of Excitement

Four days after the Browns' loss to the Vikings, Sam Rutigliano received a letter from Cleveland Mayor George Voinovich:

> I'm writing to you and the team before the outcome of Sunday's game is known because I want you to know that you are our No. 1 team regardless of what happens at Riverfront Stadium. You have given us a season of joy and delight that Browns fans won't soon forget.
>
> Thank you again for providing football fans everywhere with more excitement and entertainment than any other Browns' team.

Nobody, not even the mayor, needed to point out to the Browns the importance of the situation in which they now found themselves.

It was going to be the biggest regular-season game for the Browns in sixteen years, when they faced a similar situation in the 1964 season finale. After dropping a frustrating match to the St. Louis Cardinals in the next-to-last week, the 9-3-1 Browns needed a win over their archrivals, the New York Giants, at Yankee Stadium to capture the Eastern Conference title and an appearance in the NFL Championship Game. The Browns responded by blowing the Giants out of the Bronx. Quarterback Frank Ryan completed twelve of thirteen passes and threw for five touchdowns in a 52-20 throttling. More than 5,000 fans greeted the Browns at the airport, and the next week they shocked the sports world by blowing out the heavily favored Colts for their fourth NFL title, 27-0.

Following their nearly incomprehensible loss in Minnesota the mission was clear for the 1980 Browns: win in Cincinnati and take home the division crown and a playoff berth. A Browns' loss would give the Houston Oilers the AFC Central title regardless of what they did in their finale with the Vikings. Though there was still another possibility for the Browns to sneak into the postseason if they fell, it was a long shot. For Cleveland to back in, the New England Patriots would have to lose to the 1-14 New Orleans Saints in the Superdome. Essentially if the Browns fell in Cincinnati their season was over.

"We had created a situation where all our eggs were in one basket," Dick Ambrose said. "Cincinnati was definitely gunning for us and they didn't have the pressure on them that we had. We knew the respective records of the teams went out the window for this game. All that mattered is that it was Cleveland-Cincinnati."

It was not an unfamiliar situation for Sam Rutigliano's club. It would mark the third consecutive year that the Browns would finish the regular season at Riverfront Stadium and the second straight time they'd have a chance to make the playoffs with a win over the inferior Bengals. In 1978, Brian Sipe was knocked out of the game with a head injury on the Browns' first series, and Cincinnati rolled to a 48-16 blowout, denying the Browns a winning season. A year later the Browns appeared to have victory literally in their hands at Riverfront, but Sipe's last-gasp pass in the final seconds glanced off Ricky Feacher's paws and fell incomplete. Both times the Bengals closed a 4-12 season with a victory but, more importantly for Paul Brown, denied Art Modell a trip to the postseason.

The 1980 Browns' team was far better than the 1978 and 1979 versions, and for this squad to come so far and be denied would be incredibly heartbreaking. "Who wants to go to Cincinnati with Paul Brown and Forrest Gregg there?" Sam Rutigliano said years later. "If we lose to Cincinnati, we're 10-6, we don't win the division, we're not in the playoffs. 10-6 is not a bad year, but for all intents and purposes in this case, it would have been a downer."

For the Bengals and owner Paul Brown a third straight season-ending triumph over Modell's Browns in 1980 would be the crowning jewel of them all. For one, after winning three straight going into Week Sixteen, it was apparent that the young Bengals were headed in the right direction. To finish 7-9 would set the right tone for 1981, when expectations would be high. Even more important for Brown and Forrest Gregg, though, would be the opportunity to keep the Browns out of the playoffs. Rumors swirled that Brown had offered a large bonus to the Bengals' players if they beat the Browns. However, the Bengals' players didn't need much motivation to make them want to beat their interstate rivals. "If we win, it will be something to keep us warm all winter," Cincinnati running back Pete Johnson said. "Think how much fun it will be kidding those Browns about it."

Certainly no one in the Browns' camp wanted to lose to Cincinnati and then spend the off-season brooding on the matter. "It would be the longest winter of our lives if we were to lose," said Mike Pruitt, who before the game called it the most important one he'd ever been a part of.

And a loss would make it a long winter for Cleveland sports fans as well. It had been nearly five years since the city of Cleveland had enjoyed any kind of title in any major sport, that being the NBA Cavaliers' 1975–1976 "Miracle in Richfield" Central Division championship. But that had been a relatively short-lived ride via a team that Cleveland hadn't enjoyed a long-term relationship with, at least not to the extent the city had embraced the Indians and Browns over the years. Reflecting that reality the week before the Bengals game Cavaliers' owner Ted Stepien said in a *Cleveland Press* interview that there was a possibility he would move the team out of Cleveland (though actually the Cavs already had been playing their games south of the city in Richfield) and that he was "tired of being pictured by the part of the media as an idiot."

It had been twenty-six years since the Indians had appeared in the postseason and eight since the Browns had done so. It had been nine years since the Browns' last division title, which had come before the Oilers or Steelers had mobilized themselves for their successful 1970s runs. In 1971 the Central Division was still a novelty, an interesting byproduct of the AFL-NFL merger. By 1980 it was the toughest division in football, arguably in all of professional sports, and the Browns were one win away from being crowned its champion.

After the way the city had fallen in love with the 1980 Browns and the positive energy and optimism the team had injected into the populace, a playoff-preventing loss to their in-state rival would be a crippling blow to the city, the team, and its fans. Because of the Kardiac Kids, Cleveland was alive again. There was something to be proud of, something to give the city hope.

And everybody on the Browns—from the owner to the coaches to the players—wanted to bring that gift home to Cleveland. "Even in our bad years, the fans were more merciful in Cleveland than nearly anywhere else in the league," Mike Pruitt said the week before the game. "You may be sure that your Browns and mine will be thinking of that . . . In many ways, we're in this battle together."

Many felt a loss to the Bengals would serve as a bridge, connecting the ineptitude of Cleveland athletics in the 1970s to an entirely new decade. The poor economy, the hurtful jokes, and the civic problems had conspired to make it a long, dark era for the residents along the North Coast, and no one wanted to see it extended.

Cleveland needed a champion.

A win over the Bengals, a team created by the same man who created the Browns, coached by the same man who had guided the Browns during a difficult stretch of the previous dreadful decade, would mean the world to the denizens of Cleveland, Ohio. Conversely a loss would rip out their hearts. And nothing would please Brown and Gregg more.

"This is not a war against coach Forrest Gregg or owner Paul Brown," Mike Pruitt said. "It is the ultimate challenge of proving we are the best under the most exacting pressure-packed conditions. It is what the exhilaration of success in sports is all about."

While the players prepared for the game two distinctive camps of Browns' fans were locked in a debate over the likely outcome of Sunday's game. Browns' optimists pointed out that, while a head coach with Cleveland and then with Toronto in the Canadian Football League, Gregg had never won the final game of the season. Browns' pessimists recalled that Rutigliano never had either, and that the Browns hadn't won a season finale since 1972, their last playoff year. Optimists countered that the Browns were due for a win in Cincinnati. But pessimists focused on the fact that the Browns had lost six of their last seven at Riverfront. Ironically, Cleveland's only road win at Cincinnati in that stretch was in 1977 under Forrest Gregg.

This was the Super Bowl for both teams regardless of what happened afterward. It didn't matter what had transpired previously in the season. The Browns couldn't take comfort in their 31-7 stomping of the Bengals in Cleveland four weeks earlier because Cincinnati had played without several key regulars. Most had returned, namely wide receiver Isaac Curtis and fullback Pete Johnson, who had missed five games in the middle of the season with ligament damage in his knee. Johnson returned the week after the Browns beat the Bengals and had rushed for more than one hundred yards in his next four games. Ken Anderson probably wouldn't start at quarterback because of a sprained ankle, but Jack Thompson had showed improvement over the course of the year and was capable of beating the Browns. Of course after what Tommy Kramer had done to the Cleveland defense some felt any quarterback in the league was capable of beating the Browns.

Early in the week it became clear that the Browns would have to recover quickly from the shocking loss in Bloomington. Tom DeLeone exemplified the average response of the players when he woke up at 5:30 A.M. Monday, too upset to sleep, and shoveled manure at his Medina farm.

Understandably, Rutigliano gave the players Monday off in addition to the usual Tuesday off-day to let them recover mentally and collect themselves emotionally before returning to work. "Sleep on tomorrow's plans," he told the team, "and don't be awakened by what happened yesterday." He also didn't want the Browns watching the films from the Minnesota game. In other words it was time to look forward, not back. Following that sentiment, Rutigliano reminded his team that if he'd told them following the preseason that they'd have a chance to win the division going into the final week of the schedule, they'd be thrilled. "I didn't emphasize anything about that game," Rutigliano said of the Minnesota loss. "I said, 'We just lost the battle, now we've got a chance to win the war. Let's refocus on Cincinnati. That's all that matters.'

"I didn't act like a doting parent and try to point the finger at why we lost the game and how we could have won the game. I just encouraged them. I didn't coach them a bit that week, just encouraged them."

Still there was concern in some players' minds that week.

"Then, more than any other time during that season, we may have thought, 'Uh-oh, did we give something away?'" Cody Risien said. "I felt after that (Minnesota) game that we were a little scared. There was a reason to push the panic button."

But as the week wore on the players took the cue from their coach. "Finally around Wednesday or Thursday, I came out of it," said Thom Darden. "Those are your biggest preparation days. You have to focus on what's ahead. You can't remember what happened the week before and do well the following week. I finally got to the point where I had to let it go and I did. I think that's how most of the guys felt."

"It wasn't difficult to prepare for Cincinnati," Mike Pruitt said. "Everybody knew this was a game we had to win somehow. We knew they were going to be playing just as hard to knock us out. Everybody was really focused and serious."

And that intensity showed on the practice field. "Before that, when we were winning, practice was a little relaxed," Pruitt said. "That week, there was some serious, serious practicing going on."

Still the fans and media took a few more days to get over the loss in Minnesota. After his admission that he nearly lost his mind while watching the final minutes of the Vikings game, Hal Lebovitz announced his mental strategy for the Cincinnati contest, one that many fans in Cleveland seemed to be adopting as well. He said he would watch the game expecting the Browns to lose. "I'm not predicting they're going to lose, but I'll even do that if it will help," he said. "This way, I can watch the game, certain of the outcome, not be disgusted when, or if, things turn against the Browns. And should the Browns win, I'll be surprised and jubilant.

"I hope it works because otherwise, I might as well order my straitjacket now."

At the time it made perfect sense. That week Cleveland had become a nervous wreck, wobbling between manic depression and paranoia. "The only happy sports fans around town today are family doctors, bartenders and television repairmen," Bob Sudyk wrote in Tuesday's *Cleveland Press*. "The fans' Kardiac Kondition suffered trauma only treatable by medication, stiff drinks and punting a hole in the TV picture tube to release emotions."

As a result of those emotions a group of local entrepreneurs devised yet another piece of ingenious Browns' merchandise. It was called the "Cardiac Brick," a piece of orange rubber shaped just like a regular brick but soft to the touch (and incapable of breaking any television sets.) In its marketing literature, the Cardiac Brick was said "to relieve frustrations many Browns fans have."

Dan Coughlin listed times in his life when he felt worse than he did after Ahmad Rashad's miracle catch. The list included when he had appendicitis, when his dog was run over, when he had his broken nose straightened, and when he met Doug Dieken.

Several writers for both Cleveland papers continued to grill Rutigliano and the coaching staff for the decision to pass in the final minutes that led to the interception that turned the game around. It was as if they were already preparing to label that as the play that ultimately cost the Browns the playoffs.

In his Tuesday column Coughlin reassured Brian Sipe that it was after all only a game. However, "He should also remember," Coughlin continued, "that if he ever puts the ball into the air again with two minutes left when he is trying to run out the clock I'll put sugar in his gas tank, salt in his whiskey, goats in his living room, chickens in his garage, goldfish in his bathtub [the latter three referring to a recent Dieken prank on him] and his phone number on men's room walls.

"And I'll kick in the screen of his television set, just as I did to my own television set."

But reflecting the frenzied thinking of the typical Browns' fan that week, Coughlin also tried to stay positive. "Just because Sipe cannot always leap over tall buildings is no reason we should jump off one," he said. "This is no time to put pistols to our temples or stick our heads in ovens.

"What the Browns encountered in Minnesota was a minor setback. Everyone has minor setbacks which ultimately sweeten victory. Ask Richard Nixon."

According to Coughlin's logic, had Nixon defeated John Kennedy for the presidency in 1960 he would not have felt as good as he did when he finally was elected in 1968. For the Browns, however, going through the valley of the Minnesota loss would only make the peak of beating Cincinnati that much more satisfying.

Not everyone in the Browns' camp was buying the theory that a history of suffering and setbacks is a great way to make a football team feel satisfied when it finally reaches its goal. "It [beating Minnesota and clinching a playoff birth] wouldn't have been nearly as fun," Rutigliano admitted. Nonetheless he said, "I would have preferred to win the Minnesota game, but [losing] put everything back on the table. Now we had everything to lose and Cincinnati had nothing to lose."

The Browns' players had been facing similar "do-or-die" scenarios all season long and, despite the scrutiny of the Cleveland media and fans, were taking the upcoming Queen City showdown in stride. "I think the questions within the media were more questions of pressure," Doug Dieken said, looking back to December 1980. "That team was one that felt, 'So what? That's how it's been all year. We'll show up and give you your money's worth.' Our backs were to the wall, but we'd been there before."

Eventually the questions posed to Rutigliano began to focus on the Bengals. And when they did Rutigliano demonstrated not only his own grace under fire but also the tone around Browns' camp that week. One writer asked him if the Browns would have a psychological advantage over Cincinnati.

"Well, after talking to my psychiatrist, he thinks we will have an edge because we're 10-5 and they're 6-9," said Rutigliano.

Another reporter began a question, then paused in the middle to collect his thoughts. "Will there be an attempt made. . . . "

"On my life?" Rutigliano replied.

Another asked if the Browns would be haunted by the Minnesota loss.

"We don't believe in ghosts," Rutigliano said.

In another interview in Rutigliano's office the coach would repeatedly follow up his answers by opening up a desk drawer and shouting, "Are you listening, Forrest?" comically suggesting the Browns' former coach had taken a cue from Richard Nixon prior to departing Cleveland.

"It is only Rutigliano," Sudyk wrote, "who can muster the Browns from the ashes of Met Stadium in Bloomington, Minnesota."

"You don't have to worry about this team," Sipe said. "We are in exactly the right frame of mind. Sam is a master at getting us ready to play, making sure we are thinking about the right things."

"In fact," Rutigliano added, "if I can go any more low-key, I will."

"It was just Sam Rutigliano," Cody Risien said. "I don't think it was anything necessarily that week that Sam came up with or that he acted any different that week than any other week. It was just Sam being Sam."

As they struggled to fight their way out of the dark shadow of the Minnesota loss, a bright light shone on the Browns and gave them a much-needed boost of confidence. On Wednesday the NFL announced the rosters for the annual Pro Bowl, which would be played February 1 in Honolulu. Five Browns were named to the AFC team, the most since eight had made the team following the 1969 season. Brian Sipe, Doug Dieken, and Joe DeLamielleure were all selected as Pro Bowl starters based on voting by players and coaches. Mike Pruitt and Tom DeLeone made the squad as backups, and Lyle Alzado was selected as an alternate—if one of the already chosen defensive lineman couldn't play due to injury, Alzado would also make the team. "We're finally getting the national publicity that has evaded us for so long," said Mike Pruitt, who entered Week Sixteen with 983 rushing yards, just seventeen away from his second straight one-thousand-yard season. "We've been on national TV a few times. People around the league get to know most of us by name."

Even as honors were bestowed upon the Browns, their behavior and demeanor reflected the light-hearted atmosphere Rutigliano had created that week. He called a special team meeting on Wednesday to make the Pro Bowl announcements. When he said Dieken had been named a starter, there were some groans from the players.

"I'm a little short of oxygen," said Calvin Hill. "Could you clarify that?"

"You can call me *Mister* Dieken from now on," Dieken replied, up to the verbal challenge.

For DeLamielleure, it was his sixth straight Pro Bowl selection and justified the Browns' trade for him. Those who had criticized the move in September couldn't be found in December.

Sipe meanwhile became the fifth Browns' quarterback to make All-Pro, joining Otto Graham, Milt Plum, Frank Ryan, and Bill Nelsen. But he got an even
nicer surprise the next day when his wife Jeri gave birth to their second daughter,
healthy eight-pound Morgan Lynn Sipe.

Though the upcoming game was big, Sipe kept things in perspective. "I wasn't
worried about being distracted because we have a big game coming up Sunday,"
he said. "When you measure the two events, the birth of the baby and the game,
there is no contest. The birth is so much more important."

The entire organization was proud of its five representatives, but several felt
there could or even should have been a few more invited to Honolulu. The most
disappointing, at least in Rutigliano's mind, was the oversight of Ron Bolton. Bolton
was wrapping up a great year despite not having many interceptions or tackles
because teams were respecting his talents and not throwing in his direction very
often. If Bolton was disappointed he did a good job hiding the fact. "I'm not
going to let it bother me," he said. "I just want to go to the Super Bowl and they
can stuff the Pro Bowl."

Though the players were honored, it didn't take long for their focus to get back
to business. "It's nice individually, but I'd trade it in a minute for a win Sunday,"
DeLamielleure said of his Pro Bowl selection. "I want to be on a division champion first."

As the week went on comments like that flooded out of Berea as the Browns
regained their confidence and cockiness. "We definitely will take no prisoners,"
said Henry Sheppard. "There is no malice against any individual, but this is an
all-out war."

Never afraid to speak his mind Alzado proclaimed, "The Bengals don't have a
chance. We'll be on top of them from the first play. Losing last Sunday really helped
us because it made us realize we're not unbeatable; that we need to play with
intensity all the time."

"And we know, too, that we are the better team," added Thom Darden. "We
already have proved that, and we're ready to prove it again."

The lack of respect the Browns showed for the Bengals was a two-way street. A
Cincinnati Enquirer reporter took an informal poll of Bengals' players as to which
team would win the AFC. The almost-unanimous choice was the Houston Oilers.
Only one Bengal picked the Browns.

As the Browns marched off the field following Friday's practice a reporter asked
Alzado if that had been the team's final practice until the following July. "Hell
no!" Alzado snapped back. "We are planning to be back here Monday and for a
while after that." Alzado felt there was good reason to be optimistic heading into
the Cincinnati game and believed that the Browns had learned a valuable lesson
in Minnesota. "When you're in a winning streak, as we were, sometimes you think

you just have to walk out on the field and you'll win," Alzado explained. "I'm not saying that's what happened to us in Minnesota, but losing to the Vikings made us more aware of what we've got to do in Cincinnati."

Several players took Alzado's cue and believed that the Vikings loss would *help* the team. "It bothered all of us the same way, which is why we're all more determined now to beat the Bengals, and go on into the playoffs as division champions," Sipe said. "In that respect, maybe losing to Minnesota will prove to have been a blessing in disguise."

Come what may, the players would not go it alone along the banks of the Ohio River. When the Bengals couldn't sell all the remaining tickets for the game in the Cincinnati area by midweek, they allowed the remainder to be purchased via Ticketron outlets in Cleveland. It was like throwing raw meat to savage dogs. The tickets were devoured by Browns' fans hungry to see their team play for the division title, and thousands of Clevelanders—more than had ever attended any game in Cincinnati—prepared to make the four-hour trek south down Interstate 71.

Reflecting the added importance of the contest Cincinnati radio station WLW and Cleveland's WWWE would simulcast a combined sports talk show on Friday night and take calls from fans of both teams around the state. Since both were fifty-thousand-watt stations, every radio in Ohio was able to tune in.

It would be only the second sellout of 1980 for the Bengals, but because more temporary seats had been added following the conclusion of the baseball season it would be the largest crowd of the season at Riverfront Stadium. It only seemed appropriate. After all, how important would this game have been had Ahmad Rashad not made his one-handed catch in Minnesota the week before? The Browns would already have clinched a playoff spot, and while they still would be motivated to play for the division title and home-field advantage, the drama surrounding the contest would have been far less. As it was the Browns had created a scenario that, as author Bill Levy would note, Ernest Hemingway couldn't have written better.

Instead of melting under the pressure Sam Rutigliano was glowing in it and facing it with grace. "I look at the whole thing this way," he said. "It is fun to play a game like this, with everything at stake. If you planned it in advance, for the maximum of excitement, this would be the way to do it.

"This is the way it should be. If we're not good enough to beat the Bengals, we don't deserve to be in the playoffs."

Rutigliano knew the Bengals would be "loose as a goose," so he wanted his team to be the same way. "But," he added, "the game means a great deal to us." "We have come a long, long way and we don't intend for it to stop now."

Even before the team left for Cincinnati it encountered some good fortune.

On his way to the airport on Saturday through foul weather conditions, Greg

Pruitt skidded off the road on Interstate 71 and crashed into an embankment. Luckily he wasn't hurt, though his pickup truck was totaled. Ron Bolton had been following Pruitt and he stopped and helped his teammate. They eventually drove to the airport together. It was the second car accident for a Browns' player in less than two weeks, but neither incident resulted in any major injuries. Pruitt suffered only minor bruises on his head, shoulders, and legs. Just as the birth of Brian Sipe's daughter reminded him of what was most important in life, Greg Pruitt's car accident seemed to highlight the same lesson.

As the Browns arrived in Cincinnati their focus returned to the game of their lives. They knew the key would be their defense, which had been skinned like an onion the week before and had surrendered 397 yards to the Bengals in Cleveland in November. Marty Schottenheimer knew that if his squad gave up five hundred yards for a second straight week, they'd be in for a long vacation.

On the flip side of the ball, quarterbacks coach Jim Shofner believed that the Browns would have to mix up their play calling after they'd picked up a mere thirty-one yards on the ground in their first meeting with Cincinnati. True, the way Sipe and the passing game had moved the ball seemingly at will the Browns didn't necessarily *need* to run the ball well to win the first game back in November, but Shofner didn't anticipate seeing a rerun of the same Bengals' defensive game plan this time around. He expected the Bengals to blitz early and often in an attempt to get to Sipe. Cincinnati's defense had improved dramatically during its winning streak and was now ranked fifth in the conference.

But players and coaches knew this game would boil down to more than just Xs and Os. It would come down to who wanted it more. Which would prove to be more powerful: the fear of failure or the power of pride? Before the first player set foot on the frozen turf that sunny, crisp-but-cold Sunday afternoon, the contest already had become one of the most important in Cleveland sports history.

"I guarantee you, this will not be an ordinary game," Darden wrote in his weekly *Plain Dealer* column. "But the Cleveland-Cincinnati rivalry usually transcends the ordinary."

The contest held on December 21, 1980, would be no different.

As the team rode on the bus from the hotel to the ballpark that Sunday morning it was clear everyone knew what was at stake. Art Modell had taken his usual spot in the front seat behind the driver and Sam Rutigliano sat in his usual spot across the aisle from him. As they neared their destination Modell slid over to Rutigliano. The pair hadn't talked much during the week, each understanding the importance and consequences of this game.

"Listen, Sam," Modell said, "regardless of what happens today, it's been a great year."

Rutigliano paused, looked Modell right in the face, and smiled. "Art," he replied, "you're full of shit. You want this game more than you want to breathe. It's going to be tight, but I think we're going to win the game."

A few minutes later the bus arrived at Riverfront Stadium.

"I remember everybody got there early," Mike Pruitt said of that winter morning. "Usually we're laughing and joking around before the game, but it was silent. Everybody was concentrating. Everybody was a little nervous and you could feel that nervous tension going around. Everybody just wanted to get it done. I think the anticipation of the game was probably the biggest nervousness I've ever had."

Rutigliano was also aware of the atmosphere of the locker room. "Look men," he told them as they prepared to take the field, "there are 800 million Chinese who don't give a damn if we win or lose."

It was a memorable comment that would be associated with the coach for the rest of his NFL career. "The reason I said that," Rutigliano said, "is I wanted them to look at me and see that I could have some fun and that I could be myself and not be all tight inside."

As the team marched down the tunnel to take the field Lyle Alzado pulled several members of the defense aside. He forcefully told them how the team simply *had* to win this game. Then he started listing Bengal players he wanted to take out of the game.

"It was a little bit of a mercenary twist to the whole game plan," Dick Ambrose said. "Certainly not one we intended to carry out, but it showed the personal intensity that he felt for this game. We each expressed that in our own way out on the field. It was intense from the beginning."

That intensity was apparent from Don Cockroft's opening kickoff, with the sellout crowd snapping and humming in the background like live electric wires.

The Bengals picked up a pair of first downs on their initial possession before being faced with a third-and-six situation at the Cleveland forty-six. Jack Thompson fired a pass for wide receiver Pat McInally over the middle, which McInally had his hands on at the Cleveland thirty-nine. A split-second later Thom Darden came out of nowhere and delivered a vicious blow to McInally's upper body, separating him from the ball. The hit also separated the wide receiver from his consciousness, and he fell to the ground. Darden was penalized fifteen yards for unnecessary roughness, giving the Bengals a first down at the Cleveland thirty-one. McInally stayed on the ground for ten minutes before being carted off on a stretcher into the Cincinnati locker room. Though it didn't seem possible after a week of hype Darden's hit had just made the tension surrounding this game even thicker.

"He should have been thrown out of the game for that hit," Forrest Gregg would say later. "There is no place for something like that in football."

"That's how I was taught to play football," Darden countered. "We all knew this was going to be an aggressive, hard-hitting game. That hit set the tone for the game."

Darden was eventually fined $1,000 by the league.

The Bengals failed to pick up another first down, and Jim Breech, who had been working at an Oakland paper company a month earlier, was called on to attempt a forty-two-yard field goal. The kick was right down the middle but barely crawled over the crossbar. Nonetheless it gave the Bengals an early 3-0 lead and shifted more pressure onto the Browns.

Things looked even more foreboding on the Browns' first play from scrimmage. A designed screen pass was fouled up from the start as Sipe was quickly put under heavy pressure. He dumped the pass off for Mike Pruitt, who caught it but was immediately tackled by Cincinnati left end Eddie Edwards for a twelve-yard loss. The Bengals' fans at Riverfront went wild. After a short Sipe completion on second down his third-down toss was nearly intercepted by cornerback Louis Breeden. The Browns' offense had been hammered on its first series. The Cincinnati crowd roared as Johnny Evans was called on to punt.

It looked like the Bengals were destined to score again when, after a short Evans punt, they drove to the Cleveland thirty-seven. But a false-start penalty on rookie left tackle Anthony Munoz led to a third-down Thompson incompletion, and Cincinnati punted back to the Browns. With McInally, also the team's punter, out, Breech was called on to boot the football. He looked as if he'd been doing it for years when he pinned the Browns back at their own twelve. And even worse for the thousands of Browns' fans who had traveled to Cincinnati and the even greater number watching at home, the visitors looked no better on their second possession.

A short Sipe-to-Mike Pruitt pass over the middle gave the Browns their initial first down at the their own twenty-six, but a play later Sipe slipped on the icy Astroturf while pulling away from center. He fell flat on the ground but managed to get up in time to throw the ball away over the middle. On third down the Bengals sent ten men crashing through the line, and Sipe was again lucky to get rid of the ball for an incompletion. The Browns were forced to punt.

Cincinnati again moved into Browns' territory on its next series, but the Cleveland defense once more prevented the home team from adding to its lead. From the Cleveland thirty-seven Breech punted into the end zone for a touchback, and the Browns' offense was finally ready to make some noise.

On the first play of the second quarter, third-and-five from the Cleveland twenty-five, Sipe looped a pass for Logan, streaking down the right sideline. In typical Dave Logan fashion he out-leaped Louis Breeden to catch the football at the Cleveland forty-eight. "I hit the ball," Breeden said, "but he's tall and rangy and has better concentration than most guys in the league. He's been making those plays all year." Breeden fell down and Logan raced down the empty sideline. He was finally pulled down at the Cincinnati nine after a sixty-five-yard gain, the longest play from scrimmage for the Browns all year. This time the other half of Riverfront Stadium snapped to life.

The bad news for the Browns was that Logan got up limping after injuring his left ankle and knee on the tackle and was helped off the field. Though the Browns' leading yardage receiver on the season would return, he would not catch another pass in the most important game of the year.

Logan's play appeared to be the icebreaker the Browns' offense needed. With a score here, fans figured, maybe they'd have some much-needed momentum and wouldn't need Logan. But on first-and-goal from the nine Sipe fumbled the snap from Tom DeLeone. The ball squirted back to the fifteen, chased by a handful of players who attempted to pounce on it. It bounced off them and rolled back to the Cincinnati twenty-four where Cody Risien leaped down, at first appearing to recover the football. Instead it was Bengal Eddie Edwards who recovered, taking away any momentum the Browns had mustered. So far for Browns' fans it looked like a Riverfront replay of 1978 and 1979.

But things would get even worse for Cleveland. On a third-and-one play for the Bengals at the Cincinnati thirty-three Thompson handed off to Charles Alexander who crashed off right tackle through the Browns' line and into the secondary. He sailed down the right sideline and was finally dragged down by Darden at the Cleveland thirty-five after a thirty-two-yard gain. Even worse Darden was called for his second personal foul of the game after grabbing Alexander's facemask on the way down. After the fifteen-yard penalty was assessed the Bengals had a first down at the Cleveland twenty.

Following a pair of handoffs to Alexander up the middle Thompson dropped back to pass on third-and-three at the Cleveland thirteen. Seeing no one open he stepped up in the pocket and raced through a gaping hole in the Cleveland defensive line. He bounced off hits by Dick Ambrose and Clay Matthews inside the five before diving into the end zone for the first touchdown of the game. Again the Cincinnati faction of the crowd celebrated, and Breech's point after gave the Bengals a 10-0 lead with 10:39 remaining in the first half. Browns' fans were having flashbacks of the 48-16 nightmare two years earlier.

The nightmare became even more vivid in the next three plays. After a Sipe incompletion on first down from the Cleveland thirty-four he was sacked by Edwards for a four-yard loss to the thirty. Then after a delay-of-game penalty on the Browns made it third-and-nineteen, Edwards again sacked Sipe, this time for a five-yard loss. It appeared that the Browns would have to punt again, and with their defense on its heels and the Bengals destined for good field position, a 17-0 deficit seemed imminent.

But Cincinnati nose tackle Wilson Whitley was flagged for a personal foul after hitting Doug Dieken with a cheap shot after the play. Had Whitley simply kept his temper and walked off the field the Bengals would have gotten the ball back. Instead they were penalized fifteen yards, and the Browns were granted an automatic first down. Though Whitley's blunder didn't seem like a big deal at the time, when the game was settled that afternoon it would turn out to be one of the two biggest plays of the game—possibly of the season for the 1980 Browns.

From the Cleveland thirty-six Sipe hit Reggie Rucker for a ten-yard gain, and a play later the pair connected again for nine more to the Cincinnati forty-five. After Mike Pruitt picked up two on third-and-one, Sipe hit Rucker again but this time for a much bigger play.

Rucker, lined up on the right side, blew past Louis Breeden, and after a pump fake Sipe looped a perfectly thrown pass down the sideline. Rucker reached out and made a fingertip catch at the Cincinnati fifteen and marched untouched into the end zone for the touchdown that announced the Browns' arrival in the contest. *There will be no blowout,* the Browns seemed to be saying, *for we are the Kardiac Kids.*

And it was a good thing too because word had just reached Cincinnati that the Patriots had overcome an early 10-3 deficit in New Orleans and now led the Saints, 17-10. Don Cockroft's extra point made it 10-7, Bengals, with 7:06 left until halftime.

The Browns really appeared to have momentum on their side a few moments later when the defense forced a Cincinnati punt after three plays. Pat McInally, who had just returned from the locker room moments before, jogged out onto the field to punt on fourth down and received a standing ovation from the Cincinnati crowd. He got his punt off, but Oliver Davis ran into him at the Cincinnati nineteen, drawing a flag from the officials. Davis was called for a five-yard roughing-the-punter penalty, which gave the Bengals an automatic first down. McInally, who many were feeling sorry for a half-hour earlier, smiled as he ran off the field.

The Davis penalty didn't cost the Browns, however, as the Bengals were forced to punt from midfield. The Browns took over at their own twenty-nine, but Mike Pruitt was called for holding on first down, wiping out a six-yard completion from Sipe to Ozzie Newsome. After Pruitt could gain only one yard on a second-down draw Sipe dropped back to pass on another third-and-nineteen. With Bengals leaking through the Browns' offensive line Sipe scrambled away from two sets of potential tacklers before lobbing a wobbling floater of a pass over the middle, which was reeled in by wide receiver Willis Adams at the Cleveland forty-six for a twenty-six-yard gain and a Browns' first down. It was yet another clutch play by Sipe as he proved that his selection to start in the Pro Bowl was no mistake.

A third-down completion to Cleo Miller two plays later gave the Browns a new set of downs at the Cincinnati thirty-eight. On the next play, however, Sipe was sacked for a ten-yard loss by Bengals' right end Ross Browner, marking the fourth time in the game Sipe had gone down. Sack Number Four sabotaged the drive, and two plays later Evans was called on to punt again from the Cincinnati forty with just forty-six seconds remaining in the half.

Evans' third punt sailed deep into Cincinnati territory. Not wanting to risk any fumbles or other critical mistakes just before halftime the Bengals had no one back to receive it. But the ball came down at the Cincinnati seventeen, right onto the foot of Cincinnati linebacker Reggie Williams. It bounced forward to the nine where Dino Hall recovered the live ball for the Browns with thirty-four seconds left in the half.

After the game Williams explained how he came to be struck by the punt, even though the Bengal strategy was to keep all eleven members of their punt return team away from the ball. "It was my thinking," Williams said, "to get back and stop someone so they couldn't get to the ball before it got to the end zone."

The Browns had caught a huge break, and as Sipe and Company jogged back out onto the field many fans had to wonder what the odds were of a punted ball coming down directly on the foot of an opposing player who had his back turned to the play—probably about the same as the Browns winning the AFC Central back in September.

Despite their stroke of good fortune Sipe fired three straight incompletions, and the Browns couldn't take the lead. On fourth-and-goal Cockroft connected on a twenty-seven-yard field goal to tie the game with fourteen seconds before the half. After the ensuing kickoff Thompson kneeled down at the Cincinnati twenty-four, and the teams went to the locker rooms in the same condition they'd come out of them: even.

That would change less than forty seconds into the second half.

Shortly after the intermission in Cincinnati there was another at Public Music Hall in downtown Cleveland during the Cleveland Ballet's performance of *The Nutcracker*. During the break one member of the audience pulled a tiny portable television out of his coat and tuned into the Browns' game. Though many in the audience had smuggled transistor radios and earplugs into the performance, dozens flocked around him to see how the Browns were doing.

After Dino Hall returned Cincinnati's third-quarter kickoff thirty-five yards to the Bengals' forty-seven the Browns appeared poised to take the lead. But then Mike Pruitt was dragged down for a two-yard loss on a sweep toward left end on first down, bringing up second-and-twelve.

Sipe dropped back to pass, spotted Calvin Hill cutting open on a quick-out pattern in the right flat, and fired a pass toward him. The problem was Sipe led Hill too much. Hill dove for the football, but it was out of his reach and sailed right into the arms of cornerback Ray Griffin—younger brother of Ohio State legend and teammate Archie Griffin—at the Cincinnati forty-eight with nothing standing between him and the end zone.

Fifty-two yards later the Bengals had taken the lead back just thirty-four seconds into the second half. "We were in two-deep coverage," Griffin explained. "I got a jar on the wide receiver. Then I saw Hill coming out and stepped in front of the ball." Most of the Bengals' bench cleared and surrounded Griffin in the end zone. Once again the hometown crowd was delirious and Cleveland backers were silent. Breech's extra point gave Cincinnati a 17-10 lead. The Browns had screwed up again.

"We came out at halftime saying our whole season, our whole magic season, depended on that half of football," Brian Sipe would say. "Then what did I do? My first pass goes the other way for a touchdown. That probably was about the most bone-headed thing I could have done.

"When I ran to the sideline after the interception, the looks on the guys' faces were like, 'Well, it's been a great ride, but maybe it just wasn't meant to be.'"

If Wilson Whitley's personal foul was the most important play in the first half in terms of shifting momentum, Griffin's interception would be the most important of the second. Though it gave the Bengals an emotional lift for the moment, it also served as a definitive wakeup call for the Browns, who realized they could not afford to keep squandering opportunities.

"I got mad when that happened," Sipe said of the interception. "I think we all got mad. After Griffin ran it back, I felt more aggressive than I had at any time in the game, and I was determined that they wouldn't beat us.

"I remember thinking this was one of those moments when you find out what kind of character you have. A lesser team would have folded."

As he awaited the kickoff on the sideline Sipe walked up to Rutigliano. "Don't worry, Sam," he said. "We're going to win the game."

"That's fine," Rutigliano replied. "But you gotta promise to start throwing the ball to *our* guys."

When Cleveland got the ball back the determination was evident. Sipe completed three straight passes to Newsome, covering nineteen yards, the last of which combined with a roughing-the-passer penalty on Ross Browner to move the Browns to the Cincinnati thirty-five. A play later Sipe dropped back to pass, rolled right to avoid the oncoming Bengals' rush, and spotted Ricky Feacher streaking down the right sideline past Louis Breeden, just as Reggie Rucker had done in the second quarter. Sipe lofted another perfect pass down the sideline, which Feacher, seeing increased playing time due to Logan's injury, caught at the goal line over the outstretched arms of Breeden. The man who couldn't catch the potential game-winning pass at Riverfront a year earlier tumbled into the end zone for a thirty-five-yard touchdown reception, his third of the season. Cockroft's extra point tied the contest at seventeen with 12:21 to play in the third quarter. It had taken the fed-up Cleveland offense barely two minutes to make up for its mistake, and the visitors had the momentum once again.

The gaggle around the tiny television set at Public Music Hall applauded, and some jumped up and down. Intermission was almost over, and as they settled back into their seats the Browns' fans in the audience felt good about what was happening in Cincinnati.

Those who plugged back in to their radios felt even better when Ron Bolton intercepted a Thompson pass intended for Dan Ross at the Cincinnati forty-one. If there was a time in the game to this point in which the Bengals didn't want to give the ball to the Browns' offense, this was it.

A Sipe-to-Rucker eleven-yard pass gave Cleveland a first down at the Cincinnati thirty-one, but then Sipe was sacked for the fifth time, this time on a combination of efforts by Edwards and Browner. On the next play Sipe rolled to his left and fired the ball deep into the end zone, where it sailed over cornerback Ken Riley and into the hands of the player who seemed to be trying to add his name to the AFC Pro Bowl roster through the exploits of a single afternoon—Ricky Feacher. One hundred and forty-eight seconds after he'd caught his third touchdown of the season, Feacher snagged his fourth, which was also his third against the Cincinnati Bengals. It was also Sipe's thirtieth touchdown pass of the year, breaking the team record of twenty-nine set by Frank Ryan in 1966.

"Both were ad-lib plays," Sipe said of the two Feacher scores. "Ricky wasn't the intended receiver either time, but I went to him because of the way the coverage developed. They forced us to make longer throws than we had planned; they took away our short stuff."

Feacher, the man his teammates called "Hollywood Dude," had become a star. Ironically on the bus ride to Riverfront that morning Feacher had predicted that he would score two touchdowns.

Perhaps Feacher's sudden lethalness was due to his footwear. Ignoring the NFL dress code he'd donned his black practice shoes with the rest of the team wearing white shoes. Though he expected someone to make him change shoes, no one ever did.

With the Browns leading 24-17 with 9:53 to play in the quarter, a quick stop by the Cleveland defense and another score might do in the young Bengals. Less than five minutes earlier Cincinnati had been in control of the game. But thanks to Ricky Feacher and Ron Bolton, a whirlwind of big plays had given command back to the Browns.

On the Bengals' first two plays from scrimmage after the kickoff it appeared that that's exactly what would happen. On first down Thompson was sacked by Dick Ambrose for a three-yard loss, and on second down a screen pass to Archie

Griffin was read perfectly by the Browns, and Griffin was stopped for a seven-yard loss, setting up a third-and-twenty. But just as a costly personal foul had killed the Bengals in the first half, the Browns would be haunted by one in the second. Marshall Harris was penalized for roughing the passer, a fifteen-yard offense and an automatic Cincinnati first down at its own forty-seven. Though the Bengals were forced to punt a few plays later McInally's kick pinned the Browns back at their own six. Had it not been for Harris's penalty the Browns' red-hot offense may very well have had the football near midfield. What's more, the Bengals' extended drive seemed to cool the Cleveland attack.

After a short Mike Pruitt run on first down a pair of Sipe passes glanced off his receivers' hands, first off Mike Pruitt's, then off Rucker's. Johnny Evans was called on once again, and after another sub-par kick and short return the Bengals took over at the Cleveland thirty-eight.

With the game and emotions seesawing back-and-forth there came good news for the Browns from Louisiana. The Saints had wiped out a 24-13 New England advantage and grabbed a 27-24 lead on the Patriots late in the third quarter. It seemed the Saints were playing with the same intensity and focus as the Bengals.

That focus was exemplified two plays later when Thompson faced third-and-five at the Cleveland thirty-three. Flushed to his right he threw on the run and hit Isaac Curtis over the middle for fourteen yards and a very big first down. After failing to move the chains again the Bengals called on Jim Breech to attempt a twenty-eight-yard field goal on fourth-and-six. Breech's kick sailed wide left, and the Browns' lead remained seven. As the third quarter was running down, most in the stadium felt that Breech's missed chip shot would come back to haunt the Bengals. It would.

Unfortunately the Cleveland offense still couldn't return to the impressive level at which it was running earlier in the period, and after two more Sipe incompletions Evans punted back to the Bengals. Cincinnati wide receiver Cleo Montgomery caught, then dropped, the punt at the Bengals' forty-four. For the second time on the afternoon Dino Hall recovered a muffed Cincinnati punt, and the Browns were back in business at the Bengals' forty-three.

Just as was the case with Feacher's two touchdowns, Hall's heroics seemed more than just random coincidence. The man who had coughed up two fumbles that cost the Browns the final game of 1979 at Riverfront Stadium had now recovered two in the 1980 finale in Cincinnati. The Browns' dramatic engine was revving at full steam.

But once again the Cleveland offense stalled. Sipe threw two more incompletions, making it six straight since hitting Feacher for his second touchdown, then was quickly flushed backwards out of the pocket on third down. Eddie Edwards, who was becoming Sipe's nemesis on this day, finally pulled the Browns' signal-caller down at his own thirty-seven after a twenty-yard loss. Not only had the

Browns failed to move the football forward, but also by going backwards they'd taken away a good chunk of field position. Even worse, the score came across the Riverfront boards announcing that the Patriots had taken a 31-27 lead on the Saints.

After another short Evans punt the Bengals took over at their own forty-one with time left for just one more play in what had been a wild and wooly third quarter. Fittingly that final play was the crowning jewel of the period.

Thompson dropped back, pumped right, and floated a deep pass for McInally down the left sideline. McInally separated from Oliver Davis—the same man he'd enticed the roughing-the-punter penalty from in the second quarter—and caught the ball over his shoulder at the Cleveland fifteen. But Davis recovered and caught up to McInally as he sprinted inside the ten. He attempted a diving tackle at the five and was successful in knocking McInally down. The problem was that as he came down McInally bounced off Davis and landed in the end zone for a touchdown.

It was an almost surreal play. McInally, who had his clock cleaned by Thom Darden in the opening minutes of the game, had now made a fabulous catch-and-run that brought the Bengals back to life and back even with the Browns. After Breech's point after tied the game at 24, the teams entered the fourth quarter still with nothing settled.

The entire Browns' season—all the crazy comebacks, the exciting games, the fantastic finishes, the praise, the criticism, the tears, and the toil—would come down to one quarter. No one was surprised.

Fifteen minutes remained in the Cincinnati Bengals' season, and everyone knew it. In those fifteen minutes the Bengals would try to ensure that it was also the Browns' last fifteen minutes. With so much on the line for Cleveland in the final quarter it seemed more than just mere coincidence that the period began with a kickoff. It felt more like sudden-death overtime.

Over the next few minutes it appeared that the Browns also knew they were playing in a virtual sudden death and seemed to freeze up. After picking up a first down at midfield they punted back to the Bengals, who took over at their own fourteen and looked just the opposite of the Browns. Forrest Gregg's offense, though young, looked and played like it had nothing to lose.

On third-and-seven from the seventeen Thompson executed a perfect quarterback draw up the middle for fifteen yards. When third-and-nine arose two plays later Thompson rolled right and hit Dan Ross for a thirty-four-yard gain to the Cleveland thirty-three, and the home crowd was rocking once again.

Following a false-start penalty on right tackle Mike Wilson and an Alexander run for no gain, Thompson hit McInally for a sixteen-yard completion that gave the Bengals a first down at the Cleveland twenty-two. Now it was Thompson, not Sipe, who looked like the All-Pro quarterback. But after a two-yard draw by Pete

Johnson, Thompson showed his age. On second down Thompson was quickly put under pressure by Charlie Hall and Henry Bradley and forced a quick throw over the middle. The toss sailed over an open Ross and was picked off by Thom Darden at the Cleveland nine.

Darden scampered upfield and was finally tackled at the Cleveland thirty-three with 7:50 remaining. "If I had dropped that," Darden said, "I was going to run right out of the tunnel." For the second time in less than a quarter, the Browns had dodged a huge bullet as the Bengals failed to cash in on a perfect scoring opportunity.

But a play later Sipe returned the favor. His second-down pass intended for Feacher was short and was picked off by Ken Riley at the Cincinnati thirty-four. While the Bengals were happy to have the football back they were still nearly a half-field away from where they had turned it over, and the Cleveland defense made sure they wouldn't get a drive going this time.

After Johnson gained six up the middle on first down, Archie Griffin was stuffed for no gain on second, and then Thompson's third-down pass glanced off the hands of Curtis and fell incomplete. McInally, the Bengals' inspirational hero on this day, was called on to punt from the Cincinnati forty. It was at this point that McInally's day changed dramatically.

He shanked the kick and it traveled just fifteen yards before going out of bounds at the Cleveland forty-five with 6:04 left. It was just the break the Browns needed.

By this time *The Nutcracker* was long since over at Public Music Hall in downtown Cleveland, but still dozens of fans remained, surrounding the tiny television, not wanting to miss a thing.

Meanwhile, back in Cincinnati, Sipe called the first-down play in the huddle.

"Look," he added to his teammates, "if we're going to be champs, we've got to do it now. We've got to control the ball and get some points. This is it."

On first down Mike Pruitt picked up four yards on a draw, then Sipe hit Newsome for seven and a first down at the Bengals' forty-four. Sipe connected again, this time with Hill for seven more, and the Browns took time out before facing second-and-three.

It was time to change gears. Sipe's magic arm and his cadre of talented receivers had gotten the Browns this far, but now they would need the offensive line to prove it could do more than just pass block.

A hole opened up the middle for Cleo Miller, who picked up four and a first down at the thirty-three. Now milking the clock Sipe called another draw, this time to Mike Pruitt, who exploded through the line for fifteen yards to the Cincinnati eighteen.

"Those were memorable runs for me," Pruitt said of the final drive. "Even though they weren't that long, they were getting us closer. I was talking to the offensive line and they were talking to me: 'Don't go down, just hold onto the ball. We're going to make a hole for you.'

"It was pure determination at that point. They were moving them out and I was doing my best not to be tackled."

The Browns could taste it now. It was a good thing too since the scoreboards flashed a final from New Orleans: Patriots 38, Saints 27. The Browns' thin safety net had been removed. They would have to win this game or go on vacation.

On first down from the eighteen Miller plowed up the middle for four more, and then Mike Pruitt crashed through the line again, this time for nine yards to the Cincy five as the officials stopped the clock for the two-minute warning. For the twenty-fourth time in their last thirty-two games the Browns' fate would be determined in the final two minutes.

On first-and-goal, Pruitt was finally collared for a one-yard loss, and the Bengals took their second time out. On second down it was Pruitt again, this time on a sweep around left end, which the Bengals strung out nicely. But Pruitt quickly cut upfield through a tiny hole and for one brief moment it appeared that he would score. Instead he was dragged out of bounds at the two after a four-yard gain. Though it was a good play, it stopped the clock and saved the Bengals from taking their final time out. With third down upcoming the Browns would have one more shot at the end zone before calling on Cockroft, who was warming up on the sideline.

With one last chance Sipe figured the best way to fool the Bengals was to fool his own offense. He called a play designed to be a handoff to Cleo Miller up the middle, but as the team broke the huddle Sipe told Miller he wasn't going to hand off to him. Instead Sipe said that he would fake the handoff and run a naked bootleg around left end, figuring if members of the Browns' offensive line didn't know he was doing it they couldn't tip off the Bengals. It was, in Sipe's own words, a "feast-or-famine play."

"We didn't want a handoff, chancing a fumble," Rutigliano would later explain. "We sent the flow one way, hoping they'd overreact and let Brian sneak in to the opposite direction."

Sipe took the snap, faked the handoff to Miller, and then bootlegged to his left. It was nearly the perfect call. Except that Ken Riley was the one man who wasn't fooled by it, and he stood between Sipe and the end zone.

"I thought for an instant I could put a move on Riley," Sipe said, "but I figured I'd only embarrass myself, so I went down." Riley brought the quarterback down at the five for a loss of three, bringing up fourth down. Yet few criticized the call.

"In the past," Hal Lebovitz wrote, "Sam has been known to go to the air for a touchdown try in such instances on the premise that the Browns' attack is based on the pass."

Though Riley's play had kept the Bengals' hopes alive, the home team made a critical mistake after the tackle. Twelve seconds elapsed before the Bengals called their final time out. They would have been wiser to either call a time out right away or not call time out at all. This would prove to be a crushing mistake.

Cockroft took the field with 1:29 remaining for what would be a twenty-two-yard field-goal attempt. Browns' fans had to be thinking the worst, remembering the ten field goals and six extra points Cockroft had missed over the course of the season. This would be the most important kick of the year, probably the most important kick of Cockroft's career. If he missed, it was doubtful that the Browns could survive one more huge momentum swing.

Cockroft did his best to stay calm. "I can't think too much about what it means if I miss," Cockroft said. "That's negative thinking. I don't even watch what's going on in the game.

"Was I nervous? Sure. Inside it's churning, but you can't let it get to you."

Across the nation Browns' fans closed their eyes and hoped for the best. The entire legacy of the Kardiac Kids now rested on the foot of Don Cockroft.

After the time out that seemed to last three weeks the Browns lined up. Gerry Sullivan's snap was good, and Paul McDonald's hold was perfect. Cockroft's kick followed suit, splitting the uprights, and with 1:25 remaining the Browns had taken a 27-24 lead.

But there was no celebration taking place on the field or on the Browns' sideline. If there was one thing they had learned in Minnesota it was that any time left on the clock is too much time. The Bengals may have been out of time outs, but they had eighty-five seconds and needed just a field goal. Tommy Kramer and the Vikings had had just fourteen seconds but had gone eighty yards. Eighty-five seconds was an eternity.

"For the offense, it was pure hell," Mike Pruitt said. "We wanted the ball in the last two minutes, not the other team. It was all in the defense's hands."

Still the Browns' offense had done its job and done it well. It had given the Browns a lead while milking as much time as possible off the clock. High above the field in the press box Lebovitz noted the lessons the Browns had learned from the week before. "This is the way it should be," he wrote in his notes. "This is the perfect finish to the script. If the Browns hold, they belong. If they blow this, they don't."

There is a longstanding tradition in the student section at Texas A&M football games. When things get tight the male contingent of the student body stands up and squeezes their left testicles as hard as they can in the hopes of pushing the Aggies to victory. They called themselves the "Squeeze Army." ("I'm just glad I went to San Diego State," Brian Sipe once said. "When things got tough there, we just ordered another beer.")

Even though he was only a rookie in 1979, by the end of that nail-biting season former Aggie Cody Risien had the entire Browns' sideline squeezing their "armies" as they tried to pull out another close victory. "I ran the risk of being ridiculed when I first brought that up," he said. "But I didn't get ridiculed. After I brought that up in a meeting one time, the next game, we had a tough moment and Tom DeLeone is over 'squeezing army' with me. Before long, we had a little group." It got to the point where his teammates would begin yelling, "Squeeze Army! Squeeze Army!" before he could even bring it up.

Now with the entire season hanging in the balance, the Browns' offensive line placed their hands not on their hearts but upon the other portion of their bodies to which they pledged their allegiance.

Many would argue this is typical lineman behavior, that in doing what they do for a living, grabbing one of your nuts *would* seem like something that would bring good luck.

But right there with them was Brian Sipe, the brain of the outfit.

"There wasn't any group of people I would have rather shared that moment with," Sipe said. "Those guys lived and died with every moment of mine."

But right now the Browns' collective ball was in Cincinnati's court.

Cockroft's kickoff sailed to the Cincinnati twenty where Cleo Montgomery caught it and raced to the thirty-two before being tackled with 1:18 showing on the clock when the Bengals' offense took the field. But instead of Jack Thompson jogging out to call the play in the huddle Forrest Gregg was sending in Ken Anderson on a gimpy ankle. Though Thompson had played well Gregg figured Anderson's experience would be more important in this situation. Appropriately the Browns' defense would have to stop one of the best quarterbacks in the NFL to earn the division title.

On first down Anderson hit Isaac Curtis over the middle for three yards, a play the Browns happily accepted since it was minimal yardage and kept the clock running. The Bengals scurried up to the line of scrimmage for second down, on which Anderson fired a pass for Pete Johnson at the Cincinnati forty-two. Johnson dropped what would have been a first-down catch. It brought up third-and-seven with forty-nine seconds remaining.

Anderson dropped back and hit wide receiver Steve Kreider over the middle at the Cleveland forty-three for twenty-two yards and a first down. Clay Matthews tackled Kreider in bounds with forty-two seconds left, and the clock kept running. Cincinnati raced up to the line of scrimmage.

Anderson took the snap with thirty-one seconds left and fired another pass toward the left side. This one was caught by Dan Ross at the Cleveland thirty-four, but again he was tackled in bounds by Judson Flint with twenty-four ticks left, and the clock continued to run. Anderson and Company rushed up to the line, and the ten-year veteran from Augustana fired a pass out of bounds intentionally to stop the clock with eleven seconds to play. Forrest Gregg now had to make his final decision of the 1980 season.

Jim Breech was the fourth kicker the Bengals had used on the season, but his clutch kicks the previous two weeks seemed to show he had a long and prosperous career ahead of him in Cincinnati. However, much like the three kickers that had preceded him, Breech was not a long-distance kicker, and anything over fifty yards was not a high-percentage attempt. Barely clearing the crossbar, his forty-two-yard field goal in the first quarter, kicked in the same direction the Bengals were now heading, was evidence of that. Gregg could roll the dice and send Breech out for a fifty-one-yard attempt to tie the game. The odds were slim, but were they better than running a play?

With no time outs the Bengals could not use the middle of the field. They had two options: (1) call a quick-out for the sideline, hope someone would get open in a hurry; Anderson would hit him for a ten-to-fifteen yard gain, and he'd get out of bounds before being tackled. Breech could then attempt a field goal from forty yards or less; or (2) go for the end zone.

"We wanted them to throw the ball inside," Ron Bolton said, "but we expected them to throw outside so that whoever caught the pass could get out of bounds."

A third possible option, some felt, was to try the type of sandlot play the Vikings had used on the Browns to get them to midfield the week before. But considering Minnesota's play took ten seconds and that it was unlikely the Browns could be beaten by the same trick two weeks in a row, it was an improbable choice. If, however, the Bengals had the twelve seconds they'd wasted before calling their final time out, more options would have been available. The difference between eleven seconds and twenty-three seconds is a lifetime in the NFL.

Gregg decided against the field goal, and Anderson called a play in the huddle.

For the second time in 371 days the entire Cleveland Browns' season would boil down to one play on the slick Astroturf of Riverfront Stadium.

Anderson took the snap and dropped back. He looked momentarily at the right sideline, waiting for someone to break open on the quick-out, but no one did. With eight seconds left he lobbed the ball deep for Kreider. Ron Bolton, playing a safety position, saw the pass coming and had a decision to make. "I could have intercepted the ball, or even knocked it down," he said. "But I didn't want to take any chances. If the pass was incomplete, they would have had another play. I knew that if he caught it and I could keep him in bounds, the game would be over."

Kreider caught the ball at the Cleveland thirteen with six seconds left and an instant later was crushed by Bolton and hit the ground in-bounds with four seconds remaining.

"When he caught it, I laid it on him pretty good," Bolton said. "He felt it." The veteran cornerback then lay atop the wide receiver. "I had him down and I got on top of him and I looked up at that clock," Bolton said. "I saw the seconds ticking down and I just laid on top of him."

Bolton watched as the clock changed to three. Then to two. Then to one.

Then to zero.

It was over. The Cleveland Browns were the champions of the best division in football.

"Scripted in heaven or Hollywood," the *Press*'s Jim Braham would write, "what other ending could have fit Cleveland's 'Kardiac Kids?'"

The Cleveland bench exploded onto the field. Sam Rutigliano ran around like a wild man, hugging each and every player he could find.

"We did it!" he kept screaming. "We won the damn thing!"

Art Modell embraced every person sitting in his box with him.

"You'd think we won the Super Bowl," Mike Pruitt said. "There's no feeling like that. You've come so far and you've had some ups and downs, but you accomplished what you set out to do. It was a great moment for the team and the city."

As he made his way toward the tunnel leading back to the locker room Rutigliano was accosted by Reggie Rucker and Lyle Alzado. They hoisted him up atop their shoulders and carried him off the field. "Each guy had one of my legs," Rutigliano said. "I thought they were going to make a wish."

But the Browns' primary wish had come true. What had seemed possible only in their wildest imaginations as late as early October had become reality, even if it didn't seem like it.

"I was numb," Sipe said afterward of his initial reaction. "We finally did it. I am still in a state of shock. I'm so used to bad things happening to us at the end of the season—but I like this much better."

"It was just another chapter in a kind of fairy-tale book," Doug Dieken said.

"It was more relief than anything because of the intensity and the impact," Thom Darden said. "We had to win that game. All of our emotions were put into that game."

And by game's end, players and coaches alike were exhausted, physically and mentally.

"In my 13-year career, I was never so tired after a football game," Tom DeLeone said. "In the locker room after that game, I was on my knees and I could barely keep my head up. That was one of the hardest-hitting football games I ever played in. I remember thinking, 'Thank God we have a bye.'"

The epic victory also capped off quite a week for the Browns' quarterback: in five days Brian Sipe had received a newborn daughter, an All-Pro selection, and now a division title and playoff berth. "I always heard good things come in threes," he said, "and I had two good things happen to me last week so I figured we were in for a good game."

The Browns hadn't played perfectly—"It might not have been an artistic victory," Rutigliano said, "but that's much better than an artistic defeat."—but they had won.

For most of the Browns, however, it was more than just a good game and a big win. "This is the happiest moment of my life," Mike Pruitt said. "Nothing compares. This is something I will remember for the rest of my life. I can always say I was on the 1980 Central Division champion."

"I have never felt this good before in my life," Ozzie Newsome said. "But now that we've gotten this far, I want the Big One. I want to go to the Super Bowl."

"I'm as exhilarated as I've ever been," said Calvin Hill. "The only thing close was my second year with Dallas and we went to the Super Bowl. The city and its teams have been downtrodden for too long. The people identified with us. The people felt they were winners when we won."

Reggie Rucker echoed that sentiment. "I'm so happy for the fans," he said. "This is a hell of a love affair we have with these fans. It's a hell of a Christmas present."

Certainly Brian Sipe had been instrumental in tying the ribbon, completing twenty-four of forty-four passes for 308 yards, his sixth three-hundred-yard game of the year. Six of his completions went to Mike Pruitt, who set a new team record for catches in a season with sixty-three, breaking Mac Speedie's mark of sixty-two set in 1952.

But in terms of setting records the day belonged to Sipe. He ended up with new season team marks in passes attempted, completed, and yardage, plus the new mark for touchdown passes. And he'd done it in the face of a kamikaze Cincinnati pass rush that threw Sipe six times after he'd only been sacked seventeen times in the previous fifteen games. Looking back on the Bengals' defensive play that afternoon Doug Dieken remarked, "Because they had nothing to lose, that was a defensive lineman's holiday."

Sipe, the "destination" of choice for that Sunday's Bengal defensive lineman's holiday, concurred. "I never saw a team play defense like the Bengals did today," Sipe said. "That's the most aggressive I've seen any team. They teed off on us from the first play. They were in a sprinter's stance. They were inspired. I can't imagine why," he added with a grin.

"They shut down our passing game," Sipe continued. "We hit some long passes that were critical, but that was the result of the blitzing. They forced us out of our game plan. But we have enough talent to be a good running team and that's what we turned to on the final drive. The guys up front flexed their muscles and controlled the line of scrimmage."

Though the Browns gathered only fifty-seven rushing yards on the afternoon, thirty-six of them came on their final drive when they needed it most.

The Cleveland defense also deserved credit for keeping the Bengals at bay while the Browns' offense struggled. The Browns' D hit an all-time high on Marty Schottenheimer's scoring scale, winning forty-eight of Cincinnati's sixty-nine plays for a score of 69.5 percent. Though the Bengals outgained the Browns in total yardage 375 to 313, Jack Thompson was limited to twelve completions in thirty attempts, and Pete Johnson, who the Browns had worried about all week, was held to forty-two yards on sixteen carries. Another Bengal the Browns were concerned with was Isaac Curtis, and he was held to two receptions for seventeen yards. Ironically, it was Pat McInally who was the largest thorn in the Browns' side, shaking off Darden's ferocious hit to catch three passes for eighty-six yards in the second half. McInally's return to form after being KO'd early in the game didn't surprise the man who delivered the hit. "I knew he was all right when he tried to clip me on one play when he got back," Darden said.

But more important than statistics was that the Browns' defense was able to shake off the ill effects of the final fourteen seconds in Minnesota and prevent the Bengals from scoring on the final drive. Sure, they'd cut it close, but they did the job. "I kept thinking of that . . . as the Bengals came down the field in the last few seconds," Art Modell confessed. "They didn't have any time outs, but neither did the Vikings. It scared me half to death."

That fear was released in a grand locker-room celebration as the champions basked in the glow of their achievement. But there was no champagne flowing. For one reason, these Browns knew there was still work to do, and for another, "We're not a bunch of out-of-shape degenerates like baseball players," as Doug Dieken put it.

"We've got a game ball," Calvin Hill cried from the center of the room, "for everybody!"

True to his word, Hill made sure each and every player on the Cleveland roster—and every member of the medical staff—received a game ball. "Calvin is unbalancing the budget, he's giving away so many game balls," Rutigliano quipped. The Browns also gave a game ball to reporter Jim Sweringen, who covered the team for the *Warren Tribune* and had been ill for several weeks.

After all the initial shouting and screaming Rutigliano eventually quieted the team down. "I've got my best line of the year, men," he said, as the room hushed. "Bum Phillips knocked at the wrong door!"

After the team exploded in cheers Rutigliano continued. "You did it with a flair for the dramatics. It's the greatest thing that's ever happened to me, and the most important thing is that we can all share it together. Hey, we're No. 1, right?"

Though everyone was a hero in this moment, Rutigliano was held above the rest. With his back against the wall in a must-win situation for a must-win franchise in a must-win city he'd gotten the most out of his team. "Last week very easily could have been the toughest week of preparation we've ever been involved with," Sipe said, "but Sam wouldn't let it, and that's another reason he deserves credit. Give the credit for what we've accomplished to Sam. He is the miracle worker around here, he really is."

Even the Cleveland media seemed willing to appreciate the success of the man they had so often criticized during the season. "Those of us who criticize him for losing occasional battles must heap laurels upon the man who won the war," Bob Sudyk wrote in Monday's *Press*.

Again exemplifying the selflessness with which he had encircled the team all season Rutigliano wryly pointed out that "Our guys gave it all they had all season and won in spite of the coaching."

The man nobody had ever heard of, the man that Art Modell had hired three years earlier because he believed he'd be a winner, had proven he was. It was a similar situation for many of the Browns' players who had been told they'd never make it but now were on their way to the playoffs on board the hottest team in football. Three years earlier guys like Brian Sipe, Mike Pruitt, Dave Logan, Marshall Harris, and Henry Bradley were not familiar football names across the nation. They were second-rate players on, at best, a second-rate team. Now they were the talk of the NFL.

Modell, the figurehead of the outfit, circled the room, embracing the players and coaches who had just pulled off one of the biggest victories in franchise history. When he reached Brian Sipe's locker he thanked him for everything he'd done in getting the Browns where they were.

"Don't thank me yet," Sipe said. "We're not done yet."

Neither was the celebration. On the contrary it was just beginning.

Modell joined the players in song on the bus ride to the airport as they belted off several verses of "The Twelve Days of a Cleveland Brown Christmas." When they reached the airport Calvin Hill purchased five-dozen cigars and passed them out on the plane where the celebration continued on the hour-long flight back to Cleveland. Champagne flowed (perhaps, in Dieken's view, well-trained athletes simply don't drink it *in the locker room*), and the singing continued. At one point the players actually raised their voices in a chorus of "God Bless America."

The last time the Browns felt this good on a plane ride they were welcomed home with the surprise of nearly ten thousand people waiting for them at the airport. This time the Browns knew what to expect. While the team partied soaring high above the frozen Ohio landscape the city of Cleveland was beginning a massive celebration unequalled since their beloved Indians had won the World Series thirty-two years before.

Moments after Ron Bolton tackled Steve Kreider and time expired at Riverfront Stadium 250 miles away, the party began. The celebrations could be heard all over Cleveland, from Rocky River to Berea. From Public Music Hall to Medina. While all of the joyous reactions were spontaneous and fueled by the same emotion they differed as much as the ethnic makeup of the city they took place in.

It was families running shoeless out into the snow to dance in the suburban street and patrons drinking champagne straight from the bottle at a bar in the Flats. It was people remaining at Public Music Hall after the end of the ballet to see the finale of Cleveland's true dramatic artists and Christmas shoppers flocking around television displays at May Company to see the exciting conclusion. It was the city of Cleveland as happy as it had ever been.

As a result airport officials were blessing the decision of having the Browns arrive at the Tank Plant as thousands of fans congregated to welcome their conquering heroes home.

They began arriving at 5:30 P.M., barely an hour after the game had finished, prepared to wait for the team's scheduled 7:50 arrival. By 6:00 the flow into the plant was heavy. By the time 7:30 rolled around the roads were clogged once again with thousands of cars trying to plow through traffic toward the Tank Plant. When the team finally arrived at 8:00 police estimated there were between fifteen thousand and eighteen thousand fans there braving the eleven-degree chill. It would have been more had it not been for the traffic jams on the outlying roads.

When the players began deboarding they were once again treated like rock stars, almost like Greek gods as the scene "held the imagination of a Fellini movie," Sudyk wrote.

After returning from a trip that "had all the panics and pitfalls of *The Poseidon Adventure*," as W. C. Miller of the *Plain Dealer* put it, the players appeared just as happy to see the fans as the fans were to see the players. First Brian Sipe and Cody Risien did a victory dance on the giant flatbed truck they disembarked onto. Then McDonald Oden and Clarence Scott performed a combination Irish jig-disco-style dance. Lyle Alzado pumped his bag into the air like a giant pom-pom. Marshall Harris threw his ten-gallon cowboy hat over the fence into the crowd.

"Thank you very much," Rutigliano shouted to the crowd through a large bullhorn. "We really appreciate your coming out here. This win belongs to the city of Cleveland."

But several scribes noted that Rutigliano seemed somewhat subdued at the celebration, almost as if he was afraid he'd suddenly wake up and find himself in bed at Kent State five months earlier on the first morning of training camp.

"We won this one for you, Cleveland! There's no greater place in the world," Brian Sipe shouted, along with a few other comments that weren't audible over the roar of the crowd.

"What it means to Cleveland is important," Modell said. "It is very important to the community. It seems to give so many a sense of purpose to see us win. That's my reward. It's important to the town and to our players."

"This is the best thing that's happened to the city since I've been mayor, next to getting out of default," George Voinovich said. "But maybe this is more important."

It mirrored the feeling Rutigliano expressed when the mayor greeted him with an embrace off the plane.

"This is really just super-super for the city!" Voinovich said to the coach.

"That's what I'm happiest about," Rutigliano replied.

The Browns were in the playoffs, but on this night no one was concerned with who their next challenger would be. "Right now I don't care who we play or when," Rutigliano said. "We can play Carnegie Tech for all I care. I just want to enjoy this accomplishment. I'll think about who we play later."

In this moment the playoffs seemed almost anticlimactic. Certainly the Browns wanted to go further, but they'd already accomplished more than most ever thought possible, and Cleveland's self-esteem was higher than it had been in years.

An editorial above the banner of the *Cleveland Press* the following afternoon seemed to sum up everything this football team had done for its city:

> An exciting, winning sports team doesn't turn a city around, but, thanks to the Browns and their story-book performances, Cleveland today has taken a brisker step as a city on the way back.
>
> Regardless of what the playoffs hold in store, the message today is: Thanks, Browns. For everything.

It had been a long ride for the 1980 Cleveland Browns, but they'd finally reached the pinnacle: a playoff berth for the first time in eight years and their first division title in nine.

"The most significant part of it," Rutigliano said, "is that, during the course of the three years I've been here, I've always been aware of the hallowed ghosts . . . of the Cleveland Browns.

"Traditionally, the Browns are the flagship of the fleet. Their record proves that, in terms of Hall-of-Famers and all the people who have been here. As we all dream and fantasize, I dreamed and fantasized about winning the Central Division and bringing a championship back to Cleveland.

"And so, with all due modesty, I feel this is the most rewarding experience I've ever had in my career."

"I never felt closer to a team than I did that night," Brian Sipe would say nearly twenty years later. "I'm more proud of that game than maybe any other I'd played in."

From the airport Rutigliano went with Art Modell back to Modell's home in Waite Hill where the pair celebrated quietly on their own for about fifteen minutes. Then Rutigliano went home. "I spent the rest of the evening with my family," he said, "which was important because after we lost those tough games to Denver and Pittsburgh, I spent the evening with them, too, and it didn't matter to them that we had lost."

Even for the members of the media, who were falling over one another to compliment the Browns, the mistakes of the past four months—or even the past eight years—didn't matter. For the Browns and the city of Cleveland, next year was now.

"On the way they have learned some lessons," Hal Lebovitz wrote. "And they have learned about themselves.

"They have what it takes. They're champions. That's happiness."

For the next thirteen days the Browns and the city of Cleveland would submerge themselves in that happiness in an era of good feelings with a legacy that would last forever.

11 · The Thirteen Days of a Cleveland Browns Christmas

After the Browns returned to Cleveland as champions on that cold Sunday night, they and their fans would have two full weeks to bask in the glory before the next hurdle. If the thirteen days in October of 1962 that made up the Cuban Missile Crisis were the most important two weeks of the twentieth century in terms of world history, then the thirteen days that followed the 1980 Browns' AFC Central Division title were possibly the greatest two weeks in the history of Cleveland sports. As Bob Sudyk wrote, Cleveland, Ohio, had become "a town that is *somebody* once again."

No one seemed to remember that this city had declared bankruptcy just two years before or that it had desperately sold off many of its assets to try to pay its bills. The Hough and Glenville riots, Dennis Kucinich's disastrous mayoral administration, and the Cuyahoga River fires were all ancient memories. So were the Cleveland jokes. For the next two weeks Cleveland was once again on top of the world thanks to its football team, something that steelworkers and stockbrokers, blacks and whites, could agree on.

It had seemed like an eternity since the Browns were last involved in a playoff game. In reality it had been just over eight years (and 118 regular-season games) since they'd given the undefeated Miami Dolphins all they could handle in their divisional playoff on Christmas Eve, 1972, at the Orange Bowl. That day, despite Mike Phipps's first pass being intercepted and Don Cockroft's first-quarter punt being blocked and returned for a Miami touchdown, the Browns didn't fold. The Dolphins, thirteen-point favorites, took a 10-0 halftime lead, but the Browns rallied to go up 14-13 on mighty Miami with just over nine minutes to play. A long drive engineered by quarterback Earl Morrall resulted in the go-ahead touchdown on an eight-yard run by Jim Kiick, but the Browns weren't done yet. A last-gasp drive ended when Miami linebacker Doug Swift stepped in front of wide receiver Fair Hooker to intercept Phipps at the Miami thirty with twenty seconds to play. The Dolphins went on to complete their perfect 17-0 season with a 14-7 win over the Washington Redskins in Super Bowl VII, while the Browns began a stretch of ineptitude that would span the rest of the decade. But with the win in Cincinnati, that period was officially over.

And with Christmas now just days away, Northeast Ohio was overflowing with good will and holiday cheer. Thousands of fans broke out the traditional holiday colors: red, green . . . brown and orange. "In Cleveland, whatever the holiday, people would always decorate," Cody Risien said. "Around Christmas, people would have Christmas lights and wreaths and such. There was nothing but brown and orange that year."

It didn't matter that temperatures were in the teens or that snow blanketed the ground all over the area. The Browns were champions and were in the playoffs for the first time in eight years.

"Between Christmas and the Browns, everyone is in a good mood," one store-owner told the *Cleveland Press*. "It's a helluva good thing for the community and it gives everyone a good attitude. If this is what a winning team brings, it should happen more often."

"There are a couple of reasons for that," Art Modell said. "Most fans didn't expect us to get this far. People identify with underdogs and this has been a pleasant surprise."

And in those next few days the Browns and the holidays combined to provide a powerful one-two punch for area retailers, who couldn't keep Browns' merchandise in their stores. The last-minute rush for Christmas gifts, usually for items like perfume, cologne, slippers, and ties, was now for anything with an orange helmet on it. T-shirts, hats, pennants, clocks, buttons, and of course the hit record, "The Twelve Days of a Cleveland Brown Christmas," were all in demand. In one four-hour period that week one record store sold more than two hundred copies of the song and by Christmas Eve had sold more than a thousand. Customers placed hundreds of orders for the division championship commemorative mug, and a local supplier unveiled a new ice cream called "Super Bowl Sundae."

Everyone wanted to cash in on the Browns. A camera store advertised it would mark 20 percent off its merchandise for anyone bringing in a ticket stub from the playoff game. Halle's department store announced it would offer a $1,000 college scholarship to a local high school football player in honor of the Browns.

Even the players were showered with good will. Thom Darden's weekly jazz radio show on WMMS was flooded with calls from well-wishers more interested in talking football than music. The team received an average of a thousand letters a day from fans, not to mention various edibles. "If I ate every mouth-watering cookie that we've received," Mike Pruitt said, "I'd balloon myself out of the National Football League."

At one point during this epidemic of Browns Fever a group of players and their wives went out to dinner at a restaurant in Middleburg Heights. As the rest of the diners realized who had just walked in, the restaurant staff had to form a halo around the players' table to keep the fans back. Then as the players were finishing their meals their waiter came up to them. "Look," he said, "we can't hold these people back anymore. You'll never get out through the front. You'll have to go out through the kitchen."

So they did.

"It felt like we were the Monkees or the Beatles, escaping out the back," Cody Risien said. "We jumped in our cars and then the fans saw what was going on. They were out the front door and into the parking lot trying to get to us."

"What is happening means so much to this city," Rutigliano said. "We've seen what the Steelers have done for their city."

Thom Darden, who grew up an hour west of Cleveland in Sandusky, Ohio, reflected on what the team meant to the city of Cleveland in 1980.

As a football player, sometimes you look at adulation and think it's warranted after what you have done on the field. But in actuality, it's not warranted. It's not like we're finding a cure for cancer or doing anything to better society. But then you realize there are people who significantly feel what you're doing. People who get through you a sense of belonging. Then you understand why that entertainment is so important, because a lot of these people did not have positive things in their lives that they could attach themselves to. Or a lot of people wanted to be athletes, but for whatever reason weren't. They could live vicariously through you. To be able to provide that was a tremendous feeling and to see how people responded made you feel accepted and appreciated.

Doug Dieken remembered telling a friend about the mania surrounding the Browns at the time. "This place is wild," he told him. "[Longtime Browns' guard] Gene Hickerson has been out of the game for 10 years and he's still getting lucky off this one."

The mania even spread to the Browns' mild-mannered coaching staff. Special teams coach John Petercuskie, fifty-five years old, got a Browns tattoo on his rear end. But in that town at that time it made perfect sense.

Employees on the second floor at the East Ohio Gas Company on Superior Avenue downtown hung large signs with letters that spelled out GO BROWNS for all the city to see. The problem was that the building's lease didn't permit any signs such as those hung without the permission of the building management.

Within a few days management asked the employees to take the letters down. It just didn't fit the image of a professional office building, the management said regretfully. "Don't make it look like we hate the Browns," one of its representatives told the *Plain Dealer*. But it did look that way, and there was a huge public outcry. The company received dozens of angry phone calls and eventually allowed the letters to stay.

On the Tuesday after the win over the Bengals May Company pulled off a public relations coup: from 7:00 to 9:00 that evening there was a different Browns' player at each of the ten area May Company department stores. In addition to that event Browns' vice president of publicity Eddie Uhas received twenty-one calls on Monday requesting player appearances.

Weeks later one writer summed it up by saying it was as if Cleveland was working up for a second Christmas Day. Considering what the out-of-town visitors would spend for the playoff game through hotel reservations, restaurant tabs, and parking, the expected $2 million injected into the city's economy would be quite a stocking stuffer.

But the real madness on that Tuesday following the Cincinnati win wasn't in any stores or malls; it was at Cleveland Stadium where playoff tickets finally went on sale at 10:00 A.M. Though the Browns didn't know whom they would be playing, they knew when: Sunday, January 4, at 12:30 P.M.

After waiting nearly a month for the other shoe to drop Browns' fans were prepared and dedicated to snagging seats to the first postseason football game in Cleveland since 1971 when the Browns lost a divisional playoff to the Baltimore Colts, 20-3. Fans began arriving at the stadium ticket gates as early as 4:00 P.M. Monday, and several hundred camped out all night. With only about twenty thousand tickets being made available at the Stadium and at select Ticketron outlets—with the others going to season-ticket holders, the visiting team, league officials, and so forth—each buyer was limited to four tickets.

By 9:00 A.M. Tuesday more than four thousand people were in line at the Stadium. An hour later the crowd had grown to nearly five thousand. Browns' officials arranged for portable toilets to be set up and served coffee and doughnuts to those standing by. When the ticket windows finally opened, they didn't stay that way for long. The twenty-thousand-plus tickets sold out in two hours.

Ironically the fans were probably working harder than the Browns that week. With an extra seven days to prepare for their next game the Browns did what most teams in their situation did: took it easy for a while.

Monday was celebration day at Browns' headquarters. Players were treated to a lunch buffet of corned beef sandwiches and champagne and then given the rest of the day off. After the usual off-day on Tuesday, the team was also off Wednesday and Thursday for Christmas Eve and Christmas Day, then returned to practice Friday and Saturday. They received Sunday off to watch the Wild Card games on television then returned to their normal routine the following Monday with a specific opponent to prepare for.

"It was an exciting two weeks, but there was that anxiety," Mike Pruitt said. "We wanted to get the next step done. To me, it would have been better not to wait two weeks. There was too much anticipation."

Rutigliano had spoken with several of his coaching friends who had been in the same situation and had been planning for a few weeks on how he'd handle the potential extra week for winning the division. The consensus was to give the players some time off to recharge their batteries both mentally and physically but not to stay away from football for too long.

"I think it depends on how you use the time," Rutigliano said. "I don't think it's wise to take off a whole week as some have done."

Few were criticizing him. Rutigliano seemed to benefit the most from the championship as his players and the press revered him all week. "It's your turn to second-guess the Good Old Boys in the media," Sudyk wrote of Rutigliano. "Your won-loss record is better than any of ours."

"Sam is unique in that he is like a father, friend, another player, as well as a coach," said Reggie Rucker. "He has insight to deal with all people. I am sure if Sam left coaching, he would be a success in anything he tried."

"He has captured the town in a personal sense," Art Modell added. "No one in sports has done this in the 20 years I've been here. The elite, the steelworker, they all love him and that's part of the job."

"I'd do anything for that man," Lyle Alzado said. "I think we all feel that way because he is such a good human being, which is a reason he is such a hell of a good coach."

Someone jokingly suggested Rutigliano should turn his attention to baseball, possibly to turn the Indians around as he had done the Browns. "Anytime you're working with more than nine people, it's a zoo," Rutigliano said. "And after 162 games, they would be calling me John Phillips Sousa or the Music Man."

Despite the general optimism that had infected even die-hard pessimists, some worried that the Browns might have felt a little too satisfied after the division championship to get up for the next challenge. For example, many noticed just how *much* some of the Browns were enjoying their success. Even some of the Browns' players noticed. "We played well together, we partied well together," Dieken said. "But that was always a concern because we did have some more football left."

Dan Coughlin wasn't concerned though, and he answered the theory that the Browns were enjoying themselves too much with his own theory.

Champagne gives you bad breath and a headache. Whiskey makes you throw up and hurt all over. Beer increases your circulating volume, makes your heart work harder and gives your kidneys a good gallop.

This is all part of training. It toughens them for the playoffs. The Browns are a wonderfully conditioned team. They punish their bodies with unprecedented dedication.

But I'm not certain it will be in their best interests to win the Super Bowl. If they do, they will immediately begin training for next season and half of them will be dead within six months due to cirrhosis of the liver.

Coughlin's humorous analysis aside, his column, like many other views that week, brought up the "S" word (or more specifically, words): Super Bowl. Or as it was better known in Cleveland at the time, "Siper Bowl."

But the Browns weren't there yet, and no one knew that more than Sam Rutigliano. "Let's not get caught up in the merry-go-round," Rutigliano told his players on Monday. "The biggest thrill of all is to win it all. It's just a lot of fun. Now we need to do it three more times." Plus there were only three players on the Cleveland roster who had ever played in a Super Bowl, Calvin Hill, Lyle Alzado, and Reggie Rucker, and just five players remained from the Browns' last playoff appearance in 1972, Doug Dieken, Don Cockroft, Charlie Hall, Thom Darden, and Clarence Scott.

Nonetheless even the players who *had* been to the Super Bowl were not entirely immune to the playoff fever that had inundated Cleveland. "I'm still a little intoxicated," Calvin Hill said Monday morning, being literal and figurative at the same time. "The fans are crazy, but it's great.

"Now it's a crap shoot. Two games to go to the Super Bowl. We're capable. Now we can't think our task is done."

"We're not a great team yet, but we're on the verge of being a great team," Mike Pruitt said. "We're getting better and better with age."

"The Super Bowl? Why not?" Sudyk asked. "Such a dream holds more reality than anything anyone imagined the Browns would have accomplished three months ago."

But as this era of good feeling swelled across northern Ohio, some odd clouds formed over the parade as a pair of Browns ran into legal trouble that Tuesday.

Mike Pruitt was arrested at his Westlake home for failure to appear in Municipal Court stemming from a charge of driving without a license on March 6. It was a minor violation, and Pruitt was released on $200 bond, but it was still somewhat shocking for fans to learn that one of the classiest, most respected members of the team had been arrested in what was supposed to be the happiest week of the year.

The other incident was even more peculiar. A University Heights man filed a suit against Thom Darden in Common Pleas Court, claiming that he'd never been compensated for medical expenses stemming from a car accident in which Darden rear-ended his car. Darden remembered the accident and said that he thought his insurance company had taken care of it. His insurance company had settled the damages to the car but not the medical expenses. But what was odd was the timing of the lawsuit. The accident had taken place in August 1979, some sixteen months earlier. Darden wasn't the only one questioning why the suit was filed now, when the Browns were the top story in Cleveland.

Perhaps the Browns were learning first-hand the price of success in professional sports. Both legal cases were settled quietly without further newsworthy incident.

As the dust settled on the celebrations and the legal obstacles fans began to turn their attention to just who else had joined the Browns in the postseason tournament. The Buffalo Bills via their 18-13 win over the San Francisco 49ers the previous Sunday had captured the AFC East title and was one of the two possible teams the Browns would play on January 4. The other was Oakland, which had defeated the New York Giants in Week Sixteen to clinch a postseason spot but lost out on the division title when San Diego defeated Pittsburgh—which had already been eliminated when New England defeated New Orleans—on Monday night to secure the AFC West. But it had been necessary to go to the fifth tiebreaker for San Diego to surpass the Raiders. The teams had (1) split the regular-season series, (2) had the same division record at 6-2, (3) had the same conference record at 9-3, and (4) had the same record against common opponents at 10-4. The fifth tiebreaker was best net points in division games, which gave the Chargers the edge, plus-60 to plus-37. The Chargers—who along with the Browns, Raiders, and Bills were 11-5—had also locked up home-field advantage throughout the conference playoffs due to a better AFC record (9-3) than either the Browns or Bills (8-4).

The Houston Oilers with their narrow 20-16 win over the Minnesota Vikings had clinched the second Wild Card spot and would travel to Oakland the following Sunday. The Raiders earned the home field for the Wild Card game due to a better conference record than Houston (9-3 to 7-5).

For the first time in NFL history all five playoff teams from a conference had qualified with the exact same record. As a result there was no clear-cut favorite to win the Super Bowl. San Diego, because of its home-field advantage, had the best Las Vegas odds at 3-1. The Browns were at 4-1. The longest shot in the AFC was Oakland at 15-1.

In the NFC things were much simpler. The 12-4 Philadelphia Eagles, though they lost in Dallas in Week Sixteen, took the title in the East the same way the

Chargers did in the AFC West: on the fifth tiebreaker. But the 12-4 Atlanta Falcons had home-field advantage through the playoffs due to a 20-17 win over the Eagles in Week Fourteen. The Vikings had clinched the Central with the Hail Mary that beat the Browns. And as expected the Los Angeles Rams took one Wild Card spot and the Cowboys took the other. The two would square off at Texas Stadium the following Sunday.

The Browns would not know their first opponent until after the Raiders and Oilers played. The conference tournaments were structured so that the winner of the Wild Card game would face the top seed, in this case San Diego. If Houston defeated Oakland everything would remain as designed. The Oilers would travel to San Diego for one divisional playoff, while the Bills and Browns would square off in Cleveland in the other. (The Browns incidentally topped Buffalo for the Number Two seed because of a better winning percentage in common games: .714 to .625). But because of an NFL playoff rule stating that two teams from the same division could not face one another in the divisional playoffs (which almost sounded like an oxymoron), if the Raiders defeated the Oilers the structure would be altered. The Bills would take on the Chargers in San Diego, while Oakland would travel to Cleveland to face the Browns.

So the question around Cleveland all Christmas week was which do you pre-fer: Oakland or Buffalo?

In an unorthodox move for a coach in his position Sam Rutigliano came out and said he'd like to face the Bills. "I'd rather play Buffalo because I think we match up better against them," he said. "We have the capacity to match up well with any team that runs the ball."

That was a glaring understatement. The Browns' defense was rated second-to-last in the conference in terms of total yards allowed and dead last in passing yards allowed. But Cleveland was fourth in the AFC in stopping the rush. Buffalo on the other hand had the eighth-best offense in the conference, eleventh in pass-ing and second in rushing. It appeared that would work to the Browns' favor. Another plus was that the Browns were a bit more familiar with the Bills after having scrimmaged them in early August. On the flip side, Buffalo also had the top pass defense in the AFC, which could potentially give the Browns' Number Two passing attack troubles.

Joe DeLamielleure was looking forward to that possibility, however, for obvi-ous reasons. There were still hard feelings between him and the Bills after his September trade, and the six-time All-Pro guard would have enjoyed nothing more than to beat his former team to move one step closer to the Super Bowl.

Ironically the Buffalo Bills were thinking the same thing about a potential game with the Browns. Buffalo's players and coaches felt they matched up better with the

Browns than they did with the Chargers. Furthermore they figured their victory in San Diego in October would probably just motivate the Chargers even more.

Another reason Rutigliano and the Browns were already thinking about facing the Bills was that they expected the Oilers to knock off not only the Raiders but then the Chargers the following week. If that were to transpire and the Browns would defeat Buffalo, they would host the Oilers for the AFC Championship, a possibility that intrigued some of the Browns. "I want Houston to win because I really want to play them again for the whole ball of wax," said Dave Logan, who was still limping around on his sprained left knee and ankle but said he'd be ready for the playoffs. "They are not convinced that we are worth a damn, and I want to prove that we're the better team."

The only way the Browns could host the conference championship was if they won their game and someone defeated San Diego. Since Buffalo and Houston were the only teams that would potentially have a shot at the Chargers in the divisional playoffs, most of the Browns figured the Oilers were the only one that had a legitimate chance to defeat them.

Plus Houston had history on its side. The last two seasons the Oilers had made the playoffs as a Wild Card and won three games on the road to twice make it to the AFC Championship. They'd lost both times to Pittsburgh, but Houston had the experience that many felt would carry it over Oakland. "From a personnel standpoint, there's no doubt in my mind that the Oilers are better," Rutigliano said. "They also have been there before. Judging from what I know about our division, I have to go with the Oilers."

Still many Browns weren't concerned with whom they played or how they matched up with anyone. They were happy to be where they were and would accept any challenge placed before them.

"I don't have any interest in any team other than ours, though I admit everybody that gets to the playoffs is good," Lyle Alzado said. "I just want them to knock the hell out of each other, and then we'll play one of them."

Clay Matthews may have had the best answer. "I'd rather play Iowa State," he said.

An interesting motivating factor in rooting for Oakland, however, was geography. Or more specifically, the climate differences between the eastern and western United States. While the Buffalo Bills would be used to playing in the cold, snow, and wind, the Browns figured the Oakland Raiders would not. Plus there was the circadian rhythm factor. When teams from the west traveled to play games that started early in the afternoon in Eastern Standard Time, it would feel to them like they were playing at 10:00 in the morning. Those two conditions combined, many conjectured, would mean advantage: Cleveland.

"I'd like to get Oakland here in Cleveland," said linebacker Don Goode, "because the cold weather won't have that much of an effect on Buffalo."

"We get either team, Buffalo or Oakland, at home, so that's all that matters," Henry Sheppard said. "All I hope is that the weather is about 10 below when we play."

Someone should have warned Sheppard about being careful what he wished for.

The first Wild Card game that Sunday wasn't much of a surprise. The Cowboys rolled over the Rams, 34-13, earning a trip to Atlanta. The second game, however, was the first eyebrow-raiser of the playoffs. The Raiders routed the Oilers, 27-7, to set themselves up as the Browns' opponent the following Sunday. The Raider defense was masterful, sacking Ken Stabler seven times in his first return to Oakland since the trade and holding Earl Campbell to a mere ninety-one yards, including just twenty-nine in the second half. "That's the best I've seen any team play in 10 or 11 years," Bum Phillips said after the game.

Still the Raiders hadn't dominated the entire contest. They led just 10-7 going into the fourth quarter, then Jim Plunkett hit running back Arthur Whittington for a forty-four-yard score on the period's opening play. It was one of just eight completions for Plunkett on the afternoon, but it broke the game open. A key third-quarter interception in the end zone by Raiders' cornerback Lester Hayes had maintained the Oakland lead, then a second Hayes pick, which he returned twenty yards for a touchdown with just over five minutes to play, sealed the deal.

The Browns were surprised but not concerned. "I'm certainly not disappointed that it worked out the way it did," Rutigliano said. "A little surprised, yes, but that's all. We're just happy to be in the thing. It's fine with us to be playing anybody at this point."

Thus it would be Oakland coming to Cleveland on January 4. And the Raiders' reputation of being one of the toughest—and dirtiest—teams in the NFL through the 1970s preceded them.

"Stock up on the digitalis," warned Bob Schlesinger of the *Cleveland Press*. "Get the batteries recharged on your pacemakers. Leave the kids and old ladies at home. This one's gonna be strictly X-rated.

"The Raiders are coming! THE RAIDERS ARE COMING!"

Schlesinger added that Oakland, "the team you love to hate," was a team that plays "with all the subtlety of a punch in the mouth." The Raiders would bring a triple-threat attack to Cleveland Stadium: "Rape. Pillage. Plunder."

"Primarily, there are two things we must do to win," Rutigliano said shortly after the Raiders' victory when the weeklong preparation process began. "No. 1, we've got to be sure to protect Brian Sipe because I am sure the Raiders will come after us with a lot of blitzes and try to force us into second-and-long situations.

"And No. 2, we've got to find a way to contain their three fine receivers—Cliff Branch, Bob Chandler, and Raymond Chester—which Houston couldn't do.

"I don't want to take anything away from Oakland, because they played well, particularly on defense. They forced the Oilers to make a lot of errors.

"But Houston did NOT play well."

Though he said the loss to the Raiders wasn't the sole motivating factor in his decision, three days later Oilers' owner K. S. "Bud" Adams fired Bum Phillips as head coach and general manager. Adams cited the lack of a consistent attack on offense and the fact that Phillips wouldn't hire an offensive coordinator. A few days after that Adams promoted defensive coordinator Ed Biles to the head position.

After the Raiders had dispatched the dark horse of the AFC playoffs many wondered how the Browns could fare better against Oakland than the Oilers did. "We have more of a wide-open offense than the Oilers," Rutigliano answered. "We are not nearly as predictable, and also, that place [Oakland] is a tough place to play. The playoffs are a time when the home-court advantage really is an advantage." History backed up that statement. Since the NFL began playing a postseason in 1933 the home team held a record of 86-43 in playoff games.

For those who thought the Oilers were the better team when the Browns defeated them in the Astrodome a month earlier, seeing the Raiders dissect Houston was simply a prelude, they figured, to what Oakland would do to the Browns. Or conversely perhaps Oakland's surprisingly easy triumph proved that the AFC Central wasn't the toughest division in football as previously believed by many.

"Now the Browns remain the only team from the supposedly toughest division still in the chase," said Hal Lebovitz that Monday. "Is it the toughest division? It wasn't yesterday. Next Sunday we'll know."

"Do I think the Browns are the best team of the eight left in the playoffs?" Rutigliano asked himself at his Monday press conference. "Certainly we are. But if I didn't think so, I wouldn't tell anybody."

Rutigliano also looked at Houston's elimination in a different light. "Frankly, I'm somewhat relieved that the Oilers are out," he said. "They are a great team, and Buffalo beat San Diego in the past and is capable of doing it again."

True the Bills had defeated the Chargers in San Diego in Week Five, 26-24. But this was the playoffs. Home-field advantage took on a whole different meaning.

"We have an excellent chance to beat Oakland because, for one thing, playing at home is a great asset, especially if the weather is what it can be expected to be," Rutigliano said. "I'm just happy to be where we are, and playing Oakland in Cleveland is a bonus—although I'd play them in Death Valley if necessary."

Fueling the "warm-weather-team-in-a-cold-weather-environment advantage" theory the Cleveland media was quick to point out that the Raiders hadn't looked too sharp in their Week Sixteen victory over the Giants in the Meadowlands where it was ten degrees and snowing.

"I don't know, but I don't care," Sipe said when asked of the importance of playing the Raiders at home in the cold. "We can beat them anywhere."

"It would be a factor if it were down around zero," said second-year Oakland coach Tom Flores, "but then it would affect everybody."

Lyle Alzado didn't think the weather would matter much either way. "It won't make a difference to either team," Alzado said. "Myself, I've always been a cold-weather guy. I like it because when it's cold, you don't get as tired as you do when it's hot."

Mostly because of the home-field advantage the Browns were labeled as 3½-point favorites over Oakland. Another factor was the Raiders' recent postseason struggles away from home. The Raiders held a record of just 1-6 in road playoff games with the sole victory coming in a 1977 divisional playoff overtime thriller over the Baltimore Colts.

Still the Browns not only had the Raiders' victory over Houston to remind them of how tough Oakland could be, but they also had the memory of their last meeting just over a year earlier. In Week Fifteen of the 1979 season the Raiders, behind a blitzing and aggressive defense, soared to a 13-0 halftime lead on the Browns, and the visitors couldn't recover, falling to the Raiders for the fourth straight time. The Browns lost, 19-14, in a game that combined with the loss in Cincinnati in the finale kept Cleveland out of the playoffs.

"Last year we fell into the same trap Houston did this year," Rutigliano said. "Most of our problems were because we didn't pick up some blitzes early, then we lost our composure. As a result, they put a lot of pressure on us, and what happened should not have happened."

With a rock-solid defense the Raiders would provide quite a challenge to the Browns' offense. Oakland's secondary had surrendered a lot of passing yards during the season, but it was still capable of making the big play. The unit was anchored by Lester Hayes, who led the NFL with thirteen interceptions in 1980, at one corner and Dwayne O'Steen at the other. "They play bump-and-run against everybody because they have a lot of confidence in their people being able to cover," Dave Logan said. "But on the other hand, when you play bump-and-run, you're taking a chance of getting beat for big plays, and those often turn into touchdowns."

Safeties Burgess Owens and Mike Davis, who had been a college teammate of Dave Logan's at Colorado, were also threats to the Browns' cadre of receivers. But Ozzie Newsome, who would be matched with Davis for most of the game, thought the Browns had seen better. "Davis is good, but he's not as strong or tough as Donnie Shell [of Pittsburgh] or Vernon Perry [of Houston]," he said. "Davis is more like a cornerback than a strong safety."

But the key for the Cleveland offense would be its ability to hold back the Oakland pass rush, which, after collecting fifty-four sacks during the regular season, would be licking its chops for Brian Sipe after seeing what the Bengals had done in Week Sixteen. John Matuszak anchored the line at left end with Reggie Kinlaw at nose tackle and Dave Browning at right end. But the heart of the Raider defense was its linebackers, namely Ted Hendricks on the left and Rod Martin on the right. With Matt Millen and Bob Nelson plugging up the middle the Raiders had developed the best rush defense in the AFC. The Browns were sure to have problems running the football *and* combating the blitz.

"I know I always talk about how important it is that we get a good blend," Jim Shofner said. "But now I really mean it. We need to be able to run to complement our passing. If ever we were patient with our running game, we've got to be patient this time."

On the other side of the football the Browns were most concerned with the three receivers Rutigliano had mentioned, plus halfback Kenny King and fullback Mark van Eeghen. Leading the Oakland attack was journeyman quarterback Jim Plunkett, whom Rutigliano was quite familiar with after having worked with him in New England in the early 1970s. But Plunkett wasn't the same quarterback he was then, Rutigliano pointed out, and few would argue with him. The only reason Plunkett was the Oakland starter was because Dan Pastorini broke his leg in October and was shelved for the season. Ironically when Plunkett left the 49ers as a free agent two years earlier and was looking for a new team Rutigliano and the Browns had discussed signing him as a backup to Brian Sipe. "He was a lot like Mike Phipps," Rutigliano said of Plunkett. "The best thing that could have happened to him was to play behind somebody like Stabler as he did last year."

Still Plunkett would have outstanding protection behind the Raider line. "Oakland's line is probably the most physical in the league," Rutigliano said. "Everybody is massive . . . big . . . strong."

Right tackle Henry Lawrence, right guard Mickey Marvin, and center Dave Dalby were all solid, but left guard Gene Upshaw and left tackle Art Shell were even better. Alzado was particularly impressed with Shell, and though he didn't describe him in what would be considered complimentary terms by most people outside of football—"Art Shell is one of the meanest, vilest guys I've ever played against," Alzado said that week. "He'll cuss me, grab me, spit in my face, and I'll punch him, spit in his face, and cuss him right back."—it was evident that Shell had earned Alzado's respect. Furthermore, for a dramatic flourish, Alzado added, "People always ask me what it's like to play against Art Shell, but the only way you can describe it is to ask them 'Have you ever been attacked by wild dogs?'" Something of an animal himself, Alzado was looking forward to lining up against Art Shell.

For all the intensity and ferocity the Raiders would bring to the contest, possibly the most important ingredient in their win over the Oilers was their punter Ray Guy. "He literally won the game for them," Rutigliano said. "We'll probably drop at least four guys back just to receive his kicks." Against the Oilers Guy had punted nine times for a sterling average of 51.1 yards per kick.

If the Raiders played up to their reputation Alzado wouldn't be the only one facing a wild dog that Sunday. The Browns knew it would be a knock-down, drag-out brawl on the lakefront.

"To beat the Raiders," Rutigliano said, "we will have to run against them and throttle them down; take some pressure off Brian.

"To beat them, we will also need to stop their running game and prevent their big plays."

His years in Denver had given Alzado plenty of firsthand knowledge of the Oakland Raiders, the Broncos' bitter rival. "It will take a helluva game from us because Oakland has it all," he said. "We know we've got to go in there and kick their butts, take it to them, because if we let them take it to us, they'll beat us. Intensity is what wins in the playoffs, and we need to be as physical as we can possibly be."

While the Browns were concerned with how to stop the Raiders, the Raiders were focusing on how to stop the Browns, particularly Brian Sipe and his high-powered offense. Oakland's secondary was strong, but against Cleveland the nation would get to see just how strong.

Flores was most impressed with the Browns' offensive line, which he said was the biggest factor in the offense's success and consequently the team's leap to the playoffs. "And they do it with such a spirited enthusiasm, which is the way Sam is," Flores said. "It reflects his personality."

Early in the week it really didn't feel like winter, at least by Cleveland standards, with temperatures hovering in the mid-thirties. Oakland's Bob Chandler called his friend Joe DeLamielleure to find out just how much cold-weather gear he should bring east. "It's perfect," DeLamielleure told him. "You don't even need gloves."

But by late in the week the forecasted weather conditions didn't look so rosy. Friday's highs in Cleveland reached into the upper teens, and meteorologists were calling for more cold and snow showers over the next two days with lows ranging from five above to five below. The forecast for Sunday was about the same, though weathermen knew they couldn't gauge how much of a factor the Lake Erie wind would have on the temperature. They did call for gusts of about fifteen miles per hour off the lake and a potential wind chill of ten below.

The Raiders, departing sunny California and fifty-five-degree temperatures, arrived in Cleveland on Friday night with thermometers reading fifteen. Never one to keep his opinion to himself frosty Raiders' owner Al Davis sniveled about how NFL playoff games should be played at neutral warm-weather sites. Some of his players shook off the cold conditions, but some were clearly affected.

To some extent so were the Browns earlier that day. After practicing outdoors all week (usually before large crowds of fans overlooking the Baldwin-Wallace practice fields) the Browns moved inside, holding practice at the Tank Plant warehouse near where they had arrived from their last two road trips.

The Raiders had arranged for several "Hot Seats," electrically heated benches, to be delivered to Cleveland from Philadelphia after the Eagles-Vikings game on Saturday. Since NFL guidelines stated that one team could not have access to a piece of sideline equipment without its opponent also having access the Browns would have their own "Hot Seats." However, if Rutigliano had his way there would be no electric benches for either team. He believed that heaters and other such equipment played more of a psychological role on the players and forced their attention to stray from the game. "The weather can be to our advantage if they overreact to it, if they have to pull them off the bleachers to get away from the heaters," he said. "However, we're not counting on the weather winning the game for us."

While the weather was the primary third-party concern for the teams and fans alike going into the playoff game, the second-most important factor would be the playing field at Cleveland Stadium and how it would be able to withstand the poor weather.

It would be the latest into the winter a professional football game had ever been played in Cleveland and the first time the Browns would ever play a home game in January. The previous latest date was December 29 for the 1968 NFL Championship. As a result, the Stadium grounds crew had its work cut out that week. Beginning on Monday they removed the tarps that had blanketed the field to air it out and expose the grass to what little sunlight there was. The tarps were replaced each night. Art Modell agreed to pay for heating units to be put beneath the tarps, which would help dry out the field and keep the ground from freezing. The structure of the Stadium itself, however, made this nearly impossible.

The entire building was constructed on a landfill over Lake Erie, and the playing field was actually about fifty feet below street level. These two factors combined made it a hopeless task to try to dry out the field, which had been soaked for months. Basically the quest now was to prevent it from freezing solid before the game.

Additionally what was left of the grass had already gone through a rough few months. After a rain-soaked rock concert on the field in July, an Indians doubleheader in August was followed by a day of steady rain. Then the day after the Browns played an exhibition game on the damaged turf. The same situation preceded the Browns-Oilers Monday-night game in September: an Indians doubleheader followed by steady rain. A month later, after a seven-hour high school football doubleheader prior to the Browns-Packers game in October was played amidst rain and sleet, the field was damaged beyond repair, at least until new sod could be planted in the spring.

The Browns had been lucky so far. They had played their last home game on an unseasonably warm December day and hadn't yet been forced to play on the Stadium turf on a day when the temperatures dipped far below freezing. For as much work as the grounds crew would do on the field prior to the Oakland game, they, along with the Raiders and Browns, were essentially at the mercy of Mother Nature. If January 4 turned out to be mild, like the Browns' final home game, the field would be in decent shape.

But if it didn't, if January 4 was a typical January day in Cleveland, no one could really foresee what would happen to the field.

As the Raiders and Browns made final preparations on Saturday, most got to watch the two playoff games that afternoon. The Eagles romped over the Vikings, 31-16, at Veterans Stadium in a sloppy game. The late contest was a nail-biter right down to the wire between the Chargers and Bills in San Diego. Buffalo led, 14-13, with less than three minutes left, but Dan Fouts hit little-used wide receiver Ron Smith for a fifty-yard touchdown pass with 2:08 remaining to propel San Diego to a 20-14 win. The Chargers advanced to the AFC Championship and crushed the Browns' hopes for playing it in Cleveland. Whoever won Sunday's matchup at the Stadium would be going to San Diego to play for a trip to the Super Bowl.

The field of twenty-eight teams that had begun practice in the scorching July sun nearly six months earlier had been whittled down to six. By sundown Sunday two more would be eliminated, but most Cleveland scribes didn't think the Browns would be one of them. Chuck Heaton of the *Plain Dealer* said the Browns would pull it out, as usual, with some last-quarter heroics.

"This is the kind of game for a Sam Rutigliano gamble," wrote the *PD*'s Bob Dolgan in a stream-of-consciousness type of column. "Blood and thunder . . . Hell for leather . . . Let's do it with style. . . . That's the kind of football that got us here. . . . Don't change now. . . . Just don't fumble."

"Maybe the weather will prove to be an edge for the Browns, but don't count on it," wrote Bill Scholl in the *Press*. "The better team usually finds a way to win under any conditions."

"I don't care what the temperature is," Thom Darden wrote in his weekly *Plain Dealer* column, "I won't feel it. . . . This could be our last at-bat, so we won't think about being cold."

"It will be a war, a cold and bitter war," wrote Mike Pruitt in his column, "and I have a strange and nagging feeling that the winner of today's game is destined to reach the Super Bowl. In fact, I'll go one step further and predict that today's survivor will win the Super Bowl.

"Guess who I'm picking!"

"Assuming Lady Luck plays no favorites," Bob Schlesinger wrote, "it should add up to a Browns victory. But it should be one more heart-wrenching experience along the way."

He had no idea.

12 · One Last Kiss

Sometimes it's hard being a weatherman. When you correctly predict the weather and people don't like it, they sometimes subconsciously blame you. When you correctly forecast good weather, on the other hand, even those who enjoy it don't associate their appreciation with you. Conversely when you forecast bad weather and then Mother Nature provides an even worse reality than you predicted, you probably won't have many friends that day.

On the morning of Sunday, January 4, 1981, there weren't too many kind words or thoughts being expressed about weathermen in downtown Cleveland. The cold weather they had predicted all week had instead morphed into one of the most brutally bitter days in Cleveland history. Instead of temperatures climbing into the low teens thermometers read one degree Fahrenheit. Instead of the occasional gusts off Lake Erie the winds swirling through downtown regularly reached twenty miles per hour. But the real prize of the day was the combination of the two. The icy temperatures and blustery winds mixed to create a wind-chill factor of thirty-six degrees below zero. "I was hoping they'd postpone it," Ron Bolton said of that day's playoff game. "I didn't think anyone could play in weather like that."

Still there was magic in the air.

Nearly two years later after watching a rebroadcast of the game, Calvin Hill said that even the magic of television couldn't convey the excitement in the city at the time. "The city of Cleveland was on fire," he said, using a metaphor that was ironic in more ways than one, "and while the announcers alluded to that fact several times, mere words could not describe the degree of passion. It was a nice time to be alive and in Cleveland." But make no mistake about it, it was not a nice day for playing football. In fact it was not a nice day for anything.

Tom DeLeone thought he'd wandered into a parallel dimension when he arrived at the ballpark. When he looked out at Lake Erie he noticed waves were frozen in mid-air.

It was the kind of day the term "fit for neither man nor beast" was created for.

"It hit us as soon as we got off the bus at the Stadium," Mike Pruitt said. "We couldn't believe how cold it was. We went out for pre-game practice and couldn't believe it."

Oakland wide receiver Bob Chandler couldn't believe it, either. He quickly found Joe DeLamielleure, whom he'd asked for packing advice. "You son of a bitch," Chandler told him. "You said I didn't even need gloves!"

Some Oakland linemen tried to get a psychological edge over the Browns during warm-ups (a true contradiction in terms on a day like this) by coming out with short-sleeved shirts on.

"You wanna be macho, that's fine," a bundled-up Dick Ambrose thought to himself. "Just wait until you fall on the turf or you get hit by a helmet on your raw flesh that's freezing cold. Then we'll see how tough you are."

Sam Rutigliano later described the clouds of breath rising above the bench as "a scene out of Doctor Zhivago." Oakland safety Mike Davis would say, "It was so cold you had to lick your Gatorade from a stick."

"This is the worst I've ever seen," said NBC color man John Brodie, there to broadcast the game with Don Criqui. "I've never played or broadcast in weather any worse than this."

"It was a week before I really felt normal again because it was so cold," Sam Rutigliano later said. "You couldn't put enough clothes on. It was absolutely awful."

It was in this setting that the Cleveland Browns would play their first playoff game in eight years.

As thousands of fans made their way to Cleveland Stadium via car, bus, train, or dogsled team, it didn't take long for the comparisons to be made between this day and the most famous cold football game of all time: the 1967 NFL Championship between the Dallas Cowboys and Green Bay Packers, better known as the "Ice Bowl." The setting for that game, played on the frozen tundra of Lambeau Field in Green Bay, was even colder than this day in Cleveland. It was fifteen below when the Packers and Cowboys took the field, and the winds were even stronger, dropping the wild chill to thirty-eight below.

Those who figured the Browns would have an advantage in these conditions because they would be playing a team from California should have referred to the Ice Bowl as a reality check. The Packers were much more accustomed to playing in frigid temperatures than the Cowboys were, yet the teams were memorably well-matched. Dallas rallied from a 14-0 halftime deficit to take a 17-14 advantage early in the fourth quarter. Only a last-minute Packer drive and a memorable one-yard touchdown plunge by quarterback Bart Starr with thirteen seconds remaining gave the Packers a 21-17 win and a trip to Super Bowl II. If the temperature had been twenty degrees the Packers might have had an advantage. But at fifteen below everybody was suffering.

Though the media had warned Browns' fans going to the game to dress warmly there would still be some victims of the weather before the day was through. Thirty-five people would receive extended treatment at the Stadium's first-aid station, mostly for exposure, and dozens more were treated for minor ailments. Still there was considerably less mayhem in the stands, which were packed full of 77,655 fans. "It's too cold for anyone to misbehave," one Cleveland policeman said, a sentiment echoed by a large banner hung in the Stadium, which read, "God, it's cold."

"It was cold, but I can't imagine what the fans went through," Doug Dieken said. "If you were moving, you got a little bit of a sweat and some body heat kept your temperature up, so it wasn't that bad. But those people sitting up there in the stands, oh my God, I can't imagine what that was like. For them, it had to be unmerciful."

"The real problem was standing on the sidelines and going in and out of the locker room," Dick Ambrose said. "You got into the warmth of the locker room and your body got accustomed to the warmth, then when you went back on the field it was twice as cold."

It was also no picnic for the media either as about three hundred total reporters—several from out of town—were forced to sit in the baseball press box. Those scribes would have been right behind home plate if the Indians were playing the Athletics but were seemingly four-and-a-half miles away from the action for the Browns-Raiders game, high above the end zone in the closed end of the field. Even those who were in the unheated football press box above midfield knew they were in for a long afternoon when the windows frosted over prior to kickoff, and they resorted to scraping off the ice with their credit cards.

Before the game started it appeared the closed end of the field would be particularly treacherous. "The field was like we needed ice skates," said Lyle Alzado, whose problems were compounded since he was also fighting a bad case of the flu.

During warm-ups some players couldn't even stand up straight on that portion of the field, which was completely frozen over. And if you slipped it would be "like falling on a block of ice," Mike Pruitt said later.

"In some ways it was a lineman's delight because you knew the defensive guy wasn't going anywhere quick," Dieken said. "If he tried to do anything cute, he was going to fall on his butt."

As the afternoon wore on the conditions would take their toll on the players. Even though many wore gloves they found frozen perspiration beneath their fingernails and several wound up with frostbite. Players' nostrils froze. Sweat also froze in some players' beards, making them look silver.

"We had those hot benches and we just didn't want to get off them," Mike Pruitt said. "It was so cold it got to a point where you didn't care who won. You just wanted to get in where it was warm."

The Browns' equipment crew had its hands full as the players tried to figure out what kind of shoes would work best. "That was a big concern before the game," Cody Risien said. "We'd go out and test this shoe, then go out and test another one, checking them out and letting everybody else know which ones seemed to work best."

They experimented with cleats, Astroturf shoes with tiny rubber cleats, and shoes used for broomball, essentially basketball shoes. The latter was traditionally used on slick fields but weren't much better than the others on this day.

"Everybody brought an extra pair of shoes onto the field [for the game]," Risien said, "just in case the conditions changed."

The Browns also wore scuba-diving gloves, introduced to them by Joe DeLamielleure, who had used them in the cold in Buffalo.

"In my mind, they should have called the game," Thom Darden said. "Reschedule it or send it out to Oakland or something. We couldn't do anything."

Prior to kickoff there was already a kind of insanity surrounding this game. No matter what the result everyone present as well as those watching on television would remember this game for years. It would become "that Raiders game in the cold."

And just as the Ice Bowl was forever frozen in the collective memory of professional football, so too would the Browns-Raiders playoff game.

Early in the first quarter something was bothering Ron Bolton. As he was covering Bob Chandler he noticed how easily Chandler was able to make cuts on the glassy turf, while Bolton could barely stand up. Then after Chandler hit the ground going for an incomplete pass Bolton got his answer. Chandler had filed his spikes to the point they looked like a series of ice picks sticking out of his feet.

Bolton went to the closest official.

"Hey, you've got to make him take those shoes off," he said, pointing to Chandler. Bolton's request went unheeded.

A few plays later he walked up to the same official.

"Look," he said, "if he steps on me or hurts me in any way with those shoes, I'm going to sue you and the NFL."

On the next play the official told Chandler to change his shoes.

Despite Chandler's early advantage it was clear from the first two possessions that neither offense was going to be able to do what it wanted. The Raiders started at their own thirty-one, and after Mark van Eeghan was stuffed for one yard on first down Jim Plunkett fired incomplete passes on second and third down that weren't close to being caught. Ray Guy was even affected by the cold on his first punt of the afternoon, booting it just forty-two yards into a swirling wind. Keith Wright returned it to the Cleveland thirty-one, and the capacity crowd roared (though the roar was somewhat muffled by gloves and scarves) as the Browns' offense took the field for the first time in the playoffs.

Brian Sipe and Company could do little better. Sipe dropped back to pass on first down and lobbed one down the right sideline for Dave Logan, who came nowhere close to catching it. Calvin Hill, getting the start at halfback, picked up four yards on second down on his second carry of the season but dropped a third-down pass from Sipe in the flat that would have resulted in a Cleveland first down. Johnny Evans punted thirty-seven yards back to Oakland.

After van Eeghan was stuffed on first down and Plunkett hit running back Kenny King for four yards on a second-down screen pass, the ten-year veteran from Stanford dropped back again on third down. He spotted Bob Chandler streaking down the right side and fired a pass toward him. However, on the glassy field (and without his modified cleats) Chandler's speed was not the same as usual, and the pass was overthrown—for Chandler anyway. It was right on the money for Ron Bolton, playing in front of Chandler, who simply slowed down and intercepted the pass at the Cleveland twenty-seven. Bolton's pick excited the crowd and the Browns' sideline, but the play was almost the same as the net result of an Oakland punt: forty yards. Still it was something to cheer about, and more importantly something to keep the Browns and their fans warm for a few minutes.

The home team picked up the initial first down of the game two plays later as three Mike Pruitt draws resulted in ten yards to the thirty-seven. Another obvious indication of how ridiculous the playing conditions were came on the next play. Sipe dropped back and fired for Dave Logan, who was open at midfield. The pass was right on the money, but it bounced off Logan's hands incomplete. It was the second dropped pass in as many series for the Browns, but this one was dropped by Logan, the most sure-handed receiver on the team. After Mike Pruitt slipped in the backfield on second down and was covered for a loss, a Sipe-to-Hill screen only picked up four yards on third down. Evans punted again, a beauty, and the Raiders took over at their own eleven in the shadow of their own goalpost at the closed—and frozen—end of the field.

Once again Oakland went nowhere. This time it was King who dropped a third-down pass from Plunkett after a hit from Clay Matthews, and Guy was called upon again. The Browns took over at their own forty-eight, and Sipe went right back to Logan on first down as Cleveland's leading receiver ran a deep out pattern. Again Logan was open, and Sipe put the ball where it needed to be, right at the Oakland twenty-three. But once again the ball caromed off Logan's hands and out of bounds. For Logan to have two drops in a season was probably typical, but to have two drops in a game? No matter what anyone had said before or would say after, the playing surface and the weather conditions were definitely affecting play. "It was not a perfect field," Newsome said. "But we're in Cleveland and you expect it to be cold. It was nothing we weren't used to. We both played in the same conditions. We had to round off our cuts, but the defenders were slipping at the same time, so it evened out."

"A great play out there was simply making the catch," Reggie Rucker concurred. "Your feet are numb. Your hands are numb. You can't feel the ball."

After another Sipe incompletion on second down he underthrew Rucker crossing over the middle on third down, and the pass was picked off by Lester Hayes at the Oakland thirty-five. It was Hayes's third interception in five quarters of playoff football, and it evened the turnover ratio. But just as was the case with Bolton's interception the recipient could do nothing with its windfall. Guy punted, this time just thirty-two yards, back to Cleveland.

Sipe threw deep for Rucker on a streak pattern down the right sideline on first down, and again the ball would have probably been caught on a sunny September Sunday, but it glanced off Rucker's fingertips incomplete. Mike Pruitt picked up seven yards on a second-down draw and then two more on a delayed handoff up the middle on third-and-three, but it wasn't quite enough. Evans punted back to the Raiders, who in turn punted back to the Browns three plays later. Keith Wright received Guy's punt at the Cleveland twenty and scampered twenty yards upfield before being tackled at the forty. As he came down his head snapped back and cracked against the rock-like surface of the field, and Wright had to be helped to the locker room. He had suffered a concussion and would not return to the game, the first official casualty of the weather.

On first down the Browns finally made a pass play work when Sipe hit Rucker zipping across the middle for twenty yards to the Oakland forty. The frozen crowd came to life again as the home team was now presented with its first real opportunity to put a scoring drive together. A Sipe-to-Ozzie Newsome six-yard pass on second down was followed by a three-yard draw by Mike Pruitt on third which gave the Browns another first down at the Oakland twenty-nine with less than twenty seconds to play in the first quarter.

Noticing that time was running out and wanting to take one quick shot at scoring before having to switch ends of the field and contend with the swirling winds Sipe hurried the team to the line of scrimmage to get the play off before time expired. He did and fired deep down the right side for Rucker, who had the ball on his fingers for a split second in the end zone. But Rucker lost it, and then lost his center of balance as his momentum carried him out of the end zone and toward the visiting team dugout fifteen yards behind it. Unable to stop, Rucker floundered and slid through the ice and snow and fell down the dugout steps and out of sight. Luckily for the Browns he wasn't hurt. Unluckily they would now have to go to the other end of the Stadium, which was even more of a minefield.

In the first quarter the Browns had tallied just fifty-eight yards of total offense (twenty-eight rushing and thirty passing), while the Raiders had accumulated a mere nineteen (fourteen rushing and five passing).

As the second quarter began Sipe's second-down pass for Newsome was overthrown, and his third-down pitch to Greg Pruitt was broken up by linebacker Ted Hendricks. On fourth-and-ten from the Oakland twenty-nine Sam Rutigliano sent out Don Cockroft to attempt a forty-eight-yard field goal. The snap and hold were good, but Cockroft's kick was flat and short, landing about three yards deep in the end zone. The Browns had let their first scoring opportunity slip away.

A play later, however, it appeared they would have another. After Plunkett hit tight end Ray Chester on a slant for eleven yards to the Oakland forty, the Raiders' playcaller couldn't get away from Henry Bradley, who charged up the middle on the next play. Bradley knocked the ball out of Plunkett's hand and onto the frozen ground, where it bounced backward and was eventually recovered by the Browns' Marshall Harris at the Oakland twenty-three. Now the crowd, which had been silenced by Cockroft's miss, was back on its feet.

The fans kept cheering on the next play as Sipe scrambled for ten yards to the thirteen. But after Cleo Miller was stuffed for no gain up the middle on first down, Sipe's second-down alley-oop for Logan in the end zone was broken up by Raiders' corner Dwayne O'Steen. On third down it appeared that the Browns had taken the lead when Sipe hit Rucker in the right corner of the end zone for a touchdown. But the officials ruled that Rucker hadn't had two feet in bounds. The crowd went from ecstatic to outraged, but replays showed the call to be correct. Cockroft was called upon again, this time for a thirty-yard attempt.

But for the second time in five minutes he didn't deliver. Cockroft missed the would-be chip shot wide left and the crowd settled back into its seats, a little colder. The Browns were dominating play—at least as much as play *could* be dominated on a day like this—but had nothing to show for it. This was no way to win a playoff game.

Fortunately for the Browns the Raiders' offense still was in no shape to make an impact. King was dragged down for a three-yard loss on a poorly executed sweep, and Plunkett's third-down pass for wide receiver Cliff Branch fell incomplete. Ray Guy punted for the fifth time, and once again the Browns had good field position, starting at the Oakland forty-nine.

An offsides penalty on the Raiders and a five-yard draw by Mike Pruitt gave the Browns a new set of downs at the Oakland thirty-nine, but they could go no farther. Sipe was thrown for an eleven-yard loss by Hendricks on third down, and Evans punted back to Oakland, which took over at its own twenty-six.

Two plays later the Raiders were faced with third-and-four at their own thirty-two. Plunkett dropped back to pass, looking along the right sideline for Chandler.

Plunkett released the football just as Chandler broke open, but as the ball neared him he slipped and lost his balance.

It was the break the Browns had been waiting for.

Ron Bolton stepped in front of the pass and intercepted it at the Oakland forty-two with nothing between him and the end zone but his own clouds of breath. The throng of Browns' backers in the stands suddenly forgot about the cold and what was becoming a very frustrating first half and cheered Bolton as he motored down the field. He crossed the goal line untouched, ran up the snowy hill between the field and the fence separating it from the bleachers, and handed the football to a fan in the crowd. As he came back down the hill a slew of Bolton's teammates were waiting for him. The Browns led, 6-0, and the way this game was going six points seemed like twenty. The fans were feeling so good they didn't give much thought to the Browns' kicking team coming onto the field for the extra point. They probably should have.

Cockroft's point-after attempt was even more woeful than his last field-goal try. "In this case, the snap was inside and low," said holder Paul McDonald. "I barely had time to get my right hand up and Don was ahead of himself. It was fortunate he even got to kick the ball." Partially blocked by Ted Hendricks, Cockroft's kick barely quacked over the line of scrimmage and fell short of the goalpost. It looked like it was the first time Cockroft had ever kicked a football, and it was his third miss in less than fifteen minutes.

"When you block a kick early," said Oakland defensive end John Matuszak, "it makes them think about it the rest of the game." And indeed the Browns would think about the missed kicks later in the game—and for a long time afterward.

Still with offense hard to come by, the Cleveland defense had given the home team a 6-0 lead with 6:10 remaining in the second quarter. All the Browns' defense had to do was keep up its dominance of the Raiders, and they would be San Diego-bound.

But as is the case with all good teams, they respond when needed and answer any challenge laid before them. The Oakland offense, which had picked up just twenty-four yards on its first eight possessions, ignored the weather and put together the most impressive drive of the afternoon. A sixteen-yard pass from Plunkett to Chandler moved the Raiders into Cleveland territory, where they picked up another key first down three plays later when Plunkett improvised a blown third-and-one play and simply dove over the line of scrimmage for a first down.

The Raiders continued to inch their way into Browns' territory until they were faced with a third-and-thirteen at the Cleveland twenty-eight with just under two minutes remaining in the half. There Plunkett hit Chester for twenty-six yards to the Cleveland two, and the Browns' 6-0 lead wasn't looking quite as comfortable as it had when Bolton crossed the goal line. Oakland caught a break when a fumbled handoff on first down bounced off a lineman's leg and van Eeghan recovered at the two just before Clinton Burrell could pounce on it. When a second-down pass fell incomplete it appeared that the Browns might be able to get out of the situation with little damage, but on third-and-goal with twenty-two seconds remaining van Eeghan blasted off left tackle and into the end zone for the game-tying touchdown.

But now for the hard part: the extra point. The Raiders' Chris Bahr, who had started the season with Cincinnati, jogged out onto the field knowing all eyes would be on him. True he wouldn't have to contend with the winds that Cockroft did at the opposite end of the field, but he would have to kick off what was essentially a sheet of marble. Nonetheless after a perfect snap and hold Bahr looked good as gold as he split the uprights to give the Raiders a 7-6 lead with eighteen seconds left in the half.

After Cleveland received the kickoff Sipe threw two more passes before the half expired. From the Cleveland thirty-five following the kickoff he hit Rucker for seventeen yards on an out pattern then lobbed a desperation pass for Logan with eight seconds remaining, which was intercepted by Lester Hayes at the Oakland five. It was Hayes's fourth interception of the playoffs and his seventeenth of the year.

The Browns headed for the warmth of the locker room knowing they should have been ahead. They'd squandered two golden scoring opportunities and trailed because of a flubbed extra point. Granted the playing conditions weren't ideal, but the veterans knew if the Browns didn't start cashing in on their chances it would be the Raiders who would be booking a flight to sunny San Diego. Plus as the half wore on it was clear that the teams were adjusting to the elements. The second quarter had seen much improved offensive play than the first, and Oakland's long drive proved that it could be done. It would all now come down to the final thirty minutes: who could make the least mistakes and who could cash in on what mistakes were made.

The good news for the Browns to start the second half was that they would be traveling east to west into the closed end of the Stadium, where the turf was more frozen but the winds weren't as strong. Quickly taking advantage of the logistics the Browns took the third-quarter kickoff and marched down the field, resembling their usual selves on offense for the first time on the day.

Sipe hit a sliding Ozzie Newsome for thirteen yards to the Oakland forty-eight and a play later Calvin Hill took a sweep around right end and found daylight thanks to a key block by Henry Sheppard of Burgess Owens at the Oakland thirty-five. Hill rambled down the right sideline with a clear path of daylight with nothing standing between him and the end zone. The bad news was that Hill was angled toward the sideline as he cleared Sheppard's block. Though there wasn't a defender within five yards of him Hill ended up running out of bounds, not being able to stop or change direction on the icy turf. On a normal day it would have been a forty-six-yard touchdown run and might have changed the complexion of the contest. Instead it was just an eighteen-yard gain to the Oakland twenty-eight.

A five-yard facemask penalty on John Matuszak following a three-yard Sipe run was followed by a six-yard pass to Newsome to the Oakland fourteen. But the Raider defense dug in. Mike Pruitt was stuffed for one yard up the middle, and then Sipe overshot Dave Logan in the corner of the end zone. In Logan's attempt to reel in the pass, his momentum took him out of bounds, and just like Rucker in the first quarter he couldn't stop. He ended up crashing into a three-foot snow bank beside the stands.

Thus the Browns were forced to attempt another field goal, and they'd already had their share of adventures with the kicking game thus far. Whether it was kicking at the opposite end of the field or just a better display of execution, Don Cockroft finally came through with a thirty-yard field goal that split the uprights and gave the Browns back the lead at 9-7 with 11:29 remaining in the third quarter. The drive seemed to fill the capacity crowd with relief. The Browns had proved that they could march down the field and, possibly even more important, kick a field goal. If the Cleveland defense could shake off the ill effects of the final Oakland drive of the first half, the Browns would be in good shape.

As the fans hoped, the Browns' defense came out with fire in its eye. Van Eeghan was stuffed for four yards on two carries, and a third-down Plunkett pass was nearly intercepted by Clarence Scott at midfield before falling incomplete. Ray Guy punted back to the Browns, who were now poised to take control of the game.

On second-and-ten from the Cleveland thirty-six Sipe floated a pass for Greg Pruitt who spun around linebacker Rod Martin to make the catch for a twenty-five-yard gain, which warmed the still-frozen crowd a bit more. A play later Sipe hit Logan over the middle for fifteen yards, but shortly after the Browns were faced with another third down, this one with four yards to go at the Oakland eighteen. Oakland right end Dave Browning steamed up the middle of the Cleveland line and forced Sipe to throw his pass away. On fourth down Sam Rutigliano called on Cockroft again, this time for a thirty-six-yard attempt.

Before the crowd could discover if Cockroft was on a roll Paul McDonald had trouble with Gerry Sullivan's snap. Kneeling down, he had to reach over his lap to catch the football on his hip, and the ball slipped in his hands as he brought it down. Rather than holding the football for a kick that would almost certainly be blocked, McDonald got up with it and started running to his right, hoping the Raider rush might have overpursued. Instead McDonald was mauled at the Oakland twenty-nine for an eleven-yard loss. The Browns gave the ball back to the silver and black as the result of yet another blown scoring opportunity.

Once again the Cleveland defense shut the Raiders down and kept them from prying the momentum out of the Browns' hands. Oakland went three-and-out and punted back to Cleveland. Dino Hall received the kick at the Cleveland forty and found daylight down the right sideline. He was knocked out of bounds by Ray Guy, saving a touchdown, after a sixteen-yard return to the Oakland forty-four.

The Browns' offense picked up right where it had left off. Sipe hit Logan over the middle for twenty-one yards then a play later fired for Logan again. The pass fell incomplete, but Dwayne O'Steen was called for pass interference, giving Cleveland a first down at the Oakland nine. But once again the Browns' offense stalled in the shadow of the goal post. A second-down fumble by Sipe was nearly recovered by Oakland's Ted Hendricks, but Joe DeLamielleure saved it, limiting the damage to only a four-yard loss. On third down from the twelve Sipe fired over the middle for Logan again, and for the third straight time Logan was open, this time at the goal line. But the football went through Logan's grasp and fell incomplete as the crowd groaned in both disappointment and shock. Logan dropping passes was extremely rare, especially in the end zone, and this drop appeared especially costly. It would have given the Browns at least an eight-point advantage, meaning that the Raiders would have had to score twice to take the lead, a doubtful proposition considering the conditions and the way the Cleveland defense was playing.

Once again Rutigliano called on Cockroft, and the sellout crowd at Cleveland Stadium held its breath. Not only were the frozen turf and Cockroft's leg reasons for worry but now McDonald's hands as well. But this time McDonald handled the snap and Cockroft booted the ball high and long and through the uprights from thirty yards away, giving the Browns a 12-7 margin with 2:40 to play in a fast-moving third quarter. The Raiders could still take back the lead with one score, but now it would take a touchdown, not just a field goal. The Browns liked those odds on this day.

For the third straight possession a Cleveland drive and field-goal attempt was followed by a three-and-out series by the Raiders, and after another Guy punt the Browns took over at their own twenty-three with less than a minute remaining in the third quarter. In the fourth they would change ends, and Cleveland would have to drive into the open end of the Stadium. Life would be a lot easier if the Browns could tack on another score or at least get a drive going before having to switch direction.

Instead they moved backward. Cleveland's first infraction of the day, an illegal-motion penalty on Mike Pruitt on first down, set the Browns back five yards. After a pair of runs by Greg Pruitt, the Browns were faced with third-and-five at their own twenty-eight. The snap slipped out of Tom DeLeone's hands and past Sipe without the quarterback even seeing the football. A mad scramble into the backfield ensued, but luckily for the Browns the ball rolled right behind Doug

Dieken's legs. Dieken continued to block, not knowing the football was inches from him and simply by standing still inadvertently prevented Oakland's Mike Davis from getting to the football. Sipe dove back and recovered at the nineteen for a nine-yard loss, but the damage was minimal. Johnny Evans punted the football to the Oakland forty-seven where it hit the frozen turf and rolled another twenty-seven yards before it stopped, a season-best (and weather-aided) sixty-one-yard kick.

A play later the third quarter ended, and the Browns were fifteen minutes away from San Diego. But they'd have to get there without the help of their defensive leader. Lyle Alzado left the game for the locker room early in the fourth because his flu symptoms were too much to handle. He would return to the sideline but not to the game.

The fears the Browns had about the side change for the final stanza were well warranted. After a quarter of ineptitude trying to drive east the Raiders' offense suddenly came to life as it drove west, toward San Diego.

On third-and-four from the Oakland twenty-six Jim Plunkett stepped forward to avoid the Cleveland pass rush and flipped an underhand pass to Mark van Eeghan who rumbled for thirteen yards and a first down. It was the spark Oakland needed. A play later Plunkett hit Kenny Branch for eighteen over the middle, and a play after that hit a leaping Raymond Chester for twenty-six yards at the Cleveland sixteen. The Browns' lead was in danger.

The Cleveland defense held, forcing third-and-eight from the fourteen and appeared to be in the clear when Clarence Scott sacked Plunkett. But the Browns were penalized for being offside, and on the replay Plunkett hit Kenny King for six yards and a first down at the Cleveland three.

Van Eeghan plowed ahead to the one on first down but was stuffed for no gain on second. The crowd swelled to its frozen feet. If the Browns could keep the Raiders out of the end zone here, Oakland would have to put together another drive to take the lead. But if they couldn't stop the Raiders from scoring the pressure would be put back on the Browns.

Oakland went back to van Eeghan on third down, and he blasted off left tackle and into the end zone for the go-ahead touchdown. Chris Bahr made his second extra point of the game, and with 9:22 remaining in the contest the Raiders led, 14-12, following a twelve-play, eighty-yard drive that consumed nearly six minutes.

Dino Hall returned the kickoff twenty-four yards to the Cleveland forty-one, but the Browns went nowhere. Three straight Sipe incompletions—two of which were in and out of his receivers' hands—forced another punt, and the Raiders took over at their own twenty-seven with 8:45 to play. They managed to pick up a first down but couldn't reach midfield, and Ray Guy punted for the ninth time, pinning the Browns back at their own twenty-five with 4:39 remaining.

Everyone in the crowd knew it. Everyone watching on television at home knew it. The situation was the perfect cue for the Kardiac Kids to take center stage. It didn't matter what had happened before on this afternoon. It was time for Brian Sipe and the Browns' offense to lead one last heart-pounding march down the field. It appeared this drive would be their last chance.

On first down Sipe dropped back to pass and found no one open. He scrambled to his left and dashed through an opening along the sideline. He crossed the thirty and then the thirty-five then was blasted by Burgess Owens and Mike Davis at the thirty-six. The football popped loose.

It sailed high into the air, almost looking as if it had been thrown backward rather than jarred loose by a tackle. It landed inside the Cleveland thirty, and defensive back Odis McKinney recovered for the Raiders at the Browns' twenty-four with 4:23 remaining. Sipe peeled himself off the frozen tundra and slowly walked back to the sideline as the Raiders' offense jubilantly jogged onto the field.

The crowd was stunned. After a season of heart-stopping finishes and excitement it didn't seem right that it should end this way. Sipe was the greatest thing to happen to the Cleveland sports scene in years. He'd already been deemed a hero by thousands. They didn't want to admit he was now the goat.

The Raiders were surprised that Sipe had been so aggressive in that situation. "No quarterback should expose himself to that kind of danger in this type of game," Mike Davis said. "Sipe was in mortal terror of losing his head."

"I was surprised with Sipe," Owens added. "He kept running, wouldn't slide like he normally does."

The Raiders' offense had looked unstoppable on its last drive—now that it was going in the right direction—and it was unlikely the Browns would be able to stop them with so little territory to defend. Even if Cleveland could keep the Raiders out of the end zone Chris Bahr and the Oakland kicking team weren't having the kind of day that Don Cockroft and the Browns were. At this end of the field, Bahr could probably put the ball through the uprights even if the Raiders didn't move another yard. Any way you looked at it things looked bleak for the Browns. "I thought the game was over then," Owens said later.

Still, if Cleveland could keep the Raiders from adding a touchdown Sipe and Company could get one last chance. A Bahr field goal would only put Oakland up by five, and a Cleveland touchdown could still win it—if the Browns' offense had enough time to get down the frozen field.

Ironically, after all the media attention and national spotlights that had been shone on the Browns' offense over the previous six months, the fate of the entire 1980 season now rested on the Cleveland defense.

The Browns stuffed van Eeghan for one yard on first down, but he crashed through left tackle for eight yards to the fifteen on second down, bringing up third-and-one with just over three minutes to play. Everyone in Northeast Ohio knew who was going to get the ball, and Oakland coach Tom Flores was in no position to get creative to try and fool them. The call was a draw to van Eeghan who gained a half-yard before Dick Ambrose halted him just shy of the fourteen-yard line. It brought up fourth down.

Flores now had a decision to make. Bahr had made his two extra-point attempts at this end of the field with no problems. This would be a thirty-two-yard field-goal attempt, and the odds were good that Bahr would make it. It would give the Raiders a 17-12 lead, but they would have to give the ball back to the Browns with just under three minutes remaining to drive the field with all three time outs and the two-minute warning in their pocket. Flores knew as well as anyone that was a lot of leeway to give the Kardiac Kids.

On the other hand the Raiders needed less than two feet for a first down. If van Eeghan could simply muscle forward on fourth down to pick up what he'd gained on third down, Oakland would move the chains. A Raiders first down would force the Browns to start calling their time outs, and after three more running plays the Browns would be out. Then even if the Raiders couldn't pick up another first down Bahr could kick a shorter field goal with less time remaining, and the Browns would be unable to stop the clock after the two-minute warning. The decision came down to one question: could van Eeghan pick up eighteen inches? Flores decided he could. The Raiders' offense remained on the field to go for it on fourth down.

The capacity gallery at Cleveland Stadium rose once again, knowing the importance of this one play. The odds were stacked heavily in favor of the Raiders, but it seemed that's when these Browns performed best. The Browns' defense, which had nearly been blasted out of Cleveland following the preseason and the first two games of the year, now had a chance to show the world how much it had improved since July. The entire 1980 season came down to one play.

The playcall was the same as the one on second down that had gained eight and the one that resulted in Oakland's two touchdowns: van Eeghan off left tackle. Plunkett took the snap and handed off to van Eeghan who began to angle his way into the line. Suddenly he was thrown violently backward as if he had hit a brick wall. It wasn't a wall but rather the combination of Robert L. Jackson and Dick Ambrose crashing into him at the fifteen-yard line and sending him flat on his back on the marble-like surface.

The tension-filled silence in Cleveland Stadium snapped in a flood of screams and cheers. It appeared the Browns had held. The defense remained on the field as the officials spotted the football and called over the chains to measure. As expected the football was about six inches shy of the marker, and the Browns' defense exploded off the field, leaping and celebrating. They had given the offense one last chance.

"I wouldn't feel too good if I was an Oakland Raider right now," NBC color man John Brodie said.

"The Kardiac Kondition once again found itself in the perfect environment for yet another victorious heart-pounding climax," Bob Sudyk would write.

As the roar of the crowd continued and the Cleveland offense took the field most fans figured that whatever happened next would be remembered in this city for a long time. What they didn't know was just how long or to what extent.

Brian Sipe and Company formed a huddle like they had thousands of times over the past half-year. But this huddle was different.

"This is it," Sipe said to his teammates. "Here's where we win the game."

"It was virtually the same as it had been the entire year," Dave Logan would say. "We knew we were going to win. There was no doubt in anybody's mind that we were going to go down and score."

"It was like any other game," Dieken concurred. "It was like 'Here we go. Let's just keep it going and somebody will make a play and we'll get it done.'"

The attitude was the same on the Cleveland sideline. "We said, 'Here they go again,'" Thom Darden said. "We expected it. We expected they would score."

"Sipe's like Roger Staubach with two minutes left in a game," Mike Davis said. "He had too much time. In the huddle we were thinking 'big play.' Fumble. Sack. Big hit."

The clock read 2:22. The Browns were at their own fifteen, trailing by two. The kicking game was unsure so they very well might have to drive eighty-five yards for victory. With the entire season hanging in the balance it was the ultimate Kardiac Kids situation.

"They are ready for another Cleveland Browns finish," Don Criqui told his television audience. "Fasten all seat belts."

NBC couldn't have asked for a better finish to boost the ratings. "I love that team," said NBC publicity director Tom Merritt. "The Browns are the best TV team in the world."

On first down Sipe fired for Reggie Rucker on the right side, but the pass fell incomplete. Some groans trickled out of the stands—the fans probably realized the lopsided course of this game. Prior to the Browns' last drive there had been fifteen drives going toward the closed end of the Stadium. Four of them had ended with the offense scoring. In contrast there had been eleven drives going toward the open end of the Stadium, and none had resulted in a score. Whether or not a team was incapable of scoring at that end of the Stadium on this day remained to be seen, but a good question was whether or not the teams were psychologically convinced they couldn't score at that end and therefore believed they couldn't drive toward that end. These thoughts seemed to hang in the air with the frozen clouds of breath as the Browns lined up for second down at the fifteen.

Sipe dropped back and nearly fell down as he slipped on a patch of ice. But he regained his composure and fired a long, lofty pass down the left sideline. It was short of its intended target, Ozzie Newsome, but that worked to the Browns' benefit. Newsome stopped to wait for the pass and his defender, Odis McKinney, tried to do the same. Instead McKinney slipped and fell to the ground, leaving Newsome all alone. He caught the pass at the Cleveland thirty-seven and turned upfield with nothing in front of him. But McKinney kept his wits about him while still on the ground and grabbed Newsome's ankle. The third-year tight end out of Alabama tried to escape his grasp but fell down at the Cleveland forty-four after a twenty-nine-yard gain that ignited the crowd and, at least for the moment, brushed their concerns away.

The play also brought the Browns to the two-minute warning, stopping the clock. Sipe jogged to the sideline for instructions from the coaches during the television commercial break then returned to the field and gave the playcall to his teammates in the huddle. As the Browns came up to the line the crowd grew even louder in excitement, anticipating what was going to happen. It grew so loud that Sipe raised his arms up and down in a flapping motion to quiet the fans. They did as instructed.

Sipe's first-down pass was intended for Greg Pruitt, but it was overthrown on the left side. On second down Sipe dropped back again and slipped. He recovered and rushed forward, just getting back to the line of scrimmage before being tackled with 1:54 left and the clock running. The Browns needed another big play and fast.

On third down Sipe fired for Rucker on the right sideline, but once again the pass fell incomplete. For a split-second the fans saw the entire season once again coming down to a crucial fourth-down play.

Then they saw the flag.

Dwayne O'Steen was penalized five yards for illegal contact on Rucker, but more importantly the infraction resulted in an automatic first down at the Cleveland forty-nine with 1:19 remaining. The Browns were off the hook, at least for three more plays. On the next snap it appeared they were off the hook permanently.

Sipe dropped back and shuffled slightly to his left in the pocket, looking for a receiver. He found one and fired the football downfield where Greg Pruitt caught it just behind Lester Hayes along the left sideline at the Oakland twenty-eight. Pruitt stepped out of bounds following the twenty-three-yard gain with 1:12 left, and the Stadium was shaking with the noise of the fans. The sellout crowd seemed to know it was witnessing the consummate Kardiac Kids performance.

"That was a fantastic pass Sipe threw to Greg Pruitt, just beautiful," Burgess Owens said. "It's the way Cleveland does things. They're masterful late in games."

On first down from the twenty-eight Sipe looped a sideline pass for Newsome who caught it at the twenty-one but was ruled out of bounds incomplete. It brought up second down with 1:06 to play, and the Browns decided to try to cross up the Oakland Raiders.

The drive was seven plays old, and each of the seven plays had been a pass. It only seemed natural that the Browns would keep passing until they got to where they needed to go or at least until they got near the ten-yard line since neither team had been able to muster much on the ground. But the Browns decided to take a bit of a gamble and see where it took them.

On second down Sipe dropped back again but then handed off to Mike Pruitt on a delayed draw. Pruitt scooted around left end through a surprised Oakland defense and into open field along the sideline. With the crowd growing louder with each step Pruitt crossed the twenty-five, the twenty, and then the fifteen before being tackled at the Oakland fourteen following a fourteen-yard gain. The gamble had worked. The Browns called their first time out with fifty-six seconds to play.

For better or worse the Browns were now in what was under normal playing conditions Cockroft's field-goal range. If they didn't gain another yard Cockroft's attempt would be from thirty-one yards. Rutigliano and his staff knew that and were prepared to send Cockroft out, but they weren't sure enough to fold up the tents and simply play for the field goal.

On first down from the fourteen the call was to Pruitt again, and he fell into the line for one yard to the thirteen. The Browns called time out again with forty-nine seconds remaining. Brian Sipe came to the sideline to get the call from his coaches. Don Cockroft got up off the bench and began warming up. "There was no doubt in my mind that we were going to give Cockroft another try," Tom DeLeone said. "That's how much confidence I thought everybody had in Cockroft. He'd played there for years. He knew how the field played."

It was second-and-nine at the Oakland thirteen. Conventional wisdom whispered that the Browns would simply run up the middle again to melt some more clock and avoid a turnover and then either run again on third down or attempt the field goal. On a normal day with a consistent kicker Rutigliano may very well have played it just that way. But this was about as abnormal a day you'd ever find weather-wise, and after the shaky season Don Cockroft had experienced there were no guarantees even when the weather wasn't a factor.

"We felt a field goal was no gut cinch," Rutigliano would say later. "It was our plan to throw on second down, then run the ball on third down, and if we didn't get it into the end zone by then, go for the field goal."

"I expected another running play to set up the field goal when I went to the sidelines," Sipe said. "I did question the call. A run seemed the logical thing then.

"The coaching staff was adamant. They thought they had a play that would score a touchdown. It's their decision."

"That's the way we did it all year," Doug Dieken said. "That was our style. We lived on the edge and somebody always made a play."

The play called for Dave Logan to start on the left side and cross over the middle underneath to the opposite corner. Logan would be the primary target. Meanwhile Reggie Rucker and Ozzie Newsome would start on the right and cross over the middle going left, clearing out the right side for Logan. The key to the play would be Oakland safety Burgess Owens. If he picked up Logan, Sipe was encouraged to throw the ball away.

But as Sipe prepared to head back to the field Rutigliano delivered a warning: "If the situation gets tight," he said, "if the defense looks like Times Square on New Year's Eve, if you feel at all that you have to force the ball, throw it into Lake Erie, throw it into some blonde's lap in the bleachers, but *don't* throw the ball into the middle of the field."

As Sipe returned to the field Rutigliano turned and looked at Don Cockroft. Cockroft nodded to Rutigliano, signifying he was ready.

Once again the Browns were about to cross up the Raiders. Oakland was so sure Cleveland would run that they left their nickel defensive package in the game and remained in man-to-man coverage off the line. Even several members of the Browns' offense were surprised when Sipe told them the play.

"When they called that pass, I wanted them to call time out," Tom DeLeone said. "I couldn't believe it."

"We didn't want to throw a pass," Mike Pruitt said. "It had worked for us all year, but at that point and time with the weather conditions, you just don't want to throw because of the footing. Everybody said OK, but I think everybody wanted to run the ball, call time out, kick, and go home.

"I think everybody went along, but nobody wanted to run that play."

But not everyone in the Browns' huddle was opposed to the play. "When the play came in, I don't remember going 'What the hell is he thinking?'" Cody Risien said. "I was thinking, 'Hell, let's score the touchdown. We've always gotten it done and we're going to get it done now.'"

"I didn't think it was a bad call," Joe DeLamielleure said. "I thought we were going to score."

Sipe and Company broke the huddle and marched up to the line of scrimmage with the frenzied crowd on its feet.

NBC's John Brodie noted that since Cleo Miller, a talented blocker, was in at fullback, he felt it was unlikely the Browns would pass. He wasn't the only one. "Before the Browns broke the huddle we figured it would be a run, but then they came out in a passing formation with two wide receivers and the tight end flexed,"

Mike Davis would say later. "It probably was a good offensive play because they anticipated us expecting a run." High above the field in the press box Hal Lebovitz leaned over to an out-of-town writer next to him. "The Browns are going to pass," he whispered. "I know Sam."

The writer looked at Lebovitz as if he were crazy.

Sipe barked out the signals and took the snap. For 2½ seconds everything went exactly as designed.

Logan crossed over the middle, covered by Dwayne O'Steen, while Newsome slanted into the end zone from the other side with Mike Davis right on him. At the same time linebackers Ted Hendricks and Matt Millen came crashing through the line on a blitz.

On the sideline the members of the Browns' defense were huddled together on the electric benches like sled dogs, mildly aware of what was transpiring on the field only by audio rather than visual input. Then the unit's leader, weary and sick, realized what was happening.

"I can't believe they're fucking passing the ball!" Lyle Alzado screamed.

Meanwhile Sipe weighed his options. His top priority was to avoid a sack, which would take the Browns out of field-goal range, so he had to decide quickly what he was going to do. As Logan crossed over the middle he had a step on O'Steen, but Owens started to move over to help. Sipe opted against throwing to Logan.

In the same instant he saw Newsome gain a step on Mike Davis in the end zone going the other direction. In that moment Sipe had to choose between throwing the ball to Newsome or throwing the ball into Lake Erie. He hadn't been the top-ranked quarterback in 1980 for throwing the ball away.

"When they blitzed, I did what we did all year," Sipe said, "go to the tight end. We've run that play for two years and have scored a lot of TDs on it.

"I'm a victim of my own programming. I'm going for it."

He cocked his arm and began to throw the football.

As if the play were in slow motion Rutigliano saw what Sipe was thinking. "Logan!" he screamed on the sideline. "Logan!"

But in that next moment as Sipe's arm began to move forward, everything about the play changed.

Owens abandoned pursuing Logan to help Davis with Newsome. Had Sipe stuck with Logan for one more instant it would have been a simple matter of pitch-and-catch for the game-winning touchdown with Logan wide open in the right corner. "I was open," Logan said. "If Brian had stayed on me longer he would have realized it. But his read on the play was to go to Newsome when the weak safety comes up on me."

Even as Sipe released the football Davis was gaining thanks to Owens.

"Owens forced me upfield," Newsome said, "he took me about two steps deeper into the end zone and that got Davis two steps closer to the ball. Up until the ball was thrown I was open."

The football wobbled through the frigid winter air as Sipe was crushed by Ted Hendricks and lay face down on the ground. Sipe never saw what happened. He heard the result of what would be the most memorable pass of his football career.

As the pass cut through the bitter lake gust Davis sliced through the cushion between Owens and Newsome. Newsome saw Davis come between him and the football but could do nothing about it.

"When I saw the ball coming, and felt Davis against my arm, I knew I was in trouble," Newsome said. "I tried to knock the ball away from him, but I couldn't reach it."

The speedy Davis already was a step ahead of Newsome who couldn't even see the ball at this point. His only hope was that Davis would drop it.

He didn't.

The football that had left Sipe's hand seemingly an eternity earlier glided into Davis's chest where he put both hands securely on it and toppled forward to the ground.

For a few brief moments no one really knew what happened. Don Criqui and John Brodie in the NBC booth were silent, not sure where the ball had gone. The fans were equally silent, afraid that their worst nightmare had come true but hoping that they hadn't really seen what they thought they'd seen. As the hush swelled through the stands like falling dominoes Sipe began to sit up. He didn't need to look over to the back of the end zone. He knew what had happened.

When Davis got up holding the football, the Oakland bench cleared, and his teammates began to pile on top of him, the crowd knew for certain what had happened. Mike Davis, a college teammate of Dave Logan, the man the play was designed for, had intercepted Brian Sipe in the end zone with forty-one seconds to play. As realization hit Cleveland Stadium became a tomb, as quiet as it had been before anyone had arrived early that frosty morning.

Bill Scholl of the *Cleveland Press* described it best: "It was like standing next to your kid's amplifiers and having the power go off."

"I've never seen that many people get that quiet that quick," Dieken said. "It was kind of eerie how quiet that place got."

"From the sideline, you could hear them hooting and hollering down in the end zone," said Dick Ambrose. "You could hear the Raiders celebrating on their sideline. Usually, you could never hear your own players twenty feet away from you on your own sideline.

"It was very surreal. It was almost as if it was a dream and it really wasn't happening. Like a nightmare."

The defense was then called back to duty.

"Someone said, 'OK, defense, back on the field. Interception,'" Ron Bolton said. "I said, 'Intercept what?' I could not believe we threw a pass in that situation."

Sipe returned to Rutigliano on the sideline and took his helmet off. The look on his face was one of pain and frustration but most of all regret.

"Brian, I love you," Rutigliano told his quarterback. "You had a great year. I know how tough this is for you, but you gotta put it behind you."

Sipe looked at him as if he were crazy.

As Jim Plunkett and the Raiders' offense came back onto the field to run out the clock Sipe paced up and down the sideline, running his hands through his long dark hair in disbelief.

In the press box the out-of-town writer turned to Lebovitz and shook his head, amazed.

Plunkett took two snaps, kneeled down, and after the Browns stopped the clock once with their final time out it finally hit zero. It was the twenty-fifth time in the past thirty-three games that a Browns' contest was decided in the final two minutes. The Raiders had won, 14-12, and advanced to the AFC Championship. It was 3:45 in the afternoon when the final gun sounded, but to many the clock had struck midnight.

The Cleveland Browns' 1980 season was over.

Rutigliano thought long and hard about what he would say as he marched the frozen forty yards from the sideline to the locker room. He knew he was about to have his own head served to him on a platter by the media, questioning his decision to throw one more pass. He knew why he'd done it and had felt it was a justified decision. "If the pass had been completed for a touchdown," he wrote in his autobiography eight years later, "they would already have started constructing my statue at Public Square in downtown Cleveland."

But trying to make others understand his view was a different story. Even Sipe sounded a bit doubtful of the decision. "I don't get paid to make the calls," he told reporters. "I just do what I'm told."

It was a comment that ruffled a few feathers of several, including Rutigliano, who felt he did what he could to protect Sipe in his postgame comments.

"The play we called was a play that has been successful in the past," Rutigliano said. "Unfortunately, it was an errant throw. But I'd rather put my money on Sipe's arm than take a chance on a field-goal attempt.

"There's no way I could have consciously played it safe and let [Cockroft] try to win the game and look those players in the face after the game. We had done this all year long."

Tom Flores, who would have been the one being grilled by the press for his fourth-down decision had the Browns pulled it out, seemed to understand Rutigliano's thinking. "I think they must have figured that one shot into the end zone and then the field-goal try if it missed," he said. "They would have been kicking into the wind and it was tough at that end of the field, and they had those earlier misses to think about."

"I believe the wind is the reason they didn't just run the ball into position for a field-goal try," Plunkett said. "It was tough at that end of the field and they had those problems earlier."

So what about that last play, the writers asked. "It's called Red Right 88," Sipe said. "I listened to [the coaches] because they are smart, they know what they are doing, and also, that play has worked often for us the last two years. But it was not the play, it was the execution that was bad."

"That's my quarterback," Logan said in defense of Sipe. "I'm in no position to ever question anything he's done all year. It was just one pass we all wish we could have had back."

"It was a good call, a great call," Newsome said. "Give Davis and Owens credit for beating it. We lived and died with the pass all year, and this time we died by it."

"Whatever they did, you'd never second-guess their decisions," Dieken said of the coaching staff. "A lot of them were good. If they made a bad one, they made a bad one."

In some ways it only seemed appropriate that the Browns should take one final shot through the air. That's what got them as far as they had come, not the inconsistent leg of Don Cockroft. They'd stuck with the girl they'd brought to the dance.

Still the critics were adamant and the opposition shocked.

"I was surprised he threw in that situation," Davis said. "I don't think anyone could have completed that pass. No way that pass would get through to Newsome."

"They were so close, he shouldn't have thrown it," Dwayne O'Steen said. "When he did, we all said, 'Whoa!'"

"We knew Don Cockroft could make that one," Mike Pruitt said. "I would depend on him to win a game. He'd been around for a while and I think he would have come through. Each week it was somebody different and I thought it was his week."

"For me, he HAD to give Cockroft the opportunity," Lebovitz wrote in Monday's *Plain Dealer*. "Not even if someone had a gun at my back would I have put the ball in the air when the Browns were on the 13-yard line . . . and a field goal would have won it.

"But if someone had a gun at Sam's back he'd play Russian roulette and hope one chamber was empty, living dangerously as always. That's his style so he'll never know if Cockroft would have made that short one or not."

"If the kicking unit was solid, I wouldn't even have had to make the decision," Rutigliano countered. "There wouldn't have been a decision to make because we would have been ahead.

"All year long, it was like the stock market, and that's a source of concern on the way we enter a game, as far as strategy goes."

It was a valid objection. Cockroft had attempted six kicks on this day and made just two of them. Two misses were the result of bad snaps, but that was just as much a reason to opt against the certainty of a field goal. Also the two that Cockroft had made were at the closed end of the field. Despite Cockroft's struggles throughout the season the kicking team's problems during the Oakland game might have been caused by the weather and field conditions more than anything else. "The biggest factor was the wind," Cockroft said, "although the field was icy in some spots which also hurt in setting the ball up."

"On that end [the open, east end of the Stadium], the moisture from the lake would come in," Thom Darden explained, "so it was a lot more slippery in that area than it was at the other end. Plus, he'd already missed three. Logic says he's not going to be successful. I understood Sam's thinking."

Not all the players followed Darden's logic. "I had all the confidence in the world that Cockroft would have made it," Joe DeLamielleure said. "I'm not questioning the call, but I think if we would have kicked, he would have made it."

Rutigliano defended the decision to pass, arguing it was better to take a chance with your strength and go down in proverbial flames than to watch a field goal fall short or hook wide. "I had no doubt before and after, even with the outcome, that we did the right thing," Rutigliano said. "I think the players, especially the offensive players, would have been extremely disappointed had we tried to kick a field goal and it failed.

"Then everyone would say, 'You were on the 13-yard line and he already missed three field goals and an extra point. With the kind of season that he had, what were the percentages of Brian Sipe succeeding as opposed to Don Cockroft?' But it's like anything else: nothing succeeds like success and nothing fails like failure."

Additionally, in the wake of the loss, Cockroft revealed that he had been kicking most of the season with torn cartilage in his left knee, an injury suffered prior to the Tampa Bay game, which led to more complicated leg and back trouble as the year wore on. "I continued to kick, but I couldn't extend my leg completely," he said. "It caused pressure on my lower back and created more trouble. It either aggravated my sciatic nerve, or there is a sciatic spur that is the source of the problem."

But Cockroft was confident that the game would have ended differently if he had been given the chance to win it. "I was thanking the Lord for the opportunity but it never came," he said. "I'd rather have had the opportunity to kick and fail than not to have had it at all. But I think what Sam said was very logical.

"Nothing is certain, of course, but I would have made that field goal."

· · ·

Monday's *Plain Dealer* front-page headline read: KARDIAC KIDS RUN OUT OF MIRACLES.

And on the sports page: KARDIAC ARREST.

The *Cleveland Press* headline declared FROZEN FANS DISPUTE *THE PLAY*" while "A pass turns Stadium into a tomb" adorned the sports page.

Though it turned out to be the Browns' worst nightmare, Red Right 88 and its aftermath were a sportswriter's dream.

"It was another Kardiac Kids finish," wrote Bob Sudyk, "except this time the patient died."

"It was truly a frozen moment in Browns' football history," wrote Craig Hitchcock in the *Press*.

"Ah, but for so many of the Browns this year, their hearts were with the queen of the aerial circus," Dan Coughlin said. "They stayed for one last kiss and it was one kiss too long."

"We won so many in the final seconds it couldn't go on forever," Lebovitz wrote, notably using "we" rather than "they." "This time, though, we threw away the opportunity. That's the only thing that really hurts."

The other thing that really hurt the Browns and their fans was the popular belief that the Raiders had won solely because of the weather. Public opinion seemed to declare that the Browns suffered more offensively because of the frozen field, wind, and frigid temperatures.

"It definitely took more away from us," Mike Pruitt said, "because we had more weapons."

"If we would have played them in Oakland," Joe DeLamielleure agreed, "we would have beat them. It was to our advantage to have a better field."

"I believe very strongly that had it been anything above freezing," Thom Darden said, "if the ground were not frozen hard as concrete the way it was, if the conditions were not as unbearable and the teams had a better opportunity to implement their offenses and their defenses, we would have won the game. There's no doubt in my mind because of the momentum and the confidence level we had. When you have that kind of confidence, you can overcome almost any obstacle."

"We would have beat them, without question," Rutigliano said. "I thought they were a pretty good football team, but I think we could have beat them. [The weather] took away everything from us.

"I don't think they could have covered us man-for-man on a better field."

"Those were the most extreme conditions I've ever seen," said Reggie Rucker. "The field was so frozen that the only way you could run was straight ahead."

"It was treacherous out there, as bad as I ever care to play in," Dave Logan added. "I dropped two passes and I don't think I dropped two all year." Actually Logan dropped three—all the more evidence in favor of a different resolution to the contest on a warm and sunny day. But Sipe may have put it best.

"In September," he said of Red Right 88, "I'm going to hit that pass every time."

Even the Raiders knew the game would have been a very different one in dissimilar conditions. "It was like roller-skating on a rink without any skates," Ted Hendricks said after the game. "Those were the worst conditions I've ever seen because of the icy field. My toes haven't thawed out yet."

"I've been playing fourteen years, and that was the worst footing ever," agreed Gene Upshaw. "After you hit a guy, you couldn't knock him around because there was no footing."

Mike Davis summed it up perfectly: "Conditions on the field take away from the talent on the field."

Though the conditions had been bad some felt that the Browns still should have had the advantage. Certainly no one truly benefits from an icy field or wind, but as far as dealing with the cold shouldn't the Browns have been better prepared for it than their Californian opponents? "As usual," Lebovitz said, "all the pre-game talk about the Browns having a weather advantage was the only hot air in town."

Still the Browns had the advantage in most of the statistics. They outgained the Raiders 254 yards to 208 and gained seventeen first downs to Oakland's twelve. They'd punted less than Oakland (six to nine), and Johnny Evans actually outperformed the heralded Ray Guy, averaging 39.5 yards per kick to Guy's 38.3. The Browns, who were only penalized twice the entire game for ten yards, also caught some breaks in the turnover department, losing just one of six fumbles while the Raiders lost one of two.

But the Raiders held the advantage in third-down conversions, which was one of the primary differences in the contest. Oakland was eight-for-twenty while the Browns were just two-for-fourteen. Successful third-down conversions resulted in the continuation of the two Oakland touchdown drives, and the failed ones led to the numerous flubbed field-goal attempts by the Browns. Plunkett completed fourteen of thirty passes for 149 yards with two picks. Van Eeghan was Oakland's leading rusher but only managed forty-five yards on twenty carries (more importantly two of the twenty resulted in both of the Raiders' touchdowns), while Mike Pruitt led the Browns with forty-eight on thirteen rushes. The Browns outgained the Raiders on the ground, eighty-five yards to seventy-six.

Sipe only connected on thirteen of forty passes for 183 yards. Two of his interceptions had little impact, but the third would be remembered for decades.

Adding insult to injury for the Browns was the way that day's late playoff game finished. In Atlanta the Falcons led the Cowboys, 27-24, with less than a minute to play, but Dallas was driving. The Cowboys reached the Atlanta twenty-three when quarterback Danny White hit Drew Pearson for the game-winning touchdown with forty-two seconds left. The Browns knew both games that day could—and maybe should—have ended that way.

"When we got to the 23," White said after the game, "I was just thinking, 'Don't throw an interception. Get a field goal and go for the tie.'"

Ouch.

The Cowboys had made the play the Browns didn't and were headed to the NFC Championship the following Sunday to face the Philadelphia Eagles for a trip to the Super Bowl. As it turned out both conference title matches would pit division rivals against one another.

"I'll tell you when we'll feel the disappointment," Joe DeLamielleure said. "Next week when we're watching Oakland and San Diego on television. That's when we'll look back on it and we'll think we should be there."

But plenty of Browns were already feeling the disappointment after the game in a locker room that felt more like a funeral parlor. "The locker room was totally silent, and I remember just sitting there for the longest time and not even moving," Logan said. "Not taking my tape off, not cutting anything off. Just sitting because it couldn't have ended that way. There had to be something next week where we would go back out. The finality didn't hit me until we got to the locker room."

"It was like, 'It can't be over, not for us,'" Mike Pruitt said. "It was almost like time stopped. It was a huge, huge stunner for everybody. I figured if there was any year we were going to go to the Super Bowl, that was it."

"We were obviously very devastated because we knew we were going to win that game," Thom Darden said. "You could not have told me that we were not going to win that game regardless of the field conditions or what the Raiders did. You couldn't have told me that we weren't going to San Diego."

"It's just like the thrill of victory," Dick Ambrose said. "It doesn't hit you for a while. The agony of defeat won't set in for a while. We're still in shock."

"I really felt we had a chance to go all the way to the Super Bowl," Mike Pruitt said. "We all did. The thing that makes it especially frustrating is that we came so close."

"You dream about something for eight months," Lyle Alzado said. "You think about it night and day. And you see it disappear with 20 seconds left.

"It's like losing somebody you love."

"It felt like someone had come up and robbed me," said Ron Bolton.

Conversely across the Stadium in the other locker room it was like New Year's Eve in Times Square. "Mike Davis, I love him!" shouted Raiders' owner Al Davis. It was Davis's fourth interception of the season and the seventh of his career, but he admitted it was the biggest play of his life. Reporters asked him what went through his mind when he realized he had the football. "Relief," he replied. "Then joy. Then 'Praise to God.'"

They asked him if he had heard about the comments Newsome had made about him the previous week, saying Davis was inferior to Pittsburgh's Donnie Shell and Houston's Vernon Perry at safety. "No, I didn't read it," Davis said, "but I'm pretty sure he's changed his mind now." Interestingly, on his first play of the Wild Card game the week before Davis had recovered an Earl Campbell fumble and set the tone for the Raiders' victory. Now on his last play of the divisional playoff he'd clinched another win for Oakland.

"When the Browns first got the ball on that last drive we said in the huddle we needed a big play," Davis said. "It just took us awhile to get it done."

While the Raiders would spend the next week trying to figure out how to get it done in San Diego, the Browns would be clearing out their lockers and booking flights home. While the frustration and disappointment echoed through Cleveland for the rest of the week, there was still an upbeat spirit flowing through Browns' fans. They figured the 1980 season was just the first step toward building a champion. They assumed that 1981 would be even better.

"It's tough to lose like we did, but really it was a great year," Mike Pruitt said. "We came close and now we're going to be a better team next season. It hurts, but you learn from these kind of disappointments, and I know we will."

"I have feelings of regret and despair about losing this game, but mixed with them is the knowledge that dammit, we had a good year," Sipe said. "I think we lifted the feelings of everybody around here, and I don't want to hear anybody bad rap us. And I don't just mean me, I mean everybody."

"This was not a fluke for us this season," Rutigliano said. "We are going to continue to improve, although I am not trying to tell you we are a shoo-in to win next year.

"Next year will be better, but it probably will be just like this one was—a dogfight again with Pittsburgh, Houston, and Cincinnati.

"I told them there is absolutely no doubt in my mind that bigger and better things are just ahead . . . we reached some of our goals this season," Rutigliano continued, "and learned a lot that will help immeasurably in the future . . . and that everybody should look ahead, not behind with any remorse."

"This is part of growing, but the best of it is ahead of us," said Charlie Hall. "There is a lot of talent here and we have a good future. . . . The only goal we failed to reach was the Super Bowl, but we have time."

Even the media carried this torch of appreciation and optimism into the off-season.

"It was a wonderful season filled with thrilling climaxes," said Bob Sudyk.

"Sports is meant to be entertainment. The 1980 Browns were a smash show. And we don't even have to wait until next year. They'll be back in July.

"They had a dream. We all shared it. It was wonderful, almost a spiritual trek for the kids. But it is over. Now they must walk as men with full reality of what awaits them in the coming season."

At the time it seemed that Red Right 88 would simply be a bump in the road in a new era of the Cleveland Browns as they traveled to their ultimate destination of a world championship. Essentially the same cast of characters would return in 1981, though no one expected it to be as exciting as 1980 even if the team went further. Fans, coaches, and players alike seemed to understand that no matter what the future held, the loss to the Oakland Raiders on that bitter January afternoon brought an end to one of the greatest chapters in the history of Cleveland athletics.

"I am not going to sing the blues because we lost," Sipe said. "We lost, but it was too great of a year to be singing the blues. We did things dramatically all season, and I guess it is only fitting that we lose in a dramatic fashion."

Epilogue: The Dynasty That Wasn't

The Sunday after the loss to the Raiders may have been even harder for the 1980 Cleveland Browns and their fans, some of whom still hadn't recovered from the icy heartbreak on the lake on January 4, 1981.

Naturally the criticism of the Browns' thinking in the final minute was sometimes harsh. A joke quickly made its way around town about Brian Sipe sitting down to dinner with his family. His wife asked him to pass the salt. He did, but it was intercepted.

"You can't go through a season winning games in the last few minutes and expect to continue to do it," Thom Darden said. "We were very fortunate to get the ones we got. I guess what makes it so amazing is that we got that many. If we'd have gotten one or two, that's one thing, but to get six or seven, that's unheard of."

Bob Sudyk wrote that the game "held all the elements of the entire wonderful and zany season—struggle, seemingly certain defeat, a final late-minute dash to the end zone and the second-guess of Sam Rutigliano."

Despite the outcry against his decision Rutigliano never doubted himself. "I never, ever questioned what I did and why I did it," he said. "I'm sure there are a lot of people who felt it wasn't the right decision, but they went along with all the other decisions when we were successful. My feeling was even though I might have been the only person who felt the way I did—which I wasn't—it didn't make me wrong."

"Whatever they called, it wouldn't have mattered," Doug Dieken said. "If we failed, we went down fighting. We put ourselves in a position to win, and be it throwing a pass or kicking a field goal, we made it possible to have an opportunity."

Joe DeLamielleure was in favor of the call but later made a confession. He said he heard the football whiz just past his head as it sailed on its ill-fated path. "I've got a fat head anyhow," he said. "I just wish my fat head would have got in the way."

While some players were surprised by the decision, they knew it wasn't a bad one.

"At the time I was surprised [that the Browns didn't kick]," said Thom Darden, "because I felt we were close enough even in the inclement weather, even in that area of the field, that if we had a good snap and a good hold, [Don Cockroft] should be able to get the ball through the uprights. But I think Sam made the right decision because of the previous misses at that end of the field. Obviously, if Brian had the pass to throw over again, he would throw it in the lake."

The Cleveland fans were also forgiving. The night of the loss Dieken was talked into going out to a bar by his brother, though he didn't feel anything like going out. Dieken just wanted to hide in the corner and drown his sorrows, hoping no one would see him. Instead fans kept coming up to him and thanking him for the magnificent season. "They weren't mad at us," he said. "They enjoyed it and appreciated it and respected it. They'd have liked to see it turn out a different way, but that's what makes playing here with these fans so great: their appreciation of what went on."

The day after the loss Brian Sipe had a similar experience. He reluctantly went out to dinner with his wife and some friends, hoping no one would recognize him. Much to his surprise when he entered the restaurant he was greeted to a rousing round of applause.

Even the wrinkle left between Rutigliano and Sipe following the temperature of the latter's postgame comments was soon ironed out. They talked in Honolulu during the week of the Pro Bowl—Rutigliano and his staff were asked to coach the AFC team—and Sipe said that he had completely agreed with his coach's strategy.

"Now I realize Sam gave me the biggest compliment you can give a player when he made the call," Sipe said in a *Plain Dealer* interview eighteen years later. "He felt I could make the play. But I let him down. I regret it very much. It was hard for me to reconcile with that."

At an honorary dinner for Rutigliano in 1999 Sipe again publicly supported the decision. "I want you to know Sam," he said that night, "that I let you down because you trusted me."

"It wasn't true," Rutigliano said of the speech, "but it was so gracious and honorable for him to say that."

And it wasn't as if the 1980 Browns were the only team in sports to be connected with a heartbreaking, gut-wrenching finish.

"Everybody goes through it if you play enough sports," Joe DeLamielleure said. "But it still makes me mad."

For example when DeLamielleure's son Todd played his final collegiate game for Hofstra in the first round of the 2001 Division I-AA playoffs against Lehigh, the Pride was poised to win. It held a 24-17 lead with three minutes to play and had driven to the Lehigh five. But a fumble turned into a ninety-two-yard Lehigh drive that ended with the game-tying touchdown with nineteen seconds left. Lehigh eventually won in overtime. "Well," DeLamielleure told his son after the game, "now you've got your Red Right 88."

Despite the heartbreak it caused, Red Right 88 left no hard feelings and more importantly no regrets.

"I got over it right away because I knew I had done the right thing," Rutigliano said. "One of the things I knew coming into this business was that the difference between a pat on the back and a kick in the butt is six inches. You make decisions and you live with the decisions you make, but more importantly, you don't dwell upon them."

But many Browns fans were still dwelling on that final decision of the 1980 team the following Sunday as they watched the Raiders battle their AFC West rival, the Chargers, for the AFC Championship in balmy San Diego. NBC must also have been a bit heartbroken that day. Certainly any AFC title game would bring in good ratings, but a Raiders-Chargers matchup would probably not have had the same viewer draw as a Browns-Chargers championship. In addition to the human-interest angle of Brian Sipe going up against his former college coach, San Diego head man Don Coryell, in the biggest game of both of their lives, it would probably have once again been wonderful football theater. Had the final forty-nine seconds of the Oakland game gone differently, a Cleveland–San Diego match would have pitted two of the greatest offenses—and more specifically two of the greatest quarterbacks—in NFL history against one another: Sipe and San Diego's Dan Fouts.

But many of the Browns, including Sipe, felt the magic carpet ride would have ended in California. "It would have been fun," Dieken said of the potential Chargers duel. "I don't think we matched up that well against San Diego. It would have been a game where it was 'Let's see who can outscore who.' It would have been tough."

"That would have been a very interesting matchup," Sam Rutigliano said. "Not a good one for us because they were a little better defensively."

On the other hand . . .

"I don't know about winning the Super Bowl," Darden countered, "but we would have gone to the Super Bowl. There is no doubt in my mind."

"Had we got past that [Oakland] game," said Mike Pruitt, "there's no way we weren't going to beat San Diego."

Whoever won, it would probably have been a high-scoring, offense-dominated contest. And knowing the Kardiac Kids it probably would have gone right down to the final gun. On paper, the 1980 Chargers were probably better than the Browns. Of course the 1980 Browns were probably inferior on paper to several of the teams they'd beaten.

Could the Browns have defeated the Chargers and earned their first trip to the Super Bowl? Probably. Especially considering that the Raiders, whom Rutigliano felt the Browns would have defeated without the brutal weather conditions, pulled another upset, and knocked off San Diego, 34-27, to punch their ticket to New Orleans for Super Bowl XV as the first Wild Card team to make the big show.

Behind the sharp passing of Jim Plunkett the Raiders soared to a 28-7 lead in the second quarter and then held off the Chargers for the remainder of the afternoon. San Diego narrowed it to 28-24 midway through the third quarter but could get no closer. After Plunkett and the Oakland offense successfully ran out the final 6:43, the Raiders were Super Bowl bound. Brian Sipe was at Jack Murphy Stadium that day but in the stands rather than in shoulder pads, watching the Raiders win. Sipe, the Browns, and their fans knew it could have been them.

DeLamielleure for example was certain the 1980 Browns would have won the Super Bowl. "I have no doubt about it," he said. "But what the hell do I know? I'm just a lineman."

Two weeks later Oakland met the favored Philadelphia Eagles, champions of the NFC, in the Louisiana Superdome to determine who would be the world champion. Thom Darden was there covering the game for radio station WHK. "I couldn't even watch," he said. "I kept saying to myself, 'We're supposed to be here. I'm supposed to be down there, not up here in the radio booth.'"

An eighty-yard third-down touchdown pass from Plunkett to running back Kenny King gave the Raiders a surprising 14-0 lead in the first quarter. Oakland never looked back, winning 27-10. It was the first time a Wild Card team won the Super Bowl, to be followed by the 1997 Denver Broncos and—ironically for Browns fans—the 2000 Baltimore Ravens.

Needless to say it was difficult for Cleveland to watch a team the Browns had on the ropes not only escape the divisional playoff but then go on to win the whole thing. But there was no reason for the Browns or their fans to plunge into despair. The year 1980 was the beginning, most figured, of what would be a long and successful run that could last much of the decade.

Art Modell, after calling the 1980 campaign the most exciting in his twenty years in football, was optimistic the Browns were in for a long run of success. If they weren't yet, he figured, they would soon become one of the elite teams in all of football. "We all know it's tougher to stay on top than it is to get there," he said. "And once we get there, I want to stay on top for a while."

It appeared that the Browns finally had the right man to lead them there. Sam Rutigliano was being praised as one of the best coaches in team history as his third season ended. He'd already won twenty-eight regular-season games, the most in a coach's first three years in Cleveland since Blanton Collier, and few doubted his success would continue into the new decade. For the second straight season Rutigliano was named AFC Coach of the Year by United Press International, the first time the same man had won the distinction in back-to-back years.

"Make no mistake about it," Bob Schlesinger wrote in a *Cleveland Press* column, "Sam Rutigliano is on the way to carving out a record as one of the game's best-ever coaches."

Many felt that with Brian Sipe at the helm on offense anything was possible. In 1980 he'd compiled the greatest season for any quarterback in Cleveland history, completing 337 of 554 passes (60.8 percent) for 4,132 yards with thirty touchdowns and just fourteen interceptions. Thanks to the "condominiums" blocking in front of him Sipe was sacked only twenty-three times all season as opposed to forty-three in 1979, and his quarterback rating was an NFL- and career-high 91.4. Appropriately he was named the NFL's Player of the Year by the Associated Press, *The Sporting News*, and the Pro Football Writers Association.

Though the Browns' aerial circus was the highlight of the season, Mike Pruitt had another outstanding year. Pruitt reached the thousand-yard mark for the second straight season with 1,034 and six touchdowns. Pruitt was also the team's leading receiver with sixty-three catches for 471 yards, while Dave Logan took the top yardage honors with 822 on fifty-one receptions. Three other players caught at least fifty passes: Reggie Rucker (fifty-two for 768 yards), Ozzie Newsome (fifty-one for 594), and Greg Pruitt (fifty for 444). But probably best demonstrating the versatility of the Cleveland offense in 1980 was Calvin Hill. The veteran running back only carried the ball once in the regular season but still scored six touchdowns, all receiving.

More than just statistics, however, the balanced offense reflected the psychological temperature of the team when things got rough. "We were a chosen team," Thom Darden said. "That was the feeling you got. Regardless of what happened, somebody was going to step up and make a play. And it changed. That was the good thing about it. It changed from offense to defense, from one guy to another guy. It wasn't the same guy all the time. That's what made it so special. You didn't know who was going to be the guy that stepped up and made the play."

Though Sipe was collecting MVP awards left and right in the off-season, the Browns were anything but a one-man show, especially in crunch time when it was anyone's guess who would take center stage. "It got to the point where it was like a smorgasbord," Rutigliano said. "That's why it was so great. Nobody knew each week who was going to do it. Everybody was always thinking and always working and always doing their best."

Against Kansas City it was Charles White. In the heat and humidity in Tampa Calvin Hill came through. Against Green Bay it was Dave Logan. Against Pittsburgh it was Ozzie Newsome on offense and Ron Bolton on defense. It was Mike Pruitt on a Monday night against Chicago. Greg Pruitt in the rain in Baltimore. In the Astrodome it was Cleo Miller, then Clarence Scott. Against the Jets, Reggie Rucker, with Lyle Alzado limping in off the bench. And at Riverfront in the season finale it was Ricky Feacher, Don Cockroft, and a gutsy performance by the entire defense that cashed in on its chance for redemption.

"When we were in those tight fits," Cody Risien said, "we all had confidence that somebody would step up."

The defense, though dramatically improved, still needed work. The 1980 Browns actually allowed more yards (5,626) than they accumulated (5,588), quite a statistic considering the brilliance of the Cleveland offense. Still, the Browns allowed nearly a thousand fewer rushing yards than in 1979 with the 3-4 alignment. With Marty Schottenheimer now in charge of the defense there was no question the improvement would continue.

The Browns were certainly an older, veteran team but appeared to be drafting well. With the Steelers and Houston Oilers in transition and the Cincinnati Bengals still rebuilding, the pieces seemed to be in place for Cleveland to replace Pittsburgh as the perennial favorite in the AFC Central for the immediate future.

The following July as training camp began prior to the 1981 season Browns' fans were certain this was their year. Tickets sold like hotcakes. Before the first exhibition game, people were talking about the Super Bowl. The team's popularity not only surfaced in more media coverage but also resulted in the creation of an entirely new forum: *Browns News/Illustrated*, a weekly newsletter produced by publisher Ray Yannucci, began printing that fall.

The media prognosticators used the same optimism the fans were enjoying for the foundation of their preseason predictions. The *Plain Dealer, Sports Illustrated*, and *The Sporting News* all anticipated the Browns to at least tie for the division crown and return to the playoffs.

Those forecasts seemed well-founded after the Browns—now going for victories in the preseason in hopes of a faster regular-season start in 1981—defeated the talented Atlanta Falcons, 24-10, in the Hall of Fame Game in Canton that August. Though Cleveland dropped three of its remaining four exhibition contests, the scores were more encouraging than they were in the 1980 preseason. Plus fans had learned the year before about the unimportance of the preseason, so a 2-3 exhibition record was nothing to be concerned about even for a team contending for the Super Bowl. The Browns' first test would come on opening weekend when the hypothetical matchup for the 1980 AFC Championship would finally be realized.

The San Diego Chargers came to Cleveland for the first *Monday Night Football* broadcast of the year, and the Stadium was ready. There were 78,904 fans packed into the ballpark, expecting to see not only a great game but also the beginning of another Super Bowl run. As it turned out they saw neither.

The Chargers rolled up 535 yards of offense on the struggling Browns' defense and completely dominated the home team in a 44-14 romp. The Browns were shocked but not panicked. After all Brian Sipe and the offense hadn't looked that terrible despite the fact quarterbacks-coach and offensive-figurehead Jim Shofner had left to become Houston's offensive coordinator in the off-season. Sipe set team records with thirty-one completions and fifty-seven attempts and tossed for 375 yards in the opener against San Diego. It appeared it would just be another case of waiting for the defense to catch up to the offense. The fans remembered the massacre in New England that opened the 1980 season and knew that one game didn't necessarily forecast the season.

In this case, however, it did.

The following week at home against Houston the Browns fell to 0-2 for the second straight year with a 9-3 defeat in a game that was frustrating on several levels. For one, just as had been the case with the Oilers' Monday-night victory in Week Two in 1980, the defense had looked better, but the offense failed to ignite due mostly to injuries to Mike Pruitt, Dave Logan, and Reggie Rucker. Also the Browns' kicking game, which had undergone a serious overhaul in the off-season, proved it was in no better shape.

Don Cockroft and Johnny Evans were both out of football, replaced respectively by Dave Jacobs, a free-agent signee from the New York Jets, and 1981 fifth-round draft choice Steve Cox. Against Houston, Jacobs missed three of four field-goal attempts as the Browns were held to their lowest point total in nearly three years.

Still it was early in the season, and the AFC Central appeared to be more wide open in 1981 than it had been in 1980. The Oilers were 2-0 as were the surprising Bengals (now wearing their new striped helmets), but the Steelers were also 0-2. The Browns figured they just needed to keep from digging too deep a hole early before they got on a roll.

Pruitt and Rucker both returned for Week Three in Cincinnati and played key roles in a big 20-17 win over the Bengals. Things got even better the next week when the Browns knocked off Atlanta, 28-17, at the Stadium to even their record at 2-2. Now it appeared that they were ready to pick up where they'd left off in 1980.

A week later in Anaheim a controversial interception by Rams' cornerback Leroy Irvin was the turning point in a 27-16 Browns' loss. Irvin, who was credited with the pick with the Browns trailing 14-10 and driving late in the third quarter, later admitted that he trapped the ball. Cleveland dropped back under .500 to 2-3, just as they had in 1980, but like with the Houston game, bad vibes emanated from the Rams' loss. The Browns had allowed 213 rushing yards and Jacobs missed a field goal and an extra point in what would be his final game in a Cleveland uniform.

Things got even worse on a trip to Pittsburgh the following week, where The Jinx was extended to twelve years following a 13-7 Steelers' victory. After Brian Sipe was knocked out of the game with a concussion late in the third quarter on a hit by Jack Lambert (for which he was penalized), Paul McDonald nearly rallied the Browns to victory. He drove Cleveland to the Pittsburgh twelve with 1:53 remaining, but a pass intended for Ozzie Newsome was tipped by cornerback Dwayne Woodruff and intercepted by fellow defensive back J. T. Thomas to clinch the Steelers' win. The Browns now stood at 2-4, below their 1980 pace for the first time.

A week later against New Orleans in Cleveland it appeared that the Kardiac Kids were back. With the Saints leading 17-13 with less than nine minutes to play, Sipe led the Browns on a seventy-eight-yard drive capped by a one-yard Mike Pruitt touchdown run. The Saints had an opportunity to tie the game, but a last-minute thirty-seven-yard field-goal attempt was no good and Cleveland won, 20-17.

The Browns turned in the finest offensive display in team history the week after that when the Colts visited the Stadium. Cleveland tallied a record 562 net yards, mostly on the arm of Brian Sipe, who completed thirty out of forty-one passes for a record 444 yards and four touchdown passes. The Browns rolled, 42-28, to even their record at 4-4.

The bad news was that Tom DeLeone suffered a broken ankle on a fourth-down play at the Baltimore goal line and would miss the remainder of the season. It was the turning point of 1981. Rutigliano later called DeLeone "the glue that holds the line together." Without DeLeone the line fell apart in the second half of the season.

Things had clearly not gone as well as expected in the first half of 1981 with injuries and inconsistency plaguing the team, but most figured the Browns still had a good playoff run in them. They were still in the running in the incredibly balanced AFC Central, tied with the 4-4 Oilers and only trailing the 5-3 Bengals and Steelers by one game. The possibility of the new era of Browns' football was still alive.

The Browns started the second half of the season in Buffalo, and DeLeone's absence was felt immediately. With Gerry Sullivan filling in at center the Bills sacked Brian Sipe six times in a 22-13 win. It was a game the Browns could have easily won had an almost-unbelievable five Cleveland touchdown passes not been negated—two because of penalty and three because the receiver was ruled out of bounds. The Browns hit a new low the following week in Denver when Calvin Hill fumbled at midfield on the first possession of overtime, and moments later the Broncos kicked the game-winning field goal in a 23-20 triumph. Everything that had gone right in 1980 was now going wrong in 1981.

A reprieve from the frustration came the following week when the Browns pulled possibly the biggest upset of the 1981 NFL season, knocking off the 8-2 and Super Bowl-bound San Francisco 49ers at Candlestick Park, 15-12. Following a late Sipe-to-Rucker touchdown pass that tied the game in the fourth quarter, the game was decided on a last-minute field goal by new kicker Matt Bahr. Ironically five weeks earlier the Browns had traded a ninth-round draft pick to the 49ers for Bahr to replace David Jacobs, who had missed an astounding eight of twelve field-goal attempts in five games. Bahr's heroics improved the Browns to 5-6, and once again there was a glimmer of hope of salvaging the 1981 season. It would be the last glimmer.

The following week the Steelers scored twenty unanswered points in the second half at Cleveland to bury the Browns, 32-10, as Brian Sipe was intercepted six times. The Bengals came to town next, built a 21-0 second-quarter lead after the Browns fumbled on their first two possessions, and coasted to a 42-21 win.

Now at 5-8 and playing simply for pride, the Browns statistically dominated the Oilers the following week in the Astrodome, doubling the home team in time of possession and total yardage. Yet the Oilers led late, 17-13. The Browns wound up with a first-and-goal at the Houston three with 1:10 to play—and couldn't score. The week after, the Browns returned home to face the Jets in a game with eerily similar circumstances to the teams' 1980 meeting, only with the roles reversed. It was the Jets on their way to the playoffs and the Browns going nowhere, but the game still went right down to the wire. Leading 14-13, the Jets successfully ran out the final 4½ minutes of the fourth quarter to clinch victory, just as the Browns had successfully run out the final five minutes the year before.

The disastrous 1981 season finally came to an appropriate close the following week in the Seattle Kingdome. It was one thing to lose to the 5-10 Seahawks 42-21 but quite another to turn the football over a record-breaking twelve times. Nine fumbles and three interceptions led to all six Seattle touchdowns. When the final gun mercifully sounded the 1981 Browns had completed their nightmarish campaign with a puzzling 5-11 record, the converse of their mark in 1980.

The Browns and their fans were baffled.

"Before they go looking for scapegoats," Brian Sipe said of his teammates in the aftermath of the Kingdome catastrophe, "maybe they should look around the bars where they were enjoying so much of their 1980 prestige."

It was a heat-of-the-moment comment that riled Sam Rutigliano, but Sipe admitted he wasn't blameless in the team's fall from grace. He threw for 3,876 yards, but his completion percentage (55.2 percent), average yards per attempt (6.3), and touchdowns (seventeen) were all down while his interceptions (twenty-five) and sacks (thirty-four) rose alarmingly from their 1980 levels.

While many members of the offense had solid years statistically, the unit as a whole suffered. The Browns would often coast up and down the field as they had in 1979 and 1980 but always seemed to stall inside the opponents' twenty-yard line. Though the Browns were second in the NFL only to San Diego in total first downs in 1981, the Chargers scored a whopping 202 more points.

After averaging more than twenty-two points per game in 1980, the 1981 Browns could manage just over seventeen per contest. The defense was no better, allowing nearly four more points per Sunday.

"We weren't quite as good as we played in 1980," Rutigliano would say. "Everybody overachieved. And I don't think we were quite as bad as 5-11 in 1981. So we can offer up a lot of excuses, and I have a closet full of them, but I don't think they hold any water."

"I noticed a little less determination than we had in the past," Sipe said after the 1981 season, "more naiveness of what it took for us to accomplish what we did last year.

"I felt it was important to come to camp with even more determination than we had. But it wasn't long before I became fearful that some of the players had taken what we had done for granted, that all we had to do was show up and the same things would happen."

Needless to say, they didn't.

Making matters worse for Art Modell were Paul Brown's Cincinnati Bengals, who won the Central and went on to capture the AFC Championship with a 27-7 win over San Diego at Riverfront Stadium on a day that was actually much colder than the day of the Browns-Raiders game, with a wind chill of fifty-nine degrees below zero. Though Cincinnati lost to the 49ers in Super Bowl XVI, the fact that the thirteen-year-old Bengals had reached the NFL's premiere showcase before the established Browns was a slap in the face to Modell and the Cleveland front office. Even worse, the optimism circulating the team and the city after the 1980 season had become paranoia that the window of opportunity for the team to capture a championship was now closed.

So how did a team that was one of the most exciting in the NFL in 1980 become a last-place club in 1981? There were several reasons.

First there was the simple expectation by some players of simply picking up where they'd left off. "We kind of forgot along the way all the things that went into making a success, all the hard work, all the dedication," Dick Ambrose said. "I think that offseason of somewhat-celebrity status ended up going to some people's heads.

"The team was not as much of a team in '81 as it was in '80. We kind of let the world get in and disrupt the closeness we had. Everybody was a little bit more of an individual in '81, and that hurt us."

Another factor that many fans didn't take into account was the departure of Jim Shofner. "That's one of the first things I point to," Cody Risien said. "Brian and Jim had a really good relationship and really worked well together. I played for some good offensive coaches in my career, guys like Jim Shofner, Larrye Weaver, Lindy Infante. In their offenses, everything seems easier. They just seem to have the knack for calling the right play at the right time."

Shofner was replaced by Paul Hackett, who was replaced by the Browns' first offensive coordinator, Weaver, two years later. Shofner would return to the Browns as offensive coordinator for the disastrous 3-13 campaign of 1990 and served as interim head coach after Bud Carson was fired after nine games.

Though the Browns' offense was still strong statistically in 1981, many felt that it didn't take much to knock the team off the contending rails. "We weren't really a dominating team," Doug Dieken said, "just a team that played well together. We had to have people making plays and we weren't good enough to lose people. Maybe we got a little full of ourselves in regard to how good we were the previous year. I'm sure that had something to do with it."

In an interview two years later when Rutigliano was asked about possibly sacrificing the present for the future good of the team, he made a comparison to the 1981 fallout.

"Sure, I want to get to the playoffs," he said, "but when I make it, I want to make it each year, as opposed to being involved in a 1980 season where we totally overachieved, misread ourselves, and didn't make the necessary moves."

"I think a lot of teams were ready for us [in 1981]," agreed Ron Bolton. "When you win one year, your schedule changes the next. At that time we needed to reload and come back with a little different stuff. I guess we stayed pat."

But perhaps more than any other factor the reason the 1980 Browns excelled so much more than they did in 1981 was due to pure dumb luck.

"The most significant part," Rutigliano said of the 1980 season, "was that we didn't lose anybody [to injury]. That's amazing in pro football. We were just lucky. And everything came together."

A perfect example of that good fortune in 1980 was the minor knee injury Sipe suffered in Seattle in Week Six. He was inches away from taking a hit that would have resulted in a season-ending ligament tear and watching from the sideline as Paul McDonald took over the offense. Instead, a week later, Sipe continued his fairy-tale season.

Injuries were a major factor in 1981, and having everyone come after you as the defending division champion was another. But the biggest reason for the drop from 11-5 to 5-11 demonstrated what was truly special about the 1980 team.

"We lost the games in 1981 that we won in 1980," Rutigliano said. "We had injuries and then we just didn't make the plays. Brian didn't get the same protection and we were more beat up in 1981 than we were in 1980."

The breaks the 1980 team got were of the once-in-a-lifetime variety. The Browns when healthy were for the most part just as talented in 1981 as they were in 1980, but luck and fate have a way of determining the outcome of sporting events. In 1980 both were on the Browns' side and combined to create one of the most memorable seasons in Cleveland history. In 1981 they weren't.

The 1981 team included almost all of the major contributors from 1980. But several, most notably DeLeone, Marshall Harris (broken hand), Dave Logan (pulled

hamstring and two broken ribs), Reggie Rucker (back, knee, and hamstring problems), and Henry Sheppard (neck surgery) suffered through season-long injuries.

Another factor in the dramatic drop-off was drug use among some of the players. Several Browns, just like many other players in the NFL, were addicted to
drugs, alcohol, or both, and it affected their play. "When people are falling asleep
in meetings, you figured it was because they were out partying the night before,"
Ambrose said. "But they would be so up on drugs they'd be awake for 24 hours
and then they'd just crash. You'd think, 'Why don't they sleep at night?' Well, they
didn't."

Drug use wasn't the primary reason why the Browns fell from the top in 1981,
but it played a significant role and led to another chapter of Rutigliano's reign in
Cleveland.

"The drug problem was a microcosm of society," he said. "It was a problem we
needed to address.

"A player came to me, walked in my office and told me of his problem. He was
very fearful of retribution. I decided at that point to sit down and talk with Art
Modell and discuss it with him. The NFL had asked us to locate a psychiatrist and
a hospital and begin to take a look at this substance abuse problem that had popped
its head in the National Football League.

"I wanted to establish my trust with them and help them. I wasn't interested in
finding out who [was using drugs] and getting rid of them."

It was the beginning of what was eventually known as the Inner Circle, an in-
house rehabilitation program within the franchise, based on counseling and peer
support.

"I began to try to educate our players," Rutigliano said. "If there was a problem
with substance abuse on this team, I didn't think we'd be morally doing the right
thing if we didn't try to help."

In the end Rutigliano said the program saved the careers and possibly the lives
of about twelve players, several of whom went on to play important roles on future Browns' teams.

"I really felt that if there was anything that I did that I was most proud of when
I was there was taking part in saving their lives," Rutigliano said. "I really felt good
about what we had done. The people that I share it with, there's a bond that you
can never, never replace."

At least two players from the 1980 Browns' team were not saved by the Inner
Circle, however, and their stories demonstrate the true danger of drug abuse in
professional sports.

Running back Charles White, after an up-and-down 1980 season, saw more
action but enjoyed limited success in both the 1981 and 1982 seasons. He missed
the entire 1983 campaign after breaking his ankle in an exhibition game and only

touched the ball twenty-nine times in 1984. The Browns gave up on him in 1985, and he wound up with the Rams. After a dazzling college career culminated by his winning the Heisman Trophy in 1979, White's stay in Cleveland was destroyed by drugs.

He had been using drugs since he was fifteen and smoked marijuana on almost a daily basis during his years at USC. A few weeks before the 1977 Rose Bowl White tried cocaine for the first time, which he got through a Trojan alumnus. In July of 1982 he publicly announced he had been hospitalized for his drug problem and said that he felt his drug use was the reason why he didn't step into a starting role with the Browns right away. Drugs had affected his performance on the field "to the extent I was more annoying to my co-workers [teammates] by not being mentally there," he said at the press conference.

White's stay in Cleveland included help through the Inner Circle. During meetings he pledged to stay clean but would sometimes make the promise while holding a bottle of clean urine between his legs in preparation for the drug tests.

In the long run the Inner Circle did work for White if only temporarily. White had been clean for nearly three years when the Browns cut him in 1985, but that changed after he signed with the Los Angeles Rams shortly after. He was back using crack and marijuana, and despite some progress, just days before the 1987 season began, White was arrested after another binge.

Despite the ominous beginning to the season White finally realized his potential with the Rams in 1987. In a strike-shortened season White rushed for 1,374 yards in fifteen games, leading the league in carries, yardage, and touchdowns as the Rams came within a hair of reaching the NFC playoffs. White retired after the 1988 season having gained just over three thousand yards in his eight-year NFL career, barely half of what he'd gained in four years at USC.

But the Browns' other casualty was even more tragic.

Lyle Alzado, the defensive leader of the 1980 Browns, began using anabolic steroids while at Yanktown College in 1969. He continued to use throughout his career and even after it ended. "Guys on the Browns came to me and asked about steroids, and I'd tell them who to call or I'd give them what I had," Alzado said in a strikingly honest reconciliatory article in *Sports Illustrated* in 1991. "They'd take them in the privacy of their own homes, and it wasn't talked about much—not in the locker room."

Alzado, who eventually had plastic surgery on his rear end to cover up the numerous injection marks, was traded to Los Angeles in 1982, where easy access to the drugs increased his usage. He retired following the 1985 season having played in 196 games in his memorable fifteen-year career and would always be remembered as one of the liveliest personalities ever to don a Browns' uniform.

But his use of steroids and other substances such as human growth hormone over the years eventually caught up with him. He was diagnosed with brain cancer in 1991 and was certain that it was caused by more than twenty years of steroid use.

Alzado, the self-proclaimed "Captain Wacko" of the NFL, died in May 1992 at the age of forty-three.

"He died at a very young age," Rutigliano said. "It was very sad. At the end, he was finally trying to tell the truth. When you're on drugs, drugs become part of your personality. You're full of denial and pathological lying. He was trying to tell the truth that he had been lying [about his drug use]. He was trying to tell the truth so that he could help some other young guys who were following the same course.

"He was a little bit of a paradox, but basically a wonderful person."

Though not a member of the Kardiac Kids, possibly the most tragic victim of drugs in NFL history was safety Don Rogers, drafted by Rutigliano and the Browns in 1984. After two strong seasons of what many expected would be a sterling career, Rogers died of cardiac arrest due to a cocaine overdose in June 1986, the day before his wedding. He was twenty-three years old.

For all the people that Rutigliano had helped save, he'll never forget the two he lost. "I felt almost responsible," he said. "To this day, I can remember Don Rogers and Lyle Alzado. We saved twelve or thirteen others. Why couldn't we have done that with them?"

By the time the 1982 team assembled for training camp it was missing several key components from the original Kardiac Kids club. Following the 1981 season the Browns made wholesale changes. In a whirlwind of activity prior to the 1982 draft, Robert L. Jackson was shipped to Denver, and Greg Pruitt and Lyle Alzado were both traded to the Raiders, who had just moved to Los Angeles after twenty years in Oakland. By the time the 1982 campaign began Reggie Rucker, Henry Sheppard, Calvin Hill, and Thom Darden had retired. Brian Sipe, Dave Logan, Mike Pruitt, Doug Dieken, Tom DeLeone, Robert E. Jackson, and Joe DeLamielleure remained on offense, but all were nearing the end of their careers. Ozzie Newsome and Cody Risien were the only long-term building blocks the Browns had on offense, which would now need a dramatic overhaul by mid-decade.

On the other side of the ball, however, things were heading in the opposite direction. "This is the first time since we've been here," Rutigliano said in the summer of 1982, "that we are looking for the defense to be more offensive, to create things, make things happen."

Marty Schottenheimer was slowly building what would eventually become one of the league's top defenses. With their top pick in 1981 the Browns drafted cornerback Hanford Dixon from Southern Mississippi and then picked linebacker Eddie Johnson from Louisville in the seventh round. The first pick of 1982 was linebacker Chip Banks from USC, and the Browns got lucky as training camp broke when they signed a young nose tackle released by the New England Patriots, Cleveland native Bob Golic.

Just before the 1982 draft the Browns traded with Buffalo for the highly touted former Ohio State and Lakewood St. Edward High School linebacker Tom Cousineau, the top pick of the 1979 NFL draft who had defected to the Canadian Football League. The Cousineau trade sacrificed Cleveland's first-round pick in 1983, but in the third round that year the Browns selected defensive end Reggie Camp from California and in the fifth, nose tackle Dave Puzzuoli from Pittsburgh. The Browns' top two picks in the 1984 draft also went to defense, with Don Rogers from UCLA going in the first round and safety Chris Rockins from Oklahoma State in the second.

The defense was still under construction in 1982 as was the labor agreement between the league and the players' association. After an impressive Browns' win in Seattle to open the season and a heartbreaking loss to the Eagles at the Stadium in Week Two, the players went on strike for two months, wiping out seven games of the 1982 campaign.

Ironically on that first Sunday during the strike when network television affiliates scrambled to air something for viewers hungry for football, WKYC in Cleveland rebroadcast the infamous Browns-Raiders playoff game.

The players returned to action just before Thanksgiving, but the Browns' early momentum was gone, and over the next seven weeks they struggled to get it back. Flip-flopping between a now-struggling Brian Sipe and an inexperienced Paul McDonald at quarterback, Rutigliano directed the Browns to a 4-5 record and a spot in the improvised conference playoff structure. Along with the Detroit Lions in the NFC that year, it marked the only time in league history a team with a losing record entered the postseason.

Though it didn't truly feel like a playoff season, the Browns faced a familiar opponent in the first round of the AFC tournament: the top-seeded Los Angeles Raiders. The home team showed that Schottenheimer's project was still a work in progress by rolling up 510 yards of offense as the Raiders coasted to an expected 27-10 victory. It was the Browns' fifth consecutive playoff loss.

By the time the team began preparing for the 1983 season it had lost several of the assistant coaches who played important roles on the 1980 squad. In addition to Jim Shofner's departure prior to 1981 four assistants left the Browns for other positions following the 1982 season, including offensive line coach Rod Humenuik, who left to run the Kansas City Chiefs' offense, and secondary coach Len Fontes, who went to the New York Giants.

The 1983 season would turn out to be the last hurrah for most of the remaining members of the Kardiac Kids and would go down in team history as the final season of the era in which they participated. "That season I thought we had some opportunities to get back to where we were in 1980," Dick Ambrose said, "but we always seemed to come up short one way or another."

With the offense still potent and the defense improving and posting back-to-back shutouts for the first time in thirty-two years, the Browns went 9-7 and narrowly missed the playoffs on the last day of the season, which saw Cleveland defeat Pittsburgh, 30-17, at the Stadium.

The following day Brian Sipe, whose contract with the Browns had expired, walked into Sam Rutigliano's office. He told his coach he had a guaranteed three-year contract offer totaling $2.2 million from Donald Trump and the New Jersey Generals of the newly formed United States Football League. Ironically the man who had set up the deal was former Browns' general manager Peter Hadhazy, who was now director of operations for the USFL. Rutigliano had seen this coming.

Sipe was thirty-four years old. If he stayed healthy he still might only be able to play for another two or three years at the most. The Generals were offering more money than the Browns, and the money was guaranteed even if Sipe didn't play out the contract or if the league folded—which it did in 1986.

Still Sipe wanted to stay with the Browns and finish his playing career in Cleveland, but he was upset over the team's lack of interest in negotiating with him during the season. Rutigliano knew this and figured he could make it happen if he really wanted to. "I said take it and run," Rutigliano said. "I was just too much of a company man."

Within the week Sipe signed with the Generals, and an era of Cleveland Browns' football had come to an end. Interestingly the Generals didn't make their guaranteed contract offer to Sipe contingent upon a passing physical—a glaring mistake that foreshadowed the future of the nickel-and-dime USFL.

As it turned out it was letting Sipe go, not Red Right 88, that would be the one irrevocable mistake of Sam Rutigliano's career with the Browns. "The Browns played poker with me and they lost," Sipe later said. "It was too bad. We had the makings of a very good team in Cleveland, a lot of talent."

At the time letting Sipe go made some sense. The extra money the Browns would have doled out to re-sign Sipe for another two or three years was money they could have spent on his eventual long-term replacement. Plus Rutigliano and the Browns' brass figured Paul McDonald was ready to step into Sipe's shoes, either as that long-term solution or at least as someone who could fill the role until the right opportunity presented itself. They were wrong on both counts.

"Paul McDonald wasn't ready to play," Rutigliano said, "and as it ended up, he was a nice kid, but he wasn't good enough."

"He was not a guy that was going to carry the team," Dick Ambrose said. "Maybe he could throw a nice ball, but he wasn't the leader that Sipe was."

"In a seven-on-seven drill where you're just going against defensive backs and linebackers and nobody is rushing you isn't the same as being out there and having guys zinging by your head," Dieken said. "That was the difference between Sipe and McDonald."

Sipe wasn't the only Brown to depart. By the time the 1984 season began Clarence Scott had retired and Dave Logan had been dealt to Denver, while Cleo Miller, Ron Bolton, and Marshall Harris had all been released. The guard was changing.

With McDonald at the helm the Browns got off to their worst start in nine years, losing eight of their first nine games, several of which were decided in the final moments. In Week Two the Browns led the Rams, 17-10, going into the fourth quarter, but a Los Angeles touchdown and then a field goal in the final two minutes resulted in a 20-17 defeat. A week later against Denver in Cleveland the Browns trailed by three in the final minute but were at the Broncos' forty-six and driving into field-goal range. But McDonald threw an interception that was returned for a touchdown, and Denver clinched victory. After a much-needed win over the Steelers, the Browns again found themselves in a tight spot with a minute to go in Kansas City, trailing 10-6. On a third down from the Chiefs' thirty, McDonald was intercepted again, ending the Browns' comeback hopes.

On October 7 the Browns' future was altered by a ghost of their past. Trailing the New England Patriots, 17-16, the Browns had the ball at the New England twenty-one with twenty-three seconds to go. Remembering that Matt Bahr had missed a field goal from the same area of the field just minutes before, Rutigliano opted to roll the dice one more time in an effort to get the Browns closer. McDonald's pass was intended for wide receiver Duriel Harris, but Harris slipped and fell. The ball was intercepted by cornerback Raymond Clayborn of the Patriots, and a few moments later the Browns dropped to 1-5, following an eerie reminder of Red Right 88.

After the game a frustrated Rutigliano marched into Art Modell's office and took full responsibility for the loss, violating his father's ingenious advice: "If you ever have an opportunity to keep your mouth shut, take it." He admitted he never should have called for the pass and should have just sent Bahr on to attempt the field goal. He said he wouldn't hold Modell to the contract extension he'd agreed to prior to the season. If Modell wanted to fire him right then and there, Rutigliano said, he'd understand.

Modell responded by saying he wasn't an impulsive and unsympathetic owner like Bob Irsay (who had moved the Colts out of Baltimore seven months earlier). He said that he didn't fire coaches in midstream and that they would get through this rough patch together. To his credit Modell was putting his mouth where his money was. He'd just signed Rutigliano to a two-year contract extension prior to the season that ensured he'd be paying his coach through 1988. Still, once his emotions cooled Rutigliano knew he had made a huge mistake opening himself up that much in front of the team's brain trust.

A week later the Browns once again appeared poised for victory against the Jets when they drove to the New York twenty-eight with 1:28 to play trailing, 24-20. But McDonald was sacked on three straight plays, and the Jets escaped. "It seems like we're getting paid back for what we did in 1980," Ozzie Newsome said afterward. In Cincinnati seven days later the Browns tied the Bengals at nine with a clutch Bahr field goal with two minutes to play, but a defensive breakdown led to a big play for the Bengals and a game-winning thirty-three-yard field goal by Jim Breech as time expired.

After returning to Cleveland that night, Art Modell fired Sam Rutigliano, replacing him with Marty Schottenheimer.

The 1984 Browns would probably not have made the playoffs, but they certainly never would have been 1-7 with Brian Sipe at the controls on offense. "There were things that didn't go well in '84, but look at some of the scores of the games," Rutigliano said. "Brian would have made those plays. But as they say, if ifs and buts were candy and nuts, it would be Christmas every day."

"That was a major downfall in what happened to Sam," Dieken said of Sipe's departure. "He lost his playmaker."

Schottenheimer split the final eight games of the season, and the Browns finished, all things considered, a respectable 5-11, but the offense was in dire straits. McDonald had thrown for better than 3,400 yards and fourteen touchdowns in 1984 but also for twenty-three crucial interceptions. He was clearly not the answer. In the off-season the Browns traded for quarterback Gary Danielson from the Detroit Lions and then got lucky.

Youngstown native and University of Miami star quarterback Bernie Kosar was going to graduate early and enter the NFL's supplemental draft that June. Kosar, touted as the best college quarterback in his class, publicly declared that he wanted to play for the Browns, whom he had rooted for growing up. After some unorthodox trade maneuvering the Browns selected Kosar in the supplemental draft.

The future had arrived. Kosar would be the Browns' starting quarterback for the next nine seasons and lead them to the playoffs five times.

"When Bernie came on board," said Cody Risien, "those of us who had been around and played with Brian asked each other, 'Who does this kid remind you of?' We all agreed it was Brian Sipe. They were very similar in terms of leadership and personal charisma."

Still the question remains: What would have happened had the Browns re-signed Brian Sipe to get the team through 1984 and then tutor Kosar as Danielson did in 1985? "I would have made it through [the 1984 season] and probably would have coached the Browns for twenty years," Rutigliano laughed. "We could have bridged the gap with Sipe."

The gap that was the 1984 season turned out to be too damaging for Rutigliano to survive and led to a new era of the Cleveland Browns under Marty Schottenheimer. Schottenheimer would lead the Browns to three straight AFC Central crowns and back-to-back appearances in the AFC Championship, coming heartbreakingly close to two Super Bowl berths.

The trademark of those teams was a great defense led by people such as nose tackle Bob Golic; safeties Al Gross and Chris Rockins; defensive ends Reggie Camp and Carl Hairston; linebackers Chip Banks, Eddie Johnson, Mike Johnson, and Clay Matthews; and cornerbacks Hanford Dixon and Frank Minnifield, all acquired under Rutigliano. On offense, wide receivers Brian Brennan and Gerald McNeil; running backs Earnest Byner and Kevin Mack; tight end Ozzie Newsome; and offensive linemen Rickey Bolden, Cody Risien, Mike Baab, Paul Farren, and George Lilja all played vital roles in the playoff years, and all were acquired during the Rutigliano era.

"Marty did a good job," Rutigliano said, "but Marty did a good job with all of the people that we picked. But I don't look back on it with any degree of 'I shoulda and I coulda.' That was one thing that I learned, that you can't look back. Those things are going to happen and sometimes it's the luck of the draw. You've just got to live your life."

Sam Rutigliano did. Though he could have continued to coach in the NFL, possibly as the headman in Buffalo in 1985, he stayed out. He served as a consultant to Italy's professional football league and then worked as a television analyst for ESPN and NBC (for which he broadcast a Browns' overtime loss in San Diego and a win over Cincinnati in 1987). He interviewed for the head coaching positions that became available at LSU and Ohio State in the late 1980s, and in 1989 he took over the job at NCAA Division I-AA Liberty University. In eleven years there he compiled a 67-53 record but was always associated with the Kardiac Kids, for better or worse. When Liberty traveled to Eastern Michigan for a game in 1989, fans hung a banner reading "Red Right 88."

Rutigliano's greatest impact as a coach was not on the fans, however, but on his players. "The guy is one of the finest human beings you'll ever meet," Joe DeLamielleure said. "And the frosting on the cake is that he's a damn good coach." And a damn funny guy in any circumstance. After Rutigliano resigned from Liberty following the 1999 season DeLamielleure called him to make sure nothing was wrong with his family or to find out if something else had gone wrong that had prompted his resignation.

"No, it's Samuel three-eight," Rutigliano replied.

"What is that, a Bible verse?" DeLamielleure asked.

"No Bible verse," Rutigliano said. "Sam Rutigliano: three wins, eight losses."

Rutigliano couldn't stay out of coaching for long. In 2000 he joined the staff of the NFL Europe's Barcelona Dragons as offensive coordinator.

"He made chicken salad out of chicken shit more than anyone I'd ever seen," DeLamielleure said. "He could do anything. He was one of the masters of offensive football."

Brian Sipe—after being traded from New Jersey to Jacksonville so that the Generals could make room for a heralded young hurler out of Boston College named Doug Flutie—hung up the cleats for the final time after two shoulder surgeries in 1985 and at least nine concussions while with the Browns. As of 2003 Sipe still held several franchise passing records, including total yardage (23,713), attempts (3,439), completions (1,944), and touchdowns (154). Though his 1980 quarterback rating would be eclipsed by Bernie Kosar in 1987, his performance that year is still the greatest single season for any quarterback in Cleveland history in terms of yardage, completions, and touchdowns.

"We were at a point where we were playing with great confidence and great flare and it was very exciting," Rutigliano said looking back on the magical 1980 season. "Brian just reveled in it. He was Tiger Woods on the 18th hole or Michael Jordan with the final shot. He was just that kind of player. Great competitor, super smart, tough, great awareness. He was special."

Sipe returned to San Diego, took a year of architecture courses at a junior college, and soon found work in the field. But he still kept his ties with football and the Browns. When Art Modell announced the team would move to Baltimore in 1995, Sipe and former teammate Jerry Sherk filmed a documentary as they drove a motor home across the country to the Browns' final game at the Stadium, stopping to visit several Browns Backers groups along the way.

"I thought I'd put football behind me when I retired in 1985," he told the *Akron Beacon Journal* that December, "then I got this news and I realized that it's still part of me."

When the new Cleveland Browns opened the 1999 regular season, Sipe was in attendance. And in 2001 he was named head football coach at Santa Fe Christian High School in Del Mar, California, and won the Division 5 state title in his first season.

After leaving the Browns and catching one pass for the Denver Broncos in 1984, wide receiver Dave Logan retired with 263 receptions for 4,250 yards in his nine-year career, placing him at seventh on the Browns' all-time receiving yardage list.

He remained in Denver and eventually became the radio color commentator for the Broncos. He was promoted to play-by-play man in 1998.

Fullback Mike Pruitt lasted two more seasons after being released by the Browns in 1985 but saw limited playing time in Buffalo and Kansas City and retired following the 1986 campaign. During his years with the Browns he became the third-leading rusher in Cleveland history, accumulating 6,540 yards in nine years, trailing only Hall-of-Famers Jim Brown and Leroy Kelly. He was one of just three Browns' running backs to ever have three consecutive thousand-yard rushing seasons (Brown and Greg Pruitt were the others).

Once his playing days were over Mike Pruitt entered automobile sales and in 1991 started his own Ford dealership in Lima, Ohio.

Running back Greg Pruitt's career followed the same path once he left Cleveland. He spent three years with the Raiders in Los Angeles before retiring following the 1984 campaign. He ranks fourth on the Browns' all-time rushing list with 5,496 yards and third on both the all-time receptions list (323) and the combined yardage list (10,700).

Tight end Ozzie Newsome was still just getting warmed up in 1980. He had his first thousand-yard receiving season in 1981 and another would follow in 1984. The tight end from Alabama was a rock of consistency for the Browns throughout the 1980s, catching a pass in 150 straight games between 1979 and 1989 and setting a new team record with eighty-nine receptions in both 1983 and 1984. He retired after the 1990 season as the Browns' all-time leader in both receptions (662) and yards (7,980) after thirteen years of service. He remained with the team as an assistant coach under Bill Belichick from 1991 to 1995, then followed Art Modell to Baltimore in 1996. There he became the Ravens' director of player personnel and helped build the 2000 Baltimore team that won the Super Bowl.

Newsome was inducted into the Pro Football Hall of Fame in 1999, appropriately just two days before the new Cleveland Browns took the field in Canton for their first exhibition game.

Reggie Rucker retired prior to the 1982 season with 447 career receptions, 310 with the Browns, placing him fifth on the all-time franchise list. He was also fifth in team history in yardage (4,953). In his twelve-year career Rucker totaled 7,065 receiving yards.

Ricky Feacher was released during training camp in 1985 but remained with the team in the player-relations department for five years. Though never a star, Feacher was a consistent contributor to the Browns for nine seasons.

Left tackle Doug Dieken remained in the hearts and minds of Browns fans throughout the remainder of the decade and beyond. He retired after the 1984 season, having started 194 consecutive games and appearing in 203 straight, a pair of records that still stood as of 2003 and is not likely to be broken anytime soon. In 1985 Dieken slid into the radio booth, joining play-by-play broadcaster Nev Chandler, as the Browns' color commentator. Dieken would hold the job for eleven years (nine with Chandler, who died of cancer in 1994) until the Browns moved to Baltimore, and then picked it up again, this time with Jim Donovan as his partner when the team returned in 1999.

Most of the remainder of the 1980 offensive line, considered by many to be the best in franchise history, did not carry over into the Schottenheimer era. Henry Sheppard retired prior to the 1982 season, while Tom DeLeone called it quits in 1984 after a thirteen-year career. DeLeone would be remembered as one of the few players in the history of the game to play each game at each level of his career—high school, college, and pro—for an Ohio team. Shortly after his football career ended he became a special agent with the United States Custom Service in Salt Lake City, Utah. In 1991 DeLeone signed on as the offensive line and special teams coach at Park City High School.

When Sipe took his headcoaching job in 2001 he asked DeLeone if he wanted to be his offensive coordinator. "I told him, 'We're not throwing the ball,'" DeLeone said. "He said, 'Forget it, then.'"

Joe DeLamielleure was released during Schottenheimer's first training camp in 1985 and finished his thirteen-year career playing for the team he'd started with: Buffalo. While he played with talented players in Buffalo, he never found an offensive line with the chemistry that matched that of Sipe's condominiums. "I played on great lines in Buffalo," DeLamielleure said, "but considering what that [1980] line was asked to do, it was one of the better lines to ever play in the NFL." After losing most of the money he'd saved from his football career in an investment swindle, DeLamielleure got into coaching, first high school girls basketball, then prep football in Charlotte, North Carolina. In 1994 he joined Sam Rutigliano at Liberty as the offensive line coach, then moved on to coach the tight ends at Duke for five years beginning in 1996. In January 2003 DeLamielleure was elected to the Pro Football Hall of Fame, becoming the second member of the Kardiac Kids' offense to join the club.

Robert E. Jackson returned to being a regular starter on the Cleveland line in 1981, when he filled in at left guard for an injured Henry Sheppard, then became the permanent starter there when Sheppard retired a year later. Jackson was replaced by George Lilja in 1985, Jackson's final year in the NFL.

Cody Risien was the lone member of the 1980 line to play an integral part on Schottenheimer's playoff teams, starting at tackle and guard through the 1989 season. Risien and Ozzie Newsome were the only two members of the offense to be a part of all seven Browns' playoff teams between 1980 and 1989. After his retirement Risien got out of football altogether. With his degree in building construction he began working for a construction company in Cleveland and eventually wound up close to his roots in Austin, Texas.

Linebacker Clay Matthews was the lone member of the Cleveland defense on board for the full 1980s run, and he not only became one of the Browns' primary weapons but also one of the NFL's most durable players. As the Browns' defense improved in the mid-1980s, so did Matthews, earning five trips to the Pro Bowl. After sixteen years in Cleveland, Matthews finished his career after the 1996 campaign following three more seasons with Atlanta. Matthews played in more games than any other player in Browns' history (232) and trails only Lou Groza's seventeen Cleveland campaigns for the most seasons in a Browns' uniform. Matthews also holds the Browns' all-time sack record with 76 1/2.

Matthews was the only member of the 1980 defense to also play on the 1985 playoff team. Most of the other members of the Kardiac Kids' defensive unit either retired or were replaced as the squad improved throughout the decade.

Lyle Alzado was traded to the Raiders in 1982, and a year later Marshall Harris was released and finished his career with New England. Elvis Franks was waived following a knee injury in 1985 and saw limited action with the Raiders and Jets before retiring after the 1986 season. Jerry Sherk tried one last time to make a comeback and saw limited action in the 1981 season finale at Seattle. But when his riddled left knee was sore for two months from the effort, he realized that he'd reached the end of his football journey. He officially retired on April 7, 1982, as arguably the greatest defensive player in Browns' history.

Sherk stayed close to the team with his second career, serving as a regular photo contributor to *Browns News/Illustrated* as well as a freelance photographer for newspapers, magazines, and wire services.

Linebacker Charlie Hall retired after 1980 following a ten-year career, and the spirited Robert L. Jackson was traded after the 1981 campaign and retired after being released by the Oilers in training camp in 1983.

Dick Ambrose helped anchor the defense through the 1981 and 1982 seasons, but a broken ankle sidelined him for the final ten games of 1983, and complications from the injury forced him to miss all of 1984. Ambrose attempted a comeback the following year but couldn't make the team and retired. He'd been working toward a degree at Cleveland-Marshall College of Law part-time since the 1982 players' strike and eventually graduated in 1987. He remained in Cleveland, practicing business litigation and employment law.

Aside from Matthews, the Browns' linebacker who probably went on to the most success after 1980 was one who garnered little attention that season. After missing the 1981 campaign with a knee injury Bill Cowher returned in 1982 but was traded to Philadelphia in 1983 and retired a year later. Schottenheimer hired him as the Browns' special teams coach in 1985, and he was promoted to defensive secondary coach in 1987. The fiery Cowher followed Schottenheimer to Kansas City after he was fired as Browns' head coach after the 1988 season and eventually was selected to replace Chuck Noll as head coach of the Pittsburgh Steelers in

1992. Cowher and the Steelers reached the playoffs in each of his first six seasons in Pittsburgh and nearly won the franchise's fifth world title in Super Bowl XXX.

The 1980 secondary was also entirely replaced by mid-decade. Safety Thom Darden called it quits after the 1981 season as the Browns' all-time interception leader with forty-five. Not far behind him is safety Clarence Scott with thirty-nine, good for third place. Scott retired following the 1983 season after a thirteen-year career spent entirely with the Browns. Fellow corner Ron Bolton was waived following the 1982 season after an eleven-year career with the Patriots and Browns and eventually served as an assistant under Rutigliano at Liberty in 1996. The following year he took the defensive backfield coaching job at his alma mater, Norfolk State.

Lawrence Johnson would see action in every game through 1983, then was traded to the Buffalo Bills in 1984. He finished his career in Buffalo in 1987. Clinton Burrell moved to safety and was a regular starter through the 1983 season before he lost his job to newcomer Al Gross and was released in 1985. Oliver Davis failed to make the 1981 roster and finished his career with two seasons in Cincinnati, while Judson Flint was waived in 1983 and saw limited action with Buffalo late in the season.

Kick returner Keith Wright's banged-up knees made 1980 his final season, while fellow return man Dino Hall stayed with the team through 1983. Hall sits atop both the franchise's all-time kickoff return list (151) and kickoff-return yardage list (3,185). The versatile yet diminutive Hall is also third on the team's all-time list in punt returns (111), fourth in punt-return yards (901), and seventh in punt-return average (8.1).

Through the rich and storied history of the Cleveland Browns the importance of the 1980 Kardiac Kids team remains clear in the hearts of the fans. "They're so fond of that team and that era," Sam Rutigliano said. "Some even say that was the best even though we didn't win it all."

While most who remember the 1980 Browns first think of Red Right 88 and the disappointment that followed, perhaps that heartbreak is what helped make the Kardiac Kids such a beloved part of Browns' history. Had they simply lost to Oakland in an uninspired effort in a drab game, the legacy of the Kardiac Kids may not have swelled to what it eventually became. "It was better we went out with a bang instead of a whimper," Brian Sipe said. "The way we lost, people will always remember us."

The 1980 Browns are memorialized as a fairy tale. The accounts of how that Browns team repeatedly overcame the odds and captured the hearts of Cleveland fans have reached legendary status. Future Browns' offenses would be held up to

Sipe and Company for comparison. Anytime the Browns win a tight game it seems at least one area writer makes a reference to the Kardiac Kids.

It would be almost exactly six years after the Oakland playoff before the Browns would host another postseason game. Following a 12-4 regular season in 1986 and another AFC Central Division championship, heavily favored Cleveland faced the Wild Card New York Jets in what would become one of the most memorable games in Browns' history.

With the Browns trailing, 13-10, with nine minutes to play, a third-down Bernie Kosar pass from the New York two was intercepted in the end zone by cornerback Russell Carter. After a commercial break NBC showed a clip of Brian Sipe's end zone interception against the Raiders paralleling Kosar's, then a banner hung from the upper deck at Cleveland Stadium that read NO RED RIGHT 88. The Browns found themselves down, 20-10, with just over four minutes to play but rallied to tie the game in the final seconds of regulation. They won, 23-20, in double overtime.

On October 23, 1994, as a part of the NFL's seventy-fifth season celebration, members of the 1980 Browns' team were invited to Cleveland Stadium for "Kardiac Kids Day." Several members of the squad were introduced at halftime of the contest with the Cincinnati Bengals, who led Cleveland, 13-10. After a rousing ceremony, the Browns ran away with a 37-13 win in the second half. Even though it wasn't a nail-biter, fourteen years later it appeared that the Kardiac Kids still had some clout.

For many, the Kardiac Kids returned during the crazy 2002 season as the Browns went 9–7 and made the playoffs for the first time in eight years—just as did the 1980 team. And just like with the 1980 Browns, thirteen games were decided in the final two minutes. What's more, in 2002, an astounding eight games were determined on the game's final play, including a heart-wrenching 36–33 loss in Pittsburgh during the playoffs.

Most fans and beat writers concurred that the 2002 Browns were the closest thing to the original Kardiac Kids Cleveland had seen in twenty-two years.

That December Terry Pluto of the *Akron Beacon Journal* concluded, "following this team is a good way for your stomach to start bleeding, for your nails to be chewed down to tiny nubs, for your head to ache, your heart to skip, your brain to burst. Sound familiar?"

Over the course of Browns' history, 1980 stands out as the most exciting single season of all. Though the Browns' four NFL championship teams—1950, 1954, 1955, and 1964—hold more respected historic platforms, none of those seasons contained the week-in, week-out excitement fans witnessed in 1980.

Even in 1986, 1987, and 1989, when the Browns were probably stronger top-to-bottom than in 1980, won the division, and went one step further than the 1980

Browns in the postseason, their overall adventures could not compare to the panache and style of the Kardiac Kids.

"In '86 and '87, we had a team that was building," Risien said. "We had a team in '80 with a lot of guys in the twilight of their careers. It was just one great year for a lot of guys. It was magical, kind of a fairy tale. It was a moment, not to be duplicated."

"We were probably of average talent," Brian Sipe once said, "but we had a big heart."

Denver quarterback John Elway's ninety-eight-yard drive in the waning moments, which eventually crushed the Browns' hopes of reaching the Super Bowl in January 1987, and Earnest Byner's fumble, which may have cost the Browns an AFC championship the following year, are often lumped together with Red Right 88 as the defining moments of the 1980s for the Browns. The heartbreak was devastating in all three instances, but fans remember the 1980 season far more clearly than they do 1986 or 1987. Not because the latter two weren't fantastic, thrilling campaigns in their own right but because the Kardiac Kids were simply on another level of excitement.

That sentiment is probably best captured by a tale from the peak of the Kosar Era in the late 1980s. Kosar went out to dinner with Brian Sipe and Cody Risien, and it didn't take long for someone to recognize the Browns' current curly-haired quarterback. The fan was energetically talking to Kosar when he realized who else was at the table. His jaw dropped. "Bernie, you're great," he said a moment later, "but Brian, you're the man!"

Another reason the 1980 Browns are more memorable was because those late 1980s teams were part of a long, dynasty-like stretch of success. The same was true of the great teams of the 1950s and 1960s. After joining the NFL in 1950 the Browns reached the league title game six consecutive years, winning three. When Blanton Collier replaced Paul Brown as head coach in 1963 the Browns embarked on another long run of success, making the playoffs five times in six years from 1964 to 1969 and playing for the NFL championship in four of those seasons.

The 1980 Browns were sandwiched between long stretches of disappointment. It had been eight years since Cleveland's last playoff appearance and—excluding the haphazard and inappropriate 1982 postseason structure—it would be another five years until the Browns earned a postseason spot again. Through Cleveland's dark years of the 1970s and early 1980s, both athletically and psychologically, the Kardiac Kids represented Cleveland's one quasar of excitement in a cosmos of frustration.

Despite the promise of the 1980 team the Indians soon returned to their usual floundering ways. In four of its next five seasons the Tribe lost at least eighty-four games, and 1980 American League Rookie of the Year Joe Charboneau vanished from stardom as quickly as he had appeared. By August of 1981 he was shipped back to the minors and, after appearing in only twenty-two games for Cleveland in 1982, saw his career come to an end.

The Cavaliers were no better. After losing fifty-four games in the 1980–1981 season, they fell to a woeful 15-67 under four (yes, *four*) different head coaches in 1981-1982. The Cavs would lose more than fifty games in six of the first seven seasons of the decade and go ten straight years without a winning record.

After the Kardiac Kids had been eliminated from the playoffs until the rebirth of the Browns in 1985, Cleveland returned to being the Siberia of professional sports just as it had been throughout the 1970s.

On paper the success of the 1980 Browns might look like a fluke. But those who experienced it know better, and they remember it for the phenomenon that it was. "There was nothing but negativism [in Cleveland] at the time," Thom Darden said. "Then you have these guys who were finding a way to win after being down. People loved that because the city was down. It was a glimmer of hope. The guys would win in the fourth quarter and people could relate to that. It just brought about a love affair."

"Cleveland is that kind of town," Rutigliano said. "They remember Rocky Colavito. They remember the Brian Sipes and the Otto Grahams and the Frank Ryans and the Marion Motleys.

"There's a lot of great sports towns, but Cleveland is real special. The traditional roots are deep."

But it wasn't just that the 1980 Browns were successful, it was *how* they were successful. Thirteen of their seventeen games were decided in the final two minutes by seven points or less. In 1979 and 1980 twenty-five of thirty-three contests were determined by a touchdown or less. No other team in the history of the game can lay claim to that kind of consistent excitement.

"Nobody got uptight," Rutigliano said. "No one ever thought that it was over. No one. In times of crises, you think of players, not plays. It got to be a lot of fun. It was electric. I guess it fed on itself."

"Who knows what that ingredient was that made this team so resilient?" said Darden. "It only happened one time in my life, and it was that year."

The 1980 Cleveland Browns did not make as big an imprint on NFL history as did the 1974–1979 Pittsburgh Steelers, but they're forever carved in the memories of their city's sports lore. They didn't win or even appear in the Super Bowl nor did they advance to the AFC Championship. But dozens of NFL teams that have gone further in the postseason than the 1980 Browns—some of which won the Super Bowl—aren't remembered like the Kardiac Kids are in Cleveland. This was a team that was not defined by the bottom line. It was a team defined by the path it took in getting there.

"It was a great team," Joe DeLamielleure said, "and some really great memories."

"I'm just happy I was there for that run," Rutigliano said. "It was a heckuva lot of fun."

The 1980 Browns will always be remembered for that. They showed their followers that anything was possible, that—for better or worse—there was always enough time left on the clock. Through the powerful medium of professional sports, this group raised the collective morale of thousands of people and symbolized what endurance, optimism, and confidence can do for the human spirit.

And along the way the team made Cleveland's heart beat a little faster.

Bibliographical Essay

During the Cleveland Browns' horrific 2000 campaign in which they finished with a 3-13 record that, incredibly, didn't truly reflect the disease that was that season, I had an outlet for my sports misery. During the week, I'd spend the bulk of two days either at the Ohio Historical Society archives and library or at the Columbus Metropolitan Library, immersed in back issues of the *Plain Dealer* and *Cleveland Press* on microfilm from twenty years earlier. It's funny how it worked out, since my research of the 1980 season and the 2000 laugh-in almost perfectly paralleled one another—in reverse.

When the 2000 Browns, alternating between Doug Pederson and Spergon Wynn at quarterback, were hopelessly shut out in their final game at Three Rivers Stadium, I spent the following week reading about their miraculous one-point win over the Steelers in Cleveland in 1980 sparked by four Brian Sipe touchdown passes. When the Browns were pummeled 92-7 in consecutive weeks by Baltimore and Jacksonville, I was swept back to their thrilling win in the Houston Astrodome and their December drive toward the division title. When Chris Palmer was unceremoniously fired the following January, I was recounting how Sam Rutigliano was being praised as one of Cleveland's greatest coaches after winning the toughest division in football.

Needless to say, it was a pretty good elixir.

Much of my other research took place at the Pro Football Hall of Fame library, which had more useful material than I ever thought possible, primarily magazine and newspaper articles on microfiche (mostly from the *Plain Dealer* and *Press* but also some from the *Akron Beacon Journal* and *Canton Repository*), old programs, and play-by-play sheets. I acquired some videotapes of some of those old games and watched them (and rewatched them) in bliss. I also spent a snowy January morning at the Cleveland State University library, sifting through old photographs and captions.

The final product was improved greatly thanks to the assistance of several members of that team who took time out of their busy schedules to speak with me at

length: Dick Ambrose, Ron Bolton, Thom Darden, Joe DeLamielleure, Tom De-
Leone, Doug Dieken, Mike Pruitt, Cody Risien, and Sam Rutigliano.

Several books came in very handy:

*The Baseball Encyclopedia: The Complete and Definitive Record of Major League
Baseball.* Tenth Ed. New York: Macmillan, 1996.

Chronicle of America. New York: Dorling Kindersley, 1995.

Gruver, Ed. *The Ice Bowl: The Cold Truth about Football's Most Unforgettable Game.*
Ithaca, N.Y.: McBooks Press, 1998.

Huler, Scott. *On Being Brown: What It Means to Be a Browns Fan.* Cleveland: Gray
& Co., 1999.

Keim, John. *Legends by the Lake: The Cleveland Browns at Municipal Stadium.*
Akron, Ohio: Univ. of Akron Press, 1999.

Kirow, Bear. *Pro Football '81: Stars, Photographs, and League Records.* Middleton,
Conn.: Weekly Reader Books, 1981.

Levy, William. *Sam, Sipe, and Company: The Story of the Cleveland Browns.* Cleveland: J. T. Zubal & P. D. Dole, 1981.

Neft, David S., Richard M. Cohen, and Rick Korch. *The Football Encyclopedia: The
Complete History of Professional Football from 1892 to the Present.* New York: St.
Martin's Press, 1994.

Porter, Philip W. *Cleveland: Confused City on a Seesaw.* Columbus, Ohio: Ohio
State Univ. Press, 1976.

Rutigliano, Sam. *Pressure.* Nashville, Tenn.: Oliver-Nelson Books, 1988.

Silverman, Matthew, man. ed. *Total Browns: The Official Encyclopedia of the Cleveland Browns.* New York: Total Sports, 1999.

Total Football II: The Official Encyclopedia of the National Football League. New
York: HarperCollins, 1999.

Van Tassel, David D., and John J. Grabowski, ed. *The Encyclopedia of Cleveland
History.* Bloomington, Ind.: Indiana Univ. Press, 1987.

Vexler, Robert I., ed. *Cleveland: A Chronological and Documentary History 1760–
1976.* Dobbs Ferry, N.Y.: Oceana Publications, 1977.

Several magazine articles also proved valuable:

Alzado, Lyle (as told to Shelley Smith). "I'm Sick and I'm Scared." *Sports Illustrated,* July 8, 1991.

Myslenski, Skip. "The Gamebreakers: Dave Logan: Getting a Chance." *Pro!,* Oct. 26, 1980.

Natal, Jim. "Finding Brian Sipe." *Pro!,* Oct. 19, 1980.

Newhouse, Dave. "Raiders Shoot Down Browns' Air Weapon." *The Sporting News,*
Jan. 17, 1981.

Newman, Bruce. "Eerie End by Lake Erie." *Sports Illustrated,* Jan. 12, 1981.

Portraits (Calvin Hill). *Pro!,* Sept. 7, 1981.

Portraits (Thom Darden). *Pro!,* Sept. 15, 1980.

Reilly, Rick. "A Visit to Hell." *Sports Illustrated,* Aug. 29, 1988.

Yannucci, Ray. "As the Press Sees It." *Pro!,* Nov. 3, 1980.

Zimmerman, Paul. "Hang on to Your Seats." *Sports Illustrated,* Dec. 15, 1980.

Zimmerman, Paul. "Pro Football 81: Scouting Reports." *Sports Illustrated,* Sept. 7, 1981.

Zimmerman, Paul. "Tick . . . Tick . . . Tick. . . . " *Sports Illustrated,* Sept. 8, 1980.

Also indispensable were old Browns, Indians, and Cavaliers media guides and back issues of *Browns News/Illustrated,* a true treasure founded by Ray Yannucci and a pioneer in the NFL weekly publication genre.

And if you liked the book, you'll love the movie: *Kardiac Kids: Again,* NFL Films' short but spectacular highlight film of the 1980 season, which came in very handy in the research process. Also helpful was the NFL Films documentary *The Cleveland Browns: Fifty Years of Memories,* released in 1996, and a segment about the Kardiac Kids attached to the 1991 team highlight film titled "To Live and Die in the Crunch."

Index

Greene, Joe, 132

Gregg, Forrest, 10, 19, 20, 22, 46, 55, 62, 69, 76, 132, 136–39, 140, 144, 169, 184, 187, 188, 189, 192, 196, 204, 208, 209; in comparison to Sam Rutigliano, 11–13, 138; resignation of as Browns' coach, 16, 137–38

Griffin, Archie, 201, 202–203, 205

Griffin, Ray, 3, 201

Grogan, Steve, 37, 38, 50, 57, 121

Gross, Al, 280, 285

Grossman, Randy, 129

Groth, Jeff, 149

Groza, Lou, 29, 157, 284

Guy, Ray, 230, 237, 238, 239, 240, 243, 244, 245, 258

Hackett, Paul, 271

Hadhazy, Peter, 11, 35, 47, 60, 92, 93, 138, 157, 277

Hadnot, James, 52, 53

Hagins, Isaac, 58

Hairston, Carl, 280

Hall, Charlie, 29, 79, 82, 94, 101, 128, 166, 205, 222, 260, 284; background of, 28

Hall, Dino, 2, 30, 65, 116, 127, 164, 166, 200, 203, 244, 245, 285

Ham, Jack, 76, 154

Hannah, John, 19

Harper, Bruce, 15, 166

Harris, Duriel, 42, 278

Harris, Franco, 89, 92, 94, 108, 123, 162

Harris, Marshall, 149, 165, 203, 213, 214, 240, 272, 278, 284; background of, 28

Hartenstine, Mike, 109

Hasselbeck, Dan, 38

Hawkins, Andy, 59

Hawthorne, Greg, 95, 96

Hayes, Lester, 226, 228, 239, 242, 249

Hayman, Conway, 44

Heaton, Chuck, 4, 14, 36, 232

Hellerstein, Herman K., 173–74

Hendricks, Ted, 229, 240, 241, 244, 252, 253, 258

Herrera, Efren, 73

Hickerson, Gene, 219

Hicks, Bryan, 141

Hill, Calvin, 38, 39, 43, 58, 60, 64, 79, 82, 84, 93, 94, 96, 130, 141, 143, 156, 161, 171, 175, 192, 200, 201, 205, 211, 212, 213, 222, 234, 238, 242–43, 266, 269, 275; background of, 22–23; Browns' acquisition of, 23

Hitchcock, Craig, 257

Holden, Steve, 15

Hood, Estus, 82

Hooker, Fair, 217

Houston Astrodome, 71, 86, 102, 145, 146, 151, 160, 227, 266, 270

Houston Oilers, 2, 9, 18, 25, 36, 37, 39, 40, 41, 50, 55, 62, 64, 69, 70, 71, 72, 77, 86, 88, 89, 102–103, 104, 108, 120, 121, 124, 134, 137, 142–43, 144, 145–47, 148, 149, 158, 160, 168, 170, 171, 172, 173, 183, 186, 188, 193, 223, 224, 225, 226, 227, 228, 230, 260, 267, 268, 269, 270, 284; and first 1980 game with Browns, 42–46, 47, 48, 49, 53, 56, 72, 133, 146–47, 231, 268; and second 1980 game with Browns, 149–54, 157, 159, 160, 227, 266

Howard, Tom, 51

Humenuik, Rod, 18, 19, 276

Infante, Lindy, 271

Inner Circle, 273–275

Irons, Gerald, 28, 31

Irsay, Bob, 278

Irvin, Leroy, 268

Ivery, Eddie Lee, 82

Jack Murphy Stadium, 265

Jackson, Bobby, 166

Jackson, Harold, 38

Jackson, Robert E., 112, 115, 142, 275, 283; and losing starting job to Joe DeLamielleure, 35, 40; background of, 18

Jackson, Robert L., 37, 43, 44, 49, 56, 65, 74, 80, 81, 82, 83, 112, 150, 247, 275, 284; background of, 28

Jackson, Tom, 65, 68

Jacksonville Bulls, 281

Jacobs, Dave, 268, 269

Jauron, Dick, 3

Jensen, Jim, 67–68

Jodat, Jim, 73, 74, 75

Johnson, Bill, 135

Johnson, Charles, 80, 81

Johnson, Eddie, 276, 280

Johnson, Ezra, 80

Johnson, Jesse, 166

Johnson, Lawrence, 37, 48, 285

Johnson, Mike, 280

Johnson, Pete, 86, 139, 187, 189, 204–205, 208, 212

Johnson, Ron, 95, 98, 102, 128, 154

Kardiac Kids

was designed and composed by Christine Brooks

in 10/13.5 Minion with display type in 20/27 Helvetica Condensed Black;

printed on 55# Supple Opaque stock

by Thomson-Shore, Inc., of Dexter, Michigan;

and published by

The Kent State University Press

KENT, OHIO 44242